MW00354212

UNEQUAL FAMILY LIVES

Across the Americas and Europe, the family has changed and marriage is in retreat. To answer the question of what is driving these changes and how they impact social and economic inequality, progressives have typically focused on the economic causes of changing family structures, whereas conservatives tend to stress cultural and policy roots. In this illuminating book, an international group of scholars revisit these issues, offering competing and contrasting perspectives from left, center, and right, while also adding a third layer of analysis: namely, the role of gender – changes in women's roles, male employment patterns, and gendered family responsibilities – in driving family change across three continents. *Unequal Family Lives: Causes and Consequences in Europe and the Americas* adds richness and depth to our understanding of the relationship between family and economics in the United States, Europe, and Latin America. This title is also available as Open Access on Cambridge Core at http://dx .doi.org/10.1017/9781108235525

Naomi R. Cahn is the Harold H. Greene Chair at George Washington University Law School.

June Carbone is the Robina Chair in Law, Science, and Technology at the University of Minnesota Law School.

Laurie Fields DeRose teaches in the Department of Sociology at Georgetown University and is Director of Research for the World Family Map project.

W. Bradford Wilcox is Director of the National Marriage Project at the University of Virginia, Professor of Sociology at the University of Virginia, and Senior Fellow at the Institute for Family Studies.

Unequal Family Lives

CAUSES AND CONSEQUENCES IN EUROPE AND THE AMERICAS

Edited by

NAOMI R. CAHN

George Washington University Law School

JUNE CARBONE

University of Minnesota Law School

LAURIE FIELDS DEROSE

Georgetown University

W. BRADFORD WILCOX

University of Virginia

CAMBRIDGE
UNIVERSITY PRESS

CAMBRIDGE
UNIVERSITY PRESS

University Printing House, Cambridge CB2 8BS, United Kingdom

One Liberty Plaza, 20th Floor, New York, NY 10006, USA

477 Williamstown Road, Port Melbourne, VIC 3207, Australia

314–321, 3rd Floor, Plot 3, Splendor Forum, Jasola District Centre,
New Delhi – 110025, India

79 Anson Road, #06–04/06, Singapore 079906

Cambridge University Press is part of the University of Cambridge.

It furthers the University's mission by disseminating knowledge in the pursuit of
education, learning, and research at the highest international levels of excellence.

www.cambridge.org
Information on this title: www.cambridge.org/9781108415958
DOI: 10.1017/9781108235525

First published 2018

Printed in the United Kingdom by TJ International Ltd. Padstow Cornwall

A catalogue record for this publication is available from the British Library.

ISBN 978-1-108-41595-8 Hardback

To our families

Contents

List of Figures   *page* ix

List of Tables   xiii

List of Contributors   xv

Acknowledgments   xix

Introduction   1
Laurie Fields DeRose, Naomi R. Cahn, June Carbone, and
W. Bradford Wilcox

PART I THE INCREASINGLY UNEQUAL SOCIOECONOMIC
CHARACTER OF FAMILY LIFE   19

1   Families Unequal: Socioeconomic Gradients in Family
    Patterns across the United States and Europe   21
    Marcia J. Carlson

2   Families in Latin America: Dimensions, Diverging Trends,
    and Paradoxes   40
    Albert Esteve and Elizabeth Florez-Paredes

PART II THE CAUSES OF INCREASINGLY DIVERGING
FAMILY STRUCTURES   67

3   How Inequality Drives Family Formation: The Prima
    Facie Case   69
    Andrew J. Cherlin

4   Universal or Unique? Understanding Diversity in Partnership
    Experiences across Europe   83
    Brienna Perelli-Harris

5   Family Structure and the Decline of Work for Men in
    Postwar America   105
    Nicholas Eberstadt

    PART III CONSEQUENCES OF GROWING DIVERGENCE   141

6   Single-Mother Families, Mother's Educational Level,
    Children's School Outcomes: A Study of Twenty-One
    Countries   143
    Anna Garriga and Paolo Berta

7   Family Structure and Socioeconomic Inequality
    of Opportunity in Europe and the United States   165
    Diederik Boertien, Fabrizio Bernardi, and Juho Härkönen

8   Families and the Wealth of Nations: What Does Family
    Structure Have to Do with Growth around the Globe?   179
    W. Bradford Wilcox and Joseph Price

    PART IV BRIDGING THE GROWING FAMILY DIVIDE   197

9   Family Policy, Socioeconomic Inequality, and the Gender
    Revolution   199
    Frances Kobrin Goldscheider and Sharon Sassler

10 Where's the Glue? Policies to Close the Family Gap   216
    Richard V. Reeves

    PART V COMMENTARY AND CONCLUDING REFLECTIONS   235

11 The Pathology of Patriarchy and Family Inequalities   237
    Lynn Prince Cooke

12 Concluding Reflections: What Does Less Marriage Have
    to Do with More Family Inequality?   261
    W. Bradford Wilcox

13 Commentary, Afterword, and Concluding Thoughts on
    Family Change and Economic Inequality   265
    June Carbone and Naomi R. Cahn

    References   284
    Index   324

Figures

1.1 Crude marriage rates across OECD countries, 1970–2014 *page* 26

1.2 Women's mean age at first marriage across OECD countries, 1990–2014 26

1.3 Crude divorce rates across OECD countries, 1970–2014 27

1.4 Cumulative proportions of women repartnering ten years after union dissolution by cohort 28

1.5 Proportion of births outside marriage across OECD countries, 1970–2014 29

2.1 Maps of four dimensions that characterize families in Latin America, 2000 44

2.2 Trends in selected key family life indicators in Latin America over recent decades and cohorts 46

2.3 Percentage of mothers among women aged from 25 to 29 by union status, educational attainment, and census round 51

2.4 Percentage of women aged from 25 to 29 who reside in an extended household by motherhood status, educational attainment, and census round 54

2.5 Percentage of women aged from 35 to 44 who are household heads by partnership/motherhood status, educational attainment, and census round 55

3.1 Percentage of children living with single and cohabiting mothers, by mother's education, 1980–2010 74

4.1   Percentage of nonmarital births in selected countries,
      1980–2014   84

4.2   Percentage of births outside marriage, 2007   87

4.3   Percentage of policy areas (out of 19) that have addressed
      cohabitation and harmonized them with marriage in selected
      European countries   90

4.4   Mean values and confidence intervals for outcome variables
      in selected countries   99

5.1   Employment-to-population ratio, US males, selected age
      groups: 1948–2016 (seasonally adjusted)   107

5.2   Percentage of civilian noninstitutionalized prime-age (25–54)
      males without paid employment: USA 1948–2017
      (seasonally adjusted)   110

5.3   Males (25–54) unemployed vs. not in labor force: USA
      January 1948–May 2016 (seasonally unadjusted)   112

5.4   Labor force participation rates for males aged 25–54: USA
      vs. twenty-two "original" OECD member states, 1960–2015   112

5.5   Distribution of prime-age males by race, 1965 vs. 2015   115

5.6   Work rates for prime-age males by race, 1965 vs. 2015   115

5.7   Distribution of prime-age males by race and ethnicity, 1971
      vs. 2015   116

5.8   Work rate for prime-age males by race vs. ethnicity, 1971
      vs. 2015   117

5.9   Distribution of prime-age males by nativity, 1994 vs. 2015   118

5.10 Work rates for prime-age males by nativity, 1994 vs. 2015   119

5.11 Distribution of prime-age males by educational attainment,
      1965 vs. 2015   120

5.12 Work rates for prime-age males by educational attainment,
      1965 vs. 2015   120

5.13 Distribution of prime-age males by marital status, 1965 vs. 2015   123

5.14 Work rates for prime-age males by marital status, 1965 vs. 2015   123

5.15 Distribution of prime-age males with children under the age of 18 living at home, 1968 vs. 2015   124

5.16 Distribution of prime-age males by family status and presence of child (<18), 1968 vs. 2015   124

5.17 Work rates for prime-age males by family structure, 1968 vs. 2015   125

5.18 Conditional compositional effects on prime-age male work rates and NILF rates in 2015   131

5.19 Labor force participation rate for males aged 25–54 by marital status and race: married Black vs. never-married White   135

5.20 Labor force participation rate for males aged 25–54 by marital status and educational attainment: never married with bachelor's degree or higher vs. married high school dropout   135

5.21 Rate of nonlabor force participation from 1965 to 2016: US civilian noninstitutionalized males aged 25–54   137

5.22 Nonlabor force rates among prime-age males by state (2015)   138

5.23 Labor force participation rate for males aged 25–54 by marital status and educational attainment lower than a high school diploma   139

7.1 Actual and predicted university attainment in hypothetical situation "where all children grow up with both parents in the household"   175

8.1 Gross savings as percentage of GDP, by proportion of children being raised by two parents: 2001–2015   183

8.2 Percentage of 25–50-year-old men employed, by marital status and fatherhood: 1979–2013   184

8.3 Male labor force participation, by proportion of children in two-parent families: 2001–2015   186

8.4 Female labor force participation, by proportion of children in two-parent families: 2001–2015   187

8.5 Homicide rate, by proportion of children in two-parent families: 2001–2015   189

10.1   Intergenerational mobility by wealth quintile at birth and family inequality   220

10.2   Staying together: married vs. cohabiting parents   222

10.3   Unintended pregnancy rates are much higher among unmarried couples   226

10.4   Impact on test scores of low-income children during the school years: reports in effect size of $1,000 of public expenditure on family support, class size reduction, or school readiness   231

11.1   Nested intersections of institutions, family processes, and outcomes   239

Tables

2A.1   Results of factor analysis of family indicators in Latin America, 2000   *page* 61

2A.2A   Percentage of mothers among women aged from 25 to 29 by union status, educational attainment, and census round   62

2A.2B   Percentage of women aged from 25 to 29 who reside in an extended household by motherhood status, educational attainment, and census round   63

2A.2C   Percentage of women aged from 35 to 44 who are household heads by partnership/motherhood status, educational attainment, and census round   64

5.1   US male employment-to-population ratios: 2015 vs. selected depression years   109

5.2   Who is more likely – and who is less likely – to be in the 7 million pool of prime-age NILF males? Relative odds by demographic characteristic: 2015   128

6.1   Percentages of children by family types, PISA 2012   153

6.2   Logistic regression coefficients of mother's education on the probability of being a single mother   154

6.3   OLS and logistic regression coefficients of effects of children's family structure and mother's education on math test scores, grade repetition, and truancy   155

6.4 OLS regression coefficients of main effects and interaction terms of children's family structure and mother's education on math test scores for each country — 158

6.5 Logistic regression coefficients of main effects and interaction terms of children's family structure and mother's education on grade repetition for each country — 159

6.6 Logistic regression coefficients of main effects and interaction terms of children's family structure and mother's education on truancy for each country — 160

7.1 Countries according to the percentage of mothers who are single and the educational gradient in single motherhood — 171

8.1 GDP growth by proportion of adults who are married, country-level regression — 192

8.2 GDP growth by proportion of children in two-parent homes, country-level regression — 193

11.1 Labor market polarization across Europe — 242

11.2 Female labor force participation rates over time (age 25 to 54) — 243

11.3 Gender inequality, social expenditures, and percentage of children under 17 living in poverty in two- vs. single-parent families, circa 2010 — 252

Contributors

Fabrizio Bernardi is Chair in Sociology and Head of Department at the Political and Social Sciences Department of the European University Institute, Fiesole, Firenze.

Paolo Berta is Assistant Professor in Statistics at the Department of Statistics and Quantitative Methods of the University of Milan–Bicocca, Milan. His scientific research activity primarily concerns the application of multivariate statistical analysis techniques and mixed effects models to cross-sectional and longitudinal data.

Diederik Boertien is a postdoctoral researcher at the Centre for Demographic Studies of the Autonomous University of Barcelona (UAB). In 2017, he coauthored "Non-Intact Families and Diverging Educational Destinies" (with Fabrizio Bernardi), published in *Social Science Research*.

Naomi R. Cahn is the Harold H. Greene Professor of Law at George Washington University Law School. She is the coauthor of *Marriage Markets: How Inequality Is Remaking the American Family* (2014) (with Professor June Carbone).

June Carbone is the Robina Chair in Law, Science and Technology at the University of Minnesota Law School. She is the coauthor of *Marriage Markets: How Inequality Is Remaking the American Family* (2014) (with Professor Naomi Cahn).

Marcia J. Carlson is Professor of Sociology and Director of the Center for Demography and Ecology at the University of Wisconsin–Madison. She coedited (with Daniel R. Meyer) a 2014 volume of the *ANNALS of the American Academy of Political and Social Science* on "Family Complexity, Poverty, and Public Policy."

Andrew J. Cherlin is Benjamin H. Griswold III Professor of Sociology and Public Policy at Johns Hopkins University, Baltimore, Maryland, USA. He is the author of *Labor's Love Lost: The Rise and Fall of the Working-Class Family in America* (2014).

Lynn Prince Cooke (DPhil Oxon) is Professor of Social Policy at the University of Bath and a research fellow at the Berlin Social Science Center. She specializes in comparative, including historical, analyses of gender inequalities in paid and unpaid work and their impact on family outcomes. She is currently Principal Investigator on a European Research Council Consolidator Grant analyzing the "new" shape of family-related gender stratification in Finland, Germany, and the United Kingdom.

Laurie Fields DeRose teaches at Georgetown University, and she is Research Assistant Professor for the Maryland Population Research Center, Director of Research for the World Family Map Project, and Senior Fellow at the Institute for Family Studies. Her early research on sub-Saharan African demography laid the foundation for her current focus on global family studies. Her work, coauthored with World Family Map academic partners, "Maternal Union Instability and Childhood Mortality Risk in the Global South, 2010–2014" appeared in *Population Studies*, May 2017.

Nicholas Eberstadt holds the Henry Wendt Chair in Political Economy at the American Enterprise Institute in Washington, DC; his most recent book is *Men without Work: America's Invisible Crisis* (2016).

Albert Esteve is a demographer. He is currently the Director of the Centre for Demographic Studies at the Autonomous University of Barcelona (UAB). He completed his undergraduate studies in geography and has a PhD in Demography from the UAB. His research interests lie in the area of family and household demography, including topics such as marriage, cohabitation, assortative mating, and marriage markets. He has focused on the implications of structural changes on the marriage markets (e.g., gender-gap reversal in education, the expansion of college education, or international migration) and on family dynamics in various regions of the world, with a focus on Latin America. Most of his work is cross-national and makes intensive use of census and survey microdata. He spent three years at the Minnesota Population Center actively participating in the first release of international census microdata within the Integrated Public Use Microdata Series Project. He has been Marie Curie Fellow at the National Institute for Demographic Studies and Visiting Fellow at Princeton University. His research has been published in prestigious demographic journals and funded competitively by European, Spanish, and Catalan research agencies, including the European Research Council.

Elizabeth Florez-Paredes is a sociologist from the Central University of Venezuela with a PhD in Demography from the Autonomous University of Barcelona. Her research focuses on family systems in Latin America, with particular focus on marriage, cohabitation, households, and transitions to first union and child. She specializes in large comparative and cross-national research based on international census and survey microdata. Her work has been presented at major international conferences such as those of the Population Association of America and the Latin American Studies Association.

Anna Garriga is a postdoctoral researcher in the Department of Political and Social Science at Pompeu Fabra University. Her research mainly focuses on the causes and consequences of the increasing diversification of family structures in European countries. In 2017, she coauthored "The Change in Single Mothers' Educational Gradient Over Time in Spain" (with Clara Cortina), published in *Demographic Research*.

Frances Kobrin Goldscheider is University Professor Emerita of Sociology at Brown University and College Park Professor of Family Science at the University of Maryland. Her studies include analyses of trends in living alone among the elderly; leaving and returning home among young adults; entry into unions; men's, women's, and children's roles in the household division of labor; and new forms of fatherhood, including single, absent, and stepparent. Her current research focuses on men's roles in the family in the United States and Sweden. A recent major paper is "The Gender Revolution: A Theoretical Framework for Understanding Changing Family and Demographic Behavior" (with Eva Bernhardt and Trude Lappegård), *Population and Development Review*, 41(2):207–239, 2015.

Juho Härkönen is Professor of Sociology at Stockholm University. In 2017, he coedited a special issue (with Fabrizio Bernardi) of the *European Journal of Population* on the effects of family dynamics on children's life chances.

Brienna Perelli-Harris is Associate Professor of Demography at the University of Southampton, United Kingdom. She recently completed a European Research Council Starting Grant on *Childbearing within Cohabitation: Trends, Policies, and Consequences*.

Joseph Price is Associate Professor of Economics at Brigham Young University (BYU) and a Fellow at the Austin Institute. He is the author of over fifty academic articles and is the Director of the BYU Record Linking Lab (http://rll.byu.edu).

Richard V. Reeves is Senior Fellow in Economic Studies, Codirector of the Center on Children and Families, and Editor-in-Chief of the Social Mobility Memos blog at the Brookings Institution. His research focuses on social mobility, inequality, and family change. Prior to joining Brookings, he was Director of Strategy to the UK's Deputy Prime Minister. His publications for Brookings include *Saving Horatio Alger: Equality, Opportunity, and the American Dream* (2014), *Character and Opportunity* (2014), *The Glass Floor* (2013), and *The Parenting Gap* (2014). He is also a contributor to the *Atlantic, National Affairs, Democracy Journal,* the *Wall Street Journal,* and the *New York Times.* Richard is the author of *John Stuart Mill: Victorian Firebrand* (2007), an intellectual biography of the British liberal philosopher and politician.

Sharon Sassler is Professor of Policy Analysis and Management, and Sociology, at Cornell University. She is the coauthor (with Amanda Jayne Miller) of *Cohabitation Nation: Gender, Class, and the Remaking of Relationships* (2017).

W. Bradford Wilcox is Professor of Sociology at the University of Virginia and Senior Fellow of the Institute for Family Studies. He is the coauthor of *Soul Mates: Religion, Sex, Love, and Marriage among African Americans and Latinos* (2016).

Acknowledgments

This book has been years in the making and is only possible because of the work and support of so many people and institutions.

First, we thank the Social Trends Institute (STI), a nonprofit international research center based in New York that sponsored the Experts Meeting on family inequality in Rome in 2017, which made this volume possible. STI is dedicated to fostering understanding of globally significant social trends. To this end, STI brings together the world's leading thinkers, taking an interdisciplinary and international approach. We are especially grateful to Carlos Cavallé, the President of STI, and Tracey O'Donnell, the Secretary General of STI, for their guidance and support. More information on STI may be found at www.socialtrendsinstitute.org.

Second, we thank all of our contributors for your energy and your responsiveness as we returned yet another double-edited draft. We are also grateful to Alysse ElHage and Rich Brake at the Institute for Family Studies for their work in managing this effort, especially the Experts Meeting in Rome. ElHage also learned how to create an index, and she finalized the Index for this book.

Finally, we thank our research assistants, Carl Briggs and Nicholas Leaver. Leaver played an integral and tireless role in compiling the references for the book, as well as formatting the book. We are grateful for their substantial work on this volume.

Introduction

Laurie Fields DeRose, Naomi R. Cahn, June Carbone,
and W. Bradford Wilcox

What is the relationship between family structure and economic inequality?
Family structures in Europe and the Americas have changed and marriage has
declined since the mid-1990s (OECD 2016a). Moreover, increasing economic
inequality in these countries has become the object of considerable concern
among scholars, policymakers, and journalists. The conversation about
inequality, however, has not systematically focused on the ways in which
changes in family structure may be connected to economic inequality, both
as a consequence and a cause of this inequality. Existing debate has often
unfolded as though the economic and the cultural changes are two independent events: Progressives have focused on the economic causes of changing
family structures, while conservatives have stressed the cultural and policy
roots of these changes. Underlying both are not fully explored assumptions
about the impact of the transformed nature of women's roles, male employment patterns, and the gendered division of family responsibilities that may
affect the relationship between family inequality and socioeconomic
inequality.

This volume explores what is actually happening to the family in
Europe and much of the Americas. It discusses contextual factors that
underlie variations in family structures, and it also explores the ways in
which economic and cultural changes reinforce one another. Moreover,
because conversations about economic inequality and family structure
have too often focused either on single regions, such as northern
Europe or southern Europe, or even just the United States, this volume
brings together scholars from different countries. Accordingly, our hope is
that *Unequal Family Lives: Causes and Consequences in Europe and the
Americas* adds richness and depth to our understanding of the relationship
between family and economics.

BACKGROUND

Throughout much of North America, well-educated and more affluent families tend to be headed by stably partnered parents who enjoy comparatively high levels of relationship quality. Working-class and poor families face higher levels of family instability and single parenthood, and lower levels of relationship quality. Moreover, trends in fertility, frequency of assortative mating (similarly educated individuals forming families with one another), and rates of education may contribute to larger variations in earnings between household types. Across a wide variety of countries, the number of household types at higher poverty risk (such as single-parent families) is projected to increase (OECD 2011a). The consequences of the rise in "at risk" families are still unknown, however, as living arrangements may have less of a connection to inequality in Europe than in North America (European Commission 2013).

Family has become more central to the discourse about inequality in the United States than elsewhere, largely owing to Sara McLanahan's work on "diverging destinies" (McLanahan 2004). She argued that some trends in modern family life increase children's resources while others decrease them, but that the net change is by no means equally distributed across social class. But the United States remains an outlier among advanced economies with its low levels of public support for families, high rates of income and wealth inequality (Table 2, http://inequality.stanford.edu/sites/default/files/Pathways-SOTU-2016.pdf), and its high rates of union disruption (both divorce and the dissolution of cohabiting unions), so a comparative approach provides critical perspectives. Accordingly, this book puts family change at the center of the conversation about growing economic inequality across Europe and the Americas. Using evidence from countries that vary in both culture and public policy context, we gain more insight into how family inequality is entwined with inequalities of class.

We speak of family inequality rather than family diversity. Diversity simply means variety, and if a growing variety of family trajectories were unrelated to inequality, there would be no need for this book. Instead, our collection serves to highlight the similarities and differences in the relationship between family instability and economic inequality across contexts.

The Social Trends Institute invited professors and scholars of law, sociology, economics, public policy, demography, and political economy to an experts meeting in Rome (February 16–18, 2017) to present new research on family inequality from a comparative perspective. The invited authors not only represented various academic disciplines but also contributed diverse perspectives to the debate surrounding issues of family inequality. There was broad agreement that class inequality affects patterns of partnership and child-bearing and, in turn, family change feeds economic inequality. Nonetheless, this volume, resulting from that meeting, also reflects pronounced differences in what various scholars conceived to be of prime importance with respect to growing inequality, and differences in how each might approach turning the vicious cycles into virtuous ones. All agreed that combatting growing economic inequality requires understanding what conditions this complex relationship as well as what mediates it. Cross-national comparisons are crucial for gaining this kind of understanding.

The Parts in this book bring together economics and the family, and they are organized as follows: Part I describes the unequal character of family life in Europe and the Americas, Part II explores its causes, Part III describes various consequences of diverging family structures, and Part IV presents potential solutions for bridging the growing family divide (or minimizing its consequences). The final Part provides commentary and concluding reflections on the overall questions explored throughout this volume.

DETAILING THE INCREASINGLY UNEQUAL SOCIOECONOMIC CHARACTER OF FAMILY LIFE

Two chapters describe family inequality: Marcia Carlson's on Europe and the United States, and Albert Esteve and Elizabeth Florez-Paredes' on Latin America and the Caribbean. Both chapters start with a description of change over time in family life. Carlson accomplishes this using indicators commonly associated with the "second demographic transition," a label commonly used to refer to the transition to below replacement fertility, but that is better understood as family patterns resulting when individuals have a great deal of autonomy in how they progress through the stages of their lives (Lesthaeghe 2010). The second demographic transition is typically characterized by less marriage, more cohabitation, more divorce, and more nonmarital childbearing; Carlson compares trends in these indicators between the United States and European countries as well as among European countries. She also makes cross-national comparisons with respect to multipartnered fertility and children's experience of family instability. Instead of using these indicators that have emerged from studies of northern fertility regimes, Esteve and Florez-Paredes start with an exploratory factor analysis to determine the dimensions that structure families in Latin America. They then organize the rest of their chapter around union and childbearing calendars, household complexity, married and unmarried cohabitation, and the nature of female household headship.

Both of these chapters in the "descriptive" Part of our volume lay the foundation for a discussion of how family change influences socioeconomic inequality. Before we can know whether the destinies of children are diverging with changing family patterns, we have to know what the trajectories of family change are. Both chapters contribute this, and they also document diversity within regions.

Additionally, both chapters take the crucial next step in exploring the extent to which family patterns have been unfolding differently along class lines. Carlson reviewed European evidence on educational differences in marriage, divorce, nonmarital fertility, multipartnered fertility, and children's experience of family instability. Although the more educated are more likely to marry in the United States, this pattern is less consistent across European countries, and holds most strongly in countries where women commonly expect continued labor force participation after marrying (Kalmijn 2007, 2013). Alternately stated, education has its strongest positive relationship with marriage where marriage does not substantially increase the chance that women will drop out of the labor force. Educated women are more likely to eschew marriage where gender roles are more traditional, a pattern Göran Therborn (2014) assumingly characterized as a "*Lysistrate* rebellion," referring to the women in Aristophanes' comedy who boycotted traditional marital expectations while waiting for men's behavior to change.

Carlson further reviewed fairly mixed evidence from across Europe on the relationship between education and divorce that therefore indicated that the concentration of union instability at lower socioeconomic levels in the United States was far from universal. Similarly, repartnering and multipartner fertility did not have consistent socioeconomic patterns across different contexts. In contrast, the concentration of nonmarital childbearing at lower socioeconomic levels was far more consistent across countries (Perelli-Harris et al. 2010).

Finally, with respect to family instability for children, the indicator most closely related to "diverging destinies," the (rather thin) evidence Carlson reviewed indicated that class differences in instability might be growing in Europe, but remain small compared to the US. She also highlights the fact that class differences in instability matter less for overall inequality in Europe where fewer children experience instability (see also Chapter 7).

Esteve and Florez-Paredes' chapter on families in Latin America addresses a context in which recent expansion in cohabitation has been concentrated among those with *higher* socioeconomic status (as proxied by educational attainment). In the United States and Europe where marriage increasingly occurs only after other achievements in adult life like college graduation and stable employment, those with less access to higher education and good jobs have become more likely to have children in cohabiting unions. In contrast, cohabitation and cohabiting childbearing have been long-standing lower class phenomena in Latin America and the Caribbean, with the more marginalized (especially the indigenous groups) opting for cohabitation, and the relatively elite choosing marriage (Esteve and Lesthaeghe 2016). Work on the region even refers to a "dual nuptiality system" (e.g., Castro-Martín 2002). Then some of the same forces that have affected family life in more developed countries – e.g., the rise of individualism, consumerism, and women's economic independence – have had the greatest impact among those with high socioeconomic status in Latin America and the Caribbean. This led to increased nonmarital childbearing (both births to lone mothers and in cohabiting unions) among upper-class individuals within the region (Esteve, Lesthaeghe, and López-Gay 2012). Historically, children born in cohabiting unions were concentrated at the bottom of the income distribution, but the socioeconomic gradient for cohabiting births has weakened in Latin America and the Caribbean.

Esteve and Florez-Paredes' work is richly descriptive. They show that despite the better-educated starting to "catch up" to their more marginalized counterparts in terms of cohabitation rates, cohabitation remains more common among women with low education. Furthermore, early union formation, early childbearing, single motherhood, and union dissolution are all more concentrated at low socioeconomic levels. In short, disadvantageous family behaviors remain correlated with social class. In this respect, Latin America and the Caribbean resemble the United States. Nonetheless, they argue that with the historical legacy of high cohabitation rates among indigenous groups, modern family transitions have not created diverging destinies as "Destinies have been diverging for centuries" (Chapter 2). Latin America is the most unequal region in the world for reasons that include, but are by no means limited to, family forms. Indeed, there are many diverse and long-standing reasons for inequality that may be partly reflected in contemporary family patterns, but cannot be understood by a study of recent changes in family patterns by women's education.

In addition, Esteve and Florez-Paredes emphasize a theme that also emerges in Brienna Perelli-Harris' work (see Chapter 4): Context sometimes dwarfs overall patterns. What this means in Latin America and the Caribbean is that even though there is a fairly consistent overall relationship between family patterns and social disadvantage, "two individuals with similar profiles regarding education, ethnicity, and religion may show quite different family behaviour depending on the region where they live, proving that 'individuals have histories but regions have much longer histories'" (Esteve and Lesthaeghe 2016, p. 269). Historical differences among Latin American countries and between Latin America and Europe with respect to the evolution of and function of marriage still seem to condition individual marital choices, even though there are advantages associated with marriage across contexts.

Esteve's previous research had shown that cohabitation patterns depended on geohistorical legacies, and the contribution in this volume extends that argument to other family patterns (especially single and cohabiting child-bearing). Overall, he and Florez-Paredes show that context is a more important determinant of family behavior than class, but that the class patterns showing up in Latin American family change resemble those documented in the United States (and to a lesser extent Europe). Notably, the rise in upper-class cohabitation coincided with postponed childbearing, whereas low-educated cohabiting women have not been postponing childbearing within their unions. There is therefore potential for destinies to diverge even when cohabitation grows most among the elite.

Their chapter makes a further contribution to cross-country analysis when it highlights an aspect of family life in Latin America and the Caribbean that has, to date, been resistant to change: Women start childbearing relatively early in life. Age at first birth in the region has not increased appreciably – even with lower overall fertility, increases in women's education, and increases in women's labor force participation. Esteve and Florez-Paredes show that only university-educated women have come to postpone childbearing more over time. Among primary- and secondary-educated women, first births have remained early.

EXPLORING THE CAUSES OF INCREASINGLY UNEQUAL FAMILY LIFE

Part II of the volume on causes of inequality in family life includes contributions from Andrew Cherlin, Nicholas Eberstadt, and Brienna Perelli-Harris. Each has a different emphasis. Cherlin draws the causal arrow from economic inequality to family formation and dissolution, arguing that when men's job opportunities suffer, so does marriage. Eberstadt assigns more importance to policy and cultural causes of the retreat from marriage, while Perelli-Harris maintains that context matters more for class differences in family patterns than any universal explanations.

Cherlin argues that unequal labor market opportunities drive the retreat from marriage. He nonetheless fully concedes that economic forces only erode marriage *after* culture change has already opened up multiple possibilities for adult lives and childrearing – e.g., the Great Depression did not cause a surge in nonmarital births – but he holds that now that choices are available, the economically disadvantaged will have more nonmarital childrearing.

Cherlin's "prima facie" case for the importance of the economy as a driver of change is that moderately educated Americans saw the most pronounced retreat from marriage during the same era (starting in the 1980s) that men's labor market opportunities declined more dramatically for moderately educated Americans than for either the less or more educated. Men's earning power remains an important component of their "marriageability": It is required even in an egalitarian marital bargain where both partners share in paid and domestic work. Thus, socioeconomic inequality drives family inequality.

In contrast, Eberstadt documents that prime-age men have been progressively less likely to work in every birth cohort over the last fifty years in the United States. He emphasizes that the "flight from work" (see Chapter 5) has also in large part been a flight from marriage and parental involvement. In one of the exercises in his chapter, Eberstadt explores how the changing composition of the American population – in terms of race, education, nativity, education, and family structure – are related to men's work rates. His findings are striking, for instance that the positive effect of half a century of improvements in educational attainment has been more than canceled out by changes in marriage patterns. He also includes engaging comparisons showing that marital status is more strongly associated with work than other factors associated with disadvantage, like race. Eberstadt readily acknowledges that these parts of his analysis leave causal questions completely open.

In fact, Eberstadt gives much credit to "demand side" hypotheses (see Chapter 5) like Cherlin's – those that assert that marriage rates have fallen because changes in the economy make the kind of stable employment that contributes to marriage less likely. He nonetheless maintains that the decline in employment among prime-age men over the past two generations cannot be fully explained by the demand side. His evidence includes both that men's inactivity at the national level has increased smoothly over time, despite demand-side "shocks" like the North American Free Trade Agreement (NAFTA) agreement that should arguably have had a more detectable effect on joblessness, as well as state-level employment patterns that are far more variable than demand-side theory would predict. Eberstadt adds the reverse causal arrow to demand-side theories, claiming that men oriented toward marriage and parenthood commit themselves to jobs. He bolsters this

contention by showing nearly identical employment rates for married high
school dropouts and unmarried college degree holders from 1994 to 2015.
In other words, he discounts job prospects as the sole driver of family change
by showing that marriage seems to enhance job prospects.

Perelli-Harris makes her case for the importance of context in addressing
the relationship between family inequality and socioeconomic inequality in
four distinct ways. First, she shows through the geographic concentration of
nonmarital childbearing that evidence of history, religion, policy, and culture
all appear in contemporary geographic variation in nonmarital childbearing.
Next, she reviews how different European countries have extended (or not
extended) rights to cohabitants and unmarried fathers, and discusses the
potential implications of these variations for the class divide associated with
cohabiting childbearing. Third, she presents focus group research that demonstrates just how different the meanings assigned to cohabitation are across
countries. Fourth, she presents evidence from a study she led that systematically tackled some of the methodological obstacles to properly testing
whether marriage per se (as opposed to simply being in a union) makes
a difference for adult well-being.

One of the only commonalities across countries was that marriage was
universally viewed as an expression of commitment. Importantly in the context of the current volume, none of the focus groups across eight European
countries put an emphasis on the need for economic stability prior to marriage – a factor that is so much a part of the discourse on the class divide in
marriage in the United States. Thus it is possible that selecting marriage on the
basis of economic stability is less a part of the European family inequality story.

Her final discussion of adult outcomes (mental well-being, health, life
satisfaction, and wage differentials) provides a nice segue to Part III of the
book on consequences of growing family instability. The results fully supported Perelli-Harris's major theme (see Chapter 4) that country context
conditions the effects associated with cohabitation. She says: "Overall, the
results suggest that taking into account the heterogeneity of cohabiting unions
(as measured by union duration and shared children) as well as selection
mechanisms from childhood can explain many of the marital benefits to well-
being, but country context, such as welfare state regime and social norms, also
matters."

While most of Perelli-Harris' chapter emphasizes diversity in timing and
pace of family change, she did find more evidence of a class divide in
nonmarital childbearing than other new family formation behaviors. "Across
Europe, higher educated individuals are more likely to marry before a birth
(Mikolai et al. 2016), and lower educated individuals are more likely to

separate after a birth (Musick and Michelmore 2015)" (Chapter 4). Thus while she rightfully calls for more research to understand the complex relationships between context, selection, socially constructed meanings of cohabitation and marriage, and changes over individual life courses, she does point to an important similarity between the United States and Europe: Childbearing within marriage occurs more often among the advantaged.

CONSEQUENCES OF GROWING FAMILY INSTABILITY

The fourth section of Perelli-Harris' chapter (Chapter 4) examines how adult outcomes vary between cohabitants and married individuals, and Part III of our book supplements this concern for adult well-being with analysis of potential consequences of family inequality for the reproduction of inequality (Diederik Boertien, Fabrizio Bernardi, and Juho Härkönen, Chapter 7; Anna Garriga and Paolo Berta, Chapter 6), and for the growth of national economies (W. Bradford Wilcox and Joseph Price, Chapter 8).

Garriga and Berta address the question of whether children's destinies are diverging across twenty-one Western countries, and they approach their comparative inquiry in an unusually thorough manner. First, they explore to what extent there is a general pattern in Western countries of single motherhood being more common among women with less education; there is. Despite substantial cross-national differences in the relationship between mothers' education and single motherhood, they confirmed that a negative relationship between mother's education and single motherhood holds in most Western countries.

Second, they use three outcome variables that, while all related to education, are nonetheless distinct: Standardized math test scores, grade repetition, and truancy. While most previous comparative work had used standardized test scores, grade repetition, and truancy are both strongly associated with labor market outcomes and risk behaviors, such as drug abuse or crime (Garry 1996; Jones, Lovrich, and Lovrich 2011; Range, Yonke, and Young 2011). In other words, these additional two outcomes tell us more about the likelihood that destinies will diverge than cognitive achievement alone does; they have strong behavioral components. Garriga and Berta found that children in single-mother families had lower math test scores in seventeen of the twenty-one countries, plus that they were more likely to repeat a grade or truant practically everywhere. Further, higher levels of maternal education seemed to compensate for the negative effect of single motherhood on test scores, but much less so for the other two risk-related outcomes.

Finally, Garriga and Berta consider the question of whether the effects of single motherhood are greater or lesser among children of more highly educated mothers. Destinies might actually converge if family structure had little effect at lower socioeconomic levels where many children have relatively poor educational outcomes, compared to higher socioeconomic levels where a second parent in the household might help prevent subpar outcomes. Their findings here were quite mixed: For some outcomes and in some countries, children of less-educated mothers experienced greater consequences associated with single motherhood, while for other outcomes and/or other countries, it was children of more-educated mothers whose outcomes were most strongly related to family structure. This means that the general tendency for single motherhood to be more common at lower socioeconomic levels would sometimes result in diverging destinies: Where educated mothers compensate for the disadvantages their children would otherwise experience with single motherhood or the consequences are the same regardless of maternal education, but that sometimes high prevalence of single motherhood is coupled with low associated costs, thus limiting the extent to which destinies would diverge.

Boertien, Bernardi, and Härkönen's chapter (Chapter 7) on whether family inequality contributes to national-level increases in socioeconomic inequality is like Garriga and Berta's chapter in that they focus individually on each of several conditions that would together make diverging destinies likely. They briefly discuss critical reviews of how much difference family dynamics really matter for child outcomes, with a focus on both the magnitude of the association and how much of it is properly interpreted as being causal. Next, they examine the extent to which lower income children are overrepresented among those experiencing disadvantageous family dynamics. Third, they engage with the question of how the "penalty" associated with disadvantageous family dynamics varies by socioeconomic background: The same question Garriga and Berta take up in their third and final section (see Chapter 6).

In their own final section, Boertien and his colleagues (see Chapter 7) discuss recent evidence from the United States, the United Kingdom, Germany, and Italy that quantified the overall contribution of family structure to inequality of opportunity at the societal level. "Overall" includes the size of the effects, the distribution of the affected population by socioeconomic status, and the variability in the size of effects by socioeconomic status. They conclude that even though family structure is an important factor determining life chances at the individual level, family inequality does not explain growing socioeconomic inequality within societies. In the United States and the

United Kingdom, nonintact families were concentrated among the disadvantaged, but the consequences were smaller among the disadvantaged – thus explaining the small net impact at the societal level. In Germany, children whose mothers had intermediate levels of education were the most likely to have nonintact families, while in Italy, very few children were disadvantaged by family inequality in any socioeconomic group. Thus for different reasons in disparate contexts, family inequality did not have sizable effects on the distribution of educational attainment (attending tertiary institutions). They leave open the question of whether children's destinies diverge with respect to other outcomes.

While the first two chapters in Part III focus on inequality, Wilcox and Price (see Chapter 8) investigate the association between prevalent family structures and rates of economic growth. They show that countries where two-parent families are more common, as well as those with higher marriage rates, enjoy higher rates of economic growth (using data from 2001 to 2014 and controlling for individual country fixed effects).

While emphasizing that these correlations may not be causal, Wilcox and Price nonetheless describe potential causal pathways and provide cross-country evidence testing various mechanisms. Specifically, they show that countries with higher proportions of children living with both biological parents have: (1) higher savings rates and (2) lower homicide rates. Labor force statistics, however, did not support their argument, as intact families did not predict higher men's labor force participation rates, and were associated with lower women's labor force participation rates. Their evidence nonetheless opens the door for further investigation of the idea that intact married families do not just confer benefits on their members but that they may also help nations prosper by promoting savings and public safety (as well as other potential mechanisms like supporting educational attainment).

BRIDGING THE GROWING FAMILY DIVIDE FOR CHILDREN

Part IV of our volume addresses how the impact of family inequality on children can be reduced. Both chapters are essentially optimistic. Frances Kobrin Goldscheider and Sharon Sassler (see Chapter 9) explain why it is reasonable to expect that the more equal gender bargain that characterizes marriage among those with more education, will also become characteristic of unions regardless of the socioeconomic position of the couples. They believe that cultural diffusion will lessen family inequality (with or without strong state support for families). Richard V. Reeves' (see Chapter 10) optimism comes from accepting that new family forms present policy challenges, and also believing that policy levers to effect change are available and reasonable.

Goldscheider and Sassler frame their chapter around the question of whether the gender revolution will characterize only those with higher education unless governments provide structures that support gender equality (e.g., individual taxation, generous family benefits). Gender equality is of central concern in a chapter about reducing inequality for children because of the assumption that when men are more involved in domestic life, families are stronger and more stable. While the rise in women's labor force participation – the first half of the gender revolution – has come to affect family life in all socioeconomic strata, the rise in men's domestic work participation – the second half of the gender revolution – is concentrated among the more educated. Countries with the most generous policies for reducing work–family conflict provide the exception to this rule: There is less of a class divide in men's domestic work participation in northern European countries. Hence their central question is whether either the lack of social equality or the lack of strong state support for families will stall the gender revolution, leaving families without the benefits of the no longer realistic male breadwinner system nor men's enhanced involvement at home.

Goldscheider and Sassler begin by emphasizing that the relationship between female labor force participation rates and fertility at the national level has changed: It used to be that countries with more traditional gender roles had higher fertility, but now, among advanced countries, it is those with relatively egalitarian gender roles that have higher fertility. It thus appears that even if the educated led the *"Lysistrate* rebellion" against traditional gender roles, the results are profound enough to show up in national-level statistics: The traditional gender bargain is not supporting childbearing. Nonetheless, Goldscheider and Sassler recognize that it is the same countries that have both the most egalitarian gender roles and the most generous policies for reducing work–family conflict.

In direct response to the contention that the second half of the gender revolution cannot take hold without strong state support, they refer to work showing that the levels and trends in men's share of housework and child-care time are very similar in the United States and Scandinavia (Stanfors and Goldscheider 2017). They even argue that the *lack* of state support for families in the United States may have increased the need for men's involvement in child-rearing since, for example, publicly funded universal preschool is not available.

Their paradigm for overcoming class barriers is one of diffusion. The more educated often lead many types of social change "so that differences by education widen early in the change process and then attenuate as the new behavior diffuses more generally" (Chapter 9). From this perspective, family inequality may be a transient problem that subsides when the less educated adopt more egalitarian gender roles. The chapter reviews both quantitative and qualitative evidence, suggesting that less-educated men are becoming increasingly invested in directly caring for their children. They further suggest that although couples with egalitarian orientations used to select cohabitation, egalitarianism is beginning to promote marriage. The diffusion of egalitarian attitudes could then contribute to stability in children's lives both directly through men's involvement and indirectly through marriage.

The social diffusion arguments that Goldsheider and Sassler make by no means render policy unimportant. For example, they applaud maternity leave benefits that are tied to the level of prebirth earnings because this creates an incentive to avoid teen childbearing that, of course, contributes to family inequality. They also note that family-friendly policies have been diffusing even within the United States. Provided that the Trump administration does not derail this process, more parents will have support for combining work and child care. Consistent with their gender revolution approach, the policies that they identify as being the most pro-family (in terms of encouraging more childbearing) are those that encourage men to share more of the family leave. They also recommend an income "floor" to support men's financial contributions to their families. In other words, supporting men and women as earners and nurturers is key to promoting strong families.

Reeves acknowledges a literature that points to parental union transitions as problematic for children across a broad range of outcomes. Of particular significance for combatting "diverging destinies," children reared in stable married parent families have the best chance of upward intergenerational mobility (Reeves and Venator 2015), plus children in communities with more single mothers are less mobile (Chetty et al. 2014a). Reeves assumes parental union transitions will happen, but he wants to see fewer of them, and lower costs for the children involved. He thus advocates for strategies that both prevent family instability and mitigate its consequences.

Because Reeves agrees with his colleague Isabel Sawhill (2014) that "family formation is a new fault line in the American class structure": Preventing family instability must include reducing unintended pregnancy rates. Neither shotgun marriages nor shotgun cohabitations provide the kind of stability for children that unions formed before conceptions do (Lichter et al. 2016). Reeves highlights the rapid liberalization of social norms regarding sex across all socioeconomic groups, but uptake of effective contraception (especially long-acting reversible contraceptives like intrauterine devices and injectables) primarily among the most educated. Ensuring access to affordable, effective contraception is therefore not just "the most powerful pro-family policy available" (Chapter 10) but also a means of combatting family inequality. He also argues for affordable, effective contraception as key to promoting a social norm of responsible parenthood.

The other policy recommendations on Reeves' "prevention" list is to enhance the stability of families that already have children. To enable better earning power among the less educated, he would like to see more vocational apprenticeships and strengthening of community college capacity/effectiveness. In addition, he recommends two policies that make the work–family balance more practical: Enhancing the predictability of work schedules and providing paid leave. Goldscheider and Sassler would add that some of the paid leave should not be transferable between parents as employers seem to respect men's right to use use-it-or-lose-it leave.

Reeves' "mitigating" list includes increasing material resources to unmarried parents; improving parenting skills, especially among the less educated; and enhancing children's learning opportunities outside the home. In all cases, the fundamental idea is that parental union instability costs, that it costs the already disadvantaged more (something that Garriga and Berta as well as Boertien, Bernardi, and Härkönen question – at least for some children's outcomes), and that therefore interventions that disproportionately help the disadvantaged will help mitigate the impact of family inequality. The only interventions that made his list were those patterned after programs that had actually been shown to work (those with an evidence base).

BRINGING IT ALL TOGETHER? COMMENTARY ON THEMES

In Chapter 11, Lynn Prince Cooke focuses on gender and cross-cultural issues. She emphasizes that the magnitude of the family changes, and especially their negative outcomes, varies across cultural, economic, and political contexts. She argues that the patterns of cross-contextual variation are critical to understanding the differences in life chances across family types, and that these differences are minimized where institutional arrangements, unlike in the United States, support greater gender along with class equality. It is, she suggests, a pathology of *patriarchy* (not of matriarchy) that disproportionately hurts the life chances of boys and men.

The chapter then highlights how structural changes over the past half-century make patriarchal assumptions untenable for a growing proportion of men. Cooke concludes by arguing that only fully institutionalizing gender equality will minimize negative outcomes associated with family change. She observes that gender equality ensures children will have access to the economic and emotional resources that are critical to their development, regardless of family form, and that it encourages development of new normative masculinities that support greater family stability.

In their commentary and concluding thoughts in Chapter 13, June Carbone and Naomi R. Cahn analyze the differing approaches to the relationship between economic inequality and family structure that are apparent throughout the contributions to this volume. One approach suggests that family change – particularly class-based increases in relationship instability, nonmarital cohabitation, and single-parent births – makes an independent contribution to societal inequality beyond that which is explained by economic change. Another approach sees economic change as the source of both greater inequality and family transformation, and favors solutions that provide greater support to those left behind – both for poverty alleviation and to enhance relationship stability. Carbone and Cahn point out that both groups agree that a new information-based society has witnessed a series of overlapping changes: Greater demand for women's market labor, an elite shift to later marriage and relatively more egalitarian relationships, declining wages for unskilled men, greater tolerance for nonmarital sexuality, and lower overall fertility. While the approaches overlap, they differ in their identification of causation, preferred family strategies, and proposed government interventions.

Their commentary highlights where grounds emerge for at least tentative agreement, the issues likely to remain subjects of intense disagreement, and the areas that have yet to be fully explored. Their goal is to move the focus from the areas of disagreement toward positive policies with proven impact. Ultimately, Carbone and Cahn believe that economic inequality and cultural values interact with each other in an iterative fashion. In short, they require a dynamic systems analysis, not just the isolation of individual causal agents.

Wilcox's concluding reflections in Part V, Chapter 12 encourage scholars and policymakers to think about how the global retreat from marriage is connected to greater family instability and, in some places, more family inequality in Europe and the Americas. In particular, Wilcox contends that the retreat from marriage and the rise of cohabitation throughout Europe and the Americas has led to more family instability and single parenthood in many countries across these three continents, in countries as diverse as the United States, France, and the Dominican Republic. Wilcox believes that cohabitation, insofar as it less institutionalized than marriage, is generally less stable than marriage for children; this is why the rise of cohabitation may be fueling growing family instability in parts of Europe and the Americas. Moreover, in some of these countries, such as the United Kingdom and Sweden, family instability has grown most among less-educated and lower income families. Even though in some contexts family instability does not contribute as much to disadvantage among those that are already of lower socioeconomic status (Boertien, Bernardi, and Härkönen, Chapter 7), Wilcox argues scholars concerned with growing family inequality in family stability need to pay closer attention to the ways in which the retreat from marriage may be contributing to inequality and the stability and structure of family life.

ANSWERED AND UNANSWERED QUESTIONS ABOUT FAMILY INEQUALITY

Together, the contributions in this book highlight some useful themes for understanding the patterns, causes, consequences, and potential remedies for family inequality. We have, of course, not solved the complex puzzle nor identified everything that contributes to diversity of outcomes across contexts. We nonetheless came away from our meeting in Rome knowing more, and knowing more about what we do not know.

What we know:

(1) Socioeconomic inequality predated "new family forms" and will survive regardless of future family trajectories. The questions for the present moment are whether new family forms are making it more difficult to combat socioeconomic inequality and, if so, what can/should be done about it.

(2) The emergence of postindustrial economies and globalization have changed job markets in ways that can have profound effects on socioeconomic inequality and family inequality: One of the reasons the two have grown at the same time is that they have common causes.

(3) Recent and current changes in job markets are far from gender-neutral. Thus, the implications of economic change for family stability are importantly conditioned by the gender norms prevailing in the most affected subpopulations. Reorganization in the public sphere is going to prompt reorganization in the private sphere, but whether that is going

to result in couples that are highly interdependent in ways very different from Beckerian specialization (especially with both partners invested in child care) or increasingly fragile families is likely to be context-dependent.

(4) Different aspects of family change affect various classes differently. Some indicators associated with "the second demographic transition" (e.g., repartnering, multipartner fertility) show inconsistent relationships with social class. Class patterns of marriage and divorce also vary in both magnitude and direction across countries, but within countries, divorce tends to become concentrated at the lower end of the socioeconomic spectrum over time. Nonmarital childbearing is universally more common among women with less education, as is lone child-rearing. Children with less-educated mothers are also more likely to experience union instability.

(5) Levels of union instability condition the potential social consequences of new family forms. Thus policy that strengthens unions or keeps children from being born to unstable unions can be helpful, whether or not family inequality is an important cause of socioeconomic inequality. Similarly, delayed childbearing is a feature of the second demographic transition that could combat inequality if it could be successfully promoted among the disadvantaged.

What we do not know:

(1) Does the lack of emphasis on a need for economic stability prior to marriage in European discourse on cohabitation (Perelli-Harris, Chapter 4) help explain why the United States has the sharpest class gradient in cohabitation? Would it be useful to try to "export" an ethos that makes marriage more about commitment and less dependent on financial success?

(2) Given that welfare state regimes and social norms condition how similar outcomes for children with various family histories are, which gaps can be closed by policy? More specifically, can state policy help narrow behavioral differences associated with family structure (such as truancy) as well as cognitive ones (like test scores)? More generally, what can we learn from which outcomes are most universally related to family inequality versus which ones seem to respond well to policy?

(3) Is family inequality a transient problem that will subside when some of its causes like the decline of the male breadwinner system are relics of a distant past, or will the rise in individualism associated with

postmodern societies make family instability and thus family inequality an ongoing issue? If it is an ongoing issue, will family formation continue to be a "fault line" in class structure? Where?

(4) How is race part of the family inequality story? Various chapters allude to the importance of race, but, given that the meaning of race depends on context, we did not even try to draw any meaningful conclusions across Europe and the Americas. This volume focused on class, and in so doing it left many unanswered questions about the importance of race in family inequality, the intersection of race and class in conditioning family inequality, and how historical legacies with respect to race play out in different countries.

(5) To what extent is economic instability a cause of family inequality? There are several important issues buried in this question. First, good jobs that do not last do not provide the same kind of foundation for marriage and child-rearing as do more secure jobs. In the face of perpetual uncertainty, choices like delaying childbearing make less sense than under conditions where there are known benefits associated with waiting. Yet most of our evidence on family/economy connections focuses on employment rates, and not employment stability. How would what we know change if we knew more about instability? Second, are labor regulations that make employment more stable in many European countries part of the reason that the families are less unequal in Europe than the United States?

(6) What other contextual factors are we missing? While we are happy to have put together a volume that highlights political history, religion, family policy, gender roles, and labor policy as factors conditioning both the causes and consequences of family inequality, we suspect that future research will identify more important aspects of context that contribute to the great diversity across time, space, and various children's outcomes.

With all of these explored and unexplored questions, this volume contributes to an improved understanding of the core issues involved in the relationship between family and economic inequality.

PART I

THE INCREASINGLY UNEQUAL SOCIOECONOMIC CHARACTER OF FAMILY LIFE

Families Unequal: Socioeconomic Gradients in Family Patterns across the United States and Europe

Marcia J. Carlson[*]

INTRODUCTION

Dramatic changes in marriage, divorce, cohabitation, and fertility behaviors over the past fifty years have been observed across a wide range of industrialized countries, sometimes referred to as the "second demographic transition" (Lesthaeghe and Neidert 2006). Yet, only within the past several decades has there been growing awareness of the extent to which changes in family demography are unfolding unevenly by socioeconomic status. McLanahan (2004) was among the first to identify that differences by socioeconomic status (measured by maternal education) in a range of family behaviors were an important aspect of growing inequality ("diverging destinies") among children, especially in the United States. Other scholars have increasingly considered differences in various family behaviors by socioeconomic status across other countries (e.g., Härkönen and Dronkers 2006; Kalmijn 2013; Perelli-Harris et al. 2010), but the extent to which socioeconomic gradients in family behaviors are broadly observed across Western industrialized countries (and whether such gradients may be positive or negative) is less well understood. In this chapter, I examine whether there are differences by socioeconomic status with respect to a range of family behaviors based on the extant literature in the United States and Europe.

[*] Paper prepared for the experts meeting on "Family Inequality: Causes and Consequences in Europe & the Americas," Rome, Italy, February 15–19, 2017, sponsored by the Social Trends Institute with assistance from the Institute for Family Studies. I thank Anna Garriga, Brienna Perelli-Harris, and the editors of this volume for very useful comments. I appreciate support for this research from the Eunice Kennedy Shriver National Institute of Child Health and Human Development (NICHD) through a core grant to the Center for Demography and Ecology at the University of Wisconsin–Madison (P2CHD47873).

The striking changes in family behaviors that have been observed since the middle of the twentieth century across Western countries include a delay and decline in marriage, an increase in cohabitation, a notable rise in divorce rates (followed by a decline in some nations), a high prevalence of repartnering, and a large increase in the proportion of births that occurred outside marriage. Also, there is today striking instability and complexity in family life, as adults are likely to spend time living with more than one partner in marital and/or cohabiting unions, and children often experience several changes in the adults who co-reside with them and/or serve as parental figures in their lives. In this context, men's involvement with children has become especially precarious, since women still maintain primary responsibility for child-rearing after union dissolution (Goldscheider 2000). Taken together, these patterns suggest high levels of instability and perhaps complexity in children's family arrangements and experiences over childhood and adolescence (Furstenberg 2014).

Over the same time period that family patterns have changed, we have also observed a striking increase in overall levels of economic inequality across many industrialized countries, including those that are more egalitarian in values and public policy (OECD 2011b). The increase has been especially stark in the United States – whether measured by wage rates, earnings, family income or wealth (Brandolini and Smeeding 2006; Gottschalk and Danziger 2005; Piketty and Saez 2003). After a strong period of economic growth that benefited individuals across all parts of the income distribution from the mid-1940s to the early 1970s, US inequality rose in the 1980s, slowed somewhat in the 1990s during the economic expansion, then continued to rise as we entered the twenty-first century (Autor, Katz, and Kearney 2008; Blank 1997). Recent cross-national comparisons show heterogeneity in the levels of inequality observed across European countries (with Scandinavian countries being somewhat less unequal). Compared to industrialized OECD countries, the United States has very high levels of income inequality; in 2013, on average, the top 10 percent of US incomes were fully 19 times higher than those of the bottom 10 percent of incomes, compared to the OECD average of the top 10 percent being about 10 times higher than the bottom 10 percent (OECD 2015). It is important to note that US *market income* inequality (i.e., before taxes and transfers) is not exceptionally high compared to other European countries (Gini of 0.52, where the range is 0.43 to 0.56 across 19 OECD countries examined in 2010) (Gornick and Milanovic 2015). Rather, the United States does far less than other countries to redistribute income via social policy; after accounting for taxes and transfers, Gini coefficients across these 19 countries ranged from 0.24 in Norway to 0.37 in the United States: Scandinavian countries (Norway, Denmark, and Finland) had the lowest Ginis (0.24–0.26), Anglo-countries (Australia, Canada, the United Kingdom, and the United States) had the highest (0.32–0.37), and central/southern/eastern European countries (Czech Republic, Estonia, France, Germany, Greece, Italy, Luxembourg, Netherlands, Poland, Slovak Republic, Spain, as well as the Republic of Ireland), comprised a group in the middle (0.26–0.33) (Gornick and Milanovic 2015).

Changes in family patterns and economic inequality are not independent, especially in the United States. Indeed, many would argue that the fundamental changes in the economy that have undergirded the overall rise in inequality have also been key drivers of the changes in family patterns. Amidst rapid technological change, deindustrialization, and globalization in labor markets, "good jobs" for those with low-to-moderate education became increasingly scarce (Cherlin 2014). Starting in the 1980s, scholars began to understand that the limited job opportunities for low-skilled men, especially in poor urban areas, were shaping family behaviors among the disadvantaged (Blank 2009); the decline in "marriageable men" (i.e., men who could get and hold a steady job) was seen as a key aspect of decreasing marriage rates, especially in large US cities (Wilson 1987). Over the same period (since the 1970s), women were increasingly entering the labor market. Women's employment and earnings provided them with greater economic independence (Oppenheimer 1988), which has been an important factor that typically delays entry into marriage (Sweeney 2002; Xie et al. 2003). Once married, the influence of women's employment and earnings on the likelihood of divorce is less straightforward, and it seems the greater risk of divorce with higher female earnings is only observed for marriages of lower relationship quality (Sayer and Bianchi 2000; Schoen et al. 2002) and for marriages begun in the 1960s and 1970s – but not for marriages begun in the 1990s (Schwartz and Gonalons-Pons 2016).

While economic changes and globalization have contributed to rising inequality within (and between) most industrialized countries in recent decades (Firebaugh 2015), we know that the ultimate circumstances of individuals and families also depend on the level and type of policy supports and the degree of "decommodification" (i.e., citizens' ability to have sufficient income independent of the market) across welfare states (Esping-Andersen 1990). Overall, means-tested and targeted benefits are less effective for reducing poverty and inequality as compared to universal social insurance benefits

(Korpi and Palme 1998). As noted above, the Scandinavian countries typically offer more generous welfare policies that provide higher levels of support and allow parents to better balance work and family obligations, as compared to Anglo-countries (especially the United States) which offer minimal support, with central and' southern European countries falling somewhere in between (Gornick, Meyers, and Ross 1997). There is extensive research demonstrating that indeed social policies across countries have an important influence on levels of inequality in economic outcomes such as employment, earnings, and income (e.g., Hegewisch and Gornick 2011; Mandel and Semyonov 2005).

At the same time, differences in family patterns may also *contribute to* increasing economic inequality, both within and across generations – at least in the United States (M. Martin 2006; McLanahan 2004; McLanahan and Percheski 2008). Within the United States, changes in family structure – especially the rise in divorce and single parenthood – are shown to have increased family income inequality, although there is a range in the estimates about how big a factor these have been (McLanahan and Percheski 2008). Also, increasingly homogamous marriages at both the low and high ends of the income distribution were observed from 1960 to the early 2000s (Schwartz and Mare 2005), and the growing association in spouses' earnings served to significantly increase aggregate-level income inequality in the United States (Schwartz 2010). To my knowledge, there has been less research about how family patterns per se have driven levels of inequality in other countries. The prevalence of single parenthood has been linked with higher inequality across sixteen European countries between 1967 and 2005, holding constant the level of female employment (which is itself associated with *reduced* inequality) (Kollmeyer 2013). An analysis of Denmark shows that greater educational assortative mating has increased inequality, but due to shifting educational distributions by gender (i.e., education increasing for both men and women – but more so for women) rather than partner choice (Breen and Andersen 2012). Certainly, families with greater socioeconomic resources are able to make greater investments (of both time and money) in their children (Kalil 2015; Kalil, Ryan, and Corey 2012; Lareau 2003), and these differential investments may be an important factor in growing inequality, especially across generations (Lundberg, Pollak, and Stearns 2016; Reeves 2017). And as Cooke (see Chapter 11) describes, countries differ greatly in the share of national resources that are invested in families; when countries provide greater baseline support, there is likely less variation by parents' income in how much they invest in children. Nevertheless, differential parental investments have

a long-lasting effect on the development and attainment of the next generation, and inequality therein (Heckman 2007; Yeung, Linver, and Brooks-
Gunn 2002).

Thus, overall, it seems reasonable to expect a reciprocal and dynamic
relationship between inequality and family patterns: Aggregate-level inequality affects family behaviors and outcomes, and differential family patterns
further reify inequality and stratification (McLanahan and Percheski 2008).
In the remainder of this chapter, I will (a) provide a brief review of key
changes in family patterns that have occurred over the past half-century in
the United States and Europe, and then (b) summarize the literature about
the extent to which differentials in family patterns by socioeconomic status are
observed.

CHANGING FAMILY PATTERNS

Across most Western industrialized countries, a number of changes in family
behaviors occurred, beginning in the 1960s. Often referred to as the "second
demographic transition," there has been a similarity in the changes across
Western countries that included delayed marriage, a disconnection between
marriage and childbearing, a diversity of relationships and living arrangements, and declining fertility to below replacement level (Lesthaeghe 2010).
While not uniform across all countries or European regions (see Chapter 4),
the basic changes in family behaviors fall into predictable patterns, as
described below.

Marriage and Cohabitation. At the core of changes in family life over the
past half-century have been shifts in the nature of union formation and marital
behavior. Marriage has become less central to the life course, both because
individuals are marrying later and a small – but perhaps rising – fraction are
not marrying at all (Cherlin 2009). As shown in Figure 1.1, crude marriage rates
have significantly declined in most OECD countries over the period from
1970 to 2014.

Across nearly all OECD countries, age at first marriage has increased
over the past two decades (see Figure 1.2); women's mean ages at marriage
now range from the mid-twenties in some Eastern European countries to
the early thirties in some Scandinavian countries. In the United States, the
median age at first marriage has never been higher than since data were first
collected in 1890 – age 27.4 for women and 29.5 for men in 2015 (US Census
Bureau 2016).

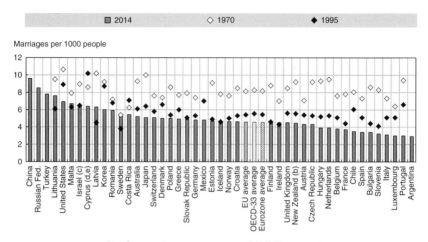

FIGURE 1.1 Crude marriage rates across OECD countries, 1970–2014
Source: OECD Family Database (OECD 2017).

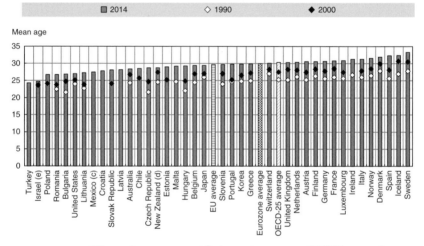

FIGURE 1.2 Women's mean age at first marriage across OECD countries,
1990–2014
Source: OECD Family Database (OECD 2017).

Also, cohabitation has increased such that today over 60 percent of US women have ever cohabited (Manning 2013), and the fraction is even higher in most European countries. Cohabitation has essentially replaced marriage as a first union for the majority of young adults, as, at least in the United States, individuals have been entering a first union at about the same average age over the past twenty years (Manning, Brown, and Payne 2014). The diverse meanings and experiences of cohabitation are an important factor in both the United States and Europe, as cohabitation may be a precursor to – or a substitute for – legal marriage for different groups or at different stages of the life course for the same individuals (Heuveline and Timberlake 2004; Hiekel, Liefbroer, and Poortman 2014; Perelli-Harris et al. 2014; Seltzer 2004). A growing proportion of first births now occur within cohabiting unions across European countries (Perelli-Harris et al. 2012) and the United States (Curtain, Ventura, and Martinez 2014). Further, many cohabiting households include children who are born to couples while living together or that one or the other partner has from a prior relationship (Kennedy and Bumpass 2008; Thomson 2014).

Divorce. Divorce has been rising across most European countries over recent decades, and there is notable heterogeneity in the patterns, causes, and consequences (Amato and James 2010). Divorce in the United States has historically been much higher than in other Western countries, and the best estimates suggesting that about half of all first marriages will end in divorce in the United States (Amato 2010). Figure 1.3 shows crude divorce rates across OECD countries for 1970–2014, ranging from the lowest European levels today in the Republic of Ireland and Italy to the highest in Lithuania, Denmark, and the Russian Federation. In many countries, divorce rates rose between 1970 and 1995 and then declined between 1995 and 2014. Across European countries, divorce tends to be higher in the West and North versus lower in the East and South.

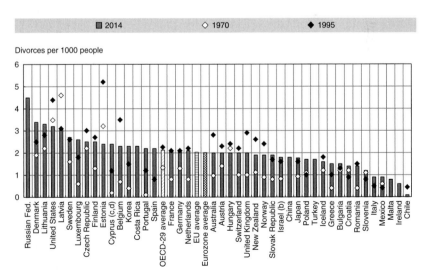

FIGURE 1.3 Crude divorce rates across OECD countries, 1970–2014
Source: OECD Family Database (OECD 2017).

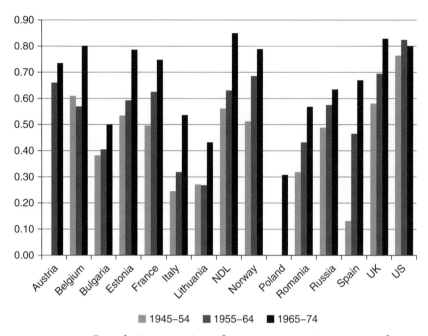

FIGURE 1.4 Cumulative proportions of women repartnering ten years after union dissolution by cohort

Repartnering. As many unions now dissolve, it is increasingly likely that individuals will have more than one partner over their life course, either by marriage and/or cohabitation. Repartnering provides a new opportunity to share economic resources, give/receive emotional support, and experience companionship and sexual intimacy, and thus may offset some of the negative consequences of divorce (Amato 2010). Yet, when children are involved, repartnered relationships may be more complicated or less "institutionalized" than first partnerships (Cherlin and Furstenberg 1994). Across Europe and the United States, there has been a notable rise in repartnering since the 1970s, although there is substantial cross-country variation (Gałęzewska 2016). Figure 1.4 (from Gałęzewska 2016) shows the cumulative proportion of women who repartner within ten years of union dissolution, across three birth cohorts. There has been a dramatic rise in repartnering over time, as, in most countries, women born 1965–1974 are much more likely to repartner than women born 1945–1954 or 1955–1964; the exception here being the United States, where repartnering was already high in the earliest cohort. For the most recent cohort, the majority of women will repartner within ten years after union dissolution across twelve of the fifteen countries examined

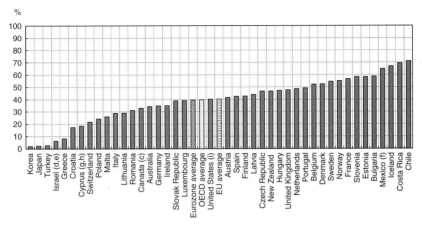

FIGURE 1.5 Proportion of births outside marriage across OECD countries,
1970–2014
Source: OECD Family Database (OECD 2017).

(the exceptions being Bulgaria, Lithuania, and Poland), and most of those unions will be cohabitations; at the same time, it is important to note that selection processes may affect the high rate of repartnering for the recent cohort, as these women were quite young at union dissolution and may differ from women who entered unions at older ages and/or had longer-lasting unions (Gałęzewska 2016).

Nonmarital Childbearing. Along with the changes in marriage patterns has been a sharp increase in childbearing outside marriage across most Western industrialized countries. In the United States, 40 percent of births are today outside legal marriage (Hamilton, Martin, and Osterman 2016). As shown in Figure 1.5, the OECD-27 average for 2014 was also 40 percent, but this belies notable variation across countries – from only 7 percent in Greece to more than 50 percent in Belgium, Bulgaria, Denmark, Estonia, France, Iceland, Norway, Slovenia, and Sweden.

While "traditional" family formation typically followed a linear course – first dating, then marriage, and then childbearing – the rise in nonmarital childbearing (along with concomitant changes in union formation) has yielded a range of complex and diverse family arrangements. This is especially true for disadvantaged individuals in the United States and the United Kingdom, who are likely to have children outside marriage in relationships that are likely to break up (Kiernan et al. 2011; Mincy and Poucy 1999). In Europe, nonmarital childbearing occurs more often within cohabitation, and cohabitation is often not differentiated from legal marriage in policy or research, especially in countries where cohabitation is quite common.

Much of the recent increase in nonmarital childbearing can be attributed to births to cohabiting couples, especially in European countries (Thomson 2014). The majority of nonmarital births between 2000 and 2004 occurred to cohabiting couples in France and Norway, and 30–40 percent in Austria, the Netherlands, and the United Kingdom (Perelli-Harris et al. 2010). In the United States, 18 percent of all children were born to cohabiting mothers between 1997 and 2001 (Kennedy and Bumpass 2008), and the most recent US data indicate that fully 58 percent of nonmarital births between 2006 and 2010 occurred to cohabiting couples (Curtain, Ventura, and Martinez 2014). At the same time, being born to cohabiting parents does not mean that children necessarily enter into a stable union, as many such unions are highly unstable – even more so in the United States than in other nations (Kiernan 1999; Osborne and McLanahan 2007). Growing evidence clearly shows that children born to married parents have much more stable families than children born to cohabiting parents across European countries as well (DeRose et al. 2017; Sánchez Gassen and Perelli-Harris 2015; Henz and Thomson 2005; Liefbroer and Dourleijn 2006). Recent research using data from the Generations and Gender Surveys and other comparable sources across Europe and the United States suggests that children born to cohabiting parents are far more likely to see their parents separate by age 15 (ranging from 13 percent in Georgia to fully 73 percent in the United States), compared to those born to married parents (ranging from 8 percent in Georgia to 34 percent in the United States and 36 percent in the Russian Federation) (Andersson, Thomson, and Duntava 2016). In other words, even in more egalitarian countries, marriage in the context of childbearing is associated with greater union stability (perhaps due to the selection of those who choose to have children within legal marriage versus cohabitation).

Multipartnered Fertility. Amidst high levels of union dissolution and nonmarital childbearing, a large fraction of adults today have (or will have) biological children by more than one partner, sometimes referred to as "multipartnered fertility." All things being equal, overall fertility rates are shown to be higher in countries where policies allow women to better balance work and family commitments (Castles 2003; Duvander, Lappegård, and Andersson 2010; Rindfuss et al. 2010), but multipartnered fertility will also be higher in contexts of high union dissolution (Thomson 2014). Recent studies focused on the United States have identified that a sizeable fraction of individuals across various demographic groups have children by more than one partner

(Guzzo and Dorius 2016), including low-income teenage mothers (Furstenberg and King 1999), national samples of adult men (Guzzo 2014; Guzzo and Furstenberg 2007b), adolescent and early adult women (Guzzo and Furstenberg 2007a), unwed parents in large US cities (Carlson and Furstenberg 2006), and mothers receiving welfare (Meyer, Cancian, and Cook 2005).

This phenomenon is not unique to the United States, and a growing literature has explored multipartnered fertility across European contexts, especially with respect to its prevalence and predictors. In a study comparing two Anglo-countries and two Nordic countries, Thomson et al. (2014) found that the fraction of all mothers who have children with two or more fathers was 12 percent in Australia, 16 percent in Norway, 13 percent in Sweden and 23 percent in the United States; the higher prevalence in Australia and the United States is likely due to the greater proportion of births that occur to lone mothers in these two countries (Thomson 2014; Thomson et al. 2014). Other studies have shown that childbearing across partnerships, or "stepfamily childbearing" (Thomson 2014), is not uncommon in Sweden (Holland and Thomson 2011; Vikat, Thomson, and Hoem 1999) and Norway (Lappegård and Rønsen 2013).

Family Instability for Children. Taken together, at the intersection of patterns of union formation and dissolution with fertility behavior, are the family experiences of children. Within the United States, a growing literature has examined the prevalence and consequences of family instability for children. While much of the early literature focused on being in particular family types – first, intact versus nonintact families, then various longitudinal categories of family structure during childhood (e.g., Astone and McLanahan 1991; Cherlin 1999; McLanahan and Sandefur 1994) – more recent studies have identified family transitions or instability (i.e., changes in family type) as an important factor predicting children's well-being. This literature consistently shows that greater family instability is associated with disadvantageous outcomes for children across a range of academic and behavioral domains (Davis et al. 2009; Fomby and Cherlin 2007; Osborne and McLanahan 2007).

There is a growing literature about the prevalence of family instability experienced in other industrialized countries, including several cross-national, comparative studies. Using data from the UN's Fertility and Family Surveys (FFS), Andersson (2004) and Heuveline, Timberlake, and Furstenberg (2003) found that the United States is an outlier with respect to family instability, with fully half of US children experiencing their parents' union dissolution by age 15; at the other end of the spectrum, only about one in ten of children in Italy will see their parents' union dissolve by age 15, while most other countries in Western and Eastern Europe fall somewhere in between – with about one quarter to one third of children experiencing the dissolution of their parents' union by age 15. The United States has a higher fraction of children born to single (i.e., not cohabiting or married) mothers than other countries; however, across nearly all countries, including the United States, children are more likely to live with a single parent as a result of parental separation than being born to an unpartnered mother.

Swedish register data (i.e., data about the entire population of Sweden) offer a particularly rich source of information about parents' union histories (and hence children's family structure), including cohabitation, which is often not accurately or regularly measured in surveys. Thomson and colleagues have several papers exploring family (in)stability in Sweden, finding that one quarter to one third of Swedish children have experienced their parents' union dissolution by age 15, depending on whether survey data or register data are used (Kennedy and Thomson 2010; Thomson and Eriksson 2013).

Research suggests that children who live apart from their biological fathers do not fare as well on a range of outcomes as children who grow up with both biological parents, especially within stable married families (Amato and Anthony 2014; McLanahan, Tach, and Schneider 2013). The research evidence is especially strong in the United States, although parents' union dissolution has been linked with various adverse outcomes across European and Anglo-countries as well (see Chapter 6; Härkönen, Bernardi, and Boertien 2017; McLanahan, Tach, and Schneider 2013). There is mixed evidence about whether there is an educational gradient in the effects of single parenthood on children's outcomes; recent reviews of the literature (see Chapter 6; Bernardi et al. 2013) note that some studies show single parenthood to be more detrimental for children of higher educated parents, while other studies show single parenthood to have greater negative consequences for children of lower education.

Children in single-mother families are often deprived of two types of resources from their fathers: Economic (money) and relational (time) (Thomson, Hanson, and McLanahan 1994; Thomson and McLanahan 2012). The economic circumstances can be most easily quantified: Single-parent families with children have a significantly higher poverty rate (43 percent in 2015) than two-parent families with children (10 percent in 2015) (DeNavas-Walt, Proctor, and Smith 2010), and an extensive US literature shows that living in poverty has adverse effects on child development and well-being as well as adult socioeconomic attainment (Duncan and Brooks-Gunn 1997; Duncan, Ziol-Guest, and Kalil 2010; Duncan et al. 2012; Hair et al. 2015). Yet, it is important to recognize the effects of family structure on economic well-being are not necessarily (or entirely) causal, though there is evidence of some causal effect of marriage on family income (Sawhill and Thomas 2005; Waite and Gallagher 2000). Also, at the aggregate level, geographic regions with a higher proportion of intact families are shown to experience greater economic growth (Lerman et al. 2017) and higher intergenerational mobility (Chetty et al. 2014a). Children in single-parent families also receive less parental attention and emotional support from their fathers: Nonresident fathers see their children less often than resident fathers, and lack of interaction decreases the likelihood that a father and child will develop a close relationship (Carlson 2006; Seltzer 1991).

Overall, dramatic changes in family behaviors have occurred over the past half-century, resulting in new and more diverse patterns of family experiences for adults and for the children with whose life courses they overlap. While there is some variation in breadth and scope, these patterns are generally observed across Western industrialized countries. In the next section, I turn to the extent to which these family patterns appear to systematically differ by socioeconomic status.

FAMILY CHANGE AND INEQUALITY

Although the "second demographic transition" – with the incumbent changes in marriage, divorce, cohabitation, and fertility – has been recognized as occurring across a wide range of industrialized countries (Lesthaeghe 1995, 2010), only within the past fifteen years has there been clear recognition of the extent to which changes in family demography are unfolding unevenly across the income distribution. McLanahan's 2004 presidential address at the Population Association of America noted that differences in family behaviors (including divorce, single parenthood, maternal employment, and fathers' involvement with children) by socioeconomic status (measured by mothers' education) were an important aspect of growing inequality among children, or what she called "diverging destinies" (McLanahan 2004; McLanahan and Jacobsen 2015). Although the bulk of her evidence was focused on the United States, she included international comparisons for maternal age, maternal employment, and single motherhood by mothers' education for six European countries, using data from the Luxembourg Income Study; in all cases, she found notable gaps by education in the prevalence of each.

Subsequent studies have provided additional evidence about the extent to which family demographic patterns diverge by socioeconomic status (and whether this divergence may be increasing).

Marriage. Extensive evidence has shown that the retreat from marriage is much more pronounced among the less-educated in the United States. Those with a college education are much more likely to marry compared to those with less (Cherlin 2009; Goldstein and Kenney 2001; White and Rogers 2000). An educational gradient in marriage is less consistently observed across European countries, although whether, and in what direction, a gradient is observed may depend on the degree of gender segregation within countries (Kalmijn 2007, 2013). Analyzing union formation across Canada, Italy, Sweden, and the United States in the early/mid-1990s, Goldscheider, Turcotte, and Kopp (2001) found that the educational gradient for marriage was steepest in the United States, where those with a college education were more likely – and those with below high school were less likely – to marry than those with a high school degree. There was no discernible gradient in Canada or Sweden, and in Italy, those with both lower education and with higher education were more likely to marry than those with a high school education. Using data from the European Social Survey from 2002 to 2010 for twenty-five countries, Kalmijn (2013) found that for women, higher education is negatively related to marriage when gender roles are highly segregated but is positively related to marriage in gender-egalitarian countries; in other words, highly educated women are more likely to marry when societal expectations about marriage include continued involvement in the paid labor market. For men, there is a positive gradient overall, but it is weaker in traditional countries and more strongly positive in egalitarian societies. At the same time, higher education is associated with a delay in marriage in a recent study across fifteen Western countries (Perelli-Harris and Lyons-Amos 2016).

Divorce. There is mixed evidence about how education is related to divorce, with some countries showing a positive gradient, others a negative gradient, and some no detectable gradient. In the United States, a notable negative educational effect on divorce has emerged since the 1970s, as those with a college degree are much less likely to divorce then their less-educated counterparts (S. P. Martin 2006; Raley and Bumpass 2003; White and Rogers 2000). Using data on first marriages in seventeen countries from the Fertility and Family Surveys with event-history techniques, Härkönen and Dronkers (2006) found that higher education is associated with a higher risk of divorce in France, Greece, Italy, Poland, and Spain and with a lower risk of divorce in Austria, Lithuania, and the United States; there is no educational gradient in divorce observed in Estonia, Finland, West Germany, Hungary, Latvia, Sweden, and Switzerland – and for some models in Flanders and Norway. They attributed their disparate findings to the social and economic costs of divorce, which vary over time and across countries. They also found that the gradient is more positive in countries with more generous welfare policies, which they suggested means that social benefits may promote marital stability among the socioeconomically disadvantaged. Kalmijn (2013) also considered divorce in his paper on the educational gradient in marriage across twenty-five European countries; he found that overall, men – but not women – with a higher education were less likely to get divorced (conditional on marriage). However, the association differed by gender attitudes within countries – a higher education was associated with a lower likelihood of divorce in gender-egalitarian societies, but with a higher likelihood of divorce in more gender-traditional countries. In a meta-analysis of fifty-three studies of education and divorce across Europe, Matysiak, Styrc, and Vignoli (2014) found a generally positive socioeconomic gradient in divorce – but with variation across countries – and they note that the relationship between education and divorce has weakened over time as divorce has become more common and as women have increasingly entered the labor force.

In a recent paper that conjointly considers union formation and dissolution patterns as linked to socioeconomic status, Perelli-Harris and Lyons-Amos (2016) used data across fifteen countries with latent-class analysis to examine partnership trajectories. They found that education is consistently associated with a delay in marriage, but there is less consistent evidence for an education gradient in stable cohabitation or union dissolution. In other words, a higher education is associated with marrying later but not with cohabiting or the likelihood of breaking up. Overall, they find that country context is more important (and increasingly so) then individual-level education in predicting partnership patterns, with country context reflecting the unique combination of social, cultural, political, and economic factors within particular nations.

Repartnering. Repartnering only occurs once unions have been entered and exited, and we know that there are numerous factors that affect the likelihood of such, including both social and economic characteristics (Lyngstad and Jalovaara 2010; Xie et al. 2003). While repartnering has increased across most Western countries, following rising union dissolution rates, there does not appear to be a consistent socioeconomic gradient. In the United States, where repartnering rates are highest, greater education (especially college) is associated with a higher likelihood of remarriage – but with a lower likelihood of cohabiting with a new partner (McNamee and Raley 2011). In the Netherlands, education is associated with a greater likelihood of repartnering (either marriage or cohabitation) for men but not for women (de Graaf and Kalmijn 2003; Poortman 2007). One recent study in Flanders that considered the characteristics of new partners found that higher educated men are more likely to repartner with a childless partner (versus no union) but not with a partner who has a child (Vanassche et al. 2015); this study also found no effects of education on repartnering for women.

Nonmarital Childbearing. We know that nonmarital childbearing in the United States is strongly associated with socioeconomic disadvantage (Ellwood and Jencks 2004; McLanahan 2011). Childbearing within cohabitation is shown to follow a clear socioeconomic gradient within eight European countries, although the gap by education has not necessarily increased over time (Perelli-Harris et al. 2010); these authors find that conceptual expectations from second demographic transition theory cannot account for the gradient across countries and over time. Instead, the negative socioeconomic gradient appeared to emerge from both economic and social changes; in particular, changes in the labor market brought both greater economic uncertainty and higher employment among women, and at the same time, social values and norms were changing that increased the acceptability of certain family behaviors. Kennedy and Thomson (2010) also considered births to single and cohabiting women in Sweden, and they found a small and persistent gap by education in the fraction of births to single (unpartnered) women; of births to women with less than secondary education (tertiary education), 5 percent (2 percent) were to single mothers in the 1970s and 6 percent (3 percent) in the 1990s. While births to cohabiting women rose for all women, the relative gap by education remained similar over this time period: For women with less than secondary education (tertiary education), the fraction of births to cohabiting women rose from 45 percent (30 percent) in the 1970s to 59 percent (38 percent) in the 1990s – thus the ratio of high-to-low education was similar (at 1.5–1.6) at both time points.

Multipartnered Fertility. In the United States, we know that multipartnered fertility is much more common among socioeconomically disadvantaged men and women (Cancian, Meyer, and Cook 2011; Carlson and Furstenberg 2006; Guzzo and Dorius 2016). Thomson et al. (2014) find a similar pattern in their study of Australia, Norway, Sweden, and the United States: There is a negative educational gradient, as higher education is associated with a lower chance of having a subsequent birth to a different father. In their detailed analyses of Norwegian register data, Lappegård and Rønsen (2013) paint a more complicated picture, finding that multipartnered fertility is related to both socioeconomic disadvantage and advantage. The former can be attributable to the fact that the risk of union dissolution is higher among those who are socioeconomically disadvantaged, while the latter is due to the fact that, conditional on having broken up, the chance of repartnering is higher among the socioeconomically advantaged. Indeed, union instability during the childbearing years can serve as an "engine of fertility," because parity progression occurs more quickly in new partnerships (Thomson et al. 2012).

Family Instability for Children. While there has been less research focused on socioeconomic gradients in family instability for children in European contexts, several recent papers have provided important new insights. In work in progress by Carlson et al. (2014) analyzing fifteen industrialized countries, the authors find that between birth and age 15, US children spend on average five years living with a single (unpartnered) mother, compared to one to three years in all other countries (Russia being the second highest at three years). Further, there is a notable educational gradient in family instability; across all countries examined, children spend a higher number of years living with both parents if the mother has a higher education, but the gap in family stability by maternal education is greatest in the United States.

Kennedy and Thomson (2010), using data from the Swedish Level of Living Survey, found some evidence of a growing gap in family instability by parental education in Sweden from the 1970s to the 1990s, although the magnitude of the gradient was far less than that observed in the United States. Given the strong association noted earlier between growing up with two biological parents and healthy child development (McLanahan, Tach, and Schneider 2013), this may have broader implications for inequality. Yet, one recent paper focused on Germany, Italy, the United Kingdom, and the United States found that while indeed growing up in a nonintact family was associated with lower socioeconomic attainment, this did not explain aggregate-level differences in inequality across countries (Bernardi and Boertien 2017a); this was in part because the effects of nonintact families are actually more negative for those with higher socioeconomic status, even though the likelihood of experiencing a nonintact family is much more common for those with lower socioeconomic status. A recent working paper by Musick and Michelmore (2016) suggests that the higher proportion of unions that break up in the United States and the greater socioeconomic gradient in such compared to European countries is due to the higher prevalence of – and correlation among – behaviors linked to union instability (such as early childbearing and multipartnered fertility – which are also linked with unplanned pregnancies); this, in turn, points to greater inequality in what children get from parents in the United States compared to Western Europe.

CONCLUSION AND IMPLICATIONS

This chapter summarizes what we know about recent patterns of family change and socioeconomic inequality therein across the United States and Europe. This is an important topic because family circumstances and transitions can influence individual well-being, happiness, identity, and relationships – and also play an important role in promoting or sustaining economic well-being. To the extent that family behaviors diverge by socioeconomic status within countries, this can reflect a broader pattern of accumulating advantage or disadvantage (depending on the direction of the gradient), with long-term ramifications for individuals and society; differences in outcomes for a given generation may then perpetuate growing inequality for the next generation.

Overall, in contrast to the United States, where there are consistent socioeconomic gradients in family behaviors – with more educated individuals experiencing more "traditional" and stable family patterns – there is much greater variability in Europe. Observed variation in family patterns by socioeconomic status (SES) seems to depend on numerous factors in particular places, including gender role attitudes and other cultural attributes, as well as social policies that facilitate balancing work and family and that reduce income inequality. At the same time, there is some evidence that family instability may be rising, especially for children from the least-educated families.

Also, it is important to consider how the timing of family changes may be related to the educational gradient. Conceptual arguments about the "second demographic transition" (Lesthaeghe 1995, 2010) suggested that the highly educated would be in the vanguard of ushering in new family patterns; thus, there would initially be a positive educational gradient in "modern" family behaviors (such as delayed marriage and childbearing, and rising cohabitation, nonmarital childbearing, and divorce), but that this gradient would dissipate as the new ideas spread to lower socioeconomic strata. Here too, a consistent pattern cannot be observed across contexts, or particular behaviors, and more research over time (that allows comparisons by education across cohorts) is warranted.

Ultimately, it seems impossible to draw strong general conclusions about patterns of inequality in family behaviors – and the relationship to broader economic inequality – across Europe and the United States writ large. Instead, it appears that individual countries experience quite distinct patterns. As Perelli-Harris and Lyons-Amos observed in their recent study of partnership patterns (2016, p. 275), "macro-level country context explains more of the variance in predicted probabilities than individual-level education." Thus, we are reminded of the importance of historical, cultural, social, and economic processes within particular geographic contexts and communities as key factors that influence human behavior and outcomes.

2

Families in Latin America
Dimensions, Diverging Trends, and Paradoxes

Albert Esteve[*] and Elizabeth Florez-Paredes

INTRODUCTION

Latin America is the most unequal continent in the world. According to World Bank data, the richest 10% accumulate more than 40% of the wealth. Latin American inequality has historical roots and has been exacerbated in recent times after decades of neoliberal reforms that neither generated sustained economic growth nor bridged the gap between the very few rich and the very large number of poor. Inequality affects Latin America in many ways (e.g., health, education) and family life is no exception (World Bank 2003). A pattern of social disadvantage emerges in every category of family formation: The evidence shows that early union formation and childbearing, cohabitation, single motherhood, and union dissolution are more common among women with low education than among those with higher education (secondary and beyond completed). Although this pattern holds true across Latin America, the effects of educational and income inequality interact in numerous ways, varying considerably from context to context.

Geohistorical legacies are of paramount importance in understanding family diversity in Latin America. At the individual level, ethnicity and religion frequently interact with themselves and with education, adding endless variations to the relationship between social status and family behavior. For instance, two individuals with similar profiles regarding education, ethnicity, and religion may show quite different family behavior depending on the region where they live, proving that "individuals have histories but regions have much longer histories" (Esteve and Lesthaeghe, 2016, p. 269). This conclusion was originally drawn from cohabitation analysis but, as we will show in this chapter, it can be

[*] The research conducted by Albert Esteve has received funding from the European Research Council (RC-2014-STG grant agreement No 637768) and the Spanish Ministry of Science (CSO2015-64713-R).

generalized to other family dimensions as well. To sum up, this underscores the importance of context in the analysis of families in Latin America.

In addition to geohistorical legacies, the historical presence in Latin America of family forms that are considered a recent phenomenon by Western standards (i.e., cohabitation, union instability, and single motherhood not connected to widowhood) complicates, from a theoretical perspective, any attempt to apply Western theoretical frameworks to Latin America, in particular the male bread-winner model (Becker 1973), the second demographic transition (Lesthaeghe 1995), diverging destinies (McLanahan 2004), patterns of disadvantage (Perelli-Harris et al. 2010), and the two halves of the gender revolution (Goldscheider, Bernhardt, and Lappegård 2015). Elements of all these theories can be glimpsed. Fertility has declined rapidly across the region, sinking below replacement levels in a growing number of countries (CELADE 2013). Unmarried cohabitation has soared and marriage rates have plummeted at the same pace (Esteve, Lesthaeghe, and López-Gay 2012). More children have been born out of wedlock (Laplante et al. 2015), unions have become more unstable, and more households are now headed by women (Liu, Esteve, and Treviño 2016). However, closer scrutiny of family trends reveals some differences from Western experience. Age at union formation and childbearing has barely changed (Esteve and Florez-Paredes 2014). Household sizes have diminished but retained similar levels of internal complexity (Arriagada 2004). Furthermore, trends over time and variations across regions reveal a significant paradox: A lack of correlation between micro- and macro dimensions of family behavior and change.

Within this context, this chapter summarizes trends in family life in Latin America over the last four decades, analyzing the rich collection of census and survey microdata available in the region and the literature on family dynamics. The chapter is organized into four main sections: Dimensions, trends in independent family indicators, divergence by education, and para-doxes. In the dimensions section, we describe family regimes in Latin America across four factors/dimensions and show their variation across 368 regions and 15 countries. In the trends section, we document changes over time since the 1970s with reference to the key variables contributing to each of the four factors. For a selection of countries – Mexico, Colombia, and Brazil– we explore in the third section divergence by education in women's partnership status, extended co-residence, and household headship. And finally, in the paradoxes section, we analyze the lack of correlation between the micro- and macro dimensions of family change over time and across space. In short, this chapter provides a systematic characterization of family regimes in Latin America, trends in key indicators, divergence by educational status, and paradoxes of Latin American family change.

DIMENSIONS

The concept of a family system has been widely used to refer to the set of characteristics defining the structure and functioning of families in a society (Laslett 1970; Reher 1998). By definition, family systems have multiple dimensions, among them, when and who to marry, intergenerational transmission of property, filial obligations toward parents, and a long et cetera (Fauve-Chamoux 1984). Most research so far has been devoted to Europe and its internal diversity (e.g., Hajnal 1965), and Asia. Research on family systems in Latin America is rather scarce, scattered, and focused on specific subpopulations. Systematic study of the regional scale of the main dimensions of family change and its geographic boundaries is lacking (see exceptions in Arriagada 2009; De Vos 1987; Quilodran 1999). Recent availability of census microdata, through the Integrated Public Use of Microdata Series (IPUMS) international project, offers an opportunity for a partial yet broad description of variations in family life across Latin America. Obviously, there are many features of family systems that are well beyond what a census can measure, but there are others for which censuses can provide reasonable approximations (e.g., marriage timing, type of union, household composition, and female headship).

Hence, in this section we ask which main dimensions characterize family regimes in Latin America. We aim to identify independent dimensions of family life and trace their respective geographies using subnational-level data to account for within-country differences. We use factor analysis to identify the main dimensions emerging from 18 family life indicators calculated for 368 regions spread through 15 Latin America countries. Data come from IPUMS census microdata (Minnesota Population Center 2015). The chosen indicators are percentages of women at various ages regarding their situation with respect to marriage, cohabitation, childbearing, union dissolution, household headship, and living arrangements. In Appendix 2A.1, we show the list of the eighteen indicators for 2000 and their contribution (in technical terms, factor loads) to each dimension. The same analysis was carried out using data from the 1970s, 1980s, and 1990s census rounds. The dimensions emerging from all these rounds were virtually the same, which demonstrates their stability over time. Hence, we only present results from the 2000 round.

One of the advantages of factor analysis is that it identifies groups of indicators that are independent of each other. Mere identification of such groupings is, per se, a very relevant result, because it allows characterization of family regimes on an empirical basis. Little is known about the dimensions that structure families in Latin America, and even less about the degree of independence among them.

First dimension: Union and Childbearing Calendars

The analysis yielded four factors or dimensions. The first dimension, *union and childbearing calendars*, refers to the age at which transitions to first union and first child occur. This factor mainly captures timing dimensions of fertility initiation and union formation, but it also includes two other variables, namely the proportion of women in unions at ages 15–44 and the proportion women both single and childless women in the age range of 15–19. The timing of union formation is closely correlated with the timing of childbearing, as, for most women, the two transitions occur within a relatively short period of time. Early transitions are associated with high intensity of union formation and childbearing. This dimension distinguishes between regions where men and women form unions and have children early in life and those where unions and children come later. Regarding internal differences, Map 1 in Figure 2.1 shows the factor scores for each region. Lighter colors indicate late transitions to union formation and childbearing and darker ones the opposite. At one end, Uruguayan, Chilean, and Argentinian (Southern Cone) women experience these transitions later than in any other regions in Latin America. At the opposite end, are women from Central America (e.g., Nicaragua, Costa Rica, Panama, and Mexico). Between these two poles, there are countries with sizeable internal variations. Brazilian women in the Amazon and in the northern states show dramatic differences from those in the southern states, where there has been much recent European immigration. Even in comparatively smaller countries like Bolivia, internal variations are huge. The Andean states (Colombia, Venezuela, Peru, and Bolivia) show the largest internal variations, as they combine areas with extremely diverse ethnic, religious, and economic backgrounds.

Second Dimension: Household Complexity

The second dimension captures *household complexity*. All the original indicators (see Appendix 2A.1) measuring the complexity of living arrangements contribute to this (e.g., percentage of extended households, of children aged 0–4 in nuclear households, and of children aged 0–4 not related to the household head, among others). Positive values (darker colors in Map 2 of Figure 2.1) indicate complex household structures, which basically mean a high proportion of members and young children not directly related to the household head. Nicaragua, Venezuela, Panama, and El Salvador present the highest levels of household complexity. At the opposite extreme, Uruguay and Argentina show the lowest levels of household complexity. Showing some independence across

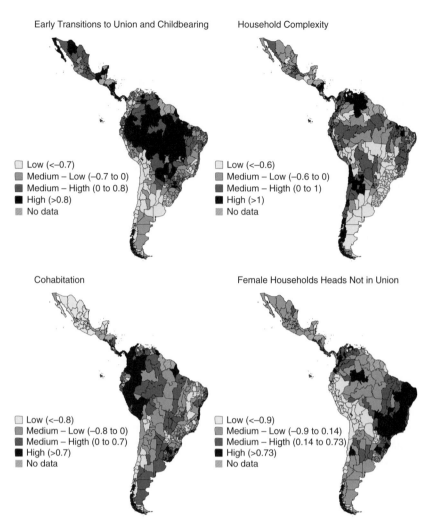

FIGURE 2.1 Maps of four dimensions that characterize families in Latin
America, 2000
Caption for top left map: Early transitions to union and childbearing
Caption for top right map: Household complexity
Caption for bottom left map: Cohabitation
Caption for bottom right map: Female household heads not in union

dimensions, Chile breaks with its concurrence with Uruguay and Argentina in
terms of late marriage while still revealing relatively high levels of household
complexity. Costa Rica, in contrast, shows relatively early transitions to union
formation and childbearing but low levels of household complexity.

Third Dimension: Married and Unmarried Cohabitation

The third dimension refers to the type of union. It distinguishes between *married* and *unmarried cohabitation*. In Map 3 of Figure 2.1, we show the factor scores for the third dimension emerging from the analysis. This dimension is constructed from all the indicators measuring the marital or nonmarital status of unions. Positive values (darker colors) indicate high levels of cohabitation, and negative values (lighter colors) the opposite. The geography of high levels of cohabitation has a distinctive profile: The highest levels of cohabitation appear in the non-Andean regions of the Andean countries (Colombia, Venezuela, Peru, and Ecuador) followed by Uruguay and Central America. Lower levels of cohabitation, hence higher marriage levels, are found in Ecuador (with some internal differences), Mexico, Chile, and Paraguay. The patterns of marriage and cohabitation basically mirror the path of history. Contrary to many Western societies, cohabitation coexisted with marriage since colonial times as a form of organizing unions among those who did not have access to the institution of marriage for many reasons. The implementation of European marriage in Latin America was uneven across regions and across population strata, as is reflected in Map 3.

Fourth Dimension: Nature of Female Household Headship

Finally, the fourth dimension, *female household headship*, consists of indicators regarding the type of female household heads rather than their numbers. It distinguishes between female household heads not in union (presumably raising children without the support of fathers) and female heads in union. Positive values (darker colors) indicate the presence of female-headed households in which women are not in union, whereas negative values and lighter colors indicate female household headship among women in union. Female household heads in Brazil, Costa Rica, Panama, and Colombia show the largest proportion of women not in a union and with children, compared to the much lower trend in Bolivia, Paraguay, and Peru. The latter countries have lower proportions of women not in union and with children than the former.

TRENDS IN INDEPENDENT FAMILY INDICATORS

As noted above, the main (census-observable) dimensions that define family regimes in Latin America have remained relatively stable between 1970 and 2010. Nevertheless, many of the indicators contributing to these dimensions

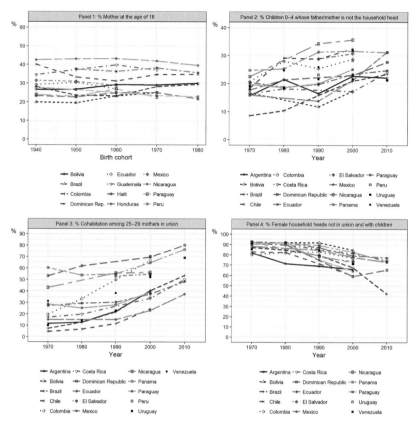

FIGURE 2.2 Trends in selected key family life indicators in Latin America over
recent decades and cohorts
   Caption for Panel 1: % mothers at the age of 18
   Caption for Panel 2: % children aged 0–4 whose father/mother is not the
household head
   Caption for Panel 3: % cohabitation among 25–29-year-old mothers in union
   Caption for Panel 4: % female household heads not in union and with children

have changed dramatically over time. We now summarize the major trends in
a selection of key variables representing each dimension. Figure 2.2 provides
graphic representation of the trends in four separate panels.

Age at First Child

Panel 1 of Figure 2.2, using all the available Demographic and Health
Survey data in Latin America, shows the percentage of women by birth

cohort who were mothers by the age of 18 in twelve Latin American countries. The timing of first childbearing has remained relatively stable over time, as has the percentage of women in a union at the age of 18 (results not shown). This suggests that trends in union formation and childbearing are strongly correlated. At later ages (e.g., 20 or 22), trends are equally stable. Such stability has been corroborated by many authors and is one of the salient characteristics of recent trends in family formation in Latin America, and sets Latin America apart from other regions where childbearing and union formation are increasingly postponed (Fussell and Palloni 2004; Heaton and Forste 1998; Martin and Juárez 1995). This has occurred amidst marked declines in fertility, increased access to contraception, even at early ages, and substantial improvements in education and female labor force participation. Signs of postponement are still modest and reduced to a small number of countries and mainly among higher educated groups (Binstock 2010; Cabella and Pardo 2014; Guzmán et al. 2006; Rosero Bixby, Martin, and Martín-García 2009).

Extended Households

Regarding household complexity, in Panel 2 of Figure 2.2, we represent the percentage of children aged 0–4 whose father/mother is not the household head. On average, one in every four children is not the son or daughter of the household head. They may be living with other relatives, including grandparents, uncles, aunts, or nonrelatives. The percentage of children in these households ranges from 8.5% in Brazil in 1970 to 35.7% in Nicaragua in 2000, but for the vast majority of countries, values are within the 15% to 30% range. On average, these percentages have increased by 8% points between 1970 and 2010.

This indicator is highly correlated with the percentage of extended households. Both indicators contribute positively to the factor on household complexity (see Appendix 2A.1). The percentage of extended households ranges, for the majority of countries, within the 20% to 30% range, and has remained constant over time (results not shown). This shows that household complexity is quite widespread in Latin America, in particular Central America. However, comparison to the meaning and function of extended households differs from that which has been described for parts of Europe (Fauve-Chamoux and Ochiai 2009). Extended households in Latin America are not seeking to secure exploitation of land and transference of property but, rather, to cope with social vulnerability and provide a refuge for family members in insecure situations (Goldani and Verdugo 2004). Few extended households in the region include two adult couples; most are comprised of a couple co-residing with other relatives (not in a union). These results reflect a very fluid system of living arrangements, in which preexisting nuclear households incorporate other relatives in need of housing (De Vos 1987). Latin America presents strong families concerned with coping with poverty, vulnerability, and uncertainty rather than with protecting family assets. For example, close to 70% of single mothers reside with their parents, and this high level has remained stable over the last three or four decades (Esteve, García-Román, and Lesthaeghe 2012).

Cohabitation

Panel 3 of Figure 2.2 shows the percentage of unions that are cohabiting but not married among mothers aged between 25 and 29, by census round and country. Among these young mothers, cohabitation is increasingly the context for childbearing. The percentage of cohabiting mothers has multiplied since the 1970s by three times or more in a number of countries, including Argentina, Brazil, Chile, Colombia, and Uruguay. Based on the latest figures available, childbearing within is more frequent than outside cohabitation in ten out of the sixteen countries represented in Panel 3.

Of all dimensions considered in this analysis, cohabitation is the one that is changing fastest. Marriage rates have dropped across Latin America. The decline of marriage has been completely offset by the rise of cohabitation. Hence, age at union formation has barely changed. The rise of cohabitation cannot be attributed to a single factor. Some authors suggest a partial fit to the theory of the second demographic transition (Esteve and Lesthaeghe 2016), whereas others emphasize a continuation of the historical pattern of disadvantage (Rodriguez Vignoli 2005). Analysis of World Values Survey for Latin America shows a major transformation of values toward post-materialist values consistent with the second demographic transition, including greater acceptance of homosexuality, euthanasia, and abortion, especially among the better-educated respondents (Esteve, García-Román, and Lesthaeghe 2012). However, the absence of postponement in union formation and childbearing does not fit with second demographic transition theory, and neither does the fact that a large part of early cohabitation takes place in complex and extended households (Esteve, García-Román, and Lesthaeghe 2012).

A combination of factors would therefore seem to be the most plausible explanation. Women with high levels of education are not only choosing cohabiting unions over marital unions more often but they are also postponing union formation and childbearing, whereas the least-educated women are choosing cohabitation more but without postponement. Recent research suggests the presence of (at least) three types of cohabitation: Traditional, blended, and innovative. Each type has its specific traits with regard to age at union formation, education, number of children, and stability (Covre-Sussai et al. 2015). Traditional cohabitation is defined by early union formation and childbearing and is more frequent among women with low levels of education. At the opposite end, innovative cohabitation is associated with later union formation and a higher level of education. In between the traditional and the innovative cohabitation, the blended cohabitation has features of both types (e.g., early pregnancy and a higher level of education). Future research should inquire further into the different meanings of cohabitation and their implications for union stability and consequences for children.

Female-Headed Households

Finally, female headship has increased dramatically since the 1970s (Liu, Esteve, and Treviño 2016), but still the vast majority of female household heads are women not in a union and with children. Panel 4 of Figure 2.2 shows the percentage of female heads between the ages of 35 and 44 who were mothers but were not in a union at the time of the census, either because they were single mothers or because they were separated, divorced, or widowed. In the 1970s, more than 80% of female heads across all countries fell into this category. These high figures remained relatively stable until the 1990s. The rise of headship rates among married and cohabiting women or among single women (without children) has slightly changed the profile of female heads. By the 2000s, the proportion of female heads with children and not in a union had decreased by 16% points on average. The rise in female headship among women in union is mainly due to an increasing propensity among women to report as household heads, even in the presence of their spouses (Liu, Esteve, and Treviño 2016). Census forms have also reflected (and perhaps induced) this change, as they adopt more gender-neutral definitions of household headship.

Despite recent trends, the historically high levels of female-headed households in Latin America continue to be associated with the notable presence of single mothers resulting from short-lived unions due to union dissolution. Although families provide "shelter" to single mothers, many are on their own. Female-headed households have been associated with the feminization of poverty (Arias and Palloni 1999; Buvinic and Gupta 1997), but recent research has challenged the supposed relationship between female headship and poverty (Chant 2003; Liu, Esteve, and Treviño 2016; Medeiros and Costa 2008), showing that the living conditions of female-headed households are not necessarily worse than in those headed by males (Chant 2003, Chant 2007; Medeiros and Costa 2008; Moser 2010; Quisumbing, Haddid, and Peña 2001), and also that female-headed households are extremely diverse.

DIVERGENCE BY EDUCATION IN WOMEN'S TIMING AND CONTEXT OF CHILDBEARING, HOUSEHOLD COMPLEXITY, AND HOUSEHOLD HEADSHIP

Most of the indicators and trends described here show a steep educational gradient. Education is one of the most significant stratifying dimensions of social and demographic behavior, and Latin America is no exception. There is ample evidence that, in Latin America, education is a strong predictor for the age at which union formation and childbearing occur, as well as whether unions are marital or not. Furthermore, access to education is constrained by social class. Despite major progress in universalizing access to primary and secondary education, schools continue to reproduce inequality (OECD 2013a).

Here we investigate whether family inequality is increasing over time. We explore divergence by education in the four family dimensions identified in the dimensions section: Timing at union formation and childbearing; household complexity; cohabitation vs. marriage; and nature of female household headship. We present results only for Colombia, Brazil, and Mexico, which are three of the largest and most populated countries in Latin America.

Timing and Context of Childbearing

The first and third dimensions are analyzed together in Figure 2.3 (see exact figures in Appendix 2A.2A). Three-dimensional histograms with stacked bars represent, on the z-axis, the percentage of mothers among women aged between 25 and 29. Among mothers, we distinguish between married, cohabiting, or single (not in a union). On the x-axis, we represent change over time, showing data from various census rounds. On the y-axis, women are classified according to their level of education: Primary or lower; secondary completed; and university.

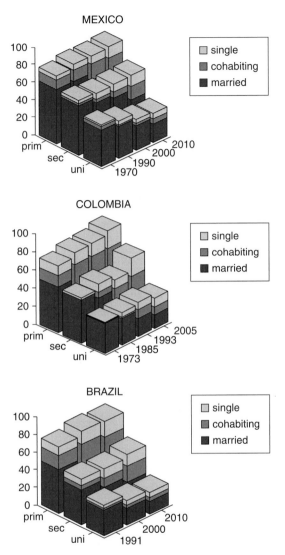

FIGURE 2.3 Percentage of mothers among women aged from 25 to 29 by union status, educational attainment, and census round
Caption for top: Mexico
Caption for middle: Colombia
Caption for bottom: Brazil

Despite being three different countries, the patterns and trends in Mexico, Brazil, and Colombia are quite similar. First, the percentage of women who are mothers is highest among those with primary or lower education, intermediate among women with only secondary education, and motherhood is least common at ages 25–29 among women with a university education. This indicates that highly educated women have children, if any, at later ages when compared with women of lower levels of education.

Second, the proportion of women who have become mothers by 25–29 years old have been almost stable among the first two groups (primary and secondary education), while over time, fertility postponement appears among women with a higher education. As shown in Figure 2.3, the percentage of highly educated women who are mothers has decreased, but the percentage for the other two groups has remained constant. Trends are diverging across educational groups. In Mexico, the percentage of women with a university education who are mothers has decreased from 47.1% in 1970 to 32.8% in 2010 and, in Brazil, from 40.3% to 23.9% between 1980 and 2010.

The most important transformation is the change in the partnership context of childrearing. This is most noticeable among women with secondary education or lower. For these two groups, the percentage of women who are mothers is stable, but the proportion of those rearing children within marriage is decreasing. Childbearing and child-rearing are increasingly taking place within the context of cohabitation and single motherhood. Trends unanimously point in this direction but the pace of change varies from country to country. Mexico has the highest proportion of mothers who are married mothers. It is still above 50% in all educational groups in 2010. In Colombia in 2005, married mothers represent less than 45% in all educational groups, dropping to 19% among the lower educated groups. Married mothers represent less than 50% in Brazil in 2010, except for those with a university education (58%). Mothers who are in cohabiting unions comprise a growing proportion of all mothers in all educational groups. The share of lone mothers, residual in the 1980s, now represent at least 15% of mothers in Mexico and 20% in Colombia and Brazil. Marriage predominates among highly educated women, but even among the highly educated, cohabitation and lone motherhood are becoming more common contexts for child-rearing. However, women with high levels of education are postponing childbearing and, accordingly, the trends in the partnership context of child-rearing are likely to be driven by selection effects.

In any case, the trends depicted so far show a clear educational gradient regarding age at childbearing and diverging trends with respect to change over time. Moreover, there is also a dramatic transformation of the family context of childbearing as marriage rates are plummeting and cohabitation and single motherhood are rising rapidly as well.

Household Complexity

Using three-dimensional stacked bar graphs, in Figure 2.4, we represent the percentage of women between the ages of 25 and 29 who reside in an extended household by year and educational attainment (see exact figures in Appendix 2A.2B). Additionally, we distinguish between mothers and non-mothers. Extended co-residence among young women has risen over time in the three countries and educational groups, except for Colombian women with primary or lower education. Mexico has experienced by far the largest increase in extended co-residence. Trends are similar across all educational groups, but the distribution between mothers and non-mothers is quite distinct, most probably because of higher educated women having children later. Half or more of women with primary and secondary education who live in extended households are mothers. Among women with a university education, this figure is lower than 50%, with the only exception of Colombia in 1993. In any case, and according to the most recent data, around one in three women in Mexico and one in four women in Colombia and Brazil reside in an extended household. In Mexico and Brazil, higher educated women are less likely to be in extended households, but in Colombia, the opposite pattern holds true. However, the gap between the higher and the lower educated group is no bigger than 5% points. This indicates that extended co-residence is quite widespread across all educational groups.

Household Headship

Figure 2.5 shows trends in female household headship among women aged 35 to 44 by year and educational attainment (see exact figures in Appendix 2A.2C). Female heads are classified according to their partnership and motherhood status. Female household headship has been on the rise in recent decades, in particular in Brazil and Mexico. Trends are less clear in Colombia because the 1973 data shows higher levels of female headship among women with primary or secondary levels of education than in 2005. In neither country is there any sign of a strong educational gradient in female headship. A look at the latest data indicates that the gap between the lower and higher educated women is less than 3% points. However, if we look at the distribution by partnership and motherhood status within educational groups, sharp differences emerge. Women with lower levels of education are more prone to head their

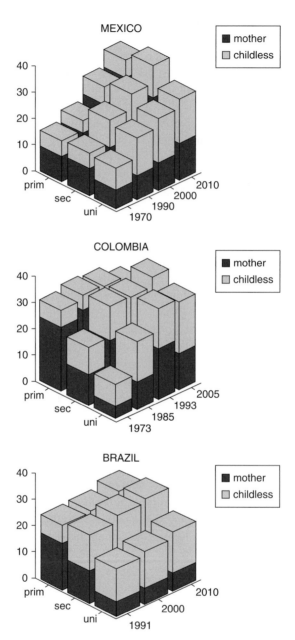

FIGURE 2.4 Percentage of women aged from 25 to 29 who reside in an extended
household by motherhood status, educational attainment, and census round
Caption for top: Mexico
Caption for middle: Colombia
Caption for bottom: Brazil

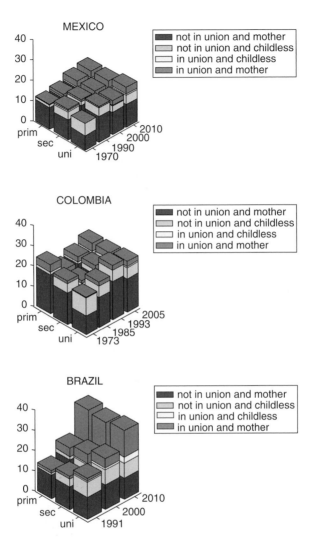

FIGURE 2.5 Percentage of women aged from 35 to 44 who are household heads by partnership/motherhood status, educational attainment, and census round
Caption for top: Mexico
Caption for middle: Colombia
Caption for bottom: Brazil

households in the absence of a spouse/partner and with the presence of children, whereas among female householders with university degrees, the proportion of single women without children is always higher than among women with secondary or lower education.

PARADOXES

Study of family change in Latin America confronts the researcher with several paradoxes. All of these can be traced back to a lack of correlation between the micro and macro dimensions of change, or in other words, between individual behavior and social change. This occurs on both temporal and regional scales. On the regional scale, family variations across regions cannot be explained by the socioeconomic characteristics of the individuals inhabiting these regions. Here we highlight two of the main micro–macro paradoxes found in Latin America.

The Paradox of Unchanging Age at First Birth while Educational Attainment Has Risen

The first paradox concerns the timing of family transitions. Despite substantial improvements in educational attainment – and education is understood as being the most robust predictor of age at union formation and childbearing everywhere (Jejeebhoy 1995; Lloyd 2005; Martín and Juárez 1995) – the age at which Latin American women have formed their unions and become mothers for the first time has hardly changed. The stability of calendars has been possible because of a rejuvenation of family transitions within educational groups. In other words, women with analogous years of schooling but belonging to different birth cohorts (at least for those born between 1940 and 1980) have formed unions and had children at different ages. Hence, if rates within educational groups change over time, predicting the effect of the educational expansion on social change (assuming constant rates) will not yield reliable outcomes, which is exactly what has happened in Latin America.

However, this is not a matter of rejuvenation within educational groups but of offsetting effects across educational groups. As we have seen in the cases of Mexico, Colombia, and Brazil, women with high levels of education are postponing transitions while other groups are not postponing or speeding up the process. As we show in Figure 2.3, the percentage of mothers among 25–29-year-old women with primary and secondary education increased in all countries between the earliest and latest year. In Brazil, 76.2% of women with primary education were mothers in 1980, compared to 79.1% in 2010. For the same group, this figure grew from 73.8% to 84.8% between 1973 and 2005 in Colombia; and in Mexico, from 77.3% to 82.2% between 1970 and 2010. As for women with secondary education, mothers represented 48.4% in Brazil in 1980 and 54.3% in 2010;

in Colombia, the figures were 50.2% in 1973 and 65.8% in 2005; and in Mexico, 62.0% in 1970 and 63.0% in 2010. These figures suggest that women with secondary or lower education in more recent times are becoming mothers at younger ages than women with analogous levels of education born three or four decades previously. By contrast, the proportion of mothers among women with a university education has decreased in the three countries, dropping in Brazil from 40.3% to 23.9% between 1980 and 2010; in Colombia, from 34.4% to 33.5% between 1973 and 2005; and in Mexico, from 47.1% to 32.8% between 1970 and 2010.

The lack of correlation between educational expansion and postponement of childbearing has given rise to a methodological debate about absolute and relative years of schooling (OECD 2013b) and attempts to determine which measure is better able to predict the time at which women form unions and have children. The evidence from Latin America shows that the specific knowledge and skills associated with each additional year of schooling may not have triggered the expected postponement of family transitions. Access to education and, in particular, to quality education is influenced by social factors and, hence, years of schooling do not always mean more opportunities for social and economic progress (BID 1998; Hoffman and Centeno 2003; Juárez and Gayet 2014; Torche 2014). This is consistent with the fact that a relative measure of education based on quartiles of years of schooling is much more consistent with the pattern of stability (Esteve and Florez-Paredes 2014). Regardless of the absolute number of years of education, the least-educated women are systematically having children at similar ages. In support of this claim, family size preferences in Latin America have remained stable over time and, after controls, show no outstanding differences across educational groups, suggesting a normative (and homogenous) context for early childbearing (Esteve and Florez-Paredes 2014).

Social and Regional Trends in Cohabitation Going against Individual Gradients

The second paradox concerns the rise of cohabitation over time and its regional distribution. Analyses of individual profiles of cohabitants reveal a pattern of disadvantage. Across the board, women (and men) with low levels of education tend more toward cohabitation than marriage. Assuming this gradient, cohabitation should have declined as a result of the dramatic expansion of education. However, quite the opposite occurred. Unmarried cohabitation spread across all social groups and, most significantly, among the highly educated populations

(Esteve, Lesthaeghe, and López-Gay 2012). This occurred because women with analogous years of schooling in two different periods were showing quite distinct levels of cohabitation. Cohabitation has risen within each educational group, but the educational gradient has remained constant.

At the regional level, we encounter a similar paradox. Despite the importance of education at the individual and contextual level and, even more, the importance of race and religion as strong predictors of cohabitation, differences across regions remain intact after individual and contextual level controls. Multilevel models have proved that the regional variance in cohabitation rates do not change after controls, which suggests that two individuals with analogous characteristics may have very distinct cohabitation levels depending on the regions in which they live (Esteve and Lesthaeghe 2016). For instance, Blacks in Brazil with no education show very different probabilities of cohabitation depending on the region where they live. It might therefore be concluded that cultural and institutional legacies are of paramount importance when it comes to understanding the geographical distribution of cohabitation in Latin America, and realizing that individual variables, such as education and race, only add modest variations to general schemes.

In the light of these results, researchers are puzzled when handling individual and contextual variables that are significantly correlated with cohabitation and other dimensions of family change while, at the same time, they cannot predict either social change or regional variability. Surprisingly, altitude turned out to be the most significant contextual-level variable in the Andean countries when accounting for the regional variance in cohabitation (Esteve et al. 2016a). At higher altitudes, there was more marriage than cohabitation. This came as a total surprise but, once again, it signaled the importance of institutional and cultural legacies closely connected with the history of colonization in Latin America. In the Andean countries, the highlands represent the areas of most intense colonization by the Spaniards. The most important civilizations were in the Andes, and it was in those areas where the penetration of the Catholic Church was more intense, and with it, the penetration of marriage. By contrast, in the lowlands, there are the inland and remote areas of the Amazonian tropical forests inhabited by sparse indigenous populations and the coastal areas, such as those of Ecuador and Colombia, with large plantation economies and a high Black population – descendants of slavery.

DISCUSSION

In a world where family forms and norms are in constant flux, Latin America comes into play challenging many of the assumptions and frameworks that have been useful for understanding modern families in the developed world. Thanks to data offering a large regional coverage and available for a long period and, we have offered an overview of the main dimensions of family regimes, trends in key family indicators, and paradoxes between micro and macro perspectives of family change and regional variations. We have not directly addressed the consequences of such family decisions on inequality and children's outcomes, mainly because the data does not permit this.

We have identified four (independent) dimensions that define family regimes in Latin America and have explored variations across regions and countries in accordance with them. These are union formation and child-bearing calendars; household complexity; married vs. unmarried cohabitation; and the nature of female household headship. Some key indicators of these dimensions have remained stable while others have changed dramatically. The timing of union formation and childbearing remains much the same, as a result of opposite trends among educational groups: The least-educated speeding up the process and the highly educated postponing transitions. Household sizes have diminished but the household complexity has not, as shown by the constant proportion of extended households. Cohabitation, however, has increased dramatically, as well as the number of households headed by women.

A pattern of social disadvantage emerges in any cross-sectional profile of cohabitation, lone motherhood, and early childbearing. As shown for the cases of Mexico, Brazil, and Colombia, women with low levels of education have children earlier than more highly educated women. The family context of childbearing has changed dramatically for all groups, but it has changed the least among the highly educated. More and more, women are having and raising their children outside marriage, either in the context of cohabitation (the majority now in Brazil and Colombia) or as single mothers (the fastest growing category).

The rise of cohabitation and lone motherhood, and diverging trends between women with low and high levels of education, might invite one to draw parallels with the West, but the point of departure is completely different. By contrast to Europe, marriage was never universal in Latin America, and cohabitation, union instability, and female headship were normative dimensions of family life. Indeed, the rise of cohabitation observed in recent decades may give the false impression that it was rare in the distant past. Indeed, analysis of the 1930 census microdata for Mexico (the first Latin American census to ask about cohabitation) shows higher levels of cohabitation than those observed in other years, until 2000, and in some states (Esteve et al. 2016b), even higher than the figures for 2010. During the middle decades of the twentieth century, the modernization of states came together with active policies to encourage marriage. In this context, the rise of cohabitation cannot merely be interpreted as a response to secularization but also to a rapid erosion of marriage which was never strongly institutionalized.

Why has marriage never become a universal institution? Why did government efforts to universalize marriage (after the 1950s) have such short-lived effects? Why did a significant majority of men have such a weak sense of commitment to their children and wives? More importantly, why have the expansion of education and modernization of Latin America societies had so little impact on family dynamics? Why is Latin America so full of interactions and regional differences? The answers to all these questions require research going beyond the short-term causes that may be driving recent family trends. They would seem to demand a study on how the economic, social, and political history of Latin America has unfolded over vast territories.

Comparative research with other societies, Europe and Asia, will also be necessary to understand why marriage did become universal in those societies. What were the prerequisites for marriage in those societies? Was it the need to organize the inheritance of property and to establish a line of descent? Was it the powerful influence of the church? Many of these prerequisites may not have appeared in some parts of Latin America. Institutionalization of the church was rather asymmetrical; access to property was constrained to certain groups, and settlement patterns and modes of production were also very diverse. In this sense, modern national boundaries encapsulate a wide range of types of social organization and family regimes, as shown by the series of maps presented in Figure 2.1. Furthermore, the evolution of modern economies in Latin America has not contributed toward increasing levels of security among the population, distributing the benefits of economic growth to the population as a whole, or improving the stability of work, or allowing people to plan their lives on the basis of long-term income.

Given the amount of considerable preexisting inequalities and their impact on family life, it would be unfair to single out family forms as drivers of inequality. We have no quarrel with the idea that, if data were available, we would certainly find different outcomes in terms of children's health, school attainment, and job quality depending on the family contexts of their mothers and fathers. Nevertheless, we would probably also discover all sorts of micro and macro paradoxes like the ones presented in this chapter, and differences in children's outcomes by family status might disappear after proper controls. All in all, one finds a puzzle of rich interactions, regional trends, and unexpected paradoxes that should, at least, stimulate social theorists to produce frameworks that encompass both individual-level predictors and the ways in which they interact with the social context. It should not be forgotten that this is a society in which inequality is pervasive, access to resources is still mediated by social class, and expansion of education did not have the expected effect on family dynamics. The idea of a relatively homogenous society from which destinies start to diverge is not the case in Latin America. Destinies have been diverging for centuries.

APPENDIX 2A.1. *Results of factor analysis of family indicators in Latin America,* 2000

	Factor Loads			
	Factor 1	Factor 2	Factor 3	Factor 4
Indicators contributing to:				
Factor 1: Early transitions				
% women 15–19 in union	0.89	0.06	0.27	0.02
% women 15–19 with children	0.85	0.18	0.30	0.00
% women 15–44 in union	0.74	−0.48	0.01	−0.22
% women 15–19 not in union and without children	−0.87	−0.14	−0.29	0.00
Factor 2: Household complexity				
% extended households	0.15	0.88	0.13	−0.32
% children 0–4 whose father/mother is not the household head	−0.12	0.85	0.30	−0.11
% children 0–4 in nuclear households	0.01	−0.84	−0.34	0.35
Factor 3: Cohabitation vs. marriage				
% cohabitation among mothers 15–44	0.28	0.19	0.89	−0.12
% cohabitation among women 15–44	0.24	0.29	0.89	−0.16
% cohabitation among women 25–29	0.12	0.20	0.92	−0.19
Factor 4: Female household heads not in union				
% female household heads not in union and with children	0.03	−0.18	−0.14	0.93
% female household heads in union	0.04	0.24	0.19	−0.90
No Factor				
% childless among women 45–49	−0.49	−0.05	0.25	0.39
% of single and childless among women 45–49	−0.56	0.02	−0.16	0.64
% nuclear households	0.14	−0.61	−0.45	0.55
% household heads among women	−0.62	0.41	0.42	−0.28
% of female heads with children	0.56	0.69	−0.09	−0.05
% separated/divorced among women 15 or over	0.03	0.47	0.35	0.28

Source: Authors' calculations based on IPUMS international microdata.

APPENDIX 2A.2A. *Percentage of mothers among women aged from 25 to 29 by union status, educational attainment, and census round*

Census round/ Partnership status	Mexico				Colombia				Brazil			
	Single	Cohabiting	Married	Total	Single	Cohabiting	Married	Total	Single	Cohabiting	Married	Total
1970s												
Primary or lower	4.7	61.5	11.1	77.3	10.8	50.1	12.9	73.8				
Secondary completed	3.5	56.4	2.1	62.0	2.6	47.0	0.6	50.2				
University completed	1.3	41.2	4.6	47.1	1.0	33.2	0.2	34.4				
1980s												
Primary or lower					13.2	40.8	25.0	79.0				
Secondary completed					8.9	40.3	7.0	56.2				
University completed					5.3	29.1	1.6	36.0				
1990s												
Primary or lower	6.2	61.7	12.5	80.4	14.6	29.1	36.2	79.9	9.8	49.6	16.2	75.6
Secondary completed	6.6	50.2	3.9	60.7	9.6	29.2	12.2	51.0	7.0	39.6	5.1	51.7
University completed	4.1	36.3	1.8	42.2	8.0	20.0	10.0	38.0	3.7	29.2	2.3	35.2
2000s												
Primary or lower	9.2	53.5	18.3	81.0	19.8	16.0	49.0	84.8	14.9	36.6	29.6	81.1
Secondary completed	8.3	46.4	7.4	62.1	20.0	18.8	27.0	65.8	10.5	29.4	10.4	50.3
University completed	4.6	27.7	2.4	34.7	9.8	15.0	8.7	33.5	5.1	18.8	3.5	27.4
2010s												
Primary or lower	12.8	40.8	28.6	82.2					17.4	23.4	38.3	79.1
Secondary completed	13.0	35.0	15.0	63.0					12.8	23.0	18.5	54.3
University completed	6.7	20.2	5.9	32.8					5.4	13.8	4.7	23.9

Source: Authors' calculations based on IPUMS international microdata.

APPENDIX 2A.2B. *Percentage of women aged from 25 to 29 who reside in an extended household by motherhood status, educational attainment, and census round*

Census round/ Motherhood status	Mexico			Colombia			Brazil		
	Mother	Childless	Total	Mother	Childless	Total	Mother	Childless	Total
1970s									
Primary or lower	5.1	10.5	15.5	6.2	24.7	30.9			
Secondary completed	5.8	10.3	16.1	10.7	11.5	22.2			
University completed	8.3	7.5	15.8	8.2	5	13.2			
1980s									
Primary or lower				5.7	27.3	33			
Secondary completed				13.1	21	34.2			
University completed				15.1	10.6	25.6			
1990s									
Primary or lower	4.8	15	19.8	4.6	28	32.6	6.8	17.5	24.3
Secondary completed	10.9	14.2	25.1	12	21.9	34.6	13.6	12.2	25.7
University completed	14.5	9.1	23.6	15.3	19.5	34.8	12.4	5.6	18
2000s									
Primary or lower	6.8	22	28.9	4.8	24.4	29.3	6.3	18.8	25.2
Secondary completed	12.4	19	31.4	12.3	25.4	37.7	14.7	13.6	28.3
University completed	16.9	10.4	27.3	19.9	13.7	33.6	13.7	5.9	19.6
2010s									
Primary or lower	6.7	28.7	35.4				7.3	20	27.3
Secondary completed	12.1	26.3	38.4				13.4	16.3	29.7
University completed	17.2	13.8	31.1				15.5	6.7	22.2

Source: Authors' calculations based on IPUMS international microdata.

APPENDIX 2A.2C. *Percentage of women aged from 35 to 44 who are household heads by partnership/motherhood status, educational attainment, and census round*

Census round/ Partnership– Motherhood status	Mexico					Colombia					Brazil				
	Mother not in union	Childless not in union	Childless in union	Mother in union	Total	Mother not in union	Childless not in union	Childless in union	Mother in union	Total	Mother not in union	Childless not in union	Childless in union	Mother in union	Total
1970s															
Primary or lower	1	10.7	0	0.4	12.1	1.1	19.2	0.1	3.5	23.9					
Secondary completed	4.1	9.5	0.5	0.9	15.0	4.4	15.4	0.2	1.1	21.0					
University completed	6.2	6.9	0	0	13.1	8.8	9.4	0	0.3	18.5					
1980s															
Primary or lower						0.8	14.7	0.1	2.1	17.6					
Secondary completed						2.5	13.8	0.1	1.5	17.9					
University completed						5.6	14.6	0.1	2	17.7					
1990s															
Primary or lower	0.6	11.4	0	1.2	13.3	0.6	17.1	0.1	2.6	20.3	1	11.5	0	0.9	13.4
Secondary completed	2.2	12.8	0.1	0.8	15.9	2.3	16.9	0.1	2	21.3	3.8	10.9	0.1	1.1	15.9
University completed	4.4	12.6	0.1	0.8	18.0	5.5	18.7	0.2	2.3	26.7	7.6	10.7	0.4	1.2	19.9

2000s															
Primary or lower	0.6	12.6	0.1	2.6	15.9	1.1	18.5	0.2	3.4	23.2	1.1	14.3	0.2	4.2	19.8
Secondary completed	1.7	12.3	0.2	1.9	16.0	2.7	18.2	0.2	2.7	23.8	3.6	13.3	0.5	4.1	21.5
University completed	3.6	11	0.3	1.9	16.9	6.1	15.9	0.4	2.6	25.1	7.4	11.9	1.1	4.3	24.6
2010s															
Primary or lower	0.6	13	0.1	3.4	17.1						1.5	14.9	1	15.8	33.2
Secondary completed	1.6	12.6	0.3	3.1	17.5						3.5	13.5	1.6	13.9	32.5
University completed	4.4	11.3	0.7	3.1	19.4						7	10.6	2.9	13.1	33.7

Source: Authors' calculations based on IPUMS international microdata.

PART II

THE CAUSES OF INCREASINGLY DIVERGING FAMILY STRUCTURES

3

How Inequality Drives Family Formation
The Prima Facie Case

Andrew J. Cherlin

Over the past several years, economic inequality has become one of the most discussed topics in social science and social policy. Indeed, no serious discussion of contemporary social and economic life seems complete without a consideration of the growing level of economic inequality that we have seen over the past several decades. In this chapter, I will explore whether, and how, economic inequality – the distribution of income and wealth across social strata – affects the formation and dissolution of families. I write from the perspective of the United States, but I hope my view will be valuable for students of Western Europe and the other overseas English-speaking countries. I will focus on different-sex couples, for whom an historical argument can be assessed. Studies of same-sex couples are underway, and it is not yet clear whether the dynamics are different. I will examine whether economic inequality may be affecting patterns of entry into and exit from cohabitation and marriage, as well as childbearing within or outside marriage. Nevertheless, I will acknowledge that cultural change matters too. Economic conditions are not all powerful. The changes that we have witnessed in family formation would not have happened had the Western world not seen a great shift in attitudes toward marriage and cohabitation over the past half-century.

I have elsewhere referred to these cultural shifts as the deinstitutionalization of marriage (Cherlin 2004). In retrospect, I think that a more accurate, although less elegant, phrase would have been "the deinstitutionalization of intimate unions." Marriage itself retains much of its distinctive structure and legal protections, even if it has a less clear set of rules for how spouses are to behave than in the past, but it no longer has a monopoly on intimate unions. A majority of partnerships now begin as cohabiting unions. Cohabiting couples cannot rely on shared understandings and legal statutes to guide their interactions. Rather, they must negotiate how they will act in their relationships.

They exhibit a wide variation in commitment. In northern Europe, one commonly finds cohabiting couples who have had long-term stable relationships without ever marrying (Kiernan 2001), but in the United States, most cohabiting unions lead either to break-ups or to marriage within a few years (Cherlin 2009). An increasing number of American children are now born into them – one in four at the rates in 2015 (Wu 2017). In some cases, the parents may not begin to cohabit until after the woman becomes pregnant (Rackin and Gibson-Davis 2012). Children born to cohabiting couples are exposed to a substantially higher risk of parental union dissolution than are children born to married couples – a relationship common across almost all European countries (DeRose et al. 2017). Childbearing in cohabiting unions is much more common among Americans without university degrees than among university graduates (Wu 2017). A clear social-class line now divides American families at the university-degree level, with graduates much more likely to marry before having a child and less likely to end their marriages. Indeed, it almost seems as though the United States has two family formation systems that are differentiated by the presence or absence of a university degree (Cherlin 2010).

Economic inequality is relevant for explaining these divergent patterns in partnerships and fertility. A long line of research links marriage formation to labor market opportunities for young men (Becker 1991; Oppenheimer 1988; Parsons and Bales 1955). Men have been, and still are, required to earn a steady income; more recently, it has become desirable, but optional, for women to earn one too – at least among nonpoor couples. Therefore I will focus most of my attention to the changes in the labor market that have affected men. Aggregate-level (e.g., cross-national or cross-state) studies have addressed the consequences of inequality for family-related outcomes, such as the percentages married (Loughran 2002) or divorced (Frank, Levine, and Dijk 2014), and for teenage pregnancy and birth rates (Gold et al. 2001). My coauthors and I have shown that individuals are more likely to marry before childbearing in places where labor market conditions are better than in places where middle-skilled jobs are scarce (Cherlin, Ribar, and Yasutake 2016). However, statistical studies require specialized knowledge to evaluate, and their mathematical models are almost always subject to limitations. Consequently, nonspecialists often have understandable difficulties evaluating the worth of statistical claims that are made. In this chapter, I would like to present a less technical argument for the proposition that rising income inequality has been an important driver of changes in family. Think of it as a prima facie case – a set of facts that establishes the likelihood that an argument is true, even though it does not prove it. The facts, I hope, will establish the plausibility that income inequality has been an important causal factor. It will also suggest that explanations that reject the importance of income inequality and instead argue that cultural change is the sole driver (e.g., Murray 2012) are at best incomplete.

THE DIMENSIONS OF INCOME INEQUALITY

Income inequality has several dimensions. Two have received close attention in social commentary. First, much has been written about the growing proportion of income and wealth accruing to people in the highest 1% of the distribution (e.g., Piketty and Saez 2003). Between the late 1970s and the early 2010s, the amount of income amassed by the top 1% from about 10% to about 20% (Atkinson, Piketty, and Saez 2011). As dramatic as this rise has been, I would argue that it is not the most important dimension of inequality to think about when studying changes in family structure. Rather, what matters more is a second dimension of inequality: The growing earnings gap between the university-educated (by which I mean individuals with a bachelor's or university degree or higher) and the nonuniversity-educated. This gap has widened since the 1970s (Autor 2014). Prior to that time, manufacturing jobs were more plentiful in the United States. The nation had emerged from World War II as *the* economic power of the world. In 1948, American factories produced 45% of the world's industrial output, and the nation's manufacturing exports accounted for a third of the world total (Cherlin 2014). The booming economy and a relative shortage of labor (due to the lower birth rates during the Great Depression) created conditions that were favorable to unionization; and labor unions negotiated for higher wages and better fringe benefits (Levy and Temin 2010).

Yet beginning with the oil embargo by the Arab states in the Organization of the Petroleum Exporting Countries in 1973, the long postwar boom subsided. The wages of production workers remained stagnant or declined as manufacturing work moved overseas, where wages were much lower, or was automated, lowering the demand for workers. The proportion of workers who were doing what was commonly called blue-collar work – production workers, craftworkers, fabricators, construction workers, and the like – declined. In contrast, demand for high-skilled professional, managerial, and technical workers remained strong – a development that economists refer to as skill-biased technical change (Autor, Katz, and Kearney 2008). It produced a growing earnings gap between middle-skilled workers, who tend to have a secondary-school education, and highly skilled workers, who tended to have a university education. Autor (2014) has estimated that in the period from 1979 to

2012, the rising earnings gap between the typical university-educated household and secondary-school-educated household has cost the latter four times as much in lost income as has the growing concentration of income among the top 1%.

The rising earnings gap has increased inequality by hollowing out the middle of the income distribution, producing what some have called the hourglass economy – a metaphor for the pinched middle (Leonard 2011). Industrial jobs have been the easiest to automate or outsource because they require routine production that can be done by computer or robots or that can be carried out in factories situated far from the place at which the goods they produce will be consumed. In contrast, many low-paying service jobs must be done in person (e.g., waiters, gardeners); and high-paying managerial and technical jobs have remained uncomputerized and performed in the United States. as well. The polarization of low-paying and high-paying jobs, with fewer mid-level jobs in between, creates a higher level of income inequality.

INCOME INEQUALITY AND FAMILY FORMATION

How then might rising income inequality be associated with changes in family formation? My argument is that the presence of high levels of income inequality is a signal that a weakness exists in the middle of the labor market. That weakness creates the conditions that change family formation. To be sure, income inequality may not inherently be a direct causal force for family change. Perhaps other forms of income inequality in other places at other times might not be as strongly associated with the hollowing out of the middle of the labor market and therefore might have little effect. However, the inequality that we have seen in the United States *is* connected to the labor market, in that it is harder for a person with a moderate amount of skill – say, a secondary-school diploma and perhaps a few university courses – to get a decent-paying job. In turn, the difficulty of finding middle-skilled jobs depresses rates of marriage and of marital fertility.

The prima facie case for the causal importance of income inequality rests on two basic trends. The first trend is the aforementioned growth since about 1980 of the earnings differential between the university-educated and the less-educated (Autor 2014). As I have noted, this gap reflects the relative decline in job opportunities in the middle of the labor market – the kinds of jobs that people without university degrees are qualified for. In addition, among individuals without a university education, the disruption in the middle of the labor market has been sharper for men than for women. Much of the automation and offshoring has occurred among manual occupations that had been seen as men's work due to their physical, often repetitive, nature at a factory or a construction site. In the American ideal of the working-class family that was socially constructed in the late nineteenth and early twentieth centuries, men were supposed to do jobs that required hard physical labor and to bring home a paycheck for the needs of their wives and children. Sociologist Michèle Lamont refers to this conception of the male role as the "disciplined self" (Lamont 2000) and claims that it has been common among White working-class men in the United States. (Lamont found that the self-sufficient breadwinner image was less common among Blacks.) It is this type of manly work that has been subject to shortages and to wage stagnation. Initially, working-class husbands took pride in keeping their wives out of the labor force, but in the postwar period, women moved into paid employment in clerical and service work – the so-called pink-collar jobs that came to be seen as women's work. Jobs in this sector of the economy have not been hit as hard by the offshoring and automation of production. Consequently, men and women's earnings have moved in different directions. Between 1979 and 2007, men's hourly earnings decreased for all those without university degrees. For women, earnings fell only for those without secondary-school diplomas; all others experienced increases. Alone among male workers, the university graduates experienced an increase; and for women, the largest increases were for university graduates (Autor 2010).

The second basic trend consists of the divergent paths that family structure has taken during the same period, according to the educational levels of the adults involved. In the 1950s, marriage was ubiquitous. At all educational levels, almost everyone married, and almost all children were born within marriage (Cherlin 1992). The central position of marriage in family life began to erode in the 1960s and 1970s. Crucially for my argument, the trends in marriage and childbearing were initially moving in the same direction for adults at all educational levels: Marriage was being postponed, cohabitation was increasing, and divorce rates were rising (Cherlin 1992). However, since about 1980, the family lives of those with a university degree, whom we may call the highly educated, and those with less education have diverged (McLanahan 2004). Family life among the highly educated remains focused on marriage as the context for raising children, and although the highly-educated marry at later ages, they ultimately have higher lifetime marriage rates than do those with less education (Aughinbaugh, Robles, and Sun 2013). In addition, the divorce rate for highly educated couples has declined sharply since its peak around 1980 (Stevenson and Wolfers 2007). Meanwhile, the

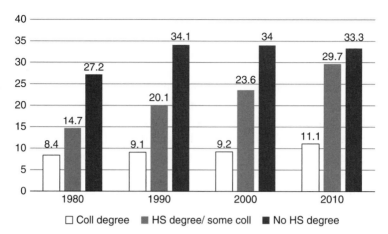

FIGURE 3.1 Percentage of children living with single and cohabiting mothers,
by mother's education, 1980–2010
Source: Stykes and Williams 2013.

percentage of births outside marriage among the highly educated has
remained low. In contrast, the family lives of people with a secondary-school
diploma but not a university degree, whom we may call the moderately
educated, have moved away from stable marriage. This group has experienced a surge of births within cohabiting unions. Unlike the typical cohabiting unions in some European countries, these unions tend to be brittle and
to lead to disruptions at a high rate (Musick and Michelmore 2015). Among
moderately educated married couples (those with secondary-school diplomas), there has not been as much decline in divorce as among the highly
educated (S. P. Martin 2006). Finally, people without secondary-school
degrees, whom we may call the least-educated, have continued to have a
high proportion of births outside marriage, although there has been less
change in their family patterns since 1980.

Consequently, the greatest change in children's living arrangements since
1980 has occurred among the moderately educated, among whom the proportion of children living with single mothers and cohabiting mothers has
increased dramatically. Figure 3.1 shows changes in children's living arrangements for the thirty-year period from 1980 to 2010. Consider the white-colored
bars, which show the percentage of children with highly educated mothers
who are living in a single-parent or cohabiting-parent family. It hardly changed during the thirty-year period – rising from 8% to 11%. In other words, there
was little or no movement away from marriage-based families for the raising of
children. Now look at the dark-gray bars, which show children living with

least-educated mothers. They were the most likely to live in single-parent or cohabiting-parent families in all years but after increasing from 1980 to 1990, the rate has held steady.

It is the light-gray bars, which show children living with moderately educated mothers, that portray the greatest changes in family structure. Here we see the substantial growth of the proportion of children living in single-parent or cohabiting-parent families – from 15% to 30%. Thus, it is among the moderately educated, that we see both the greatest change toward nonmarital, unstable living arrangements for having and rearing children *and* the greatest erosion of labor market opportunities – and we see both trends commencing at roughly the same point in time. It is among the highly educated that we see the opposite pairing of trends: Continued high levels of children living in more stable marriages centered on marriage coincided with a rise in the earnings premium for university graduates. This is the prima facie case for the proposition that rising income inequality has been an important indicator of changes in family formation – a marker for the deterioration of the middle of the labor market, especially for men, and an improvement in the labor market for the university-educated. Those who experienced a deteriorating job market trended toward less stable family environments. Those who experienced an improvement in the job market trended toward stable marriage-based family environments.

Many of the highly educated are living an advantaged family life, with two earners providing an ample household income. It is the flipside of the family troubles experienced by the moderately educated. In fact, a number of European and American researchers are claiming that the relatively stable unions of the highly educated are based on a new marital bargain in which the partners share the tasks of paid work, housework, and child-rearing more equally than in the past (Esping-Andersen 2009, 2016; Esping-Andersen and Billari 2015; Goldscheider, Bernhardt, and Lappegård 2015). For these observers, the key driver has been the change in women's roles and the normative shift it has caused. In the mid-twentieth century, marriage and family life was in a stable equilibrium based on a specialization model in which the wife did the housework and child care and the husband did the waged work. When wives began to move into the labor force, they also began to ask their husbands to do more in the home. The result, it is said, was several decades of disruption and dissension as husbands resisted taking on more of what had been seen as wives' work and as welfare states were slow to support women wage workers through programs such as child-care assistance. However, these scholars argue that a new egalitarian equilibrium is emerging that is based on the sharing of both market and housework by the partners, who may now be either married or cohabiting, and who rely on expanded state support for two-earner families. Social norms, according to this view, have evolved from a breadwinner/home-maker equilibrium in the 1950s to an egalitarian equilibrium that is emerging now.

However, an important limitation of this argument is that the egalitarian bargain rests on the availability of good labor market opportunities for men and generous family-friendly social welfare benefits for couples, such as childcare assistance and family leave. Although the husband is no longer required to be the sole earner of the family, there is still a widespread norm that a man must have the potential to be a steady earner in order to be considered as a good long-term partner (Killewald 2016). Among the moderately educated and least-educated, it is increasingly difficult for men to demonstrate sufficient potential. Consequently, the emergence of a gender-egalitarian equilibrium of committed, domestic work-sharing couples in long-term relationships is likely to be more common in the privileged, university-educated sectors of Western nations than in the less-advantaged, lower educated sectors.

THE INFLUENCE OF CULTURAL CHANGE

The main counterargument to the prima facie explanation I have presented is that changes in social norms have driven *both* the decline in earnings among the nonuniversity graduates *and* the changes in family structure that occurred over the same time span. To be sure, culture is part of the story. During the Great Depression, job opportunities were scarce and yet there was no increase in the percentage of children who were born outside marriage. The reason is that having an "illegitimate" child, as it was called at the time, was socially unacceptable and stigmatizing. Today nonmarital births are much more acceptable than in the past. Without this greater cultural acceptance of alternatives to marriage, we would not have seen the rise in births to cohabiting couples in the United States. Moreover, the weakening of marriage began in the early 1960s, well before the dramatic rise in inequality occurred (Cherlin 1992).

In fact, marriage is much less central to Americans' sense of their adult identity today than it was in the past. In the 2002 wave of the General Social Survey – a biennial survey of American adults that is conducted by the research organization NORC at the University of Chicago – respondents were asked which of several milestones a person had to accomplish in order to be an adult. More than nine out of ten selected markers such as being economically independent, having finished one's education, and not living in one's parental home, but only about half agreed that one had to be married to be an adult (Furstenberg et al. 2004). In the mid-twentieth century, the first step a young person took into adulthood was to get married. The average age at marriage in the 1950s was about 20 for women and 22 for men (US Census Bureau 2016). Only then did you leave home: 90%–95% of all young people married. Today, marriage's place in the life course, if it occurs at all, is often at the end of the transition to adulthood (Cherlin 2004). Other paths to adulthood, including having children prior to marrying, cohabiting, and perhaps never marrying, are common and largely acceptable.

A further cultural counterargument is that an erosion of social norms supporting hard work has caused the declining work rates of men, at least in the United States, and by extension, family instability (Eberstadt 2016; Murray 2012). Although we have seen changes in men's and women's work and family roles, one norm has held constant: Men must be able to provide a steady income in order to be considered good candidates for marriage. Killewald (2016) found that men who are not employed full-time have an elevated risk of divorce, but that low earnings were not necessarily a risk factor as long as the men worked steadily. Other studies suggest that while a woman might choose to cohabit with a man whose income potential is in doubt, she is unlikely to marry him – and he may agree that he is not ready. In focus groups conducted with cohabiting young adults in Ohio, several couples told the researchers that everything was in place for a wedding except for the finances, and that until they were confident of their finances, they would not marry (Smock, Manning, and Porter 2005).

It is alarming to some observers, then, that the percentage of prime-age men who are working or looking for work has declined, particularly among men without university degrees. Eberstadt (2016) reported that the percentage of 25–54-year-old men who were employed dropped from 94% in 1948 to 84% in 2015. He cites a number of factors, including the employment problems faced by the growing number of men who have returned to the general population after serving prison sentences, but he suggests that a decreasing motivation to work among certain groups of men may be part of the story. In contrast, university-educated men are working almost as hard as in the past (Jacobs and Gerson 2005). One might think, then, that university graduates prefer to work longer hours more than do less educated men.; however, that is not true.

In fact, the General Social Survey shows that there has been a decline in the desire to work long hours among both secondary-school-educated men *and* university-educated men. In several of the survey's biennial waves, respondents were handed a card showing five characteristics of a job and asked to rank them in importance. One characteristic was "Working hours are short, lots of free time." In the 1973–1984 period, the proportion of men aged 25–44 who rated it as most or second-most important was 13%; in the combined 2006 and 2012 samples, it rose to 28% (Cherlin 2014). It seems, then, the percentage of men who highly valued short working hours and lots of free time has increased. However, the increase was just as sharp for university graduates as it was for those with a secondary-school diploma but not a university degree. (There was no increase among men without secondary-school diplomas.) So both moderately educated and highly educated men seem to value working short hours more than they used to. Yet only the moderately educated men are actually working less than they used to. On the contrary, Americans working in the professional, technical, and managerial sectors of the labor force tend to work longer hours than their European counterparts (Jacobs and Gerson 2005). The survey results therefore raise this question: If both highly educated men and moderately educated men had a growing preference for shorter hours and more free time, why was only the latter group actually working shorter hours than in the past?

The answer, I would argue, is that employment opportunities and earnings levels for the university-educated men were improving so much that some of these men decided to work longer hours than they preferred: The attraction of the jobs that were available to them – notably higher wages and salaries – more than balanced their attraction to free time. Among moderately educated men in contrast, employment opportunities were not attractive enough to override their growing preference for free time. In other words, whether a man is working depends on both his preferences for work and the opportunities available to him. The decline in men's labor force participation is rooted in a cultural shift as well as a change in the labor market. Both cultural and labor market factors are necessary to explain the decline.

More generally, this example suggests how intertwined economics and culture are in producing the trends we have seen in family life. Economic sociologists have long argued that economic action is embedded in social institutions (Granovetter 1985): People make decisions about employment in a cultural milieu. Currently, that milieu may be more favorable toward other activities and leisure than in the past. Some observers might judge that milieu negatively and decry the choices working-age men may make, but cultural forces can be overridden by the opportunity for higher paying, stable work or they can be reinforced through job opportunities that are insecure and lower paying. Cultural forces do not alone determine how young adults will relate to family and work, and nor, it must be said, do economic forces.

One other cultural phenomenon may be contributing to the class differences, not by its transformation but by its stubborn persistence: Ideas about masculinity (Cherlin 2014). As I noted earlier, working-class men have taken pride in hard physical labor. Meanwhile jobs that involved caring for and serving others came to be associated with women. These caring-work jobs typically pay less than industrial jobs, which may explain some of the reluctance of men to take them, but they also seem to be devalued in status, at least among men, precisely because they are seen as unmanly jobs (England 2005). As a 53-year-old man who had lost several jobs to automation and to factories that moved to other cities, told a reporter for the *New York Times*, he never considered work in the health sector of the labor market: "I ain't gonna be a nurse; I don't have the tolerance for people," he said. "I don't want it to sound bad, but I've always seen a woman in the position of a nurse or some kind of health care worker. I see it as more of a woman's touch" (Miller 2017). What we might call conventional masculinity – and what the literature sometimes calls "hegemonic masculinity" (Connell 1995) – still prescribes that some jobs are men's jobs and others are for women. The problem is that men's jobs have been disproportionately affected by the globalization and automation of production. In the meantime, service jobs have opened up, as in the health sector, but men have resisted taking them. Working-class men's resistance to doing jobs that are not considered manly enough contributes to the difficulties they face in the labor market.

DISCUSSION

The social-class differences in family formation that are apparent today are not unprecedented. Rather, we are seeing, in a sense, a return to the historical complexity of family life (Therborn 2004). That complexity was apparent throughout the early decades of industrialization during the late nineteenth and early twentieth centuries, when there was a great growth of factory jobs. During this period, traditional-skilled jobs in the middle of the labor market, such as those performed by independent craftsmen, yeomen, and apprentices in small shops, were undercut by factory production. Independent shops either collapsed or turn into larger factories. Inequality increased, and as is the case today, the middle of the labor market was hollowed out. Sharp social-class differences in marriage rates were visible; professional, technical, and managerial workers were more likely to marry than were workers with less remunerative jobs (Cherlin 2014). The prosperous period of stability just after World War II, when almost everyone married, fertility rates were high, and divorce rates were unusually stable (Cherlin 1992), was the most unusual time in family life since industrialization and should not be taken as an anchor point.

Nevertheless, the complexity of family life we see today is different from the complexity of the past. The high rates of cohabitation and of child-bearing outside marriage that are now prevalent were rare during the disruptions of early industrialization. Nor, as I noted, were they present during the disruption of the Great Depression. The culture of family life was different; alternatives to marriage such as cohabitation and single-parent families (other than those due to widowhood) were unacceptable to most people. So if a young adult was not married, he or she probably lived in the parental home or boarded in another family's home and remained childless. The growth in the number of people who were living alone is largely a post-World War II phenomenon, as the housing stock increased and wages and salaries (and therefore the ability to pay rent) rose (Kobrin 1976; Ruggles 1988). The lives that unmarried young adults in the United States led in the past are more similar to family life today in countries such as Italy, where it is common for twenties to live at home, remain childless, and marry in their late twenties and early thirties.

One must also include the growth of a more individualistic, self-devel-opment oriented culture in the story of changes in family formation today. This cultural development may be connected to a larger shift among the population of the wealthy countries to what are called post-materialist values (Inglehart 1997). As societies have become wealthier and have solved the problem of providing basic needs, it is said individuals have come to value self-expression – the development of one's personality – over survivalist values such as providing food, shelter, and basic financial support. One aspect of self-expression is the examination of whether one's intimate partnership continues to meet one's needs. If not, the self-expres-sive individual will consider ending that partnership and finding a new one that better fits her or his continually developing self. Thus, self-expression is associated with higher rates of union dissolution and re-formation. Post-materialist values also include a decline in traditional religious beliefs; in the West that decline is consistent with a rise in nonmarital partnerships and childbearing outside marriage. Overall, a rise in post-materialist values is consistent with what demographers have called the second demographic transition (van de Kaa 1987; Lesthaeghe and Surkyn 1988): The period since the 1970s during which cohabitation, nonmarital births, and low fertility have become common in most Western countries. Moreover, during this period, there has been a decline in civic engagement – social ties, atten-dance at religious services, and participation in local associations – that has been more pronounced among those without university educations (Putnam 2015).

Note, however, that second demographic transition theory does not explain the continued strength of marriage and the decline in divorce rates that have occurred among highly educated Americans in this period. It provides no explanation for a seeming transition back toward a family form characterized by relatively stable marriage, albeit preceded by cohabitation. Highly educated young adults were previously thought to constitute the nontraditional vanguard, providing new models of family life that diffused down the educational ladder. That is not, however, what we have seen; rather, the patterns in the United States suggest a neo-traditional highly educated class and a growth of nontraditional behavior among those with less education. At least in the United States, then, second demographic transition theory cannot provide us with an explanation for the growing divide in family life.

That divide suggests a role for the momentous changes in the economy that have differentially affected the highly educated and the less educated. Nevertheless, one must be careful in attributing social change solely to economic inequality. It has become the go-to explanation for a wide variety of social phenomena. One frequently cited book claims that inequality has caused anxiety and chronic stress that has led to a long list of consequences that include poorer physical health, higher mortality, greater obesity, lower educational attainment, higher teenage birth rates, greater exposure among children to conflict, higher rates of imprisonment, more drug use, less social trust, and less social mobility (Wilkinson and Pickett 2009). All of this is deduced solely from macro-level correlations at the national or state level. It seems unlikely that any social phenomenon could have effects this broad, and in any case, macro-level correlations do not prove the case. The claims in the literature (as well as in this chapter) must therefore be carefully scrutinized and subject to further research.

This chapter also presents a very US-centric perspective that may be less applicable in Europe. The American social welfare system is well known to be among the least generous in the Western world – it is the archetype of the "liberal" (free-market oriented) welfare state in the classic formulation of Esping-Andersen (1990) – and compared to other nations, it provides a larger proportion of its benefits through programs that are contingent on work effort (Garfinkel, Rainwater, and Smeeding 2010). Therefore, it does less to support low-income families that do not have steady wage earners than do the welfare systems in other countries. It also provides less support for working parents, in terms of paid family leave or child-care assistance. This lack of support may be one reason why rates of union instability and childbearing among single parents are high in the United States from an international perspective (see Chapter 1). Moreover, the idea that a couple should not marry until they are confident that they will have an adequate steady income (Gibson-Davis, Edin, and McLanahan 2005) seems to be stronger in the United States than elsewhere. Perelli-Harris (2014) and her colleagues convened focus groups in nine settings in Europe to discuss cohabitation and marriage. They found that the rise of education has not devalued the cultural meaning of marriage; however, they did not hear much discussion of economic uncertainty and its relationship to whether a cohabiting couple should marry.

Nevertheless, the prima facie case that inequality – and more specifically the diverging labor market opportunities for the highly educated and the moderately educated – has driven family formation and dissolution seems strong for the United States. It is not the complete explanation for the great changes in these behaviors that have occurred in the past half-century or so, but it does not need to be. To be sure, had bearing children outside marriage not become acceptable, had cohabitation not become the predominant way that young adults enter into a first union, had survival values persisted over self-expressive values, we would not have seen the same retreat from marriage and marital childbearing; however, had employment opportunities for secondary-school-educated men not deteriorated and had corporations not been able to use the mobility of capital to undermine unionized factories, we would probably not have seen the same retreat either. Culture alone cannot explain the increasingly divergent paths by which the university-educated and the nonuniversity-educated are forming and maintaining families. It seems highly likely that one must take into account the economic changes that have occurred in the increasingly unequal American society.

4

Universal or Unique? Understanding Diversity in Partnership Experiences across Europe

Brienna Perelli-Harris

New family formation behaviors have increased nearly everywhere in Europe. Cohabitation, childbearing within cohabitation, divorce, separation, and repartnering have all become more common, even in places where scholars did not think that these behaviors would emerge (see Chapter 1). Recent data from the OECD (2016a) shows that nonmarital fertility, for example, increased dramatically in nearly every country in Europe throughout the 2000s, even across much of southern and Eastern Europe (Figure 4.1). However, European countries still vary widely with respect to the prevalence of new family formation behaviors. For example, in Norway, Sweden, and Denmark, the majority of births occur within cohabitation, while in other countries, such as Italy and Romania, childbearing within cohabitation is still relatively rare (Perelli-Harris et al. 2012). Figure 4.1 shows that although nearly every country in Europe experienced increases in nonmarital fertility, the year in which the increases began differs across countries, as does the speed of the increase.

The nearly universal increase in new family formation behaviors coupled with the diversity in the timing and rate of increase raises questions about whether the underlying causes are universal, or if the process of development is unique in each context. Several scholars have proposed overarching theories to explain the observed changes, the most well-known of which is the second demographic transition (SDT) (Lesthaeghe 2010; Van de Kaa 1987). Proponents of SDT theory posit that shifting values, ideational change, and increasing individualization have led individuals to choose unconventional lifestyles and living arrangements, often defying the traditional marital pathway of their parents (Lesthaeghe 2010). SDT theory also implies that those with higher education were the forerunners of the change, as they challenged patriarchal institutions and focused on the pursuit of self-actualization (Lesthaeghe and Surkyn 2002).

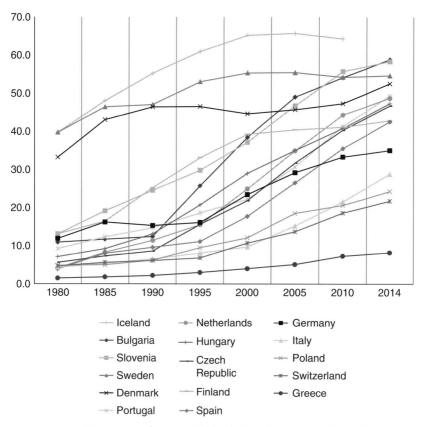

FIGURE 4.1 Percentage of nonmarital births in selected countries, 1980–2014

There is scant evidence, however, that the emergence of new behaviors is due to the pursuit of self-actualization or practiced by the more highly educated. Indeed, recent evidence (as discussed in Chapter 1) indicates that childbearing within cohabitation is associated with lower education (Perelli-Harris et al. 2010), divorce has increasingly become associated with lower education (Matysiak et al. 2014), and the highly educated are more likely to marry (Isen and Stevenson 2010; Kalmijn 2013). These studies suggest that new forms of family behaviors are associated with a "pattern of disadvantage." Although social norms have shifted to become more tolerant of cohabitation and nonmarital childbearing, the less-educated face greater uncertainty and economic constraints, which is reflected in their relationship choices (Perelli-Harris et al. 2010).

Nonetheless, despite evidence that many aspects of the family are changing across Europe, and some of these new aspects are associated with lower education, a consistent association between family change and social class has not been observed for all behaviors or in all contexts (Mikolai, Perelli-Harris, and Berrington 2014; Perelli-Harris et al. 2012). Superficial trends may be masking substantial underlying differences in specific processes and consequences. In fact, research has found that although many aspects of family formation are changing, they might not be converging in the same way or toward a similar standard (Billari and Liefbroer 2010; Sobotka and Toulemon 2008). Several studies have found that while transitions to adulthood are becoming more complex, heterogeneous, and "destandardized" throughout Europe, trajectories do not appear to be converging on one particular pattern or type of new trajectory (Elzinga and Liefbroer 2007; Fokkema and Liefbroer 2008; Perelli-Harris and Lyons-Amos 2015). In addition, while some elements of partnership formation, such as the postponement of marriage, seem to be universally associated with higher education, country context appears to be much more important for predicting partnership trajectories than individual-level educational attainment (Perelli-Harris and Lyons-Amos 2016). Thus, while some aspects of family formation, such as the postponement of marriage and fertility, seem to be changing on a wide scale, others, such as long-term cohabitation and union dissolution, seem to be dependent on the social, economic, political, religious, and historical contexts that shape family behavior.

In this chapter, I will explore the diversity and similarity of partnership experiences throughout Europe, drawing on recent research and evidence. I will focus on the emergence of cohabitation as a new family form, especially as a context for childbearing. Cohabiting unions are heterogeneous living arrangements, with some couples sliding into temporary partnerships of short duration, others testing their relationship to see if it is suitable for marriage, and still others living in long-term committed unions with no intentions of marriage (Perelli-Harris et al. 2014). Yet, on average, cohabiting unions are more likely to dissolve, even if they involve children (Galezewska 2016; Musick and Michelmore 2015). Also, as discussed above and in Chapter 1, childbearing within cohabitation is often associated with low education, resulting from a pattern of disadvantage (Perelli-Harris et al. 2010). Thus, the costs of union dissolution more commonly fall on already disadvantaged individuals, potentially exacerbating inequality.

This chapter will cover findings from a mixed methods project that examined cohabitation and nonmarital childbearing across Europe and the United States from different analytical perspectives.[1] First, I will describe the spatial

---

[1] This project was funded by the European Research Council under the grant agreement entitled CHILDCOHAB.

variation in nonmarital fertility across Europe to illustrate how patterns of family change may be influenced by political or cultural borders as well as the persistence of the past. Second, I will outline the laws and policies governing cohabitation in nine European countries to demonstrate how welfare states may be ill-equipped to deal with the new realities of more people living outside marriage. Third, I will draw on a large focus group project to describe discourses surrounding cohabitation and marriage in eight European countries to better understand similarities and differences in cultural and social norms. Finally, I will address the potential conse-quences of new partnership behaviors by summarizing a recent project that examines the health and well-being of cohabiting and married people. This section will discuss whether marriage, versus remaining in cohabitation, provides benefits to adult well-being beyond simply living with a partner. Throughout, I will speculate about why partnership behaviors differ across countries. Taken together, these studies portray a complex picture of family change in Europe today and raise questions about whether the interrelation-ship between family trajectories and inequality may be mediated by country context.

THE DIFFUSION OF NEW FAMILY BEHAVIORS: UNIVERSAL CHANGE — UNEVEN DISTRIBUTION

One of the best ways to illustrate the diversity of family formation behaviors is with a map (Figure 4.2, Klüsener, Perelli-Harris, and Sánchez Gassen 2013). The variegated landscape of nonmarital fertility can reveal clues into the fundamental reasons why marriage has declined in some countries, while remaining the predominant context for childbearing in others. Figure 4.1 shows the percentage of nonmarital births across Europe in 2007, with the lightest regions indicating that less than 10% of births occur outside marriage and the darkest regions indicating that up to 75% of births occur outside marriage. Note that the diffusion of nonmarital fertility has primarily been driven by the increase in childbearing within cohabiting partnerships, not births outside a union (Perelli-Harris et al. 2012). Thus this map portrays a rapid increase in a new and emerging behavior. More recent nonmarital childbearing statistics on the national level (OECD 2016a) suggest that the entire map has become even darker over the past seven years as the percentage of births outside marriage has reached unprecedented highs; however, these statistics are not available on the regional level. The map shown here is important for showing gradations

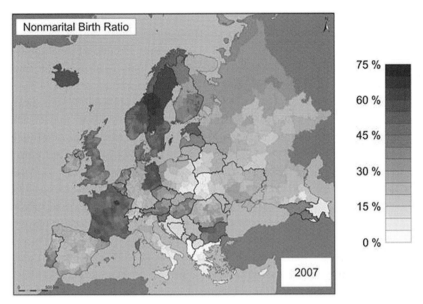

FIGURE 4.2 Percentage of births outside marriage, 2007

of patterns on the regional level, thus providing insights into the link between spatial variation and the persistence of the past (Klüsener 2015).

First, notice that the patchwork of high and low regions does not necessarily accord with particular welfare regimes, or even typical geographic areas. Nonmarital fertility is very high in the Nordic countries, with the highest levels in northern Sweden and Iceland, reflecting a long history of female independence and permissiveness of alternative living arrangements (Trost 1978). Nonmarital fertility is also high in France, where cohabitation rose rapidly during the 1980s, possibly due to policies which favored single mothers or as a rejection of the Catholic Church and the institution of marriage (Knijn, Martin, and Millar 2007). Eastern Germany also stands out as a region with particularly high levels of nonmarital fertility, dating back to the Prussian era (Klüsener and Goldstein 2014) and increasing during the socialist period through policies favoring single mothers (Klarner 2015), and after the collapse of socialism, by high male unemployment and female labor force participation (Konietzka and Kreyenfeld 2002). Of the Baltics, Estonia has the highest level of nonmarital fertility, reflecting greater secularization than in Latvia and Lithuania, which have maintained Catholic or traditional social norms favoring marriage (Katus et al. 2008). Bulgaria is another, southern European, country with unexpectedly high levels of nonmarital fertility, possibly due to cultural practices in rural areas or as a response to economic insecurity (Kostova 2007). Other regions also have surprisingly high nonmarital fertility, for example, parts of Austria and southern Portugal, which harken back to norms only permitting marriage upon inheritance of the family farm.

Very low levels of nonmarital fertility are primarily concentrated in southern Europe, for example, in Greece, Albania, and southern Italy. Studies have indicated that Italy has had a "delayed diffusion" of cohabitation, potentially because parents have opposed their children living together without being married (DiGiulio and Rosina 2007; Vignoli and Salvini 2014). The vast majority of births also continue to occur within marriage in Bosnia and Herzegovina, Croatia, and Serbia, reflecting traditional religious and cultural practices (Klüsener 2015). In addition, a large swathe of Eastern Europe has very low levels of nonmarital fertility, including parts of eastern Poland, Western Ukraine, and Belarus. Thus, this map and more recent data (OECD 2016a) indicate that some areas appear to be resistant to the changes sweeping across Europe, although some of the very low levels may be due to underreporting (Klüsener 2015).

When we look closer at the map, we can further see that both political and cultural borders can be very important for delineating the patterns of nonmarital fertility (Klüsener 2015). In some instances, distinct state borders imply that national policies and legislation can have a strong effect on decisions to marry. For example, the Swiss–French border denotes a sharp distinction between high levels of nonmarital fertility in France and low levels in neighboring Switzerland, despite sharing a similar language and employees who commute daily. The strong distinction in nonmarital fertility is most likely due to strict Swiss policies for unmarried fathers, who were not allowed to pass down their surname if they were not married to the mother of their child. Note, however, that these policies were recently relaxed, and 2014 estimates indicate rapid change with one fifth of all Swiss births outside marriage (OECD 2016a).

In some regions, however, state borders do not define patterns of nonmarital fertility, suggesting that cultural or religious influences are more important. For example, the percentage of nonmarital births is very low across the borders of eastern Poland and Western Ukraine, despite different family policy regimes (Sánchez Gassen and Perelli-Harris 2015), indicating that the long history of Catholicism in this area has maintained strong social norms toward marriage. Furthermore, some countries have strong differences within their borders, for example nonmarital childbearing varies considerably from the north of Italy to the tip of the boot. In sum, it is fascinating to stare at the map and recognize that both political and cultural factors may influence such a fundamental demographic phenomenon as the partnership status at birth. Below I investigate these factors in more detail.

POLICIES AND LAWS: UNIVERSAL RIGHTS – UNEQUAL TREATMENT

Along with complex social and cultural factors, the countries of Europe are defined by a complicated array of policies, laws, and welfare institutions, all of which shape the family and the relationship between couples (Neyer and Andersson 2008). Family demographers have long examined how welfare state typologies (Esping-Andersen 1990) and constellations of family policies influence fertility (e.g., Billingsley and Ferrarini 2014; Gauthier 2007; Thévenon 2011) and lone parenthood (Brady and Burroway 2012; Lewis 1997). Here, I will discuss the laws and policies that govern marital and cohabiting relationships. This perspective will provide insights into how legal rights and responsibilities are similar or different across countries, sometimes as a result of underlying economic and welfare state models. It is important to keep in mind that laws and regulations often provide couples with a sense of security and stability, which may influence decisions around partnership formation and marriage. In addition, depending on how they are enacted and enforced, laws and policies may also potentially exacerbate disadvantage and inequality.

Up to the 1970s, marriage was the primary way of organizing family life. European states regulated couples and families primarily through the institution of marriage by providing rights such as joint taxation, widow's pensions, and inheritance only to married couples (Coontz 2005). In addition, states regulated the relationship between parents and their children, for example, children's rights to maintenance and inheritance and parents' rights to child custody and recognition. Until the mid-twentieth century, marriage was the only living arrangement in which childbearing was legitimate, but gradually discrimination against children born outside marriage was abolished and single mothers were granted custody. By the mid-1970s, most European states had also developed legal mechanisms for dissolving a marriage that would regulate the division of assets and financial savings and provide alimony to the weaker party in case of divorce (Perelli-Harris et al. 2017a).

Over the past few decades, many states have started to extend the rights and responsibilities of marriage to couples living in nonmarital relationships (Perelli-Harris and Sánchez Gassen 2012). The extent of the legal recognition of cohabitation depends on historical developments, resulting

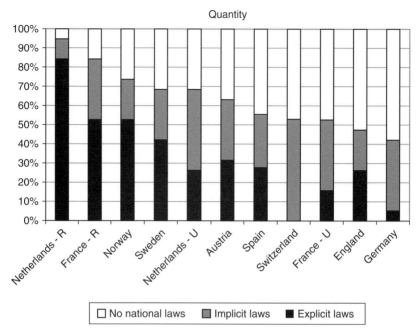

FIGURE 4.3 Percentage of policy areas (out of 19) that have addressed cohabitation and harmonized them with marriage in selected European countries

Note: R = registered cohabitation or Pacs; U = unregistered cohabitation.

in great variation in the degree of harmonization between cohabitation and marriage across the continent (see Figure 4.3). Generally, countries have taken one of several approaches to recognizing and regulating cohabitation (Sánchez Gassen and Perelli-Harris 2015). Some countries, for example, Sweden and Norway, have extended many marital rights and responsibilities to cohabiting couples, especially if they meet certain conditions such as living together for a defined period (e.g., two years) or having children together. Countries such as the Netherlands and France have implemented an opt-in approach, which entitles registered partners (in the Netherlands) or PACS (civil solidarity pacts; in France) to additional rights, such as joint income tax and inheritance, but made it easier for them to separate than divorce. Still other countries, such as England and Spain, have taken a piecemeal approach, with rights extended in some policy domains but not others. As Figure 4.3 shows, these different approaches have resulted in countries falling along a continuum in the degree to which they have harmonized cohabitation and marriage policies, with countries that have adopted registered partnerships and marriage-like arrangements at one end, and countries which favor marriage, such as Switzerland and Germany, at the other (Perelli-Harris and Sánchez Gassen 2012).

One policy area that has changed in all countries has been the expansion of the rights of unmarried fathers. Unmarried fathers have the right to establish paternity and attain joint – or sole – custody over their children; however, in all countries they must take additional bureaucratic steps to establish paternity and/or apply for joint custody. Another area which is similar across most countries is the restriction of welfare benefits for cohabiting partners. Generally, unemployment benefits are means-tested and based on households, taking into account the income of all household members (including cohabiting partners). Other policy areas depend on the fundamental relationship between the state, the individual, and the family. Tax systems in Sweden and Norway, for example, are organized around the individual rather than the couple, resulting in similar tax rules for cohabiting and married individuals. Germany and Switzerland, on the other hand, which continue to favor the male breadwinner model, only allow married couples to benefit from tax breaks if one partner earns more than the other.

One of the areas which can have the greatest consequences for the reproduction of inequality is whether cohabitants who separate are protected by the law or have access to family courts. As many studies have shown, cohabiting couples have higher dissolution risks, even when the couple has children together (Galezewska 2016; Musick and Michelmore 2016). Often these couples have lower education and income, putting them at greater risk of falling into poverty (Carlson (this volume); Perelli-Harris et al. 2010). The lack of legal protection for cohabiting couples can be especially pertinent if one partner (usually the woman) is financially dependent, due to household maintenance and child care, or gender wage differentials. In some countries, such as the UK, the lack of legal regulation may restrict the vulnerable partner's access to state resources that help to solve property disputes or apply for alimony (The Law Commission 2007). Even though the state may require unmarried fathers to pay child maintenance, the regulations may not be sufficient if the mother does not have access to the courts or the resources to hire a lawyer. In addition, cohabiting partners without children have no legal claim to resources, even if they contributed to the relationship, which could result in a substantial decline in living standards for the vulnerable partner (Sánchez Gassen and Perelli-Harris 2015).

Again, protections upon separation depend on whether the state has implemented registered partnerships and the degree to which the state organizes benefits around individuals or families. Registered partners in the Netherlands have many of the same rights as married partners in respect of the division of household goods, the joint home, other assets, and alimony. PACS in France have fewer regulations governing the division of household goods and assets, and no provision for alimony. Sweden and Norway regulate the division of household goods and assets for cohabiting couples, but the tax and transfer system is based on the individual. Most other European countries provide no legal guidance during separation for cohabitants, with the exception of provisos for those separating with children; for example, Germany and Switzerland require separated fathers to pay maintenance to their partners while their children are very young. Overall, this lack of regulation can make it very difficult for vulnerable cohabiting individuals to apply for maintenance or support, and as a result income may fall more after cohabitation dissolution than after divorce.

Nonetheless, it is important to remember that many individuals cohabit precisely because they want to avoid the legal jurisdiction of marriage. They may want to keep their finances and property separate, maintain their independence, and avoid bureaucratic entanglements. Previously married cohabitants may decide to remain outside the law to avoid a costly or time-consuming divorce or protect assets for their children. Given the variety of reasons for cohabiting, it is difficult to know to what extent laws should regulate cohabiting relationships, especially if people are likely to slide into relationships without knowing their responsibilities (Perelli-Harris and Sánchez Gassen 2012). In any case, it is important to keep in mind how legal and welfare systems may exacerbate the risk of disadvantage. The legal policies governing cohabitation, marriage, and separation across Europe may have implications for whether states protect vulnerable individuals from slipping further into poverty.

CULTURE AND RELIGION: UNIVERSAL THEMES – UNIQUE DISCOURSES

As described above, the historical, cultural, and social context is fundamental for shaping attitudes and social norms toward family formation. Social norms are reflected in how people talk about families, and what they say about cohabitation and marriage. They also provide insights into how countries are similar or different from each other. This section draws on a cross-national collaborative project, which used focus group research to compare discourses on cohabitation and marriage in nine European countries (see Perelli-Harris and Bernardi 2015). Focus group research is not intended to produce representative data, but aims to provide substantive insights into general concepts and a better understanding of how societies view cohabitation. Collaborators conducted 7–8 focus groups in the following cities: Vienna, Austria (Berghammer, Fliegenschnee, and Schmidt 2014), Florence, Italy (Vignoli and Salvini 2014), Rotterdam, the Netherlands (Hiekel and Keizer 2015), Oslo, Norway (Lappegård and Noack 2015), Warsaw, Poland (Mynarska, Baranowska-Rataj, and Matysiak 2014), Moscow, Russia (Isupova 2015), Southampton, United Kingdom (Berrington, Perelli-Harris, and Trevena 2015), and Rostock and Lubeck, Germany (Klärner 2015). Each focus group included 8–10 participants, with a total of 588 participants across Europe. The collaborators synthesized the results in an overview paper (Perelli-Harris et al. 2014) and each team wrote country-specific papers, which were published in 2015 as Special Collection 17 of *Demographic Research* (entitled *Focus on Partnerships*). The results of this project are the basis for the discussion below.

The most striking finding from the focus group project was how the discourses in each country described a vivid picture of partnership formation unique to that context. In the countries with the lowest levels of cohabitation, Italy and Poland, focus group participants responded that cohabitation provides a way for couples to test their relationship, but in Poland participants tended to emphasize the unstable nature of cohabitation. In both countries, participants discussed the role of the Catholic Church, but in Italy the emphasis was more toward the tradition of marriage and family, while in Poland it was on religiosity and the heritage of the Church. In Western Germany and Austria, participants took a life-course approach to cohabitation and marriage: Cohabitation is for young adults, who are oriented toward self-fulfillment and freedom, while marriage is for later in the life course, when couples should settle down and be more responsible. Thus, marriage signifies stability, protection, and safety, especially for wives and children.

The discourses in the other countries were also unique. In the Netherlands, a recurring theme was that cohabitation was a response to the increase in divorce. Cohabitation was a way of dealing with possible relationship uncertainty, and marriage was the "complete package," although registered partnerships or cohabitation contracts could also provide legal security. In the United Kingdom, participants expressed tolerance for alternative living arrangements, but unlike in the other countries, differences between higher and lower educated participants were more apparent. The higher educated tended to think marriage was best, especially for raising children, while the lower educated viewed cohabitation as more normative. In Russia, religion was again expressed in a different way. Orthodox Christians referred to a three-stage theory of relationships: Cohabitation is for the beginning of a relationship, registered official marriage comes soon after, and finally, when the relationship has progressed, a church wedding represents the ultimate commitment. Russian participants also discussed how cohabitation and marriage were linked to the concept of trust, which reflects the general state of a society in which individuals have difficulties trusting each other and institutions (Isupova 2015).

Finally, in some countries, cohabitation was much more prevalent and the focus group participants referred to cohabitation as the normative living arrangement. In Norway, cohabitation and marriage were nearly indistinguishable, especially after childbearing. Nonetheless, marriage was not eschewed altogether, and some still valued it as a symbol of commitment and love. Although marriage is increasingly postponed to later in the life course, often even after having children, it is still seen as a way to celebrate the couple's relationship. In eastern Germany, on the other hand, marriage held very little symbolic value. The focus of relationships was more on the present rather than whether they would last into the future, and for the most part, participants in eastern Germany thought marriage was irrelevant. Klärner (2015) speculates that the disinterest in marriage is due to the influence of the former socialist regime, which devalued the institution of marriage, but high levels of nonmarital fertility also have historical roots in the Prussian past (Klüsener and Goldstein 2014), again suggesting that culture shapes behavior.

Given the unique set of discourses within each country, it is difficult to determine which specific social, economic, or legal factors influenced the responses in each country. Some general patterns emerged, for example, in countries with more similar legal rights, such as Norway, cohabitation was perceived to be mostly similar to marriage, while in countries with fewer protections for cohabitants, such as Poland, focus group participants considered cohabitation to be an unstable relationship. However, the association with legal policies was not clear-cut – for example, discourses in eastern and western Germany differed, even though both regions fall under the same marital law regime. Further, despite the lack of legal differences between de facto partnerships and marriage in Australia, many respondents still valued marriage. These cross-national observations again provide evidence that a complex array of cultural and historical factors shape family behaviors.

Despite the distinct discourses expressed across Europe, however, some common themes emerged, which suggests that cohabitation does share an underlying meaning across countries. First, participants in all countries generally saw cohabitation as a less-committed union than marriage, saying that marriage was the "ultimate commitment," (United Kingdom), "one hundred percent commitment" (Australia), "higher quality" (Russia), or "more binding and serious" (Austria). Several distinct dimensions of marriage were revealed, for example security and stability, emotional commitment, and the expression of commitment in front of the public, friends, and family. Participants in some countries also discussed fear of commitment, especially among men, and due to the increase in divorce (see also Perelli-Harris et al. 2017a). Although the expression of commitment through marriage was a major theme in most countries, many participants pointed out that other factors, such as owning a house or having children, were just as, if not more, important in signaling commitment. In addition, in nearly every country, a few "ideological cohabitants" argued that cohabiting couples were even more committed than married couples, because they did not need a piece of paper to prove their love. Overall, however, these individuals were in the minority, and cohabitation was seen as a less committed relationship than marriage.

Another theme which emerged throughout the focus groups was the idea that cohabitation is a testing ground allowing couples to "try out" the relationship before marriage. Testing was seen as providing the opportunity for partners to get to know each other and separate if the relationship did not work out. In some countries, participants said that cohabitation was the wise thing to do before marriage (Austria), or even mandatory (Norway), but in all countries cohabitation was recognized as a period when couples could live together as if married but (usually) experience fewer consequences if the relationship dissolved. As a corollary, cohabitation was seen as providing greater freedom than marriage, since it was a more flexible relationship. In some instances this meant that partners have greater independence from each other, for example keeping finances separate, and that they can pursue their own individual self-fulfillment – particularly appealing to women who want to escape the traditional bonds of patriarchy. Some asserted that forming a cohabiting partnership was particularly important after a bad experience with divorce. Others said that the freedom of cohabitation permitted individuals to search for new partners and leave the previous partner if a better one comes along.

The focus group discussions suggested that in most of these European countries, marriage and cohabitation continue to have distinct meanings, with marriage representing a stronger level of commitment and cohabitation a means to cope with the new reality of relationship uncertainty. Yet this uncertainty was not expressed with respect to *economic* uncertainty, as has often been found in US qualitative research (e.g., Gibson-Davis, Edin, and McLanahan 2005; Smock, Manning, and Porter 2005). Although some European participants did discuss the high costs of a wedding, especially in the United Kingdom, they did not say that couples needed to achieve a certain level of economic stability in order to marry. Of course, the format of focus group research may have discouraged individuals from divulging certain reasons for not marrying, and in-depth interviews with low-income individuals may reveal different narratives, but on the whole, the focus group results suggest that the lack of marriage is not primarily about money, but more about finding a compatible partner. Thus, these focus group findings raise questions about whether cohabitation in Europe is quite different than in America, which appears to be experiencing a more extreme bifurcation of family trajectories by social class (Perelli-Harris and Lyons-Amos 2016).

CONSEQUENCES – DOES COHABITATION REALLY MATTER FOR PEOPLE'S LIVES?

While focus group participants often talked about marriage being a more committed and secure relationship, except in eastern Germany and, to some extent, in Norway, it is not clear whether cohabitation and marriage are truly different types of unions, and to what extent this matters for adult well-being. A large body of research has found that married people have better physical and mental health (Hughes and Waite 2009; Liu and Umberson 2008; Waite and Gallagher 2000), but many of these studies compare the married and unmarried, without focusing on differences between marriage and cohabitation. Studies that do examine differences between partnership types often find mixed results (e.g., Brown 2000; Lamb, Lee, and DeMaris 2003; Musick and Bumpass 2012), still leaving open the question of whether marriage provides greater benefits than cohabitation.

On the one hand, certain aspects of cohabitation do seem to universally differ from marriage. For example, research has consistently found that, on average, cohabiting unions are more likely to dissolve than marital unions (Galezewska 2016), even if they involve children (DeRose et al. 2017; Musick and Michelmore 2016). Women who were cohabiting at the time of their first child also have lower second birth rates compared to married women, unless they marry shortly afterwards (Perelli-Harris 2014). In addition, certain characteristics are consistently negatively associated with cohabitation, for example subjective well-being (Soons and Kalmijn 2009) and relationship quality (Aarskaug Wiik, Keizer, and Lappegård 2012). Thus, some differences between cohabitation and marriage do indeed seem to be universal across countries.

Nonetheless, it is important to keep in mind that many quantitative studies present average associations that do not reflect the heterogeneity of cohabitation or the potential progression of relationships. As discussed above, cohabitation is an inherently more tenuous type of relationship, and many couples use this period of living together to test their relationships. While some of these couples break up, and some eventually marry, many others will live in long-term unions similar to marriage, but without official recognition. Many of these cohabiting relationships can be nearly identical to marriage, providing similar levels of intimacy, emotional support, care, and social networks, as well as benefiting from shared households and economies of scale. Studies of commitment (Duncan and Philips 2008) and the pooling of financial resources (Lyngstad, Noack, and Tufte 2010) indicate that over time, couples in cohabiting relationships often make greater investments in their relationships, resulting in smaller differences between cohabitation and marriage. Thus, cohabiting relationships have the potential to be identical to marriage, just without "the piece of paper."

A second key issue that may account for observed differences by relationship type is selection, which posits that different outcomes are not due to the effects of relationship type per se, but instead, the characteristics of the people who choose to be in that type of partnership. As discussed in Chapter 1, many studies find that cohabitants often come from disadvantaged backgrounds, for example their parents had lower levels of education or income (Aarskaug Wiik 2009; Berrington and Diamond 2000; Mooyart and Liefbroer 2016) and might have experienced divorce (Perelli-Harris et al. 2017a). Selection mechanisms often persist into adulthood, for example men who are unemployed or have temporary jobs are more likely to choose cohabitation (Kalmijn 2011), and women with lower educational attainment are more likely to give birth in cohabitation than women with higher educational attainment (Perelli-Harris et al. 2010). Studies using causal modeling techniques to control for individual characteristics demonstrate that the union type itself does not matter for well-being; instead, the characteristics which lead to poor outcomes also lead people to cohabit rather than marry (Musick and Bumpass 2012; Perelli-Harris and Styrc 2018). Thus, although further research is needed to ensure a lack of causality, existing studies suggest that marriage does not itself provide benefits over and above cohabitation, given that the union remains intact. This is very important to note, given the common perception that cohabiting couples are less committed than married couples.

Again, however, cultural, social, policy, and economic context may be very important for shaping these interrelationships. Local and national context may attenuate differences between cohabitation and marriage in some countries but not in others. Social and cultural norms may reduce differences between the two relationship types if cohabitation is normalized with few social sanctions, or widen the gap if marriage is given preferential treatment or accorded a special status. We would expect few differences in behavior or outcomes in the Nordic countries, where cohabitation is widespread (Lappegård and Noack 2015), but we would expect substantial differences in the United States where marriage tends to be accorded a higher social status (Cherlin 2014).

The legal and welfare state system may also reduce or exacerbate differences. Legal regimes which recognize cohabitation as an alternative to marriage may provide protections that produce a stabilizing effect for all couples, thereby reducing differences in well-being. On the other hand, systems which privilege marriage – for example, with tax incentives promoting a marital breadwinner model – may result in greater benefits to well-being for marriage than cohabitation. Welfare states that provide benefits only to low-income single mothers may also discourage marriage, and even cohabitation, if benefits depend on the income of all adult household members (Michelmore 2016). Finally, selection effects can differ across countries, with cohabitation primarily practiced by disadvantaged groups in some countries, or practiced by all strata in others.

Given that countries differ by social, legal, economic and selection effect context, the different meanings of cohabitation may result in differential outcomes across countries. To test this hypothesis, I led a project to examine the consequences of new family arrangements in settings representing different welfare regimes and cultural contexts: Australia, Norway, Germany, the United Kingdom, and the United States. The team systematically analyzed a range of partnership and childbearing behaviors, with a specific focus on outcomes in mid-life – around ages 40–50, depending on the survey – after the period of early adulthood relationship "churning" and most childbearing. The outcomes included mental well-being (Perelli-Harris and Styrc 2018), health (Perelli-Harris et al. 2017b; Sassler et al. 2016), life satisfaction (Hoherz et al. 2017), and wage differentials (Addo et al. 2017). The team used a variety of retrospective and longitudinal studies, and one of the key concerns of the project was to address selection, which could explain the positive relationship between marriage and outcomes but differ across countries. We used a variety of methods, but primarily propensity score matching or propensity weighted regression, which allowed us to test whether those who did not marry would have been better off if they did marry.

Figure 4.4 shows the mean values and confidence intervals for three outcomes: Self-rated health, life satisfaction, and hourly wage in the local

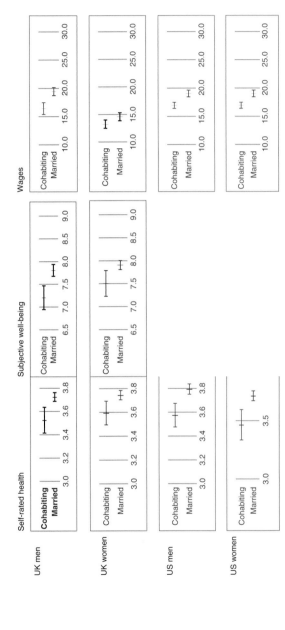

FIGURE 4.4 Mean values and confidence intervals for outcome variables in selected countries

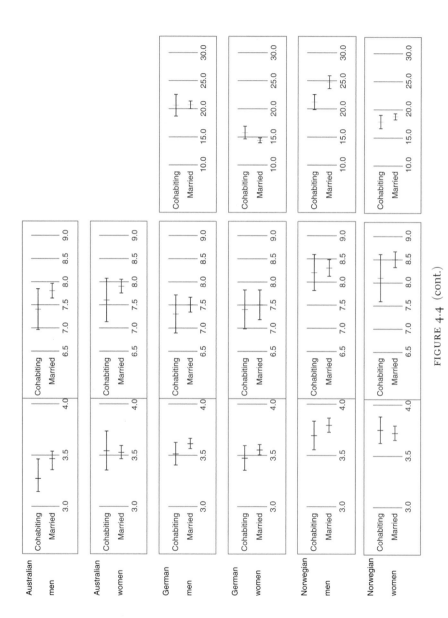

FIGURE 4.4 (cont.)

currency. The confidence intervals in bold indicate that the modeling approaches described above were unable to eliminate significant differences between married and cohabiting men and women. The results immediately confirm our main hypothesis: The benefits of marriage relative to cohabitation differ across countries, suggesting that context can shape the meanings and consequences of different partnership types. Before including controls, the confidence intervals indicate that married people have significantly better outcomes in the United Kingdom and United States with respect to self-rated health and hourly wages, and in the United Kingdom with respect to life satisfaction (the United States was not included in the life satisfaction study, and Australia was not included in the wage study). Differences in outcomes by relationship type were not as pronounced in Australia, Norway, and Germany, although cohabiting men in Norway did have significantly different wages from married men, and cohabiting men in Australia and women in Norway had significantly different mean life satisfaction from married individuals.

Once we controlled for different aspects of the union, for example union duration and prior union dissolution, the differences between marriage and cohabitation in health, life satisfaction, and wages were reduced substantially in most studies. This finding suggests that one of the reasons we see differences between cohabitation and marriage is because cohabiting unions are often a testing ground and more likely to dissolve, or they are more commonly chosen as a second union. Cohabiting unions are also less likely to have children together, and controlling for children eliminated many of the differences between cohabitation and marriage. However, one of the main reasons for differences between cohabitation and marriage in mid-life is due to selection mechanisms from childhood, such as parental SES and divorce. After including these indicators in our models, differences by partnership type were reduced substantially and eliminated in the United States. However, some puzzling exceptions remained after including controls: British cohabiting men continued to have worse self-rated health than married men, and both British men and women who were cohabiting continued to have worse life satisfaction than their married counterparts. British married women continued to have slightly higher wages than British cohabiting women. Nonetheless, despite including a large battery of control variables, we suspect that other forms of selection still might account for any effects. Overall, the results suggest that taking into account the heterogeneity of cohabiting unions (as measured by union duration and having children together) as well as selection mechanisms from childhood can explain most of the marital benefits to well-being, but country context, such as welfare state regime and social norms, also matters. Thus, it is important to keep these factors in mind when assessing the extent to which the emergence of cohabitation itself is detrimental to adult well-being; in many places, simply forming a lasting partnership seems to be most important.

CONCLUSION

Throughout this chapter, I have grappled with the idea that some processes of social change are universal and others are still shaped and reinforced by country-specific factors. I have primarily focused on one of the greatest new developments in the family over the past few decades – the emergence of cohabitation – which has challenged conventional expectations that individuals enter into a lifelong union recognized by law and society. Many people have been alarmed by this development, especially because studies indicate that rates of union dissolution are higher among cohabitants than married couples, and that cohabitation is often associated with disadvantage or low subjective well-being. However, many studies mask the heterogeneity in cohabiting couples and therefore make assumptions about cohabitation that may not be accurate, especially across different settings. In this conclusion, I will briefly summarize and reflect on the different types of heterogeneity which are important to think about when considering whether emerging forms of family behavior, such as cohabitation and nonmarital fertility, are producing and reproducing disadvantage, or whether the behaviors are simply a product of new social realities and shifting norms.

First, countries are diverse and reflect heterogeneous patterns of change. Some countries have experienced rapid increases in cohabitation and nonmarital fertility, while others have not. The variation in family behaviors across Europe reflects different cultural, social, political and economic path dependencies, and the explanations for change cannot be boiled down to one factor. The nonmarital childbearing maps show that sometimes laws and policies can produce differences in behaviors that are distinctly demarcated at state borders, while sometimes religious and cultural factors create pockets of behaviors that stretch across state borders. The discourses from the focus groups also suggest that culture and religion continue to echo in social norms today. Thus, while some general explanations may be similar, we cannot assume that all countries are experiencing the same changes in the family for the same underlying reasons, or that the family change will have the same consequences in the long run.

Second, within countries, we see heterogeneous responses to social change, with some strata of society experiencing increases in new behaviors and other strata not. On the one hand, cohabitation and increases in nonmarital fertility are occurring across all educational levels in most European countries (Perelli-Harris et al. 2010). In many countries, cohabitation is becoming a normative way to start a relationship, regardless of educational level, and as a way to test that the relationship is strong enough for marriage. Yet transitions to marriage after the relationship is formed, especially before and after the birth of the first child, may be particularly important for producing inequalities. Across Europe, higher educated individuals are more likely to marry before a birth (Mikolai et al. 2016), and lower educated individuals are more likely to separate after a birth (Musick and Michelmore 2016). These findings suggest that different groups may be responding in different ways to new behaviors, potentially leading to "diverging destinies" between the most and least educated (McLanahan 2004). Thus, social change can influence different groups of people in different ways, and it is important to continue to recognize these heterogeneous responses.

Third, the meanings of cohabitation and marriage can change across the life course, and even throughout relationships. Individuals' values and ideas undergo a process of development as they age and transition throughout different life stages, and this may result in shifting perceptions of cohabitation and marriage as they grow older. As the Austrian focus groups highlighted, people often think that cohabitation is ideal when individuals are young and free, but marriage is best when individuals are more mature and ready to take on more responsibilities, for example childbearing. This evolution of the importance of marriage may especially be embedded in cultures that perceive marriage to signify stability and security. On the other hand, the purpose and meaning of cohabitation may change as relationships progress. At the beginning of a relationship, cohabitation may be a desirable alternative to living apart and a testing ground to see if the relationship is secure, but as the partners become more committed, sharing a home and investing in a long-term relationship may be just as significant as an official marriage certificate. Thus, both cohabitation and marriage are imbued with multiple meanings that can change across multi-dimensional life courses linked to other life domains (Perelli-Harris and Bernardi 2015).

To reiterate, these different types of heterogeneity are essential to keep in mind when considering the association between partnership formation and inequality. The great complexity across settings, couples, and individuals creates challenges for understanding how family change is exacerbating or reinforcing inequalities. While some studies have begun to investigate to what extent family structure is responsible (or not) for increasing inequality (Bernardi and Boertien 2017a; Härkönen 2018), far more research is needed to understand these complex relationships, especially in different contexts.

5

Family Structure and the Decline of Work for Men in Postwar America

Nicholas Eberstadt[*]

INTRODUCTION

Over the past two generations, America has experienced an extraordinary – and yet somehow, also widely overlooked – collapse of work among its men. In the half-century between 1965 and 2015, work rates for the American male ratcheted relentlessly downward, and an ominous migration gathered force: A "flight from work," in which ever greater numbers of working-age men exited the labor force altogether. America is now home to a vast "idle army" of jobless men no longer looking for work – as of 2015, over 7 million alone between ages 25 and 55, the traditional prime of working life.

To be sure, the decline of work in America is no longer entirely delimited to men. After decades of postwar increase, the work rates and labor force parti-cipation rates for prime-age American women have likewise been falling since roughly the beginning of the new century. But the decline of work for American men is a much longer-term trend, and also one of much larger absolute dimensions – and it is that problem, rather than the similarly trou-bling decline of work for women, that is the subject of this chapter.

The general decline of work for adult men, and the dramatic, continuing expansion of a class of nonworking males (including those both ostensibly able-bodied and in the prime of life) constitutes a fundamentally new and unfamiliar sort of problem for America. It is a problem with manifold and far-reaching economic, social, and perhaps even political implications.

The implications for the state of American families are immediate and inescapable. Lest it otherwise go unsaid, these "prime working ages" in which the present male work crisis is concentrated overlap significantly with the

[*] This chapter draws heavily upon my study *Men without Work: America's Invisible Crisis* (Eberstadt 2016). The author wishes to thank Cecilia Joy Perez for her able research assistance on this chapter. The usual caveats apply.

conventional life course ages for family formation, parenting, and child-rearing for the contemporary American man.

As it happens, the long-term decline of work for prime-age men in modern America has coincided with the long-term decline of the married two-parent family structure. The correspondence and interaction of these two great sea changes in daily life for contemporary Americans is a question of obvious importance.

In the following pages, I will attempt to cast some light on the outlines of this important relationship. My exposition is intended only to be exploratory in nature: I recognize there are deep and vital questions my method and approach cannot answer, or even adequately address. It is thus my hope that this introduction will be followed by more detailed investigation into the complex dynamics in play here.

In this chapter I will: (1) present a broad quantitative overview of the ongoing decline of work for American men, and especially men 25–54 years of age, placed in both an historical and international perspective; (2) offer a corresponding quantitative overview of the attendant changes in the socio-demographic profile of prime working-age American men over this same period; (3) decompose arithmetically contributions to declining long-term work rates and labor force participation rates by major sociodemographic factors, including family structure; and (4) conclude with a discussion of what the evidence indicates, what it may suggest, and directions for further research.

WORK RATES AND LABOR FORCE PARTICIPATION RATES FOR US MEN IN THE POSTWAR ERA

One of the major and defining, if not necessarily widely heralded, social changes in postwar America has been the secular decline in employment-to-population ratios (also known as "work rates") for men. Work rates for American men have been falling for most of the postwar era.

The US government did not begin releasing continuous monthly data on the American employment situation until after World War II. (We do this today, as we have since late 1947, through the Current Population Survey (or CPS), which is maintained by the US Census Bureau and used by the Bureau of Labor Statistics (or BLS) to gauge employment conditions for the adult civilian noninstitutionalized population.) By any broad measure we choose, the US employment-to-population rates for civilian noninstitutionalized men in 2015 and 2016 were very close to their lowest levels on record – and far lower than levels in earlier postwar decades (see Figure 5.1).

FIGURE 5.1 Employment-to-population ratio, US males, selected age groups: 1948–2016 (seasonally adjusted)

Between the early 1950s and 2016 – between Eisenhower's America and Obama's America – the nation's work rate for adult men (those 20 years of age and older) relentlessly ratcheted downward. Very broadly speaking, this downward trajectory tracked with the business cycle: With each new recession, male work rates typically hit a new low – and typically failed to snap back to prerecession levels over the course of the subsequent recovery. We tend to think of the Great Recession of 2008/09 as the "epic" event in postwar labor markets, and of course the devastation that it wrought is incontestable. What is not generally appreciated, however, is that the drop in male work rates since the Great Recession accounts for less than a quarter of the total long-term downward spiral of 20+ employment-to-population ratios for American men in the postwar era. Three quarters of that slide took place *before* the crash of 2008.

Between 1948 and 2015, the work rate for American men 20 and older (all postwar employment data are for the civilian noninstitutionalized population) fell from 85.8% to 68.1% – or by almost 18 percentage points. Put another way, between 1948 and 2015, the proportion of American men 20 and older without paid work of any sort more than doubled – from about 14% to almost 32% (see Figure 5.2). This work rate for adult men in 2015 was only a little over a percentage point higher than the 2010 level (its all-time low, at least to date). It rose just a bit more in 2016, from 68.1% to 68.5%. (It registered 68.7% in July 2017, the latest reading available at this writing.) Despite purportedly "near full employment" conditions, at least according to much of the received wisdom currently circulating in business and policy circles, the work rate for the US male 20+ group was fully one fifth lower in mid-2017 than it had been in 1948, almost seventy years earlier.

Of course the 20+ work rate measure includes men 65 and older (i.e., those of classical retirement age), but when I exclude the 65+ population and look instead at men 20–64 years of age, work rates reportedly trace a long march downward here as well – from 90.8% in 1948 to 78.4% in 2015. The 20–64-year-old male work rate in 2015 was thus nearly twelve and a half percentage points below the 1948 level, meaning work rates in America for men in this "classical" working-age group were only about six sevenths as high in 2015 as they had been in the early postwar era. In 2015, the fraction of US men aged 20–64 not at work was 21.6% – 2.3 times higher than it had been in 1948 – and the situation was only very slightly better in 2016 and mid-2017, when the proportion of men 20–64 years of age without any paid work at all was reportedly 21% and 20.7%, respectively.

Note that the impact on recorded work rates from changes in the population composition within the male 20–64 age group was altogether negligible, accounting for less than one hundredth of the intervening twelve or more percentage point decline for the 1967–2015 period (Eberstadt 2016). Population structure effects likewise had virtually no effect on work rate trends for prime working-age men – the 25–54-year-old cohort, whose changing fortunes are the focus of this chapter.

Prime working-age men are a critical demographic cohort for reasons both economic and social. They comprise the backbone of the male workforce, currently accounting for roughly two thirds of the 20+ men in the US work-force today, and close to three quarters of adult US men with paying jobs (Eberstadt 2016) (see Table 5.1). They are also the group in which labor force participation tends to be highest, due to health and life cycle considerations, and of course, they are also the group arguably most central to family forma-tion and the raising of children, not only in contemporary America.

Between 1948 and 2015, for the male 25–54 age group, work rates for prime-age US males sank almost 10 percentage points, from 94.1% to 84.4% (see Figure 5.1). Since 2016 these have improved, the rate was 85.0% for 2016, and registered 85.5% in July 2017. One may say that prime-age male work rates have recovered appreciably since their nadir in the wake of the Great Recession, when they hit 80.6% in the fourth quarter of 2009. Even so, at the time of writing, prime-age male work rates are on a par with the lowest-ever BLS readings before the 2008 crash (i.e., from the depths of the deep recession in the early 1980s).

TABLE 5.1 *US male employment-to-population ratios: 2015 vs. selected depression years*

Year and source	Employment-to-population ratio, males aged 20–64 (percentage of civilian noninstitutionalized population)	Employment-to-population ratio, males aged 25–54 (percentage of civilian noninstitutionalized population)
2015 (BLS)	78.4	84.4
1940 (Census)	81.3	86.4
1930 (Census)	88.2*	91.2*^

Notes: * = calculated for total enumerated population, not civilian noninstitutionalized population
^ = 25–44 population – corresponding male 25/44 work ratio for 2015 would be 85.3 for civilian noninstitutionalized population alone
Sources:
- For 2015:
  - US Bureau of Labor Statistics. "Current Population Survey." Retrieved June 21, 2016. http://data.bls.gov/pdq/querytool.jsp?survey=ln
- For 1940:
  - Chandra, Amitabh. 2000. "Labor-Market Dropouts and the Racial Wage Gap: 1940–1990." *The American Economic Review* 90(2): 333–338. www.jstor.org/stable/117246?seq=1#page_scan_tab_contents
  - US Census Bureau. 1940. "Census of Population: The Labor Force" (Sample Statistics). Retrieved August 5, 2016. www2.census.gov/library/publications/decennial/1940/population-labor-force-sample/41236810p1_ch1.pdf
  - US Census Bureau. 2012. "1940 Census of Population." Retrieved August 5, 2016. www2.census.gov/library/publications/decennial/1940/population-institutional-population/08520028ch2.pdf
  - US Department of Defense, Progress Reports and Statistics Division. 1956. "Selected Manpower Statistics." Retrieved August 5 2016. www.dtic.mil/dtic/tr/fulltext/u2/a954007.pdf
- For 1930:
  US Census Bureau. "1930 Census of Population." Retrieved March 2, 2016. http://digital.library.unt.edu/ark:/67531/metadc26169/m1/1/high_res_d/R40655_2009Jun19.pdf

The drop in the work rate of prime-age US men did not actually commence until roughly two decades after the end of World War II. In 1948, the work rate for this cohort was 94.1% – exactly the same rate recorded in 1965. (Between 1948 and 1965, the entirety of the decline in work rates for adult men – for those 20–64 years of age as well as those 20 and older – was due to falling work rates for the cohorts 55 years of age and above.[1]) Roughly speaking, the long-term

---

[1] Between 1948 and 1965 the work rate for men 55 and older dropped by over 13 percentage points, from 68.4% to 55.0%. The 55+ male work rate continued to fall to 35.8% in 1993 – but has subsequently risen, and as of 2016, was back up to 44.4%. Ironically, just as the 55+ cohort was the only major component of the adult male population to register sustained declines over the

FIGURE 5.2 Percentage of civilian noninstitutionalized prime-age (25–54) males
without paid employment: USA 1948–2017 (seasonally adjusted)

decline in prime-age male work rate did not start until around 1965. Therefore
I shall use 1965 and 2015 as the end points for much of my analysis in this
chapter, as that timeframe neatly offers us a half-century of long-term data on
changes in prime-age male work rates and their correlates.

As Figure 5.2 illustrates, the percentage of prime-age men without paid work
rose fitfully but inexorably from the 1960s to the present. In the 1960s, the
average monthly fraction of prime-age men was 6.3% – not appreciably
different from the 6.2% of the 1950s. That mean monthly level has risen
markedly in every successive decade since the 1960s. For the decade that
commenced in 2010, the monthly average to date works out to an astonishing
16.9% – well over two and a half times the mean monthly level from the 1960s.
Naturally, this decadal average is affected by the truly awful employment
trends in the immediate wake of the Great Recession. In 2010, a monthly
average of 19% of all prime-age males had no paid work of any sort. Yet today's
"new normal" should still give pause. In 2015, the corresponding proportion
was 15.7%; in 2016 – that is to say, seven years after the end of the Great
Recession – it was still 15.0%; and for the first quarter of 2017, it was slightly
over 15%. This range appears to be the "new normal" for America today: An

first two decades of the postwar era, it is now the only major component to have registered
sustained increases over the past two decades. (Calculations based upon the US Bureau
of Labor Statistics. "Data Finder 9.0." Retrieved April 22, 2017. https://beta.bls.gov/dataQuery
/search)

employment pattern where at any given moment between one in six and one in seven prime-age men is not engaged in paid work.

This "new normal" for US male nonwork may be instructively compared to work rates for American men during the Great Depression (see Table 5.1). As we can see, work rates for both men 20–64 years of age and those of prime working age were *lower* in 2015 than in either 1930 or 1940; the same would be true for male work rates in 2016 and early 2017 if these were added to the table. Contraposition of today's rates and those from the year 1940 is most mean-ingful. For one thing, employment data in the 1940 census was for the first time recorded in a manner directly comparable with our postwar jobs data; for another, America's unemployment rates in 1940 are extremely high, pushing 15% on a nationwide basis – sharply higher than in 1930, when the Depression was just getting underway. Even so, measured work rates for prime-age men were 2 percentage points lower in 2015 than in 1940. Thus, it is empirically accurate to describe the current work crisis for American men as a Depression-scale problem.

The critical difference between the joblessness situation for men in 1940 and 2015, however, concerns the shifting balance between unemployment and economic inactivity. In 1940, the overwhelming majority of the men without jobs were looking for one: That is to say, they were unemployed in the classic definition of that term. Only a relatively small number of the men without jobs were economically inactive: That is to say, not in the labor force, neither working nor looking for work. The situation is reversed today: As of 2015, for every prime-age male formally unemployed, there were three neither working nor looking for work (see Figure 5.3). Modern America's job problem for prime-age men has principally been a long-term exodus from the labor market, a flight that started in the mid-1960s and as yet shows no sign of stopping. Nonworking (or NILF, not-in-labor-force) men are the very fastest growing component of the civilian noninstitutio-nalized prime-age male population in America, increasing at over three times the tempo of the overall cohort for fully half a century between 1965 and 2015. The decline in labor force participation rates (or LFPRs, the ratio of persons in the workforce to total population) between 1965 and 2015 amounted to 8.4 percentage points (96.7% vs. 88.3%), while the overall decline in work rates for that same period came to 9.7 percentage points (94.1% vs. 84.4%). This means the retreat from the labor force accounted for nearly seven eighths of the fall in prime-age male work rates in America over that half-century, and unlike withdrawal from the labor force at older ages, mass withdrawal from the workforce in the prime of life cannot plausibly be attributed to retirement.

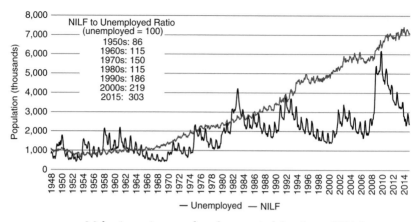

FIGURE 5.3　Males (25–54) unemployed vs. not in labor force: USA January 1948–May 2016 (seasonally unadjusted)

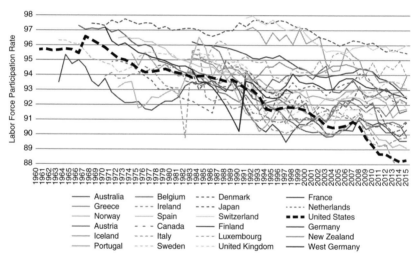

FIGURE 5.4　Labor force participation rates for males aged 25–54: USA vs. twenty-two "original" OECD member states, 1960–2015

The postwar prime-age male flight from work has been more extreme in America than in almost any other economically advanced democracy. This is apparent when I compare prime working-age LFPRs for the United States with the corresponding patterns traced out in other "traditional" members of the OECD (or Organisation for Economic Co-operation and Development, the de facto club of affluent aid-giving Western democracies) (see Figure 5.4). This grouping includes Japan, Canada, Australia, New Zealand, and eighteen

Western European nations as well as the United States: Twenty-three countries in total. Today, America is at the bottom of all these states in prime-age male labor force participation – twenty-second out of twenty-three, underperformed only by Italy. This troubling state of affairs is also puzzling in a number of respects. For the decline in US prime-age male LFPRs is more severe than in countries beset by "lost decades" of economic growth (e.g., Japan), or those burdened with notoriously *dirigiste* labor market regulations and hypertrophied welfare states (e.g., France), or even those seemingly enmeshed in perennial debt-and-austerity crises (e.g., contemporary Greece). Why male workforce participation rate performance should be poorer in the United States than in any and all of these comparator states is an important but seldom-examined question.

SOCIODEMOGRAPHIC CHANGE AND THE DECLINE OF PRIME-AGE MALE LFPRS, 1965–2015

The sea change in employment patterns for prime working-age men that took place over the years between 1965 and 2015 coincided with a sea change in their sociodemographic profiles. The population profile for American men aged 25–54 in 2015 differed markedly from half a century earlier in a number of respects. Important characteristics that registered major changes over this period included (but were not limited to): Ethnicity, educational attainment, family structure, and nativity (that is to say, whether one was native-born- or foreign-born). In this section, I examine the dimensions of some of these broad sociodemographic shifts within the overall composition of the US prime-age male population, and how these shifts related to both the overall decline of work for prime-age men and the closely related increase in the number of such men who have left the workforce altogether. (As already mentioned, the reference population under consideration here is prime-age men in the "civilian noninstitutionalized population," per CPS/BLS survey coverage.)

The availability of data series for my examination below does not always nicely match my designated 1965–2015 time frame. Over the decades under consideration, the CPS, from which the BLS' monthly employment report is derived, gradually extended its scope and asked more detailed and nuanced questions about the nation's sociodemographic profile. Often, these new questions signified official recognition of the importance of changes already well underway. Thus, in 1965, CPS already provided detailed information on educational attainment for the US population, but its breakdown of data by ethnicity or "race" was still rather rudimentary. It was not until 1971 that it was possible for respondents to identify as themselves as Hispanic, and it took over another two decades before it was possible to do so for Asians, much less multiracial. By the same token, CPS did not begin to track "nativity" (whether the respondent was foreign-born or native-born) until the early 1990s. As for family structure, back in 1965, the CPS could tell us whether a man was married, separated, divorced, or never married, but nothing else. Beginning with the year 1968, CPS started providing information about living arrangements as well, including whether men in these various marital categories were with their spouses and children under 18, and if the latter, how many. Convenient or no, my analysis must conform with the time spans for which the requisite CPS data are available.

Figures 5.5–5.17 illustrate some of the major sociodemographic shifts that have transformed the composition of the US prime-age male population over the half-century under consideration. I describe these briefly below.

Race and Ethnicity

The 1965 CPS offers just three alternatives for categorizing the "race" of the US population: White/Black/Multiracial. By 2015, the categories of Asian and Native American have also been added to the taxonomy. Between 1965 and 2015 the proportion of prime-age men identified as White dropped by about 12 percentage points, from roughly 90% to 78%. But roughly eight points of this twelve-point decline was due to the new-found availability of Asian and Native American classifications for 2015; almost all of whose contingents would have been represented as White under the 1965 schema. The only two consistent racial categories for the 1965–2015 period are Black and Multiracial/Other; the proportion of prime-age men identifying as Black rose by a little over 3 points, from around 9% to around 12%, while the proportion for Multiracial/Other rose by somewhat less than one point, from 1% to a bit less than 2%. In all, then, these "race" data do not seem to reveal any major shifts in US "racial composition" over the period in question (apart from the introduction of new categories) – in part perhaps because of the limitations of this classification system for modern America.

A more nuanced and informative picture of heritage and ancestry comes from the CPS information on "ethnicity," which in addition to counting Asian and Other/Multiracial persons, also identifies the population of Hispanic origin (both White and Black), non-Hispanic Whites, and non-Hispanic Blacks. This CPS series commenced in 1971, and the breakdown from that year for prime-age men can be compared with results for 2015.

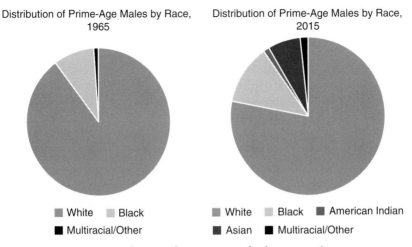

FIGURE 5.5 Distribution of prime-age males by race, 1965 vs. 2015

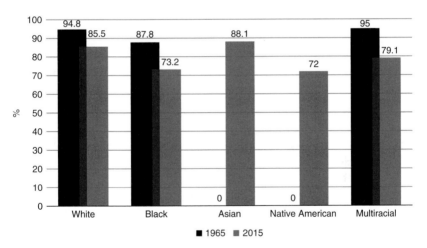

FIGURE 5.6 Work rates for prime-age males by race, 1965 vs. 2015

Between 1971 and 2015 the ethnic composition of US prime-age males changed appreciably. The most dramatic change was for the proportion of Hispanic men, which soared from under 5% to almost 18%. (Almost all of these Hispanic men classified themselves as White; as of 2015, less than 1% of all prime-age men were Black Hispanics.) In 2015, self-identified Asians comprised almost 7% of prime-age US men, and though I lack corresponding data for 1968, I may suspect the percentage was much smaller back then. Non-Hispanic Black men accounted for just under 12% of prime-age males in 2015,

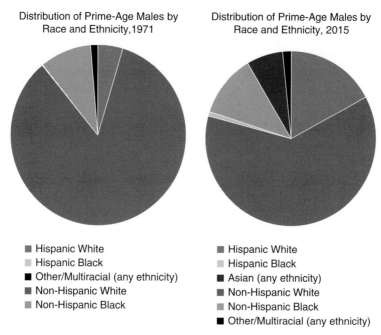

Distribution of Prime-Age Males by   Distribution of Prime-Age Males by
Race and Ethnicity,1971   Race and Ethnicity, 2015

■ Hispanic White   ■ Hispanic White
▫ Hispanic Black   ▫ Hispanic Black
■ Other/Multiracial (any ethnicity)   ■ Asian (any ethnicity)
■ Non-Hispanic White   ■ Non-Hispanic White
▪ Non-Hispanic Black   ▪ Non-Hispanic Black
                                             ■ Other/Multiracial (any ethnicity)

FIGURE 5.7 Distribution of prime-age males by race and ethnicity, 1971 vs. 2015

up about 2 percentage points from 1971. By 2015, non-Hispanic Whites (or
"Anglos") made up just 62% of the prime-age male population, down roughly
17–23 percentage points, depending on the initial number of Asians in the
prime-age male pool in 1968. This is a considerable reduction in the "Anglo"
proportion of the prime-age male population in somewhat less than half a
century, but with only a very small part of the increase in the "minority"
percentage (somewhere between less than an eighth and less than a tenth) due
to an increase in the proportion of non-Hispanic Blacks.

For prime-age men overall, work rates fell by nearly 9 percentage points
between 1965 and 2015, and by almost 8 percentage points between 1971 and
2015. Over those same years, Black and Non-Hispanic Black work rates fell
even more sharply than this: By nearly 15 points and over 13 points, respectively. By 2015, roughly 27% of all prime-age Black or non-Hispanic Black men
in the civilian noninstitutionalized population – over one in four – reported no
paid work at all. The Black/White and non-Hispanic Black/non-Hispanic
White gap in work rates widened over these decades: From 7 points in 1965/
71 to 13-plus points in 2015. White/"Anglo" work rates fell somewhat less than
the national average over these years.

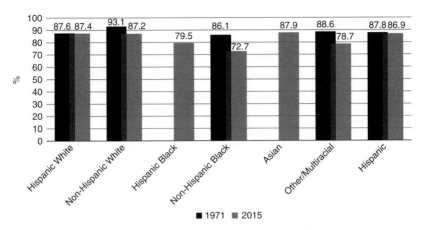

FIGURE 5.8 Work rate for prime-age males by race vs. ethnicity, 1971 vs. 2015

The work rates for non-Hispanic Blacks in the prime-age male population in 2015 are thus perhaps akin to those for the United States during the darkest hours of the Great Depression – and there are other minority groups with similar grim prospects. In 2015, the prime-age male work rate for Native Americans was just 72% – meaning 28% had no paid work. Likewise, prime-age men with Multiracial backgrounds, as well as the small contingent who self-identified as Black Hispanic, were in groupings where over 20% had no paid work.

However, the story of the collapse of work for the modern American man is by no means an unrelieved story of differentially poor performance for ethnic minorities. By 2015, White Hispanics and Asians accounted for nearly one quarter of the prime-age male population – twice the number for non-Hispanic Blacks. Of all ethnic groups whose trends can be traced over the decades under consideration, the group with the best (or perhaps I should say least-bad) work rate trends are the Hispanics, whose work rates dropped by "only" 1 percentage point between 1971 and 2015.

By 2015, interestingly enough, both Hispanic and Asian work rates for prime-age men were slightly higher than those of "Anglos." Not only has America become more ethnically diverse over the past half-century but diversity in work rates for America's ethnic minorities has become more apparent as well. At the same time, these racial and ethnic differentials help place the dimensions of the postwar collapse of work for prime-age men in sharper perspective: Work rates for Blacks in 1965 were higher than for Whites fifty years later, and rates for non-Hispanic Whites in 2015 were just about the same as they had been for non-Hispanic Blacks back in 1971.

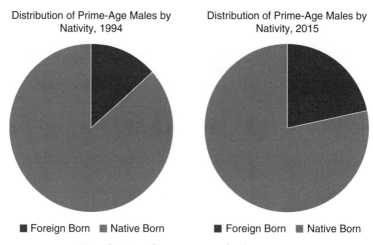

Distribution of Prime-Age Males by Nativity, 1994

Distribution of Prime-Age Males by Nativity, 2015

■ Foreign Born   ■ Native Born   ■ Foreign Born   ■ Native Born

FIGURE 5.9 Distribution of prime-age males by nativity, 1994 vs. 2015

Nativity

Most of America's changing ethnic complexion since 1965 is due to immigrants and their descendants, and much of this change is accounted for by the foreign-born themselves. CPS did not begin to track employment patterns by nativity until the 1990s, but even in just over two decades for which such data are available, we can see the impact on both prime-age male population composition and on overall prime-age male work rates.

In 1995, foreign-born men accounted for a little over 13% of all prime working-age males in the US civilian noninstitutionalized population. Just twenty-one years later, the corresponding proportion was nearly 22%. In 2015, foreign-born prime-age men were overrepresented in the employed population, meaning their work rates were higher than those of native-born men. (This turns out to be true, incidentally, for all major ethnic groups in America: Whites, Blacks, Hispanics, and Asians alike.)

Between 1994 and 2015, prime-age male work rates fell by a little over 3 percentage points, but trends for native- and foreign-born men moved in opposite directions: Down sharply for the former, up distinctly for the latter. Indeed, foreign-born men are the only group covered in my study for whom long-term work rates were reported to rise. As of 2015, work rates were over five points higher among prime-age men for the foreign-born than the native-born, and over four points higher than the national average.

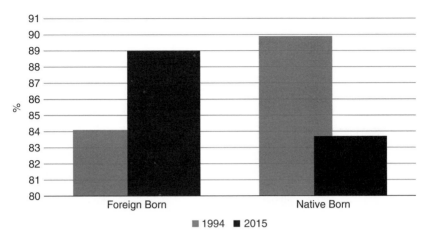

FIGURE 5.10 Work rates for prime-age males by nativity, 1994 vs. 2015

Educational Attainment

In terms of sheer years of schooling, America was a much more educated society in 2015 than in 1965 – and of course the same was true for America's prime-age men. In 1965, high school dropouts formed the largest single grouping within the prime-age male population, making up nearly 43% of the total; by 2015, they accounted for less than 12% of that population. Conversely, only 14% held a college degree or higher in 1965, as against nearly 33% in 2015. By 2015, nearly three fifths of America's prime-age men had at least some college training in their résumé, as against just a quarter back in 1965.

From 1965 to 2015, work rates for prime-age men have always tracked positively with education: The higher the level of educational attainment, the higher the work rate. Over these decades, though, the gradient has grown far steeper. Work rates have declined for every educational attainment, but they have more or less collapsed for those at the lower end of the spectrum. Work rates for men with a graduate education fell by only 2 percentage points over that half-century, yet even for men with no bachelor's degree but some college training, work rates dropped by eleven points. For men with just a high school diploma, rates plunged by nearly seventeen points, and for those with no high school diploma, they plummeted by almost eighteen points. By 2015, nearly 20% of prime-age men with high school diplomas but no higher training were jobless; the same was true for over 27% of high school dropouts, and the vast majority of these same jobless, lower educated men were entirely

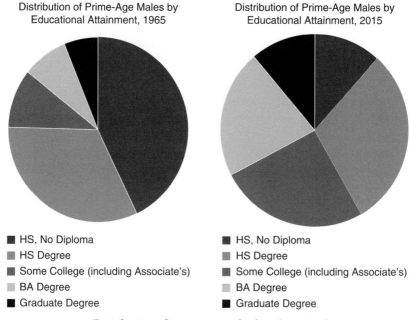

FIGURE 5.11 Distribution of prime-age males by educational attainment,
1965 vs. 2015

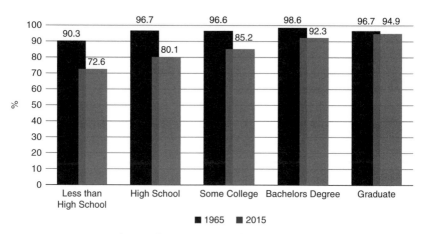

FIGURE 5.12 Work rates for prime-age males by educational attainment,
1965 vs. 2015

out of the labor market, no longer actively seeking employment. In retrospect, no less astonishing than the collapse in work for lower skilled men may be the high work rates those same educational groups still maintained just two generations ago. In 1965, after all, work rates for prime-age men with just a high school diploma were higher than those for men with graduate education today (i.e., 2015), and rates for high school dropouts in 1965 were over five points higher than the overall average for a the much more schooled prime-age male population of 2015.

Family Structure

Between 1965 and 2015, as in most other affluent Western societies, US marital patterns and living arrangements underwent upheaval, the reverberations from which are evident in my data on prime-age men. In 1965, five out of six prime-age men were currently married; by 2015, married men formed only a bare majority of that population. In 1965, less than a tenth of men aged 25–54 had never been married; by 2015, this group formed nearly a third of the entire prime-age male population. The proportion divorced or separated likewise roughly tripled over these decades. (The widowed proportion actually shrank slightly, but this was a tiny segment of the US prime-age male population: Less than 1% in 1965.)

This postwar disruption in previously extant family patterns is all the more evident from 1968 onward, once CPS began reporting on living arrangements and children. In 1968, nearly 70% of prime-age men were not only married, but married and living with at least one child under 18 years of age at home. By 2015, barely 40% of prime-age American men were married with children at home, while close to 30% were never married and currently not living with children. In all, less than half of all prime-age men – just 46% – were living with children in 2015; in 1968, by contrast, more than twice as many prime-age men had a child in their home as did not (70% vs. 30%).

This upending of previous living arrangement profiles, I should emphasize, was partly the result of declining fertility levels, which were considerably lower in 2015 than 1968 – but only partly. A major driver was the increasing likelihood that a man would not live in the same home as his children, irrespective of his marital status. By 2014, according to the Census Bureau's Survey of Income and Program Participation (SIPP) survey, only three quarters of US men were living with all their identified biological children (Monte 2017). This estimate, furthermore, only covers children those fathers reported or acknowledged. An analysis of SIPP data for the year 2004 noted that the average number of biological children reported by adult men was 20% lower than the number reported by adult women – a discrepancy possibly explained, in the words of the authors, by "underreporting in the survey or men not knowing about their offspring" (Emens and Dye 2007).

Just as we observe major differentials in prime-age male work rates – both at any given point in time and also across time – by race or ethnicity, nativity, and education, so we do with family structure. Very broadly speaking, work rates are always higher for married men than for others, and almost higher for men with children at home, irrespective of their marital status.

Let us begin by looking just at marital status. In 2015, the work rate for all married men aged 25–54 was 91% – over 6 points higher than the national average. Work rates for these married men were roughly 14 points higher than for their never-married and separated/divorced peers, and nearly 20 points higher than for their widowed counterparts (although this is a tiny population – less than two thirds of a percent of the total). Interestingly enough, back in 1965, work rates for married men were already much higher than for others: 10 or more points higher than for those never married or widowed, and 13 points higher than for those separated or divorced. Work rates for married prime-age men did decline between 1965 and 2015, but by less than for any other marital status. Some may be surprised by how little work rates fell for never-married prime-age men over this half-century: The drop was a bit under seven points, as against an average drop of nearly nine points for prime-age men overall. Part of the answer to this apparent paradox may lie in the extraordinarily low levels to which work rates for never-married prime-age men had already dropped. In 1965, work rates for never-married prime-age men were already down to 83% – over 4 points below the national average that same year for Black prime-age men; fully 7 points below the level that same year for high school dropouts; and, despite an intervening half-century of sharp work rate declines, lower than the national average for prime-age men in 2015.

Now, let us consider the matter of prime-age men with children under 18 in their homes, biologically related or otherwise. In 2015, the work rate for any prime-age men with any children at home was 91% – almost the same as for the average for married prime-age men that same year. The gap in work rates separating prime-age male homes with and without children in them was almost 12 percentage points – a differential comparable to that separating college graduates and high school graduates in 2015, and almost as large as the 2015 White/Black work rate disparity for prime-age males. An appreciable gap in work rates between prime-age male homes with and without children

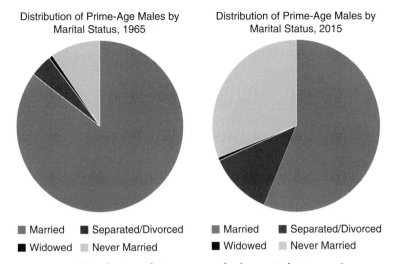

FIGURE 5.13 Distribution of prime-age males by marital status, 1965 vs. 2015

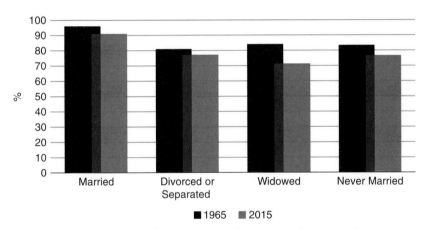

FIGURE 5.14 Work rates for prime-age males by marital status, 1965 vs. 2015

was already apparent in 1968, but by 2015, that gap had close to doubled, meaning that work rates fell much further for childless homes than those with children in them.

I can further disaggregate work profiles by both marital status and presence of children for America's prime-age men in 2015 and 1968.

In 2015, the prime-age work rate for married men with children at home was almost 93% – very slightly higher than for college graduates that same year. Married men without children at home reported work rates over six points

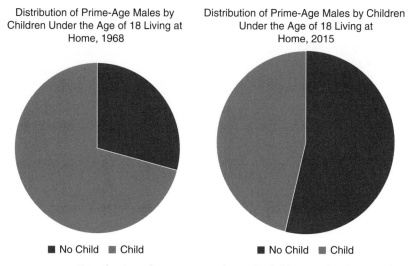

FIGURE 5.15 Distribution of prime-age males with children under the age of 18 living at home, 1968 vs. 2015

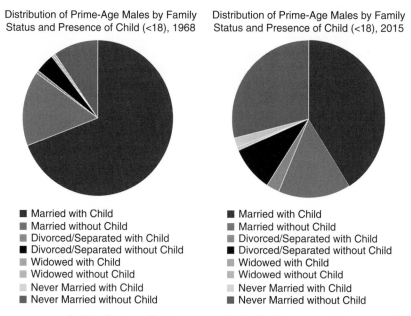

FIGURE 5.16 Distribution of prime-age males by family status and presence of child (<18), 1968 vs. 2015

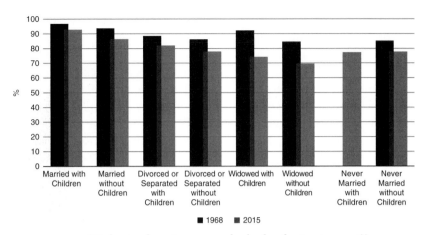

FIGURE 5.17 Work rates for prime-age males by family structure, 1968 vs. 2015

lower; even so, their rates were above the overall average for 2015, and indeed, higher than for those of any other category of men not currently married. Whether or not they had children at home, prime-age men who were separated/divorced, widowed, or never married all reported work rates below the national average, but work rates tended to be lower still for those without children (excepting only never-married men, where the rates were very slightly higher for those without children at home).

In 1968, the relationship between work rates and family structure was similar (if not identical) to the patterns witnessed in 2015. Then as now, married men had the highest work rates, with the very highest reported by married men with children at home. (In 1968 the work rate for this "married with kids" contingent was over 96%!) The nonmarried men had lower work rates than their married counterparts, and for each of the other designations for marital status, men with children at home tended to have higher work rates than those who did not.[2] For those prime-age men not currently married and without children at home, work rates were already very low by 1968 – more or less on a par with America's overall average prime-age male work rates for 2015, which, as we have already seen, were actually lower than prime-age male work rates in 1940, at the tail end of the Depression.

We can see from these comparisons that work rates had already commenced to collapse by the mid- or late 1960s among prime-age men with what we might

[2] The generalization has to be qualified because there were so few never-married prime-age men with children at home in 1968 that CPS cannot provide estimates of their work rates to match up against the work rates that year for never married without children at home.

call "nontraditional" family types (i.e., for those who were not currently married, and especially for those not currently married without children at home). The work rates for all not currently married men in 1965 were lower than the corresponding rates for either contemporary Black men or high school dropouts. Work rates for not currently married prime-age men without children at home – all "races" included – in 1968 were lower than for non-Hispanic Blacks of all family types in 1971. By such indications, the collapse of work rates for nontraditional family types preceded the great drop in work rates that were to come for both non-Hispanic Black and less highly educated prime working-age men in subsequent decades.

EXAMINING THE RELATIONSHIP BETWEEN FAMILY STRUCTURE ON PRIME-AGE MALE WORK PATTERNS

As we have seen, family structure – like race and ethnicity, nativity, and educational attainment – appears to be a powerful predictor of postwar work patterns for American men. We can begin to assess the impact of these social factors on changing male work profiles – on those major postwar declines in male work rates and dramatic upsurges in the percentages who have exited the workforce altogether – with two simple quantitative comparisons.

The first is to estimate the relative risk of being out of the workforce (or NILF, not in labor force) – a condition that mirrors the work ratio closely, albeit imperfectly – in accordance with given sociodemographic characteristics. The second is to present illustrative counterfactuals for the potential contribution of sociodemographic change on employment patterns. We derive this counterfactual by holding constant the characteristic-specific work rates or NILF rates for prime-age men for the year 2015, but applying these against the composition of the prime-age male population in 1965 (or whatever the earliest year for my analysis in the previous section may have been), so as to indicate what the NILF rates and work rates would have been like if the composition of the prime-age male population composition were the same nowadays as, say, half a century earlier.

Statistically speaking, these metrics cannot tell us how much changes in family structure have altered postwar male employment patterns. For one thing, changes in US family structure are correlated with other big social changes – in education, ethnicity, nativity, and other factors – which I do not attempt to disentangle in this section. For another, any statistical associations I uncover are just that – associations – in which questions of causation remain unanswered. Recognizing these important caveats, we can begin to quantify the relationship between family structure and the decline of work for the postwar American man.

Table 5.2 outlines the relative risk for prime-age men ending up in the NILF pool by social characteristic. The interpretation of the results is straightforward: Each cell indicates how much more likely, or less likely it is that the particular group of men in question will be represented in the NILF pool than the "average" prime-age US man in the year 2015.

Consider first the factor of race and ethnicity. In 2015, non-Hispanic Whites were about 7% less likely to fall into the pool of prime-age men neither working nor looking for work than would have been suggested by their overall numbers alone. This necessarily means that non-"Anglo" minorities as a whole were overrepresented in the prime-age male NILF population. Yet, there were strikingly divergent dispositions and risks here for different ethnic minorities. On the one hand, non-Hispanic Blacks were far more likely to be NILF than their national numbers alone would have suggested: They were overrepresented by 71%. By the same token, Multiracial men were 31% more likely to be NILF than would have been expected just from their population total. On the other hand, Asian men were less likely than "Anglos" to be NILF – 10% less likely than prime-age American men as a whole – while Hispanic men were 20% less likely to be NILF than American prime-age men overall. America's prime-age men of color, in other words, included both the ethnicities most likely to have dropped out of the labor force, and those very least likely to have done so.

Now consider the variable of nativity. On the whole, native-born men are more likely to have dropped out of the workforce than would have been predicted by their proportion in the national prime-age population: They are overrepresented by about 8% in the NILF pool. On the other hand, foreign-born men are markedly underrepresented: 28% less likely than their proportion in the overall prime-age male population would have suggested. (We may note that the great majority of foreign-born men nowadays are Asian or Hispanic – groupings, as we have already seen, distinctly less likely to be NILF; thus ethnicity and nativity appear to be significantly overlapping factors.)

With respect to educational attainment, we see a stark and already quite familiar gradient of risk. At one extreme, prime-age men with a graduate education are nearly three fifths (59%) less likely to be found in the NILF pool than the overall average; at the other extreme, prime-age men without a high school diploma are over three quarters (77%) more likely to be NILF. In between these end points, men whose highest attainment was a college degree college were 43% less likely to be NILF than the population-wide average,

TABLE 5.2 *Who is more likely – and who is less likely – to be in the 7 million pool of prime-age NILF Males? Relative odds by demographic characteristic: 2015*

Race/Ethnicity		Educational Attainment		Marital Status		Nativity	
Hispanic	−20%	Graduate Studies	−59%	Married	−36%	Foreign-Born	−28%
Asian	−10%	Bachelor's Degree	−43%	Divorced/Separated	+41%	Native-Born	+8%
"Anglo" (Non-Hispanic White)	−7%	Some College Training	−3%	Never Married	+48%		
Multiracial	+31%	High School Diploma only	+25%	Widowed	+116%		
Non-Hispanic Black	+71%	No High School Diploma	+77%				

Source: Flood, Sarah, Miriam King, Steven Ruggles, and J. Robert Warren. 2015. "Integrated Public Use Microdata Series, Current Population Survey: Version 4.0." Annual Social and Economic Supplement (ASEC). Minneapolis: University of Minnesota. Retrieved August 2016. http://doi.org/10.18128/D030.V4.0

while men with a high school diploma were 25% more likely to be NILF, and those with some college training were close to the nationwide average (3% below it). The powerful and predictable regularity of the correlation between educational attainment and employment in America is one of the widely accepted relationships in the contemporary social sciences, and Table 5.2 demonstrates the importance of this social factor with respect to prime-age NILF men.

Thus far, the strongest NILF risks identified in the US prime-age male population in 2015 are for non-Hispanic Blacks and for high school dropouts of all ethnicities: Note furthermore that the relative risk of being NILF is of roughly the same magnitude these two groups. We might assume that part of the explanation for this outcome would be the strong overrepresentation of African–American prime-age men in the pool of high school dropouts, but such an assumption would appear to be erroneous. Within the civilian noninstitutionalized population of prime-age men, the proportion of non-Hispanic Black men with no high school diploma is only very slightly higher than the national average for all races together: 10.2% vs. 9.7% in 2015.[3] Other powerful influences, apart from differences in educational attainment levels, must also be at work determining this highly unfavorable employment outcome for Black men in modern America.

Although perhaps less generally recognized than race/ethnicity and education, marital status and family structure turn out to be powerful predictors of male employment status, too. In 2015, widowed men were over twice as likely to be in the NILF pool as their totals in the overall population would have suggested, but as already mentioned, this was a very small contingent in terms of absolute numbers. On the other hand, the very large numbers of never-married men in 2015 were 48% more likely to be NILF than their population weighting would have suggested. Separated or divorced men were over 40% more likely to be NILF than the "average" prime-age man. By contrast, married men are 36% less likely to be neither working nor looking for work.

Much the same is true for the relationship between employment status and presence of children at home. In 2015, prime-age men with no children at home were 37% more likely than average to be NILF, while those with one or more children at home were 43% less likely. Even larger differentials are evident when I parse by both marital status and presence of children at

---

[3] Derived from US Census Bureau. 2015. "Educational Attainment in the United States: 2015." Retrieved November 2016. www.census.gov/data/tables/2015/demo/education-attainment/p20 -578.html

home. On the one hand, currently married men with children at home are only half as likely to be NILF (–51%) as would be expected by their overall numbers; on the other, never-married men without children at home were nearly 50% (49%) more likely to be long-term absentees from the labor force than we would have expected from their total numbers.

Those numbers underscore just how powerful a predictor of employment status for prime-age men the factor of family structure appears to be. Consider the following: In Table 5.2, the odds of being a prime-age NILF male are 50% higher for the native-born than foreign-born; 84% higher for non-Hispanic Blacks than non-Hispanic Whites; and 119% higher for men with only a high school education in relation to those whose highest degree is a college degree. By comparison, the odds of being NILF were 127% higher for a prime-age man with no children at home than one living in a home with children: A gap far larger than the Black/White differential, and indeed, slightly greater than the high school/college differential. Similarly, the odds of being NILF were over 130% higher for never-married prime-age men than for those currently married. Even greater disparities in NILF risk were evident for prime-age men who were currently married with children at home as against never-married men with no children at home: Here the odds were over 200% higher for the latter, very nearly the same differential as for high school dropouts in relation to college graduates.

Suffice it then to say that differences in marriage patterns and family structures are strongly associated with employment differentials for prime-age men in contemporary America. A quick glance at Table 5.2 offers the impression that the influence of differences in family structure may roughly in the order of differences in educational attainment for prime-age male employment, or more specifically, the risk of being absent from the labor force. That impression is reinforced by estimates of conditional compositional effects in today's (2015) prime-age male NILF rates and work rates: Holding 2015 work and NILF rates for subgroups constant, but recalculating hypothetical national rates on the basis of these subgroups' weighting in society as they were back in 1965, or some other earlier benchmark year in the previous section of this chapter (see Figure 5.18).

Perhaps surprisingly, America's shifting postwar racial and ethnic composition appears, by my calculations, to have had very little impact at all on changes in either work rates or NILF rates for prime-age men. Superimposing the 1965 "race" distribution for prime-age men on 2015 race-specific work rates results essentially in zero adjustment against either actual reported 2015 prime-age male work rates or their NILF rates. A very slight (half

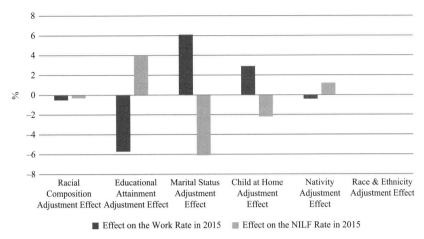

FIGURE 5.18 Conditional compositional effects on prime-age male work rates
and NILF rates in 2015

of 1 percentage point) downward adjustment in work rates would result from
matching the 1971 racial and ethnic composition of the prime-age male
population against work rates by ethnicity for 2015, while at the same time
such an exercise would result in a downward reduction of NILF rates by less
than one third of 1 percentage point. In effect, increasing ethnic diversity looks
to have had little impact with respect to prime-age male employment status:
Poor performance by non-Hispanic Blacks and some other less populous
groupings were balanced out by the above-average performance of other
groups, specifically Asians and Hispanics.[4]

The conditional compositional effect for nativity looks to be somewhat
larger than for race and ethnicity. With current (2015) nativity-specific work
rates but a 1994 breakdown of population by nativity, prime-age male work
rates would have been 0.4 percentage points lower in 2015 than those actually
recorded – actual work rates over that period declined by 2.3 points. By the
same token, the conditional compositional adjustment raises NILF rates by
over one point; in actuality, NILF rates fell by about three points over that
same period. These hypotheticals suggest that the overall employment profile
of contemporary prime-age men would look worse, not better, without the
intervening influx of foreign-born prime-age men.

[4] It may seem curious that the race and ethnicity adjustment should be negated for both work
rates and NILF rates, as such adjustments customarily would be expected to move in opposite
directions. The paradox appears to be explained by the sharp reduction in Hispanic unemployment between 1971 and 2015.

Educational attainment, however, appears to exert a larger influence on adjustments for work rates and NILF rates than either race and ethnicity, or nativity. With 2015 education-specific work rates but 1965 distributions of educational attainment, the conditional calculation for prime-age male work rates would be 5.7 percentage points lower than those actually recorded in 2015, and the conditional calculation for NILF rates would be 4 points higher. Those hypothetical adjustments can be compared with the actual drop in work rates of 9.3 points, and the jump in NILF rates of 8.8 points. By these illustrative computations, improvements in educational attainment appear to have played a very important role in preventing a far worse decline in male work over the past half-century. Hypothetically speaking, with today's education-specific rates and a 1965 distribution of educational attainment, the drop in prime-age male work rates would be over half again as dramatic as that which took place, and the jump in NILF rates would likewise be almost half again as large as what was actually recorded.

Big as these hypothetical conditional adjustment effects for educational attainment may appear, those for marital status are of the same magnitude – in fact, even a bit larger. Whereas the calculated compositional effect for changes in educational attainment for 1965–2015 on prime-age male work rates amounted to –5.7 points, it would be +6.1 points for marital status. Where the calculated compositional effect for educational attainment over those same years on NILF rates would be +4 points, it would be –5.7 points for marital status. By one reading, this might suggest that that the impact on prime-age male work rates and NILF rates from changes in marriage patterns would have been sufficient to cancel out the impact of half a century of improvements in educational attainment, entirely – and then some.

I may note as well that the conditional compositional effect for presence of children at home (using a 1968 benchmark) would adjust work rates upward by nearly 3 points (2.9 points) against their actual 2015 levels, and would adjust NILF rates downward by more than 2 points (–2.2 points). Even without more refined calculations, taking into account the marital status of men in homes with children, it is apparent that the "child at home factor" looks to be somewhat over half as large in magnitude as the educational attainment factor.

In this section, we have seen that marital status and family structure correlate strongly with employment status for prime-age men nowadays – indeed, that the predictive power of family structure on work rates and NILF rates are on a par with that of education, which is commonly recognized as an extremely powerful factor in social outcomes. We have also seen that changes in family structure over time could be associated with changes in male work patterns over time, and that, here again, the conditional compositional effect on male employment patterns over the past half-century might be of the same absolute magnitude as improvements in educational attainment, albeit weighing in the opposite. However, we need to look at these relationships more closely to draw inferences about the independent statistical contribution of changes in family structure to changes in male work patterns, to say nothing about causality or the possible casual mechanisms at play here.

IS FAMILY STRUCTURE A DETERMINANT OF POSTWAR MALE WORK PATTERNS?

Establishing a correlation or association between two factors – even a strong one – is not the same thing as establishing an independent and causal influence of one factor on the other. For one thing, such associations may be due to additional, unobserved conditions or variables with which both observed factors happen to correlate. However, even if a genuinely independent and statistically meaningful relationship can be established between two factors, that correlation tells us nothing about the direction of causality: In statistical jargon, we cannot tell which variable is independent and which is dependent simply by demonstrating that a relationship exists in the first place.

In the context of the family structure/male employment relationship, these cautionary methodological generalizations have at least two immediate and practical implications. First, it could be possible that the correlation we have detected between family structure and male employment patterns are in reality due largely, or entirely, to a deeper underlying relationship between male employment patterns and some other factor closely tracking with changes in family structure: Educational attainment, for example, or race and ethnicity, or health. Second, even if a methodologically sound and independent relationship between family structure and male employment patterns could be identified, this would tell us nothing about which variable was influencing which. Far from assuming that family structure is affecting employment patterns, one might instead make the case that the declining availability of work for men is forcing a disintegration of traditional family patterns, as ever greater numbers of disadvantaged men find it impossible to find spouses and earn the wherewithal to form families. As it happens, recent social science studies include methodologically sound research by authors pointing the arrow of causality in each of these opposing directions (Ahituv and Lerman 2007; Autor, Dorn, and Hanson 2017).

An exhaustive examination of these methodological issues cannot be undertaken in this brief section; It will suffice instead to make two simple points. First, controlling for such important social factors as race/ethnicity and education does not eliminate the strong relationship between family structure and male employment patterns. Second, while the "declining male work causes declining male marriage" interpretation of causality is inherently plausible, and may indeed persuasively speak to part of the observed association between employment and family structure for US men, it also leaves a number of important aspects of the contemporary social tableau manifestly unexplained.

Consider, to begin, the potentially confounding factors of race/ethnicity and education. It is true that each of two factors tends to correlate with family structure and male work rates at one and the same time. With respect to ethnicity, Asian prime-age men report the highest proportion of those currently married and among the highest work rates; conversely, non-Hispanic Blacks report among the lowest numbers currently married and among the lowest work rates. By the same token, with respect to education, overall work rates and proportions currently married are lowest for prime-age men without a high school diploma and highest for those with a college degree or graduate education.

Clearly, race and education have a bearing on family structure in modern America, but when I attempt to control for them, a residual independent "family structure" effect is revealed, and its association with male employment profiles appears to be a strong one.

As already mentioned, a significant differential separates workforce participation rates for currently married and never-married prime-age men of every major US ethnic or "racial" grouping: White, Black, Hispanic, and Asian. As we already know, overall prime-age male NILF rates are much lower for Blacks than Whites 18.8% vs. 10.0% in 2015. Nevertheless, workforce participation rates for prime-age married Black men are distinctly higher nowadays than those for never-married White men, and have been for decades (see Figure 5.19). In this particularly vivid example, the "marriage effect" trumps the "race effect" – and it is by no means the only such example that could be adduced.

To be sure, Figure 5.19 does not control for education, and it is possible that the educational profile of married Blacks could be different from (and more favorable than) that of their never-married White peers. However, if we look at education, we find that currently married prime-age men of all ethnicities report higher workforce participation if they are currently married than not

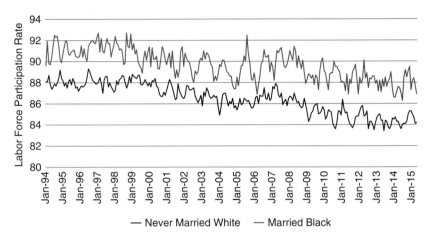

FIGURE 5.19 Labor force participation rate for males aged 25–54 by marital status and race: married Black vs. never-married White

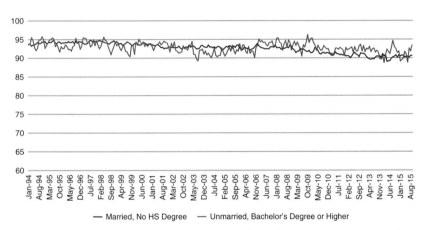

FIGURE 5.20 Labor force participation rate for males aged 25–54 by marital status and educational attainment: never married with bachelor's degree or higher vs. married high school dropout

currently married (divorced/separated, widowed, or never married) – and that this holds for every level of educational attainment. The lower the level of educational attainment, the greater the gap in workforce participation between men who are married and men who are not. Indeed, despite their ostensible disadvantages in the contemporary labor market, married high school dropouts record roughly the same workforce participation rates as never-married college graduates (see Figure 5.20). Here we see a particularly instructive instance of the "marriage effect," one in which it apparently compensates entirely for the "education effect" with regard to workforce participation rates for prime-age American men.

I could provide similar examples of the effect of marital status after controlling for race and education, and analogous examples for the influence of the "child at home" effect after controlling for other social factors, but the point should already be clear: Even after controlling for other social factors, we see a strong residual "family structure" effect in play after taking such formidable social forces as race and education into account. The plain fact is, all other things being equal, currently married prime-age men appear to have consistently higher work rates and consistently lower NILF rates than those whose are not currently married – and the same holds true for prime-age men who have children living in their home.

Isolating a "marriage effect" or a "family structure effect," of course, does nothing to clarify the direction of causality between changes in employment patterns and changes in family patterns. An inherently plausible case can be made that the decline of work is driving the decline of marriage and family formation for men. In this interpretation, the key factor in the decline of male work is a decline in the demand for male labor due to structural economic change: Technological change, globalization and trade, decline of manufacturing, outsourcing and all the rest. (The important 2016 study on the decline in prime age male labor force participation rates by the President's Council of Economic Advisers is representative of this broadly accepted school of thought.) By this assessment, for example, demand for lower skilled male labor has fallen disproportionately over the postwar era, so marriage among lower skilled men has also fallen disproportionately during the postwar era.

On the face of it, this "demand-side" hypothesis would seem to have much to commend it. I would certainly not contest the proposition that it can explain some, perhaps even much, of the decline in employment for prime-age men over the past two generations. However, it clearly cannot explain *all* of it. In a number of important respects, the labor market patterns for prime-age men that have unfolded over the past half-century look to be fundamentally inconsistent with the "demand-side" hypothesis – and thus with the assessment that causality leads from changes in work patterns to changes in family structure.

Three empirical challenges to the "demand-side" theory deserve particular attention. The first is the trajectory of the prime-age male "inactivity rate" – the percentage of men not in the workforce – over the 1965–2015 period (see Figure 5.21). The trouble for the "demand-side" theory is the remarkable

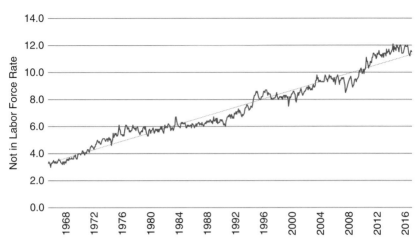

FIGURE 5.21 Rate of nonlabor force participation from 1965 to 2016: US civilian noninstitutionalized males aged 25–54

regularity of this trend: It is almost a straight line upward for fully fifty years. There is no indication whatever of any influence of the business cycle: The Great Recession of 2008/09 is not visible, nor for that matter are any of the previous six recessions that occurred over the decades between 1965 and 2008. Likewise with respect to trade shocks, it is impossible to detect the NAFTA agreement, or of China's entry into the WTO, in the steadily increasing inactivity rates over these years. As with regard to technological disruptions, it is impossible to identify from the prime-age male inactivity rate the trend line for the advent of personal computers, Internet use, or any of the other great innovations that may have had a profound or disruptive effects on the demand for labor over these years. While the remarkable smoothness of the ascent in inactivity rates does not concord with any of these many major "demand-side" shocks, we note that it does track with the relative smoothness of the trends in changing family structure over the past two generations at the aggregate or national, level.

Second, there is the curious and, for the labor market-driven causality theory, rather inconvenient pattern of prime-age male inactivity rates at the state level (see Figure 5.22). From 1980 to 2014, interstate variations in such inactivity rates steadily increased, even though one would ordinarily expect a nationwide labor market to seek equilibrium in the wake of demand shocks. Furthermore, some of the states with the very highest prime-age male inactivity rates (for example, Maine) happened to border some of the states with the very lowest inactivity rates (e.g., New Hampshire – Maine's only land

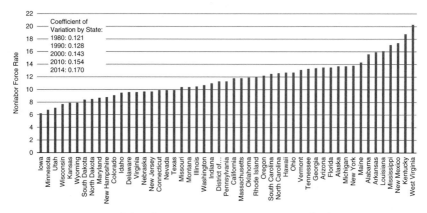

FIGURE 5.22 Nonlabor force rates among prime-age males by state (2015)

boundary within the United States). On first impression, these growing state-level imbalances do not look like "demand-side" problems but rather "supply-side" problems: Insufficiency of migration or mobility. However, it should be remembered that the family structure-to-employment profile causation hypothesis is also a "supply-side" labor theory, since it implicitly posits that men who are not currently married and/or do not have children at home are less likely to seek work than those who do.

Finally, there is the matter of the wildly disparate workforce participation rates for less skilled men in accordance with their marital status (see Figure 5.23). According to CPS data, in 2015, a gap of almost 20 percentage points separated labor force participation rates for currently married and never-married prime-age male high school dropouts. This means that between 1965 and 2015 prime-age male LFPRs fell by about 8 percentage points for unmarried high school dropouts – somewhat less than for the prime-age male population as a whole – while they fell by almost 28 percentage points for never-married high school dropouts. If we attempt to explain this extraordinary disparity in outcomes as a "demand-side" effect, we are also obliged to come up with an explanation for why the demand for labor would drop so very little for less skilled men with more traditional family structures, and so radically for those with alternative family structures. To date, I am unaware of any such theorizing yet attempting such acrobatics.

These few pages can only begin to address the complexities of a quantitative investigation of family structure as a determinant of male employment patterns in contemporary America. What I hope to have demonstrated, however, is that further rigorous examination of this topic is warranted, as there appears

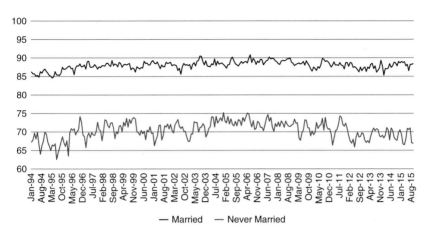

FIGURE 5.23 Labor force participation rate for males aged 25–54 by marital status and educational attainment lower than a high school diploma

to be evidence of an independent relationship between family structure and employment patterns after holding other potentially confounding variables constant – and reason as well to believe there may be some genuine causal relationship between changes in family structure and changes in male employment patterns in postwar America (in additional to whatever causal relationships may work in the other direction).

CONCLUDING OBSERVATIONS

This chapter has made the case that changing patterns for marriage and living arrangements correspond strongly with changing patterns of male employment in the United States over the postwar era, or, to offer a formulation perhaps more in keeping with the framing of this volume, that there is a strong relationship between increasing family inequality and increasing male employment inequality in contemporary America. I have offered evidence that differences in family structure track with differences in male employment patterns, even after taking account of alternative and perhaps competing social factors, such as race/ ethnicity and education. Furthermore, I have offered evidence of a causal relationship between changes in family structure and changes in male employment patterns – evidence that the competing hypothesis of employment ("demand-side")-driven changes in family patterns cannot explain readily, if at all. This chapter does not presume to undertake an exhaustive examination of the topic, but it does attempt to provide sufficient groundwork to justify and encourage further and more exhaustive research in this area.

It may be suitable to conclude by indicating some potentially fruitful directions for such work. This chapter established evidence of broad relationships on the basis of aggregate "macro"-statistics of a cross-sectional nature. For delving deeper into the dynamics of this relationship, and for teasing out possible causal mechanisms, quantitative analysis microdata would appear to be most suitable – and ideally, microdata from a longitudinal survey, as such information would help us better understand how and whether male employment behavior changes in the aftermath of changes in marital status or living arrangements.

It might also be beneficial, if possible, to add several additional social variables I did not include in my examination for this study. One of these would be prime-age male utilization of government benefits, including means-tested benefits and disability program benefits. Broadly speaking, we know that unemployed men are more likely to participate in such programs nowadays than employed men, and that NILF men are more likely to participate in them than unemployed men, but the interplay with family structure, and the issue of "demand-side" versus "supply-side" drivers of such increased participation, surely deserves more careful illumination. Another, and scarcely less important, variable would be criminal justice system history – in particular, previous criminal conviction record or comparable serious criminal history. Between the early 1960s and 2010, the number of adults in the United States with a criminal record is estimated to have more than quadrupled (Shannon et al. 2017). Rough calculations suggest that something like one in eight adult men not behind bars in the United States may have a criminal conviction in his past – the figure for prime-age men today may be even higher (Eberstadt 2016). Criminal justice status may possibly be the most important typically unexplored variable in social research on the dynamics of change in family structure and male employment. Casting light on this strangely unexplored dimension of modern American life would surely permit us to clarify and refine our understanding of the dynamics of family inequality and employment inequality in modern America.

PART III

CONSEQUENCES OF GROWING DIVERGENCE

6

Single-Mother Families, Mother's Educational Level, Children's School Outcomes
A *Study of Twenty-One Countries*

Anna Garriga and Paolo Berta*

INTRODUCTION

The increase of single motherhood and parental divorce has become of the most important social transformations experienced by Western societies in the last half-century. This change has not been even across these societies; it has started later and moved slower in some places (Härkönen 2017). Hence, there are substantial cross-national differences in the percentage of nontraditional living arrangements (Pong, Dronkers, and Hampden-Thompson 2003). It has been demonstrated that parental divorce and growing up in a single-mother family have negative effects on children's well-being (McLanahan, Tach, and Schneider 2013), and several studies have tested to what extent these effects diverge between countries and over time (see Bernardi et al. 2013 for a review). It was expected that these negative associations would be lower in countries and time periods where nontraditional family forms are more common, where there is a greater acceptance of new family forms, and where there are generous policies for single-mother families (Gähler and Garriga 2013). Surprisingly, most studies that address the variation across countries and over time show that the effects of parental divorce and family structure on children's well-being have been relatively constant (see Bernardi et al. 2013). Some studies have even found that the impact of parental divorce has increased over time, contradicting most expectations that a reduction in stigma and an increase in father involvement might mitigate the effects (Bernardi et al. 2013).

A possible explanation for why the consequences associated with single parenthood have not decreased is that over time, the prevalence of single

* This research has been possible thanks to the grants provided by the Spanish Ministry of Economy and Competitiveness (grants CSO2013-43461-R and CSO2015-69439-R) and the grant provided by Abat Oliba CEU University and "La Caixa" "Banking Foundation" (2017).

motherhood has increased faster among those with lower levels of education (Gähler and Garriga 2013). Research documenting this has mainly focused on the United States and has not considered whether or not the increasing polarization of family structure by educational level diverges between countries in different time periods (Garriga, Sarasa, and Berta 2015; McLanahan and Jacobsen 2015). McLanahan (2004) showed that in Canada, Finland, Germany, the Netherlands, Sweden, and the United Kingdom, less-educated women were more likely to be single mothers, while in Italy it was more educated women who were more likely to be single mothers. However, to our knowledge, only four studies have focused on the changes in trends in the educational differences of single motherhood from multiple causes in European countries. Kennedy and Thomson (2010) show that the probability that a Swedish child spent time in a single-mother family during her childhood increased between the 1970s and 1990s. Garriga and Cortina (2017) showed that between 1991 and 2011, the educational gradient of single motherhood reversed from positive to negative in Spain. Garriga, Sarasa, and Berta (2015) have also found that in Italy the relationship between mother's education and single motherhood was positive in 2005 and became insignificant by 2011. Härkönen (2017) is the only study that has observed the educational gradient of single motherhood in different time periods in multiple countries. Using data from the Luxembourg Income Study (LIS) Database, Härkönen showed that "diverging destinies" are not confined only to the United States, but there are nonetheless major cross-national variations. The main limitation of this study, however, is that the educational gradient of single motherhood is not adjusted for mother's immigration status. Taking this variable into account might substantially affect the results since the percentage of foreign born mothers has increased in most Western countries and, on average, they have a lower educational level than native born mothers (Garriga and Cortina, 2017; OECD, 2012).

Several researchers have argued that marked increases in the prevalence of single motherhood among the low-educated together with the well-documented negative effects of parental divorce and growing up in a single-mother family on child outcomes have exacerbated the inequality between children from different socioeconomic backgrounds and different family structures (Augustine 2014; Cherlin 2005; Härkönen 2017; Härkönen 2018; McLanahan and Percheski 2008). However, Bernardi and Boertien (2016) and Bernardi, Boertien, and Popova (2014) have argued that this conclusion is only true if a third premise is also true; namely that the consequences of parental divorce and family structure are greater among children of lower socioeconomic background, or that the consequences are the same regardless of socioeconomic background. If instead growing up in a nonintact family entails more negative consequences for children from higher socioeconomic backgrounds, they have claimed that this might actually counterbalance the increase of nonintact families among children from disadvantaged backgrounds. In other words, the increase of parental divorce and single-mother families may reduce inequality in children's outcomes and life chances between children from different socioeconomic backgrounds if these single-motherhood costs relatively advantaged children more (Leopold and Leopold 2016).

Despite the importance of the issue of varying costs of divorce and family structure by family socioeconomic background, it has not received much attention until recently. To date, the research has obtained mixed findings. Some studies have found that higher socioeconomic background can compensate for the negative effects of family structure and parental divorce, but other studies have found that larger negative effects at higher socioeconomic status. Alongside methodological reasons, two other possible explanations for why these studies may not produce consistent results are that they focus on different children's outcomes and on different countries: The conditioning role of family socioeconomic background may depend on the outcome and country studied.

Overall, this chapter aims to address these gaps in the literature by using data from twenty-one Western countries from the Programme for International Student Assessment (PISA) of 2012. First, we explore to what extent there is a general pattern in Western countries of single motherhood being common among women with less education. Second, we analyze the effects on children of being in a single-mother family on three school outcomes: Standardized math test scores, grade repetition, and truancy. Most cross-national studies on the effect of family structure on school outcomes have only focused on achievement tests, despite evidence of stronger effects of family structure on educational attainment and school behavior outcomes than on test scores (McNeal 1999). In addition, truancy or repeating a grade has negative consequences for children's educational attainment, plus both are also strongly associated with labor market and socio-emotional outcomes and risk behaviors such as drug abuse or crime (Garry 1996; Jones, Lovrich, and Lovrich 2011; Range, Yonke, and Young 2011). Third, we look at the heterogeneity of family structure effects by focusing on a specific dimension of family socioeconomic background: Mother's education.

We use this analytical approach based on the study of different outcomes and countries to address the question of whether the growing number of single mothers in Western countries generally increases or decreases inequality in children's outcomes and life chances between those from different socioeconomic backgrounds. Answering this question requires knowing: (1) whether single motherhood is generally concentrated among women of lower education in most Western countries; (2) if the effects of single motherhood matter across a range of children's important educational outcomes; and (3) whether the impact associated with single motherhood depends upon the mother's education. We argue that even if children of lower socioeconomic status are generally more likely to be in single-mother homes, the retreat from traditional family structures would increase children's inequality only if there were a consistent pattern across countries and outcomes of single motherhood having consistent negative effects on children's outcomes and life chances regardless of mothers' education, or if children with less-educated mothers have greater disadvantages associated with single motherhood. In contrast, if living with a single mother were associated with deeper disadvantage among children of more educated mothers across countries and outcomes, then the retreat from traditional family structures could decrease children's inequality.

COMPENSATORY HYPOTHESIS AND FLOOR EFFECT HYPOTHESIS

The sociological literature has developed two general perspectives about the heterogeneity of parental divorce and family structure effects by mother's education: The "compensatory hypothesis" and the "floor effect hypothesis." These perspectives are based on diverging interpretations of how various mediators of the effects of family structure on children's well-being work according to different levels of mother's education. These mediators are financial constraints, quality of parenting, mother's psychological well-being, involvement of the noncustodial father, and social support and networks (Amato 1993; Sigle-Rushton and McLanahan 2004).

The compensatory hypothesis posits that mothers with a higher educational background are better equipped to buffer their children from the negative consequences of growing up in a single-parent family and, consequently, there are no – or few – differences in children's outcomes by family types among those that have a mother with a higher educational level. On the other hand, this hypothesis states that lower educated mothers are more vulnerable to factors that intensify the negative consequences of growing up in a single-mother family. Single mothers with a low educational level are in a worse position than single mothers with high educational level, and are less likely to mobilize resources to compensate for their children's disadvantages (Augustine 2014; Leopold and Leopold 2016).

With respect to financial constraints, it is well-known that women with more education are more likely to be in the labor market and to be better paid (Pettit and Hook 2005). Highly educated women may, therefore, already have jobs before becoming single mothers. They also have better opportunities to re-enter the labor market after a period of nonemployment than women with a lower educational level (Drobnič, Blossfeld, and Rohwer, 1999). Further, research has found high levels of educational homogeneity within couples in Western countries (Blossfeld and Timm 2003). Consequently, children with a mother with a high educational level have a higher probability of having a father with a high educational level. Couples with high educational levels tend to be wealthier and, even when family income and wealth have to be divided after parental separation, mothers may retain more financial resources than their less-educated counterparts. Finally, resources may also increase mothers' ability to navigate the legal system on behalf of herself and her child to obtain child support payments. Case, Lin, and McLanahan (2003) show that mothers with a higher level of education have a greater chance of receiving child support payments in high amounts than mothers with a lower education, who often do not receive any child support.

With respect to quality of parenting, Augustine (2014) argued, that better-educated single mothers are better placed to overcome many family-structure-related barriers to maintaining higher levels of parenting quality. The first barrier is financial resources. Single mothers have less time and energy than mothers in two-parent families, and this is mainly due to task overload since they have to obtain financial resources and take care of their children alone (Astone and McLanahan 1991). Mothers with a high educational level have greater financial resources to pay for hiring domestic workers or good quality child care. These mothers also have larger and wealthier social networks that may help by taking care of the children directly or providing them with financial support. Economic resources and the related social networks of highly educated single mothers can help them to minimize their stress and task overload and hence, they may have more time and energy to provide better quality parenting to their children.

A second barrier that affects quality of parenting of single mothers is psychological well-being, and this barrier may be more consequential for less-educated mothers. In fact, research shows that mothers with lower socio-economic resources experience more psychological problems after dissolution of their unions than those with greater resources (Liu and Chen 2006; Mandemakers and Monden 2010). Better-educated mothers may also be more conscious of the negative effects of divorce and single motherhood since they may be more familiar with psychological and sociological research that has been popularized on this topic (Mandemakers and Kalmijn 2014). Therefore, despite the psychological problems that these mothers may experience, they may be more aware of the importance of providing high quality of parenting to counterbalance these effects.

In addition, several studies show that mothers with higher education are more likely to enroll their children in academically stimulating preschool programs and are more likely to sign their children up for extracurricular activities or summer programs (see Augustine and Crosnoe 2010 for a review). These pro-academic experiences provide children with learning opportunities that may not be available at home due to the task overload or psychological problems that single mothers often face. For these reasons, highly educated mothers who cannot give these learning opportunities to their children directly may plan so that children receive them indirectly. They may also monitor the results in ways that enhance outcomes.

A third impact on children's well-being is the quality of the father-child relationship (Amato and Gilbreth 1999). As mentioned, mother's education is correlated with father's education; this, in turn, is associated positively with fathers' involvement (King, Harris, and Heard 2004). Cheadle, Amato, and King (2010) show that children whose mothers have a high educational level also have a greater probability of maintaining a consistently high level of contact with their fathers over time – a precondition of having a good relationship with them. In addition, mothers who share joint physical custody have a higher educational level than those who are awarded sole custody (Juby, Le Bourdais, and Marcil-Gratton 2005), and joint physical custody may be somewhat beneficial for children when compared to sole custody (see Baude, Pearson, and Drapeau 2016 for a review). In addition to parental relationships, several studies show that the amount of social support children receive outside the home is positively related to their adjustment after divorce (Zartler and Grillenberger 2017 for review), and affluent children receive more social support (Putnam 2015).

On the other hand, in direct opposition to the compensation hypothesis, the "floor effect hypothesis" posits that the family structure penalty is smaller for children with less-educated mothers (Bernardi and Radl, 2014; Leopold and Leopold, 2016). This perspective maintains that children with less-educated mothers are less vulnerable to the negative effects of family structure given that their mothers are poor, have low psychological well-being, provide poor quality parenting, and their fathers have little involvement – regardless of whether their parents are together (Bernardi and Boertien 2017b). In other words, women with a low educational level are (Bernardi and Boertien 2017b) already in a bad situation that cannot become much worse. In contrast, children of highly educated mothers are better situated – have a higher level of family income, better maternal psychological well-being, a greater likelihood of good quality parenting, and are more likely to have an involved father – so those who become single mothers have more to lose; family structure matters more for their children.

PREVIOUS RESEARCH AND LIMITATIONS

As mentioned, the few studies that have focused on how parental divorce and family structure effects differ by mother's education have obtained mixed findings (Bernardi and Boertien 2017b). First, substantial research shows that children's educational attainment suffers less from parental divorce if they have more highly educated mothers (Albertini and Dronkers 2009; Fischer 2007; Grätz 2015). However, the two studies that used test scores rather than educational attainment obtained contradictory results. Augustine (2014), comparing children in the United States who live in intact married families to those who live in other family forms, found that the effect of family structure on math and reading achievement is greater for those whose mothers have a lower educational level. On the other hand, Mandemakers and Kalmijn (2014), using the British Cohort Study (1970), found that the effect of parental divorce on reading and math test scores did not vary by maternal education. These findings suggest that the choice of educational outcome affects the conclusions drawn from the research. In addition, outcomes such as mental health and behavior problems that have been extensively analyzed in the literature on family structure effects have not been tested for heterogeneous effects across maternal education levels (with the exception of Mandemakers and Kalmijn 2014). For these reasons, more research on other outcomes alongside educational attainment is needed in order to have a more complete picture of how mother's education conditions the effect of family structure.

An alternative explanation for the conflicting findings on test scores is that the two studies on this outcome are based on data from different countries. There are several reasons to argue that the role of mothers' education may vary by country (Bernardi and Boertien 2017b; Mandemakers and Kalmijn 2014). For example, less-educated mothers may be less vulnerable to separation-related declines in income when they live in generous welfare states where various social policies protect citizens against financial hardship (Leopold & Leopold, 2016). Mothers with a low educational level would have similar income levels regardless of whether they live in two-parent or single-mother families, since family income cannot be lower than a state-guaranteed minimum. By contrast, children with highly educated mothers should suffer more from single motherhood because they are likely to experience lower income than in two-parent families.

A third reason for these conflicting findings is that there is substantial cross-national variation in the percentage of children living in joint physical custody (Bjarnason and Arnarsson 2011), and children with highly educated mothers have a higher likelihood of living in joint physical custody (Juby, Le Bourdais, and Marcil-Gratton 2005). The number of children with highly educated mothers in this living arrangement should, therefore, be greater in countries with a high proportion of children in joint physical custody. Taking into account that joint physical custody is beneficial for children (Baude, Pearson, and Drapeau 2016), mother's education may be associated with smaller negative effects of parental divorce and single motherhood in countries with a high percentage of joint physical custody. Additionally, societal characteristics related to the outcome studied may affect the interplay between family structure, mother's education, and children's well-being (Bernardi and Boertien, 2017b). Mare (1993) argues that in a society with a high level of inequality in educational opportunity, only very talented children from poorly educated families may obtain higher education. Following this argument, Bernardi and Radl (2014) argue that floor effects are exaggerated in the most unequal societies – children from disadvantaged socioeconomic background are so unlikely to succeed in the educational system that parental divorce or the experience of single motherhood does not reduce their odds substantially. In spite of these theoretical reasons for cross-national variation, previous research was based on single-country studies (with the exception of Bernardi and Radl 2014), and a cross-national approach is required to determine whether mothers' education conditions the effects of family structure differently across countries or whether there is a similar pattern in Western countries.

DATA AND VARIABLES

For the purposes of this study, we have used data from the 2012 Programme for International Student Assessment (PISA) organized by the Organisation for Economic Co-operation and Development (OECD). PISA data provide internationally comparable measurements on the socioeconomic background and cognitive and noncognitive educational performance of 15-year-old students from OECD countries. In this study, we focus on twenty-one countries that share similar Western cultural traditions and social institutions (Garib, Garcia, and Dronkers 2007). These countries follow the well-known welfare state regime categories (e.g., Armingeon, 2001; Esping-Andersen, 1990; Ferrera, 1996). The Liberal countries are Australia, Canada, United Kingdom, Republic of Ireland, New Zealand, and the United States. The Nordic countries are Denmark, Finland, Norway, and Sweden. The Continental countries are Belgium, France, Netherlands, Austria, Germany, Switzerland, and Luxembourg. The southern Europe countries are Spain, Greece, Italy, and Portugal.

PISA data have some strengths and some weaknesses. The main strength of PISA is its cross-national comparability. The most significant weakness is the limited nature of the data collected. It is a snapshot of 15-year-old students: No information about either the children's further development or about their earlier experiences and outcomes is available (Garib, Garcia, and Dronkers 2007). For example, the causes of the current family structure are not known. Single-parent families may be due to divorce, cohabitants' separation, parental death, or the parents never having lived together. Furthermore, the most recent PISA survey, the PISA 2015, contains no information about family structures. For this reason, PISA 2012 is used in this chapter.

There are several outcome variables that measure cognitive and noncognitive performance. Cognitive performance is measured using math tests developed by PISA since *mathematical* literacy was the focus of the *PISA 2012* survey. The grade repetition variable takes into account students who repeated a grade in primary school or in secondary school (value "1") and students who never repeated a grade (value "0"). Truancy is used as a measure of noncognitive performance. Students were asked if, in the last two weeks, they had played truant for a whole day or just from some classes. Students who reported that they had played truant from classes or for days of school at least once in the two weeks leading up to the PISA test have lower scores than students who did not (OECD 2013b). The truancy variable takes value "1" when they played truant all day or from some classes one or more times during the last two weeks and "0" when the student did not.

The family structure variable is based on the child's response to the questionnaire item asking them with whom they live. This is made up of two categories: single-mother family referring to children who said that they live with only with their mother, and two-parent family referring to children who said that they live with their two biological parents or stepparents.[1]

---

[1]   Unfortunately, the PISA 2012 data do not distinguish whether the parents are natural parents or stepparents. For this reason, we include stepparent and biological two-parent families in the same category in our analysis. As Dronkers, Veerman, and Pong (2016, p. 4) suggest, "any bias resulting from this problem only makes our estimations more conservative, which means that

Mother's education is measured using the International Standard Classification of Education (ISCED) scale. Four categories are created: Lower secondary education or below (None education, ISCED levels 1 and 2), upper secondary education and non-tertiary postsecondary (ISCED levels 3 and 4), tertiary education (ISCED levels 5 and 6). The control variables are gender of the child ("1" female and "0" male), immigrant statuses of the mother and the child, and age of the child (measured continuously). The immigrant status of the child, used when predicting child outcomes, has three categories: (1) native student; (2) first-generation student; and (3) second-generation student. Mother's immigrant status, used when estimating how much education affects the probability of single motherhood, takes value "1" if she is foreign-born and "0" if she is native-born.

RESULTS

THE RELATIONSHIP BETWEEN SINGLE MOTHERHOOD AND EDUCATION

Table 6.1 shows the percentages of different family types across the twenty-one countries in 2012. As previous studies have found, there is a substantial variation in the percentage of single-mother families. In 2012, the United States had the highest percentage and Greece the lowest.

We tested whether less-educated mothers were more likely to be single using logistic regression with family structure as the dependent variable. Separate models were done for each country, and the effect of mother education was estimated controlling for whether the mother was foreign-born. Table 6.2 only presents the coefficients for mother's educational level.

In Anglo-Saxon and Nordic countries, single mothers are significantly more likely to have less education, while mothers in two-parent families are more likely to have higher educational levels. There are only two exceptions to this generalization. In the United Kingdom, the effect of tertiary education is not significant. In Denmark, lower education does predict single motherhood, but not significantly.

The Continental countries have two different patterns. In France, the Netherlands, and Belgium, less-educated mothers are more likely to be single, but the relationship is not statistically significant in Belgium. In contrast, in

we are likely to underestimate the difference between two parent families and the single mother families." Additionally, we have excluded children that live in single-father families or apart from both biological parents from my sample, since in some countries there are not enough cases to perform the analyses.

TABLE 6.1 *Percentages of children by family types, PISA 2012*

	Two Parents	Single Mother	Single Father	Not Living with Parents		N
Australia	85.7	11.6	1.8	0.9	100	13.15
Canada	86.3	10.4	2.3	1	100	9.672
United Kingdom	82.8	15	1.6	0.6	100	11.341
Ireland	88.7	10	1	0.3	100	4594
New Zealand	77	16.1	3.6	3.3	100	4.16
United States	77.9	17	3.3	1.8	100	4.466
Denmark	84.2	12.7	2.4	0.7	100	6.976
Finland	83.4	13.4	2.6	0.6	100	8.081
Norway	88.9	9	1.7	0.4	100	4.322
Sweden	89.7	7.6	1.9	0.8	100	4.289
Belgium	85.7	11.7	1.9	0.7	100	8.012
France	84.3	13.3	1.7	0.7	100	4.226
Netherlands	88.3	9.8	1.5	0.4	100	4.227
Austria	86	12.2	1.3	0.5	100	4.438
Germany	85.8	11.6	2	0.6	100	3.974
Switzerland	86	12.2	1.4	0.4	100	10.583
Luxembourg	87.1	10.7	1.6	0.6	100	4.912
Spain	89.2	8.9	1.3	0.6	100	24.797
Greece	90.2	7.5	1.3	1	100	4.834
Italy	89.9	8.5	1	0.6	100	29.719
Portugal	85.8	11	1.3	1.9	100	5.193

countries where German is spoken – Germany, Switzerland, and Austria – *more* educated mothers are more likely to be single, though the relationship is only significant in Switzerland. In Luxembourg, single motherhood is distributed almost evenly across the educational spectrum. There is no clear pattern in Mediterranean countries where more educated mothers are more likely to be single in Portugal, Italy, and Greece (not significantly in Greece), but in Spain, like Denmark, less-educated mothers are insignificantly more likely to be single mothers.

Overall, these findings indicate that in spite of the fact that there are still substantial cross-national differences in the relationship between mother's education and single motherhood, there is a general pattern toward a negative relationship between mother's education and single motherhood in most Western countries. Higher education significantly predicted greater odds of single motherhood only in Switzerland, Portugal, and Italy among the twenty-one countries analyzed, although in a few other countries, there was no significant effect. Because single

TABLE 6.2 *Logistic regression coefficients of mother's education on the probability of being a single mother*

	Lower Secondary or Below	Upper Secondary	Tertiary
Australia	Ref	−0.26**	−0.20*
Canada	Ref	−0.06	−0.33*
United Kingdom	Ref	−0.26	−0.26
Ireland	Ref	−0.38*	−0.50**
New Zealand	Ref	−0.41**	−0.31*
United States	Ref	−0.21	−0.59***
Denmark	Ref	−0.01	−0.17
Finland	Ref	−0.37*	−0.71***
Norway	Ref	−0.36	−0.47*
Sweden	Ref	−0.58**	−0.55**
Belgium	Ref	0.03	−0.19
France	Ref	−0.25+	−0.39**
Netherlands	Ref	−0.48**	−0.40*
Austria	Ref	−0.01	0.14
Germany	Ref	−0.06	0.12
Switzerland	Ref	0.06	0.25+
Luxembourg	Ref	−0.14	−0.03
Spain	Ref	−0.09	−0.07
Greece	Ref	−0.06	0.09
Italy	Ref	0.12	0.24**
Portugal	Ref	0.29*	0.22+

Note: These models control for whether the mother was foreign-born. $^{+}p < 0.10$; $^{*}p < 0.05$; $^{**}p < 0.01$; $^{***}p < 0.001$

motherhood is commonly concentrated at the bottom end of the educational spectrum, it makes sense to continue considering whether trends away from traditional family structure are contributing to an increase of inequality in children's outcomes and life chances between those from different socioeconomic backgrounds. To answer this question, as mentioned, we need to know if single motherhood matters across several educational outcomes, and if its effects vary by maternal education.

THE RELATIONSHIP BETWEEN SINGLE MOTHERHOOD, MATERNAL EDUCATION, AND VARIOUS CHILDHOOD OUTCOMES

Table 6.3 shows the main effects of growing up in a single-mother family and mother's education on math test scores, grade repetition, and truancy

TABLE 6.3 OLS and logistic regression coefficients of effects of children's family structure and mother's education on math test scores, grade repetition, and truancy

	Math Test Scores				Grade Repetition				Truancy			
	Single Mother	Lower Secondary or Below	Upper Secondary	Tertiary	Single Mother	Lower Secondary or Below	Upper Secondary	Tertiary	Single Mother	Lower Secondary or Below	Upper Secondary	Tertiary
Australia	−18.55***	Ref	18.05***	49.47***	0.58***	Ref	−0.05	−0.05	0.44***	Ref	−0.17**	−0.30***
Canada	−11.79***	Ref	27.41***	52.52***	0.52***	Ref	−0.87***	−1.43***	0.43***	Ref	−0.33***	−0.46***
United Kingdom	−24.93***	Ref	33.22***	46.79***	0.54***	Ref	−0.62+	−0.44	0.21*	Ref	−0.31	−0.33*
Ireland	−22.39***	Ref	19.22***	45.76***	0.54***	Ref	0.09	−0.03	0.43**	Ref	0.12	0.08
New Zealand	−16.45***	Ref	25.56***	59.58***	0.56***	Ref	0.03	−0.03	0.46***	Ref	−0.49***	−0.64***
United States	−22.46***	Ref	28.63***	57.91***	0.37***	Ref	−0.42*	−0.68***	0.26***	Ref	−0.38***	−0.69***
Denmark	−17.01***	Ref	18.16***	43.84***	0.51***	Ref	0.1	−0.51*	0.50***	Ref	−0.22	−0.24+
Finland	−14.59***	Ref	17.41***	43.22***	0.89***	Ref	−0.51+	−1.00***	0.48***	Ref	−0.44***	−0.53***
Norway	−8.88*	Ref	18.40***	38.88***					0.56***	Ref	−0.54***	−0.36+
Sweden	−11.14*	Ref	33.22***	46.79***	0.47	Ref	−0.57**	−0.47+	0.63***	Ref	−0.15	−0.42***
Belgium	−24.83***	Ref	24.62***	63.21***	0.73***	Ref	−0.60***	−1.10***	0.69***	Ref	−0.11	−0.20
France	−16.96***	Ref	31.84***	66.52***	0.37***	Ref	−0.69***	−1.32***	0.43***	Ref	−0.37***	−0.11
Netherlands	−23.62***	Ref	1.05	19.96***	0.21+	Ref	−0.21	−0.35*	0.33	Ref	−0.19	0.2
Austria	−9.37*	Ref	37.70***	61.65***	0.71***	Ref	−0.49*	−0.42*	0.28*	Ref	−0.43***	−0.05
Germany	−2.93	Ref	35.51***	47.10***	0.29**	Ref	−0.59***	−0.65***	0.56***	Ref	−0.16	0.15
Switzerland	−15.60***	Ref	34.70***	43.54***	0.53***	Ref	−0.46***	−0.45*	0.30*	Ref	−0.24*	0.27*
Luxembourg	−9.00*	Ref	34.86***	61.94***	0.40***	Ref	−0.54**	−0.97***	0.45***	Ref	−0.21	−0.11
Spain	−4.80	Ref	27.26***	48.90***	0.50***	Ref	−0.61**	−1.15***	0.38***	Ref	−0.21**	−0.30***
Greece	−7.60	Ref	32.17***	60.56***	0.72*	Ref	−1.17***	−1.76***	0.17	Ref	0.1	0.05
Italy	−5.37*	Ref	37.50***	37.47***	0.78***	Ref	−0.65***	−0.70***	0.22**	Ref	−0.17**	−0.14**
Portugal	−0.82	Ref	43.27***	70.13***	0.29*	Ref	−0.95***	−1.47***	0.49***	Ref	−0.01	−0.11

Note: There are no cases of grade repetition in Norway. Background control variables (children's immigration status, age, and sex) were included in all models. +p < 0.10; *p < 0.05; **p < 0.01; ***p < 0.001

controlling for sex, age, and immigration status of the child. We have performed three separate models for each of the twenty-one countries; OLS regressions for math test scores, and logistic regressions for the other two outcomes. The effect of being in a single-mother family is significant for math test scores in all countries except Germany, Spain, Greece, and Portugal. As previous research has shown, there is substantial variation in the magnitude of this effect across countries; the largest negative effects are observed in United Kingdom, the United States, Republic of Ireland, Belgium, and the Netherlands. In all countries, the effect of having a mother with tertiary education is significant and, with the exception of the Netherlands, tertiary education has a substantially greater positive effect on math ability than the negative effect of being in a single-mother family. That is, the magnitude of the effect of tertiary education is greater than the magnitude of the effect of single-mother family. For test scores, it seems that mother's education is more important than family structure.

Turning to grade repetition, the effect of being in a single-mother family is significant across nineteen of the twenty of the nations studied (there is no grade repetition data for Norway). The estimated effect in Sweden is in line with the other countries, but not significant (b = 0.47, p = 0.125). Finland, Belgium, Austria, Greece, and Italy all show very large effects associated with single motherhood. Unlike math test scores for which the positive effect of mother's tertiary education outweighed the negative effects of single motherhood in virtually all of the countries, this is only true in slightly more than half (12) of the countries when considering grade repetition. In fact, having a mother with tertiary education did not significantly affect grade repetition in Australia, New Zealand, United Kingdom, and Republic of Ireland, and the estimated family structure effect is larger than the estimated effect of tertiary education in Sweden, Austria, Switzerland, and Italy. In all eight of these countries, family structure seems more relevant in predicting grade repetition than mother's tertiary education.

The effect of living in a single-mother family on truancy is significant in all countries with the exception of Greece (p = 0.140). The largest effects of family structure on truancy are found in Sweden, Belgium, Germany, and Norway. Unlike math test and grade repetition, the estimated effect of having a mother with tertiary education is not significant in eight of the twenty-one countries, and it is greater than the estimated effect of family structure in ten other countries. Only in the United Kingdom, New Zealand, and United States does the estimated positive effect of mother's tertiary education exceed the estimated negative effect of being in a single-mother family.

Overall, our analysis reveals substantial differences in the importance of family structure depending on the outcome studied. Growing up in a single-mother family has negative effects on math test scores in only seventeen of the twenty-one countries analyzed, while children of single mothers are more likely to repeat a grade or play truant practically everywhere. In addition, the magnitude of the coefficient of having a mother with tertiary education is clearly more important than family structure on cognitive performance in all countries analyzed, while this is only true in about half for grade repetition and around a fifth for truancy.

TO WHAT EXTENT DOES THE EFFECT OF FAMILY STRUCTURE ON
EDUCATIONAL OUTCOMES DIVERGE BY MOTHER'S EDUCATION?

We now turn to investigate whether the impact of being in a single-mother family depends on the mother's educational level. We show the main and interaction effects between family structure and mothers' education for each outcome (math test scores in Table 6.4; grade repetition in Table 6.5; truancy in Table 6.6) in every country.

Our results show important cross-country differences. The interaction between family structure and having a mother with a tertiary education is negative and significant in six countries, specifically in Republic of Ireland, United States, Belgium, France, the Netherlands, and Italy. This means that the negative effect of growing up in a single-mother family in these countries is larger when the mother is highly educated. In the United Kingdom, this interaction is also negative but nonsignificant (b = −17.55, p >0.10). We cannot rule out the possibility that the interaction would be significant if United Kingdom had a larger sample size. In contrast, having a mother with tertiary education positively interacts with family structure in Germany and New Zealand, showing that the negative effect of growing up in a single-mother family in these countries is smaller when the mother is highly educated. In the other twelve countries, the penalty associated with being in a single-mother family does not significantly vary by mother's education. Unlike tertiary education, upper secondary education conditions the effect of family structure in only three countries. In the United States and the Netherlands, the negative effect of growing up in a single-mother family is greater for children who have a mother with upper secondary education than one with lower secondary education. The opposite is true in Australia.

Turning to grade repetition, being in a single-mother home increases the odds of grade repetition more for children of highly educated mothers in the Republic of Ireland, the United States, Belgium, Spain, and Greece (shown by the positive coefficient on the interaction term in Table 6.5). In other words,

TABLE 6.4 OLS regression coefficients of main effects and interaction terms of children's family structure and mother's education on math test scores for each country

	Single Mother	Lower Secondary or Below	Upper Secondary	Tertiary	Lower Secondary or Below * Single Mother	Upper Secondary * Single Mother	Tertiary * Single Mother
Australia	−27.02***	Ref	16.41***	48.18***	Ref	12.5+	9.44
Canada	−6.62	Ref	28.64***	53.03***	Ref	−9.52	−3.18
United Kingdom	−17.55	Ref	32.5***	50.5***	Ref	7.6	−22.15
Ireland	−9.10	Ref	20.92***	48.24***	Ref	−12.14	−20.46+
New Zealand	−29.62**	Ref	23.28***	55.18***	Ref	8.78	21.69+
United States	2.89	Ref	−3.15***	65.29***	Ref	−20.41+	−36.95**
Denmark	−22.63**	Ref	17.30***	42.89***	Ref	5.73	6.59
Finland	−8.13	Ref	19.65***	44.60***	Ref	−11.02	−5.60
Norway	5.65	Ref	20.88***	41.02***	Ref	−18.13	−14.39
Sweden	−10.25	Ref	27.69***	37.63***	Ref	−1.53	−6.69
Belgium	−6.17	Ref	27.23***	66.47***	Ref	−17.72	−23.31*
France	−3.42	Ref	33.69***	70.33***	Ref	−8.90	−23.78*
Netherlands	0.68	Ref	4.65	24.68***	Ref	−22.53+	−34.52*
Austria	3.82	Ref	39.51***	62.95***	Ref	−15.59	−11.32
Germany	−14.65+	Ref	34.67***	43.48***	Ref	6.95	29.66**
Switzerland	−7.00	Ref	36.12***	44.42***	Ref	−12.48	−8.16
Luxembourg	−7.93	Ref	34.95***	62.19***	Ref	−0.75	−2.15
Spain	−5.03	Ref	26.65***	49.31***	Ref	6.12	−4.82
Greece	−9.69	Ref	32.27***	60.07***	Ref	−1.5	6.15
Italy	2.68	Ref	38.15***	38.71***	Ref	−8.39	−14.61*
Portugal	3.01	Ref	45.04***	70.15***	Ref	−14.42	−1.05

Note: Background control variables (children's immigration status, age, and sex) were included in all models. +p <0.10; * p <0.05; *** p <0.01; *** p <0.001

TABLE 6.5 *Logistic regression coefficients of main effects and interaction terms of children's family structure and mother's education on grade repetition for each country*

	Single Mother	Lower Secondary or Below	Upper Secondary	Tertiary	Lower Secondary or Below * Single Mother	Upper Secondary * Single Mother	Tertiary * Single Mother
Australia	0.67**	Ref	−0.03	−0.2	Ref	−0.7	−0.17
Canada	0.5	Ref	−0.88***	−1.44***	Ref	0.05	0.03
United Kingdom	0.39	Ref	−0.60	−0.55	Ref	−0.15	0.4
Ireland	−0.13	Ref	0.02	−0.18	Ref	0.62	0.94+
New Zealand	0.5	Ref	−0.04	0.2	Ref	0.25	−0.11
United States	−0.18	Ref	−0.53*	−0.86***	Ref	0.52	0.79*
Denmark	0.11	Ref	−0.6	−0.52	Ref	0.8	0.1
Finland	1.48	Ref	−0.54	−0.62+	Ref	0.12	−1.36*
Norway							
Sweden	−0.00	Ref	−0.61	−0.60	Ref	0.16	0.82
Belgium	0.3	−0.31	−0.32	−0.33	−0.34	−0.35	0.61*
France	0.37	Ref	0.67	−1.35	Ref	−0.16	0.17
Netherlands	−0.13	Ref	−0.27+	−0.42**	Ref	0.37	0.45
Austria	1.37	Ref	−0.38+	−0.25	Ref	−0.65	−0.92+
Germany	0.53	Ref	−0.54***	−0.58***	Ref	−0.41	−0.49
Switzerland	0.45*	Ref	−0.48***	−0.46***	Ref	0.17	0.05
Luxembourg	0.69	Ref	−0.51***	−0.90***	Ref	−0.26	−0.57*
Spain	0.35	Ref	−0.62***	−1.19***	Ref	0.11	0.35+
Greece	−0.53	Ref	−1.28***	−2.12***	Ref	1.26	2.40**
Italy	0.79	Ref	−0.63***	−0.73***	Ref	−0.21	0.2
Portugal	0.26	Ref	−0.97***	−1.47***	Ref	0.09	0.08

Note: Background control variables (children's immigration status, age, and sex) were included in all models. + p <0.10; * p <0.05; ** p <0.01; *** p <0.001

TABLE 6.6 *Logistic regression coefficients of main effects and interaction terms of children's family structure and mother's education on truancy for each country*

	Single Mother	Lower Secondary or Below	Upper Secondary	Tertiary	Lower Secondary or Below * Single Mother	Upper Secondary * Single Mother	Tertiary * Single Mother
Australia	0.59***	Ref	−0.15*	−0.26***	Ref	−0.13	−0.23
Canada	0	Ref	−0.40***	−0.51***	Ref	0.55+	0.39
United Kingdom	0.52	Ref	−0.23	−0.26	Ref	−0.34	−0.33
Ireland	0.56	Ref	0.15	0.1	Ref	−0.17	−0.15
New Zealand	0.44	Ref	−0.52**	−0.61	Ref	0.15	−0.10
United States	0.16	Ref	−0.42**	−0.71***	Ref	0.17	0
Denmark	0.51+	Ref	−0.23	−0.22	Ref	0.09	−0.07
Finland	0.3		−0.49**	0.58***	Ref	0.16	0.22
Norway	0.78	Ref	−0.51*	−0.30	Ref	−0.08	−0.36
Sweden	0.95	Ref	−0.07	−0.37*	Ref	−0.70	−0.21
Belgium	0.93*	Ref	−0.08	−0.10	Ref	−0.10	−0.43
France	0.14	Ref	−0.44	−0.17	Ref	0.41	0.31
Netherlands	0.2	Ref	−0.20	0.17	Ref	0.04	0.22
Austria	0.57	Ref	−0.39+	−0.00	Ref	−0.28	−0.38
Germany	0.75	Ref	−0.17	0.24	Ref	−0.01	−0.57
Switzerland	0.14	Ref	−0.23+	0.22	Ref	−0.02	0.34
Luxembourg	0.51	Ref	−0.24***	−0.06***	Ref	0.23	−0.37
Spain	0.32	Ref	−0.23***	−0.30***	Ref	0.21	−0.03
Greece	−0.02	Ref	0.08	0.03	Ref	0.23	0.23
Italy	−0.03	Ref	−0.19***	−0.17***	Ref	0.28+	0.46**
Portugal	0.52	Ref	−0.04	−0.06	Ref	0.22	−0.37

Note: Background control variables (children's immigration status, age, and sex) were included in all models. $^+$p <0.10; *p <0.05; **p <0.01; ***p <0.001

the cost associated with single motherhood is greater among children of the more highly educated. The opposite is true in Finland, Austria, and Luxembourg where children of less-educated mothers have a greater cost associated with being in a single-mother family. Germany shows the same pattern ($b = -0.49$, $p = 0.16$). In the remaining eleven countries, the effect of being in a single-mother family does not differ significantly between children with tertiary and lower educated mothers. In addition to that, in every country the effect of being in a single-mother family did not differ significantly between mothers with an upper secondary education and mothers with less education.

In most countries, the probability of truancy does not differ by mother's education. There are only few exceptions. In Italy, the probability of truancy among children of single mothers is higher if the mother has upper secondary or tertiary education, and the same is true among those having a single mother with upper secondary education in Canada.

DISCUSSION

The goal of this study was to determine to what extent the increase of single-mother families, especially among the less educated, is associated with an increase in children's inequality in twenty-one Western countries. To do so, we first analyzed to what extent there is a negative relationship between single-mother families and mother's education in these countries. This is important because most previous evidence on "diverging destinies" has come from the United States. We also investigated the effect of being in a single-mother family, and how this effect differs by mother's education. To do so we tested the two main hypotheses developed by the literature: The "compensatory hypothesis," which posits that mothers with a high educational level are better equipped to protect their children from the negative consequences of growing up in a single-parent family; and the "floor effect hypothesis," which maintains that children with less-educated mothers are less vulnerable to single mother-hood given that their mothers are already in a bad situation than cannot become much worse. We used multiple children's outcomes and countries in order to overcome the limitations of previous research on how mother's education conditions the effects of being in a single-mother family.

Our findings highlight substantial cross-national differences in the relationship between mother's education and single motherhood. However, less-educated mothers are generally more likely to be single mothers in most Western countries. In eleven of the twenty-one countries, there was a significant negative relationship between mother's education and the probability of being a single mother, and in four more this relationship is also negative but insignificant. More educated mothers are significantly more likely to be single in only three countries – Portugal, Switzerland, and Italy – and previous research has demonstrated that the positive gradient observed in Italy is decreasing (Garriga, Sarasa, and Berta 2015). Overall these findings indicate that the negative educational gradient toward single motherhood is not only an American phenomenon. However, to what extent does concentration of single motherhood among mothers with less education increase inequality in children's outcomes between children from different socioeconomic backgrounds?

In all countries analyzed, living with a single mother has a negative effect on at least one of the three outcomes studied. However, we also found substantial differences in the importance of family structure depending on the outcome studied. Being in a single-mother family does not have negative effects on math performance in four of the twenty-one countries analyzed, while its effect on grade repetition and truancy is significant in practically all of them. In addition, mother's tertiary education is clearly more important than family structure on cognitive performance in all countries analyzed, while this is only true in about half of them for grade repetition, and around a fifth for truancy. Overall, our results highlight that the effect of family structure is more important and consistent across countries for grade repetition and truancy than on cognitive performance. This finding accords with several literature reviews that have concluded there is less consistent evidence on the effects of family structure on test scores than on educational attainment and behavioral outcomes (Amato and Keith 1991; McLanahan 1997; McLanahan, Tach, and Schneider 2013; Sigle-Rushton, Hobcraft, and Kiernan 2005). Most previous comparative work had used standardized test scores despite of the fact that grade repetition and truancy are both important outcomes since, as mentioned, they are strongly associated with labor market and socio-emotional outcomes and risk behaviors such as drug abuse or crime (Garry 1996; Jones, Lovrich, and Lovrich 2011; Range, Yonke, and Young 2011). In other words, these additional two outcomes tell us more about the likelihood that destinies will diverge than cognitive achievement alone does; they have strong behavioral components.

With respect to how the effect of family structure varies by mother's education, our results show substantial variation across countries and outcomes. Consistent with the "floor effect hypothesis," the negative impact of being in a single-mother family is greater among otherwise advantaged children on math performance in six countries, on grade repetition in four countries, and on truancy in one country. However, we also obtained a few results consistent with the "compensatory hypothesis": The negative effect associated with being in a single-mother family is smaller among advantaged children on math performance and grade repetition in three countries.

When taking into account all three of the outcomes studied in each country, we can derive the extent to which the increase of single-mother families would increase inequality between those children from different socioeconomic backgrounds. According to Bernardi and his colleagues, the rise of nontraditional family forms will only increase inequality if single motherhood has a negative effect regardless of maternal education, or if these effects are greater among children with less-educated mothers (Bernardi and Boertien 2016; Bernardi, Boertien, and Popova 2014). One of these two possibilities is the case for all three outcomes in eleven of the twenty-one countries analyzed. For this reason, it is possible to argue that in countries such as Nordic countries, Australia, and New Zealand, there is evidence that an increase in single-mother families, especially among the less educated, implies an increase in inequality on children's outcomes. In addition, it is important also to remark that only in Germany, having a mother with tertiary education compensates for the harmful effects of being in a single-mother family on math performance; the same is true for the other two outcomes, though the interaction between family structure and education does not reach statistical significance. These findings accord with those obtained by Grätz (2015) for the probability of attending the upper track in secondary school (Gymnasium) and on school grades in German and Mathematics.

In contrast, it has been argued that if the costs associated with single motherhood are greater at higher maternal education levels, the growth of single-mother families may reduce inequality in children's outcomes and life chances between children from different socioeconomic backgrounds (Leopold and Leopold 2016). In no country are the negative effects of being in a single-mother family greater at higher maternal education levels across all of the outcomes studied. Therefore, we do not have any evidence that the growing number of single-mother family structures is consistently reducing inequality in societies. In fact, we obtained mixed findings in ten countries. For some outcomes, the negative effect of family structure is greater with higher maternal education (especially math performance) and for other outcomes, the conditioning effect of mother's education is insignificant. For example, in contrast to Augustine (2014) whose results supported the compensatory hypothesis, we found that in United States being in a single-mother family was associated with lower math test scores and more grade repetition only among children whose mothers had more education, and the odds of truancy among children in single-mother families did not depend at all on maternal education. Overall, our findings reveal that in around the half of the countries studied, the growth of single-mother families increases inequality in some outcomes and reduces inequality in others.

Alongside these contributions, the study has limitations. Foremost, due to the cross-sectional nature of the PISA data, we were not able to control for selection into single-mother families on unobserved variables and therefore, the interaction effects reported in this study may be spurious due to differences between social origin groups on the probability of being in a single-mother family (Grätz 2015). The data also did not allow testing how mother's education mattered in different types of single-mother families – single mother at birth, single mother due to parental divorce, and single mother due to parental death – and between different types of two-parent families: Biological and stepfamilies.

The findings of this study demonstrate the importance of more cross-national research on how family structure effects differ by socioeconomic status. They also indicate the need for work across a broader range of outcomes than those analyzed here such as psychological well-being. Such research is essential in order to determine to what extent there is an increase of inequalities in children's outcomes due to the growing number of single-mother families. Future research should also analyze contextual mechanisms that may explain why maternal education seems to condition family structure effects differently across outcomes and countries, such as the cross-national variations on the percentage of children in joint physical custody.

7

Family Structure and Socioeconomic Inequality of Opportunity in Europe and the United States

Diederik Boertien, Fabrizio Bernardi, and Juho Härkönen

Family demography and the study of inequality of opportunity have become increasingly intertwined over the last decades (Amato et al. 2015; Bernardi and Boertien 2017a; Cherlin 2014; Esping-Andersen 2007; McLanahan and Percheski, 2008; Western, Bloome, and Percheski 2008). An important reason underlying this trend is that family dynamics are increasingly stratified by socioeconomic background in the United States and several European countries (Härkönen and Dronkers 2006; McLanahan 2004). Given that growing up in a nontraditional family is associated with various disadvantages and child outcomes (Amato 2010; Härkönen, Bernardi, and Boertien 2017), the stratification of family dynamics could have an influence on inequality of opportunity among children. Several scholars have therefore argued that family dynamics are an important engine of growing socioeconomic inequality of opportunity (Cherlin 2014; Esping-Andersen 2007; McLanahan and Percheski 2008; Putnam 2015; Wax 2014). This argument goes back to McLanahan's (2004) "diverging destinies" thesis that several developments related to the second demographic transition, and changes in family structures in particular, have increased inequality of opportunity between children from different socioeconomic backgrounds (Amato et al. 2015; McLanahan 2004; McLanahan and Percheski 2008).

The two premises underlying the diverging destinies thesis – namely that growing up in a nontraditional family is negatively related to child outcomes and that it is a more common experience for socioeconomically disadvantaged children – have been widely documented across a large body of studies (Amato 2000; 2010; Matysiak, Styrc, and Vignoli 2014). A recent update of these trends has shown that the "diverging destinies" thesis remains relevant today (McLanahan and Jacobsen 2015). However, whether and how much variation in family structures contributes to inequality of opportunity does not solely depend on these two premises.

First, the causal effects of family structure (and transitions between them) need to be strong enough to make a difference to children's life chances. If the association between nontraditional family forms and children's outcomes is weak or reflects other pre-existing differences between families rather than causal effects (McLanahan, Tach, and Schneider 2013), variation in family structures will not have a major impact on inequality of opportunity.

Second, it matters whether family structures and transitions affect children from different socioeconomic backgrounds the same way. Recently, many studies have documented that growing up in a nonintact family has more consequences for the educational outcomes of advantaged children (Bernardi and Radl 2014; Bernardi and Boertien 2016, 2017b; Martin 2012). Hence, even though children from lower socioeconomic backgrounds might be more likely to grow up without a parent present in the household, they also appear to be affected less by the absence of a parent. If that is the case, the overall impact on differences in opportunities between socioeconomic groups might be smaller than expected.

Finally, the "diverging destinies" thesis has been especially prominent in the United States where associations of nontraditional family forms with poverty and child outcomes are comparatively large (Hampden-Thomson 2013; Heuveline, Timberlake, and Furstenberg 2003; Raymo et al. 2016) and family dynamics relatively stratified by ethnicity and socioeconomic status (Härkönen and Dronkers 2006; S. P. Martin 2006). The thesis, however, has also been claimed to apply to Western countries more in general (McLanahan 2004; McLanahan and Jacobsen 2015) where the effects of growing up in a nontraditional family could be different and less stratified across socioeconomic strata. The answer as to whether family structure contributes to inequality of opportunity is therefore likely to depend on the country studied.

In the remainder of this chapter we will briefly discuss the existing empirical evidence for the different premises that together determine the influence of family structure on inequality of opportunity. The negative associations of nontraditional family forms with child outcomes, the stratification of family dynamics, and issues of causality have been subject to extensive earlier reviews (Amato 2000, 2010; Härkönen, Bernardi, and Boertien 2017; Matysiak, Styrc, and Vignoli 2014; McLanahan, Tach, and Schneider 2013). We therefore will be relatively succinct on those topics. After discussing existing evidence on the different premises, we give an overview of a set of recent studies that has attempted to quantify the overall contribution of family structure to inequality of opportunity. In that section, we built heavily on our earlier work published in Bernardi and Boertien (2017a).

Our discussion of research on family structures concentrates on (transitions into and out of) single-parent, stepparent, and biological two-parent families. The chapter focuses on the possible role of family structure in increasing differences in life chances between children coming from different socioeconomic backgrounds, but the arguments might also be applicable to ethnic inequalities (Erman and Härkönen 2017). We focus primarily on educational and other socioeconomic outcomes. Whereas the substantive conclusions of whether and how much differences in family structures matter for the reproduction of intergenerational inequality can be different for other outcomes (such as psychological well-being), the general premises outlined above are not outcome-dependent.

FAMILY STRUCTURE AND CHILD OUTCOMES

Many children growing up in households with nontraditional family structures, such as single-mother or stepfamilies, do at least as well as their peers (Amato 2010). On average, however, they are disadvantaged on a wide range of outcomes compared to children growing up in traditional two-parent families. For instance, several studies have documented that they have lower levels of cognitive ability, noncognitive skills, educational attainment, income, and psychological well-being (Amato 2000, 2010; Härkönen, Boertien, and Bernardi 2017). These associations are in general relatively modest in size (Amato 2000) in comparison to other socioeconomic background characteristics such as parental education (Bernardi and Boertien 2016), have been relatively stable across time (Gähler and Palmtag 2015; Li and Wu 2008; Sigle-Rushton, Hobcraft, and Kiernan 2005), but vary to some extent across countries (Hampden-Thompson 2013; Pong, Dronkers, and Hampden-Thompson 2003).

What is it about family structures and transitions between them that could have an influence on children's outcomes? Some authors have argued that it is the stability of a family structure rather than the particular characteristics of a family structure that matters for children's development. The transition from one family structure type to another (e.g., the exit or the entrance of a parent or stepparent) creates a new situation to which children have to adapt, this might interfere with the development of cognitive and noncognitive characteristics (Fomby and Cherlin 2007; Waldfogel, Craigie, and Brooks-Gunn 2010). To test this hypothesis empirically, several studies compared children living in stable nontraditional families to stable two-parent families and other family forms. In general, little empirical support has accumulated for the "family stability" perspective. Single-parent families often do worse compared to two-parent families also if they are stable throughout childhood (Magnuson and Berger 2010; Mariani, Özcan, and Goisis 2017), and the separation of a two-parent family appears to be more impacting for children's outcomes than other family transitions (Bzostek and Berger 2017; Lee and McLanahan 2015).

The characteristics particular to certain family structures and transitions therefore appear to be responsible for its associations with child outcomes. The specific family structures and transitions that have received most attention are single-parent families (McLanahan, Tach, and Schneider 2013), the separation of two-parent families (Härkönen, Bernardi, and Boertien 2017), and the formation of a family including a stepparent (Sweeney 2010). Characteristics held responsible for the effects of living with a single parent include less authoritarian parenting styles, obstacles to employment for the co-resident single parent, and access to resources of the non-resident parent (Amato 2010; McLanahan and Sandefur 1994; Seltzer 2000). Parental separation, besides implying a transition to a single-parent family, can also come with family conflict and financial costs (Cherlin 1999; Kalmijn, Loeve, and Manting 2007; Pryor and Rodgers 2001; Uunk 2004). Many studies find the income losses related to parental separation to be responsible for a large part of its effects on educational outcomes (Jonsson and Gähler 1997; McLanahan and Sandefur 1994; Thomson, Hanson, and McLanahan 1994). Parental separation can also have a negative impact on psychological well-being, both in the short and the long term (Amato 2010; Härkönen, Bernardi, and Boertien 2017), which can translate into poorer educational performance. Stepparents can provide time and financial resources that can compensate for some of the disadvantages experienced by single parents. Children living with a stepparent, however, appear to be more similar in their outcomes to their peers living with a single parent compared to peers living with two biological parents (Gennetian 2005; Jonsson and Gähler 1997; Thomson, Hanson, and McLanahan 1994).

The documented association between family structure and child outcomes could also be due to endogeneity, and hence be spurious. Variation in child outcomes across groups might reflect other processes that are both related to family structures and transitions as well as child outcomes. A major suspect in this respect is socioeconomic disadvantage of parents that might influence both child outcomes and the likelihood to enter a given family structure. In many countries, socioeconomically disadvantaged mothers are more likely to have children outside a union (Perelli-Harris et al. 2010) and to separate after forming a union (Härkönen and Dronkers 2006; Matysiak, Styrc, and Vignoli 2014). Associations between family structures and child outcomes might therefore reflect socioeconomic disadvantages that were already present before family formation or before a family transition took place.

In the study of the effects of parental separation, family conflict has been marked as an additional possible source of endogeneity. Many families who break up are likely to experience high levels of conflict before separation. In that case, parental conflict might both lead to a separation and have consequences for children's outcomes. The actual separation of the parents could in that case have little extra consequences for children's outcomes (Demo and Fine 2010; Dronkers 1999; Härkönen, Bernardi, and Boertien 2017).[1]

Several methods have been employed to monitor or control away the possible influence of these sources of endogeneity (see McLanahan, Tach, and Schneider 2013, and Härkönen, Bernardi, and Boertien 2017 for overviews). Whereas in some studies associations of family structure with child outcomes disappear, they persist, at least to some extent, in most studies (McLanahan, Tach, and Schneider 2013). Associations were more often found to be spurious once looking at cognitive ability, whereas they often appeared of a more causal nature once studying educational attainment (Bernardi and Boertien 2016; McLanahan, Tach, and Schneider 2013). The actual role of family structure in affecting inequality of opportunity is therefore likely to depend on the outcome variable considered. Nonetheless, given that educational attainment is a key socioeconomic outcome, family structure appears to matter for children's chances in life at least to some extent.

PREVALENCE OF FAMILY STRUCTURE TYPES AND ITS SOCIAL STRATIFICATION

Family structure does thus appear to matter at least to some extent for children's outcomes. However, whether and to what extent variation in family structure also contributes substantially to the observed inequality of opportunity between socioeconomic groups depends crucially on whether nontraditional family forms are common, and whether variation in family structures is socioeconomically stratified.

Giving birth as a single mother has been traditionally more common among women with lower socioeconomic status, but it is still an uncommon course of events in most countries, with the Czech Republic, Russia, the United Kingdom and the United States as some exceptions (Andersson, Thomson,

---

[1] Although most analyses that attempt to estimate the causal effect of (changes in) family structure have attempted to control away the effects of parental conflict, much of the conceptual discussion on parental separation and related transitions see it as a part of the separation process. The implications of this for interpreting causal effects were discussed in Härkönen, Bernardi, and Boertien (2017).

and Duntava 2016; Mariani, Özcan, and Goisis 2017). Most episodes of living in a nontraditional family therefore start after the break-up of a two-parent family. The extent to which parental separation is socially stratified (i.e., correlated with socioeconomic characteristics) differs across countries, especially once looking at the socioeconomic status of the mother (Härkönen and Dronkers 2006; Matysiak, Styrc, and Vignoli 2014). Explanations for variation in the socioeconomic gradient of divorce often go back to Goode (1962), who argued that when divorce is relatively uncommon, individuals need resources to overcome social, economic, and legal barriers to divorce. In such situations, the socioeconomic gradient of divorce will be more positive, but this gradient is expected to reverse to negative once barriers to divorce fade out and also those with fewer resources can divorce. The supposed greater stress experienced by disadvantaged couples will eventually cause them to divorce more once barriers to divorce cease to play a key role (Boertien 2012; Conger, Conger, and Martin 2010; Härkönen and Dronkers 2006). In addition to Goode's long-standing narrative about why the socioeconomic gradient of divorce would become negative, contemporary reasons have been proposed as to why the socioeconomically advantaged are less likely to divorce. These include a higher prevalence of egalitarianism among the educated, which could stabilize relationships (Esping-Andersen et al. 2013; Goldscheider, Bernhardt, and Lappegård 2015), and greater internal barriers to divorce caused by common investments and commitment to relationships (Boertien and Härkönen 2018).

Table 7.1 shows the prevalence of different family types and the extent to which they are more common among low-educated mothers across countries. If we take mother's education as a proxy for a family's socioeconomic position, these numbers provide an indication of the scope for family structure to affect socioeconomic inequality of opportunity across countries. As discussed above, disadvantageous family types should be fairly common and concentrated among socioeconomically disadvantaged families in order to make a substantial contribution to inequality of opportunity.

The table combines information on the percentage of mothers who are single and its stratification by mother's education. This classification is based on Härkönen's (2017) results using cross-sectional data from the Luxembourg Income Study (LIS) for the period 2011–2015 (or 2006–2010 if recent data are missing).

The more prevalent single motherhood, and the more negative the association between mother's education and single motherhood, the more likely family structure is to contribute to socioeconomic inequality of opportunity. Hence, in countries toward the bottom right corner of the table, such as Australia,

TABLE 7.1 *Countries according to the percentage of mothers who are single and the educational gradient in single motherhood*

	% of Mothers Single in Country		
	<12% Single Mother	>12% but <16.8% Single Mother	>16.8% Single Mother
Gradient in Single Motherhood			
Positive/No Educational Gradient	HU, IT, RS,		
Modest Negative Educational Gradient	ES, GR, IL, TW	CA, FR, NL	EE, DE(West), IS, RU
Strong Negative Educational Gradient	KR, SI, SK,	AT, CZ, FI, LU, NO, PL	AU, DK, DE(East), IE, UK, US

Note: Based on Härkönen (2017) cross-sectional estimates of the prevalence of single motherhood using Luxembourg Income Study (LIS) data. Data refer to 2011–2015 or 2006–2010 in the case of Australia, Canada, France, Iceland, Republic of Ireland, and Slovakia. Gradient considered modest if at least 2 percentage points difference in the prevalence between lower and higher educated mothers, and strong if double as large for lower educated compared to higher educated mothers.

Denmark, East Germany, and the United Kingdom, family structure is more likely to play a role in amplifying socioeconomic inequalities, whereas this is less likely to be the case in countries toward the upper-left corner, such as Hungary, Italy, and Serbia. Estimates of the accumulated exposure toward single parenthood across childhood based on union histories indicate a similar ranking of countries (for the countries with data available), but with France and the Czech Republic being among the countries with the highest percentage of children ever exposed to single parenthood (Andersson, Thomson, and Duntava 2016).

DIFFERENCES IN THE EFFECTS OF FAMILY STRUCTURE ACROSS SOCIOECONOMIC GROUPS

A final key factor that determines to what extent family structure contributes to socioeconomic inequality of opportunity is the heterogeneity in its effects on child outcomes across groups. It could be that family structure is socially stratified and that it matters for child outcomes on average, but that its effects are restricted to socioeconomically advantaged children. In that case, its effects on socioeconomic inequality of opportunity will still be limited. In contrast, if family structure especially matters for the disadvantaged, the contribution of family structure to inequality of opportunity might be bigger than expected.

Should we expect heterogeneity in the effects of family structure according to socioeconomic status of families? An in-depth of discussion of this issue can be found in Bernardi and Boertien (2017b). Two competing expectations can be formed in that regard. On the one hand, children from socioeconomically advantaged backgrounds might have more resources to deal with the challenges posed by living in a nontraditional family form. On the other hand, children from socioeconomically advantaged backgrounds might have more to lose from an absent parent. It could be harder for nonresident parents to transmit their cultural, social, and economic capital to their children (Coleman, 1988). Following Bernardi and Radl (2014), these competing expectations can be labeled as the "compensatory" and "floor effect" hypotheses respectively (see also Chapter 6). Kearney and Levine (2017) described it in more economic terms as variation in the "marriage premium for children" according to socioeconomic background.

Studies on differences in the effects of family structure according to socioeconomic background have accumulated rapidly over the last years (Bernardi and Boertien 2017b) and do not all come to the same conclusions. Studies looking at educational attainment mostly find that children from advantaged backgrounds are affected more by parental separation (Bernardi and Radl 2014; Kearney and Levine 2017; Martin 2012; McLanahan and Sandefur 1994). A recent study on the United Kingdom (Bernardi and Boertien 2016) documented how this pattern can to an important extent be explained by changes in family income following separation. Not only do children with higher educated parents lose more family income following separation, these losses in income are also more consequential for their college attainment. Given that family income matters less for the educational attainment of socioeconomically disadvantaged children (as family income could be too low to invest in education to begin with), losses in family income due to separation are less consequential for them (Bernardi and Boertien 2016).

Results from studies on other outcomes such as cognitive ability and psychological well-being come to more mixed conclusions with both possibilities finding support across studies (Augustine 2014; Grätz 2015; Mandemakers and Kalmijn 2014; Ryan, Claessens, and Markowitz 2015). Results depend crucially on whether one looks at heterogeneity according to maternal or paternal resources, as maternal resources are often directly accessible to children living with a single parent, whereas access to the resources of the father could be more complicated. The results of most studies can indeed be aligned with a narrative where effects of family disruption are larger when maternal resources are low and paternal resources are high (Bernardi and Boertien 2017b).

The context studied also appears consequential for conclusions. For instance, Grätz (2015) provided one of the few results on Germany, and found that only the school performance of socioeconomically disadvantaged children is affected by parental separation. Studies on Italy, the Netherlands, and Sweden find smaller effects for children with resourceful mothers (Albertini and Dronkers 2009; Fischer 2007; Jonsson and Gähler 1997), but larger effects for children with resourceful fathers (Fischer 2007; Jonsson and Gähler 1997). Single-country studies on the United Kingdom and the United States in general support the conclusion that socioeconomically advantaged children are affected more by separation (Biblarz and Raftery 1993; Mandemakers and Kalmijn 2014; Martin 2012; McLanahan and Sandefur 1994).

Bernardi and Radl (2014) documented the extent to which effects of parental separation on educational attainment differ by parental education across countries. They found, overall, that socioeconomically advantaged children were affected more by parental separation than socioeconomically disadvantaged children. Importantly, however, these differences in effects were smaller or even the opposite in countries where ability tracking in schools occurs at early ages. If crucial transitions in children's school careers take place at an early age, separations taking place after that age will have small effects on children's educational attainment (Bernardi and Radl 2014), reducing the estimated influence of parental separation experienced during childhood when averaged across ages.

In general, our reading of the empirical evidence is that socioeconomic heterogeneity in the effects of family structure tends to limit the influence family structure has on inequality of opportunity. In any case, there is no strong evidence that the consequences of growing up in a nontraditional family are greater for children from socioeconomically disadvantaged backgrounds, and hence, that heterogeneity in the effects of family structure would be another factor contributing to the accumulation of disadvantages. Whether this is indeed the case is an empirical question that has so far been addressed only on few occasions.

QUANTIFYING THE CONTRIBUTION OF FAMILY STRUCTURE TO INEQUALITY OF OPPORTUNITY

We are now in a position to go back to the key question of this chapter: How large is the contribution of variation in family structures to inequality? This question has been central to many studies on income inequality and poverty. Various decomposition and simulation techniques have been used to estimate how much changes in family structure have contributed to changes in income inequality and poverty over time (M. A. Martin 2006; McLanahan and Percheski 2008; Western, Bloome, and Percheski 2008). Studies on the United States in general come to the conclusion that family structure has been consequential for inequality. A review of the literature stated that between 11% and 41% of the increase in income inequality over the last decades in the United States can be attributed to increases in female-headed households (McLanahan and Percheski 2008). Evidence for other countries is more mixed with one study arguing that family structure only matters for income inequality in the United States (Esping-Andersen 2007) and other studies finding an income inequality amplifying effect for family structure across sixteen countries (Kollmeyer 2013). A comparative study on poverty among single mothers comes to a similar conclusion (Härkönen 2017).

That variation in family structures matters for income inequality and poverty, however, does not automatically imply that it also matters for inequality of opportunity between children coming from different socioeconomic groups. Few studies have, until now, aimed to quantify the extent to which family structure could explain differences in child and adult outcomes between individuals coming from socioeconomically advantaged and disadvantaged backgrounds.

Bernardi and Boertien (2017a) presented such estimates of the contribution of family structure to socioeconomic background differences in educational attainment for four countries: Germany, Italy, the United Kingdom, and the United States. Their main question was to what extent differences in the likelihood of attaining tertiary education between children with higher and lower educated parents could be explained by family structure. Their results are summarized in Figure 7.1, which displays observed differences in college attainment between individuals with a lower (ISCED 1–2) and higher (ISCED 5–6) educated mother. These observed differences are compared to predicted differences between both groups of individuals in the hypothetical situation that all children would have grown up in a two-parent family.

Figure 7.1 reveals that, in all four countries, differences in college attainment depending on maternal education are predicted to be very similar to observed differences in the hypothetical situation that all individuals would have grown up in a two-parent household. This suggests that the explanatory power of family structure is limited.

The reasons for this result differed according to country. In Italy, the number of children living in a nontraditional family was too small (see Table 7.1) to have a major impact on inequality of opportunity. In Germany, family structure was not (yet) clearly stratified according to parental

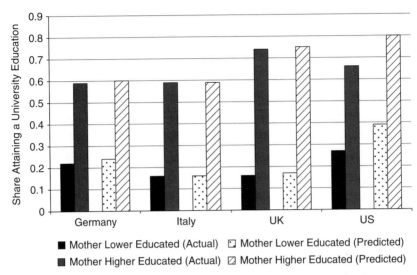

FIGURE 7.1 Actual and predicted university attainment in hypothetical situation "where all children grow up with both parents in the household"

education, preventing its influence on inequality of opportunity. In the United Kingdom and the United States children of lower educated parents were more likely to grow up in a nontraditional family structure. This was most clearly so in the United States where differences in college attainment between individuals with lower and higher educated parents were estimated to be 10% lower if family structure would not be stratified by parental education. However, in both countries children of higher educated parents were more negatively affected by growing up in a nontraditional family. This heterogeneity in effects almost entirely canceled out the effects of the stratification of family structure by parental education.

A lack of such "diverging destinies" due to variation in family structures in the United States has also been documented in another study using a similar approach (Alamillo 2016). However, evidence quantifying the possible role of variation in family structures is limited to studies on educational attainment. It could well be that socioeconomic background differences in other outcomes are amplified by variation in family structures.

DISCUSSION AND CONCLUSION

Does the result that family structure can explain little of socioeconomic background differences in educational attainment imply that family structure does not matter for socioeconomic inequality of opportunity in general? More evidence is needed before such a conclusion can be reached. The existing evidence quantifying the contribution of family structure is limited to studies on educational attainment and current research is limited to a small set of countries and time periods.

Even though tertiary education is an important socioeconomic marker, it could be that family structures and transitions between them are important for socioeconomic background inequalities in other outcomes such as income, status, health, or even secondary education. Whether this is the case depends on how strongly family structure is related to these outcomes, and how this relationship varies between socioeconomic groups. Kearney and Levine (2017) argued that the additional resources that a second parent (in their framework the father) brings to the household matter less for socioeconomically disadvantaged children when the outcome is only attained by relatively few people, as is the case with tertiary education. This may explain why higher educational attainment is the outcome for which the clearest evidence exists that socioeconomically advantaged individuals are more negatively affected by growing up in a nontraditional family (Bernardi and Radl 2014; Martin 2012; McLanahan and Sandefur 1994). For other outcomes, such as psychological well-being and cognitive ability, evidence is less uniform (Grätz 2015; Mandemakers and Kalmijn 2014).

Kearney and Levine made a contrasting argument for outcomes attained by the majority of the population, such as living out of poverty. In such cases, an inverted U-shaped pattern is predicted to be observed with both the most-disadvantaged and advantaged individuals benefiting the least from an additional parent's resources. This is because socioeconomically advantaged single parents have sufficient resources to enable their children to attain such outcomes, while for many of the most-disadvantaged children, the additional resources of a second parent would still not bring them to a level that enables them to attain "basic outcomes." If family structure indeed matters little for the attainment of "basic outcomes" by socioeconomically advantaged individuals, its contribution to inequality of opportunity might be greater once considering adult outcomes such as secondary education, employment, and living without debt. Conversely, its role in creating unequal access to outcomes attained by a smaller proportion of the population such as home ownership and other assets might be more limited because, like tertiary education, these are outcomes that advantaged individuals may be less likely to attain if they lose immediate access to the resources of a second parent in the household.

Can we expect family structure to matter more for socioeconomic background inequality of opportunity in contexts that have not been studied so far? Returning to the above discussion on the conditions under which family structure can matter provides clues to answer this question. First, nontraditional family structures have to be common and be socially stratified in order to impact on inequality of opportunity. Both the prevalence and social stratification in single parenthood have continued to increase in many countries during the latter decades (Härkönen 2017), whereas most of the above results pertain to individuals born in the 1970s and 1980s (as educational attainment was measured around age 30). Stratification in family structures can therefore have become more important for inequality of opportunity over time. The role of family structure also remains unclear in countries where educational differences in family structures are relatively large but which have not featured in previous studies (such as Australia, Denmark, and Republic of Ireland [see Table 7.1]).

Second, the (negative) effects of family structures on the outcomes studies have to be relatively strong. Family structure effects are found in each country and they have remained relatively stable over time, despite the increase in nontraditional families (Härkönen, Bernardi, and Boertien 2017). An important implication of the insight that the role of family structure in the intergenerational reproduction of inequality is contingent on effect size is that intergenerational inequality can be potentially addressed by targeting the effects of family structure on child outcomes (cf. Cohen 2015). Family structure effects on economic outcomes – such as child poverty (Härkönen 2017) – are readily modified by public policies, but findings suggesting that the effects on school performance can depend on social policies (Pong, Dronkers, and Hampden-Thompson 2003) or the features of the educational system (Bernardi and Radl 2014) support that public policies can address the consequences of family change more broadly. Family change need not inevitably lead to increasing inequality, and whether it does can depend on appropriate policy measures.

Third, the impact of variation in family structures on inequality of opportunity will be particularly large if family structure matters most for socioeconomically disadvantaged families. Many studies have shown, instead, that family structure effects are stronger for children from socioeconomically advantaged backgrounds. This particular heterogeneity in the consequences of growing up in a nonintact family reduces the contribution of family structures to the overall inequality of opportunity. It still remains unclear for many countries and outcomes whether heterogeneity in the effects of family structure exists and, if so, whether socioeconomically disadvantaged children are affected more.

All in all, however, the example from the United States is instructive. This is a context where effects of growing up in a nonintact family are large

(Hampden-Thomson 2013) and strongly socially stratified (Härkönen 2017), but nonetheless the consequences for equality of opportunity are small because of larger consequences associated with nonintact families experienced by advantaged children. Moreover, inequality of opportunity would be only 10% lower if family structure effects were homogenous across socioeconomic groups (Bernardi and Boertien 2017a). Therefore, it is unlikely that the contribution of family structure to inequality of opportunity in education will be very large in other contexts. The overall conclusion of this chapter thus remains: Currently it does not appear to be the case that family structure contributes to inequality of opportunity between children of different socioeconomic groups in a major way. This conclusion does not mean that family structure does not matter per se for children's outcomes. Children growing up in nontraditional families do, on average, differ in their outcomes from their peers growing up in stable two-parent families and are overrepresented among children living in poverty (Härkönen 2017). Family structure is therefore a factor to take into account once studying income inequality, poverty or the characteristics of the most-disadvantaged children. Overall, however, the argument that variation in family structure is a major engine behind socioeconomic inequality of opportunity is not yet empirically supported.

8

Families and the Wealth of Nations
What Does Family Structure Have to Do with Growth around the Globe?

W. Bradford Wilcox and Joseph Price[*]

One of the ironies of contemporary economics is that a discipline that has its roots in the Greek term, *Oikonomikos*, or household rules, has devoted so little attention to the familial origins of contemporary macroeconomic growth. Recent research on the sources of economic growth has instead focused largely on human capital (e.g., education) (Aghion et al. 2009), public policies (e.g., taxes and regulatory burdens) (Padovano and Galli 2001), and social norms (e.g., trust) (Bjornskov 2012; Young 1995) as drivers of growth. Important as these factors may be for growth, however, we believe that the culture, character, and composition of families in a society also matter for growth.

The importance of family composition (i.e., family structure) is the most novel of these claims. It is already recognized that the culture and character of families in different nations matter when it comes to economic growth. The East Asian family emphasis on education, for instance, may help explain the tremendous economic expansion enjoyed by the Asian tigers in the last half-century, insofar as high levels of human capital in countries such as Japan, South Korea, and Taiwan aided their rise (Hofstede and Bond 1988; Marginson 2011; Shin 2012). Undoubtedly, other features of parenting and family life are linked to patterns of economic growth across the globe as well.

We focus here on the role that family structure plays in economic growth, in particular, on how the prevalence of marriage and two-parent families is correlated with economic growth. A stable marriage matters in part because it allows couples to make decisions over time that maximize the economic prosperity of their family unit. Stably married persons have incentives to invest in their marriage and benefit from specialization and economies of

[*] We would like to acknowledge the research assistance of John Bonney and the editorial assistance of Nicholas Leaver in the preparation of this chapter.

scale; their households also tend to earn and save more than their peers who are unmarried or divorced (Stevenson and Wolfers 2007; Lerman and Wilcox 2014). Marriage also has a transformative effect on individuals, especially men. It seems to increase men's productivity at and attachment toward work, and reduces men's willingness to engage in risky behaviors, including criminal activity (Akerlof 1998; Nock 1998; Sampson, Laub, and Wimer 2006). What is more, it looks like married parenthood may be especially influential in encouraging men's engagement in the labor force (Killewald 2012). In the aggregate, then, higher levels of marriage, and probably two-parent families, should boost men's labor force participation and reduce criminal violence, both to the benefit of national economies. At the same time, insofar as motherhood tends to reduce women's participation in the labor force (Budig and England 2001), we also explore the possibility that higher rates of marriage and two-parent families reduce growth. Finally, higher rates of intact marriage foster stable two-parent families, which are more likely than single parents to supply children with the human capital they need to thrive first in school and later in the labor force (Lerman and Wilcox 2014; McLanahan and Sandefur 1994). Accordingly, the more children are born and raised in stable, two-parent families, the more a society should experience economic growth.

MARRIAGE, FAMILY, AND ECONOMIC GROWTH

The Noble Laureate, Robert Lucas Jr., has noted that once one starts to think about economic growth, it becomes hard to think about anything else (Lucas 1988). His comment reflects the fact that even small differences in economic growth rates can accumulate into very large differences in standards of living over time. Nations that create even small improvements in economic growth rates will see dramatic improvements in economic prosperity over time.

Previous research suggests that higher levels of household income and savings, male labor force participation, low levels of violent crime, and educational attainment all potentially play a role in fostering the conditions for economic growth. Here, we consider the ways in which marriage and the proportion of two-parent families in a nation may influence these factors. In this analysis, two-parent families include both married and cohabiting couples with children. Our assumption is that any effects of family structure on cross-national economic growth may be mediated in part by these mechanisms. That is, higher rates of marriage and two-parent families may foster more household income and savings, male labor force participation, public safety, and educational attainment among children, and in ways that – in turn –

promote higher rates of economic growth. At the same time, more marriage and a higher proportion of two-parent families might also inhibit growth, insofar as they reduce female labor force participation. In this section, we explore associations between the proportion of children living in two-parent families and these potential mechanisms through which we expect stable families to encourage growth. In the section that follows, we test for net effects of family structure on economic growth, controlling for country-specific fixed effects and time-varying country-level characteristics that are also likely to contribute to economic growth.

Household Income and Savings

Compared to single individuals, married households enjoy greater economies of scale, often access to more income, and higher savings rates. One might note that marriage creates a mechanical bias in household income since there are two potential earners in the family compared with only one potential earnings' stream in households with a single adult. That is exactly the point. Marriage can create two sources of income and allows the household to take advantage of economies of scale (Lerman and Wilcox 2014). Even in married households where only one spouse is in the labor force, the presence of both individuals allow them to specialize to maximize the welfare of the household and provide a natural source of insurance if the primary earner loses his or her job (since the spouse that was previously not working can enter the labor force to provide additional income) (Becker 1993). All these things are conducive to growth because they foster positive economic outcomes at the household level (which can aggregate up to the national level) (Samuelson and Modigliani 1966). They may also promote economic growth by encouraging a stronger work ethic and by reducing the need for government-funded social welfare programs (Plümper and Martin 2003).

Even compared to comparable cohabiting couples, married couples have an economic advantage. Because they enjoy more commitment and, in many cases, more legal recognition and benefits, married couples enjoy more stability. New research from the Social Trends Institute, for instance, indicates both that cohabiting families are less stable than married families in much of Europe and North America, even when they have children together, and that the growth of cohabitation across much of the globe is linked to increased family instability in countries around the world (DeRose et al. 2017). If research in the United States is representative of trends across the globe, marriage's comparative advantage in commitment and stability should

translate into higher levels of savings; married couples are also less likely to
incur expenses from a union dissolution, insofar as union instability is markedly higher in cohabiting families than in married families (DeRose et al.
2017). Indeed, stably married Americans typically accumulate more assets
than men and women who are single, divorced, remarried, or cohabiting,
even controlling for a range of background factors (Lupton and Smith 2003;
Wilmoth and Koso 2002). The income, savings, and stability advantages
associated with marriage should help to explain any advantages that countries
with more married adults and families enjoy, compared to countries with
more single or cohabiting adults.

Finally, the links between marriage and economic growth should also be
paralleled when we turn our attention to the proportion of two-parent families
in a society. Specifically, a greater proportion of two-parent families – especially when such families are stable – should promote economies of scale,
income pooling, and higher levels of savings in societies across the globe. That
is, we expect that adults in two-parent families are more likely to pool income
and devote more money to savings than adults living by themselves or heading
up single-parent families.

So, what does the cross-national evidence suggest about the links between
marriage, two-parent families, and household economic patterns? We do
not have access to data about household income in countries across the
globe, but data taken from the World Bank, the Organisation for Economic
Co-operation and Development (OECD), and the Demographic and
Health Surveys (DHS) indicate an association between family structure
and one important economic outcome, the savings rate, conducive to
growth. (For a list of the countries and years included in our data analyses
for Figures 8.1, 8.3, 8.4, 8.5, as well as for Tables 8.1 and Table 8.2, please
see our online Appendix, Table 8A.1: http://sociology.virginia.edu/media
/2696.) Specifically, Figure 8.1 indicates that the proportion of children
living in two-parent families is associated with higher savings rates in
nations across the globe. That is, in more than ninety countries, countries
that have more children living in two-parent families also have higher rates
of savings. This pattern is consistent with our hypothesis that two-parent
families foster economic behaviors conducive to economic growth.
Marriage is associated with two-parent families, but future research will
have to determine if marriage itself has a similar relationship with household saving. However, in general, we suspect that strong and stable families
foster patterns of household income and savings, both of which promote
economic growth at the national level.

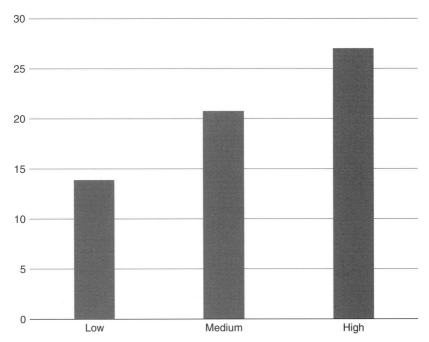

FIGURE 8.1 Gross savings as percentage of GDP, by proportion of children being raised by two parents: 2001–2015

Note: The y-axis in this figure provides the gross saving rates as a percent of GDP (World Bank national accounts data for 2001–2015). The x-axis splits the sample of countries into terciles based on the fraction of children being raised by two parentsbased on data from the World Bank, OECD, and the DHS. The sample includes 429 country-year observations from 90 countries representing the following regions: Africa (30), the Americas (11), Asia (16), Europe (30), and Oceania (3).

Male and Female Labor Force Participation

The research on men and work in the United States indicates that marriage tends to have a transformative impact on men. After marrying, men tend to work harder, smarter, and more successfully; they also are more likely to steer clear of risky activities (Nock 1998; Lerman and Wilcox 2014). In the words of Nobel laureate George Akerlof (1998, p. 290), "men settle down when they get married," adding, "Married men are much more attached to the labor force; they have less substance abuse; they commit less crime, are less likely to become the victims of crime, have better health, and are less accident prone."

The United States experience is instructive here. Over the last forty years, the drop in male labor force participation has been largest among men who are not married (see also Chapter 5). In Figure 8.2, we plot the fraction of men by family status from 1979 to 2013. This figure indicates that married fathers

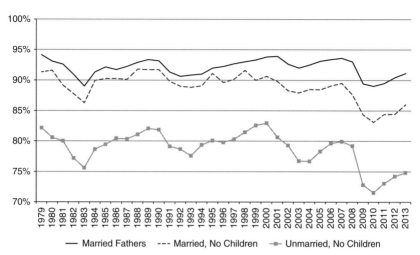

FIGURE 8.2 Percentage of 25–50-year-old men employed, by marital status
and fatherhood: 1979–2013
Note: This figure is from Lerman and Wilcox (2014).

had the smallest declines in labor force participation, whereas unmarried men
who do not live with children have seen the biggest declines in labor force
participation. That is, the fraction of married men with children who are in
the labor force has stayed relatively stable during this time period (at about 90
percent), whereas the fraction of unmarried men without children in the
home in the labor force has fallen to about 75 percent. Lerman and Wilcox
(2014) estimate that about one third of the decline in men's labor force
participation since 1979 in the United States is associated with the retreat
from marriage in the United States.

To be sure, there is a debate about whether marriage causes higher labor force
participation or vice versa. Several recent studies have noted that a contributing
factor to lower marriage rates are the lower employment prospects for less-
educated men (Carbone and Cahn 2014; Wilson 1987); however, research by
economists Ahituv and Lerman (2007) indicates that stable marriage increases
men's attachment to the labor force and their income in the United States, even
after taking into account background factors like education and job experience.
Chapter 5 also shows that less-educated men who are married are much more
likely to be working than are less-educated men who are not working.

Men's stronger connection to the labor force is also linked to a marriage
premium in personal income. Because men work more hours and work more
strategically when they are married, they tend to enjoy higher incomes than

their equivalently credentialed single peers (Lerman and Wilcox 2014). Research in the United States suggests this marriage premium is greater than 10 percent (Lerman 2011). The evidence, then, suggests that marriage is associated with both more work and more income for men in the United States. Cross-national research in fifteen countries in Europe and North America also indicates that married men enjoy an income premium in most of these countries (Geist 2006). However, much of the premium can be attributed to underlying human capital differences between married and unmarried men or to increased engagement or better opportunities at work associated with the transition to adulthood for men – rather than marriage per se (Geist 2006; Killewald and Lundberg 2017). In other words, from this research, it is not clear if marriage exercises a causal role on men's wages or, if instead, men with more human capital or better work opportunities are more likely to get and stay married.

Finally, the link between family structure and men's work seems to be particularly strong for men who are married fathers. Evidence from the United States indicates that men tend to work the most hours and garner the highest income premiums when they are married fathers than when they are in other family statuses (Nock 1998; Killewald 2012). Men may feel particularly strong internal and external pressures to provide when they are married with children to support financially. In other words, married fatherhood is associated with the greatest premium in work hours and income for men, at least in the United States.

If our expectations about marriage and fatherhood are correct, we would expect to find higher levels of labor force participation and income for men in countries with more married men or two-parent families. Here, we look at measures of men's labor force participation by the proportion of children who are in two-parent families. Specifically, we use data from the World Bank and the Demographic and Health Survey to examine the relationship between the proportion of children within two-parent families and male participation in the labor force, hypothesizing that men who are helping raise their children have additional motivation to support their families and seek employment. Contrary to our expectations, Figure 8.3 indicates that men's labor force participation for ages 15 and older is negatively associated with children living in two-parent families. Thus, at least in this international sample of more than ninety countries, we do not see evidence that more two-parent families foster higher paternal labor force participation. This runs counter to our predictions.

There is another way in which strong families, however, might weaken the economy. Strong families may reduce female labor force participation and income, which could serve as a drag on the economy. The evidence in the

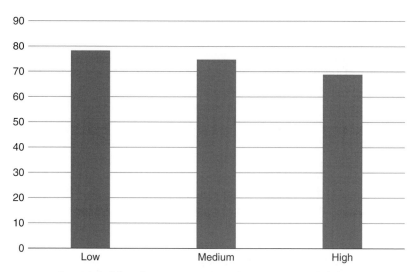

FIGURE 8.3 Male labor force participation, by proportion of children in two-parent families: 2001–2015

Note: The y-axis in this figure provides the average male labor force participation is based on the International Labor Organization database for 2001-2015 available from the World Bank. The x-axis splits the sample of countries into terciles based on the fraction of children being raised by two parents based on data from the World Bank, OCED, and the DHS. The sample includes 443 country-year observations from 97 countries representing the following regions: Africa (35), the Americas (11), Asia (18), Europe (30), and Oceania (3).

United States and Europe is ambiguous about the effect that marriage has upon women's labor force participation and income (Geist 2006; Killewald 2012; Lerman and Wilcox 2014). Motherhood, however, is associated with fewer hours, less work, and lower income for women in many countries in the developed world (Budig and England 2001; Budig, Misra, and Boeckmann 2012; Gash 2009; Harkness and Waldfogel 2003). The maternal penalty is reduced in countries where norms and public policies support mother's work (Budig, Misra, and Boeckmann 2012; Gash 2009), but the broader set of findings in this research lead us to expect that motherhood is generally associated with lower labor force participation, fewer hours, and less personal income for women.

Indeed, our analysis of data taken from the World Bank, the OECD, and DHS indicates that a motherhood penalty exists at the national level when it comes to women's labor force participation. Figure 8.4 indicates that women are less likely to be working when more children live in two-parent families. Accordingly, if

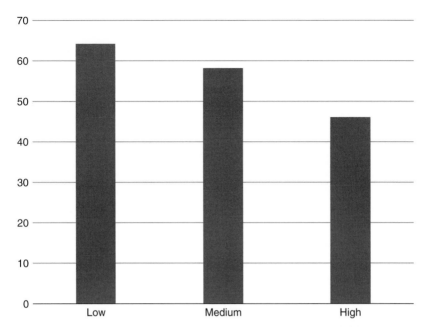

FIGURE 8.4 Female labor force participation, by proportion of children in two-parent families: 2001–2015

Note: The y-axis in this figure provides the average female labor force participation based on the International Labor Organization database for 2001–2015 available from the World Bank. The x-axis splits the sample of countries into terciles based on the fraction of children being raised by two parents based on data from the World Bank, OCED, and the DHS. The sample includes 443 country-year observations from 97 countries representing the following regions: Africa (35), the Americas (11), Asia (18), Europe (30), and Oceania (3).

strong and stable families discourage women from working, this may offset some of the positive effects that strong and stable families have on the economy.

Public Safety

The strength of the family may also influence patterns of crime at the national level. This, in turn, could have implications for the health of the economy, insofar as crime discourages economic growth (Detotto and Otranto 2010). A number of scholars (Akerlof 1998; Nock 1998; Sampson, Laub, and Wimer 2006) have argued that marriage fosters male responsibility and discourages crime. As Sampson, Laub, and Wimer (2006, p. 467) note, marriage discourages crime among men inclined to criminal activity because "it creates interdependent systems of obligation, mutual support, and restraint that impose significant costs for translating criminal propensities into action." Marriage also encourages men to engage in ordinary work-related routines, rather than deviant activities, and to spend less time with friends and acquaintances who might encourage criminal activity (Nock 1998; Sampson, Laub, and Wimer 2006). Marriage, then, is an important social control mechanism reducing the likelihood that men engage in delinquent or criminal acts.

Moreover, strong families reduce the odds that children engage in delinquent or criminal behavior as adolescent and young adults. Two-parent families tend to provide more attention and monitoring of children and adolescents (McLanahan and Sandefur 1994), both of which discourage delinquent and criminal activity. Boys, for instance, who are raised in intact-married families are less delinquent, less criminally active, and less likely to be incarcerated, according to research in the United States (Antecol and Bedard 2007; Harper and McLanahan 2004). In Sweden, substance abuse and suicide are higher among children raised in single-parent homes (Weitoft et al. 2003). At the community level, communities with more two-parent families have less violent crime, at least based on research at the neighborhood and state levels in the United States and Canada (Lerman, Price, and Wilcox 2017; Sampson 1987; Wong 2011).

The connections between family structure and crime, both at the individual and the community levels, matter because crime tends to inhibit prosperity. Specifically, high levels of crime discourage male labor force participation (Eberstadt 2016), force businesses to spend more on security, and lead to significant public-sector costs. As the economists Detotto and Otranto (2010) note, "Criminal activity acts like a tax on the entire economy: it discourages . . . direct investments, it reduces firms' competitiveness, and reallocates resources creating uncertainty and inefficiency."

How, then, is family structure associated with violent crime? Using data from the United Nations Office on Drugs and Crime (UNODC), we find a strong negative association between the proportion of children raised in two-parent families and violent crime rates. Figure 8.5 indicates that the average homicide rate is more than four times larger in the countries in the bottom third of countries in terms of children living with two parents compared to countries in the top third. This association leads us to hypothesize that strong and stable families foster higher levels of public safety. In turn, we think that lower levels of crime are linked to stronger economic growth, *ceteris paribus*, thereby helping to explain any associations between family structure and economic growth in nations across the world.

Educational Attainment

A long-standing literature suggests that higher levels of human capital increase growth (Aghion et al. 2009). Moreover, research across the developed world

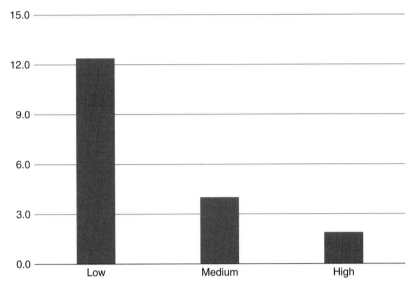

FIGURE 8.5 Homicide rate, by proportion of children in two-parent families:
2001–2015
Note: The y-axis in this figure provides the homicide rate based on data from the United
Nations Office on Drugs and Crime for the years 2001–2015. The x-axis splits the sample
of countries into terciles based on the fraction of children being raised by two parents
based on data from the World Bank, OCED, and the DHS. The sample includes 397
country-year observations from 83 countries representing the following regions: Africa
(24), the Americas (11), Asia (16), Europe (30), and Oceania (3).

indicates that children from intact, two-parent families are more likely to
flourish in school. Such children usually enjoy access to more income,
more parental attention and affection, and more stability in their lives, all of
which help them excel in school (e.g., McLanahan and Sandefur 1994). In
other words, higher rates of marriage and children being raised in two-parent
families might produce greater human capital in countries around the globe.

For instance, research in the United States indicates that children from
intact, married families are more likely to complete a high school diploma and
graduate from college, compared to children from intact families (Duncan
and Duncan 1969; Kearney and Levine 2017; Rumberger and Larson 1998;
Sandefur, McLanahan, and Wojtkiewicz 1992). Moreover, the economist
Jonathan Gruber has found that adults who were exposed to higher divorce
rates in their state as children have lower levels of educational attainment
(Gruber 2004). In general, then, research indicates not only that children are
more likely to acquire human capital in the United States when they are raised
in stable, two-parent homes, but that there are benefits to all children when
higher proportions of school children are from stable two-parent homes.

Outside the United States, children in developed countries are less likely to be held back in school and more likely to do well on standardized tests if they come from two-parent families. Children from single-parent households in countries as diverse as Sweden, Singapore, and Indonesia, for instance, are at least 70 percent more likely to be held back in school, compared to their peers from two-parent families (Scott et al. 2013). In Europe, research also indicates that children from single-parent families are more likely to skip school, compared to children in two-parent families, as Garriga and Berta point out in Chapter 6.

In general, then, in much of the developed world, children may benefit educationally from the higher levels of time, money, and stability found in two-parent families, compared to single-parent families. Given that marriage is a more stable context for the rearing of children, children are more likely to live in two-parent homes in nations where marriage is the dominant pattern when it comes to childbearing (DeRose et al. 2017). We suspect that higher rates of marriage and two-parent families, then, foster greater educational attainment. This, in turn, is probably one mechanism by which countries that have strong and stable families are likely to experience the highest rates of economic growth.

MARRIAGE AND COUNTRY-LEVEL ECONOMIC GROWTH

To test our theories about the relationships between family structure and economic growth in countries across the globe, we compile data from a number of sources. We obtain historical data on marriage rates from the United Nations Statistics Division as well as the World Values Survey (WVS), which is a survey started in 1981 designed to gather national representative samples of individuals from almost 100 countries, which collectively constitute 90 percent of the world's population, and the sample we use includes 340,000 total respondents providing on average about 4,000 respondents per country. Additionally, we merge in marriage statistics from census data from 81 countries obtained from the Integrated Public Use Microdata Series-International (IPUMS-I) database. Using the latest wave of data from all three data sets, we have marriage statistics for 129 countries scattered over a 46-year time period between 1968 and 2014, with a total of 401 unique country-year observations. Within these observations, the marriage rate is calculated as the fraction of adults who are legally married out of all adults.

We obtain historical data on the fraction of children who are living with two parents from the Organisation for Economic Co-operation and Development (OECD) and the Demographic and Health Surveys (DHS), which is a survey compilation beginning in 1984 including over 300 nationally representative surveys in over ninety countries. Combining the most recent OECD and DHS data sets, we have statistics on the fraction of children living in two-parent families for eighty-seven countries between 2001 and 2014, with a total of 416 unique country-year observations.

The other key measure of interest in our analyses is the gross domestic product (GDP) growth experienced by each country. We use data from the World Bank's World Development Indicators to obtain data on per capita GDP, adjusted for inflation. As additional controls, we also merge in information about each country's population, the fraction of the population that lives in cities, the proportion of the population under 15, the proportion of the population over 65, the education index (which taps the expected years of schooling as well as the historical average of years of schooling within each country), and the average life expectancy. Some of these measures (such as education) are likely to be influenced by family structure and so our estimates are likely to slightly the understate the actual correlation between family structure and economic growth.

We start by using a fixed effects regression to model the relationship between the economic growth and the fraction of adults who are married. The results are found in Table 8.1, indicating a positive relationship between marriage and economic growth. The coefficient indicates that a standard deviation increase (or 13 percentage point increase) in the fraction of adults who are married in a country is associated with a per capita GDP that is 8 percent higher.

The subsequent columns in Table 8.1 indicate how the size and statistical precision of this relationship between marriage and economic growth differs based on the controls that we include. Since each regression already includes country fixed effects, those fixed characteristics about each country (history, geography, natural resources) are controlled for in all of the analysis that we do. We find that the relationship is robust to the inclusion of additional time-varying controls such as population, urbanization, age distribution, education, and life expectancy. In each model, a standard deviation increase in the fraction of adults who are married is associated with about a 10 percent higher per capita GDP.

We then use a similar fixed effects model to explore the relationship between the fraction of children who are being raised by two parents in a country and its economic growth. Again, the results indicate a positive relationship (Table 8.2). The coefficient in this model is even higher and indicates that a standard deviation increase (also about 13 percentage points) in the fraction of children living with both parents is associated with a per capita GDP that is 13 percent higher. This relationship gets even larger when we include additional time-varying controls for each country. In the model with full controls, a standard deviation increase in the fraction of children

TABLE 8.1 *GDP growth by proportion of adults who are married, country-level regression*

	(1)	(2)	(3)	(4)
Proportion of Adults Married	0.0819***	0.103***	0.102***	0.106***
	(0.0297)	(0.0288)	(0.0287)	(0.0286)
Population (log)		−1.626***	−1.702***	−1.764***
		(0.377)	(0.379)	(0.377)
Percentage of Population in Cities		0.0830	0.106	0.0640
		(0.138)	(0.138)	(0.138)
Proportion of Population under 15		−0.507***	−0.526***	−0.528***
		(0.119)	(0.119)	(0.118)
Proportion of Population over 65		−0.306*	−0.304*	−0.295*
		(0.168)	(0.167)	(0.166)
Average Years of Education			−0.192	−0.206*
			(0.117)	(0.116)
Life Expectancy				0.200**
				(0.0897)
N	401	401	401	401

Note: The outcome variable is the log of per capita GDP. Each regression includes country fixed effects. All of the control variables are measured in standard deviation units. ***, **, and * indicate statistical significance at the 1, 5, and 10 levels, respectively. This includes 129 different countries. The regions represented by these countries are Africa (37), the Americas (24), Asia (32), Europe (32), and Oceania (4).

who are living with two parents is associated with about a 16 percent higher per capita GDP. Overall, then, our results indicate that marriage and family structure are both strongly linked to patterns of growth using a sample of more than eighty countries across the globe.

Our analysis has some important limitations. One of the limitations of this analysis is that we have a limited number of observations per country and can only exploit a limited amount of the full variation of data over time. In addition, the results we present are descriptive and may not represent a causal relationship for a variety of reasons, including unobserved heterogeneity and reverse causality. What we show here is that changes in the proportion of adults who are married and changes in the proportion of children who are living in two-parent homes are both strongly associated with more economic growth. We assume that shifts in family structure

TABLE 8.2 *GDP growth by proportion of children in two-parent homes,*
country-level regression

	(1)	(2)	(3)	(4)
Proportion of Children with Two Parents	0.126**	0.185***	0.192***	0.157***
	(0.0516)	(0.0505)	(0.0513)	(0.0517)
Population (log)		−0.189	−0.239	−0.242
		(0.470)	(0.475)	(0.468)
Percentage of Population in Cities		−0.0774	−0.0940	−0.134
		(0.186)	(0.187)	(0.185)
Proportion of Population under 15		−1.054***	−1.038***	−1.055***
		(0.166)	(0.168)	(0.165)
Proportion of Population over 65		−0.510***	−0.522***	−0.435***
		(0.112)	(0.113)	(0.115)
Average Years of Education			0.106	0.0232
			(0.143)	(0.143)
Life Expectancy				0.399***
				(0.121)
N	416	416	416	416

Note: The outcome variable is the log of per capita GDP. Each regression includes country fixed effects. All of the control variables are measured in standard deviation units. *** and ** indicate statistical significance at the 1 and 5 percent levels, respectively. This includes 87 different countries. The regions represented by these countries are Africa (30), the Americas (10), Asia (16), Europe (29), and Oceania (2).

predict shifts in growth, but changing economic conditions could also affect family structure. For instance, the work of economist Autor and his colleagues (2017) indicates that regional declines in employment in the United States fueled declines in marriage and increases in single parenthood in the regions most-affected by trade-related losses in employment (Autor, Dorn, and Hanson 2018).

Efforts in the future may be able to identify factors unrelated to economic growth that had an independent effect on marriage and two-parent family rates that could be used as an instrumental variable. The downside of such an approach is that it is likely that identifying factors that influence the marriage rates of a sufficiently large sample of countries may be difficult to find. We present these results as a set of interesting descriptive findings of a largely overlooked factor, family structure, which may contribute to economic growth. Future research on economic growth should seek additional ways to explore the family structure–growth connection around the world.

Research on economic growth around the globe has tended to overlook the role that family structure may play in fostering growth. This is surprising, given a large body of evidence connecting marriage and family life to factors – from education to household savings to crime – that have potential implications for economic growth. In this chapter, we hypothesize that strong and stable families are associated with higher levels of economic growth in countries across the globe.

Indeed, we find that a significant association between family structure and economic growth. Every 13 percentage point increase in the proportion of adults who are married is associated with an 8 percent increase in per capita GDP, net of controls for a range of sociodemographic factors. Likewise, every 13 percentage point increase in the proportion of children living in two-parent families is associated with a 16 percent increase in per capita GDP, controlling for education, urbanization, age, population size, and other factors. There is clearly a link between family structure and economic growth.

However, this association does not prove causation. For instance, better economic growth may encourage increases in marriage and two-parent families even as poor economic performance may discourage marriage and family stability (e.g., Autor, Dorn, and Hanson 2018). Our results cannot definitively prove that family structure has a causal impact on economic growth.

Nevertheless, we also note that the cross-national relationship between family structure, household savings, and crime are generally consistent with our expectations about how marriage and two-parent families foster a social environment more conducive to economic growth in countries around the world. It is striking that more two-parent families are linked to less crime and more savings. If nothing else, the patterns documented in this paper suggest that stronger families, higher household savings rates, less crime, and higher economic growth may cluster together in mutually reinforcing ways.

On the other hand, when it comes to labor force participation, we do not find consistent evidence that two-parent families are more or less conducive to work on the part of men or women. Not surprisingly, women in countries with a greater proportion of two-parent families are less likely to work, and surprisingly, men in countries with a greater proportion of two-parent families are less likely to be in the labor force, contrary to our expectations. On the other hand, after controlling for a number of demographic factors, our ancillary analyses indicate a positive association between male labor force participation and the proportion of children in two-parent families. Additional research ought to explore the links between family structure, men's labor force participation, and economic growth, if any.

In conclusion, this chapter indicates that strong and stable families are linked to higher levels of economic growth in nations across the globe, despite the fact that marriage and two-parent families are in decline across much of the globe. Given the potential economic importance of marriage and family stability to a nation's economic life, policymakers, business leaders, and civic leaders should pursue a range of public and private policies to encourage and strengthen marriage and stable families. That is because what happens in the family may not affect only the welfare of private families but also the wealth of nations.

PART IV

BRIDGING THE GROWING FAMILY DIVIDE

9

Family Policy, Socioeconomic Inequality, and the Gender Revolution

Frances Kobrin Goldscheider and Sharon Sassler

INTRODUCTION

As is well known, there have been major changes in family processes in industrialized countries, frequently referred to as the "second demographic transition" (SDT) (Lesthaeghe 2010; Van de Kaa 1987). These include a retreat from marriage and an increase in childbearing and rearing outside marriage, all appearing to weaken the family by reducing its centrality and stability, frequently with negative effects on its members. These changes have been linked with the growth in female labor force participation.

However, evidence is accumulating that the link between family weakening and female employment has attenuated and even reversed, at least at the macro level, as a result of continued changes in gender relationships. Female employment has become ubiquitous, even expected, suggesting that the first half of the gender revolution is advancing rapidly as women come to share the public sphere with men. Further, there is evidence that families benefit from men's increasing contributions of time to the care of their children and their homes, so that unlike the first half of the gender revolution, the second half might actually strengthen families, increasing union formation, fertility, and marital happiness, and decreasing union dissolution (Goldscheider, Bernhardt, and Lappegård 2015). Most dramatic is the fertility turnaround. The countries of southern Europe that once had the highest levels of fertility, particularly Spain, have had the lowest levels of fertility for several decades (Brewster and Rindfuss 2000; Brinton and Lee 2016). The highest fertility in Europe is now found among the countries with the highest levels of female labor force participation. However, these countries also have the world's most generous policies for reducing work–family conflict, including universal, subsidized, high-quality child care and generously paid family leave, and have the lowest levels of socioeconomic inequality of all industrialized countries (see Chapter 1).

This makes it unclear how much the pro-family effects of the continuing gender revolution are due to family policies or perhaps low levels of socio-economic inequality and how much to actual increased male family involvement. The picture is further clouded by the problem that so much research on these issues is done either in the United States, which has few policies supporting the family and drastic levels of socioeconomic inequality, or in the Scandinavian countries, which are so different in both these dimensions. There are few, if any, class differences in these pro-family patterns of increased fertility and union stability in the Scandinavian countries (Goldscheider, Bernhardt, and Lappegård 2015). In the many other countries undergoing gender change at work and at home, however, particularly those with high socioeconomic inequality, the greatest changes appear to have occurred primarily among those with the highest class positions, particularly among the most-educated (Cherlin 2016; Esping-Anderson and Billari 2015). Do these class differences challenge hopes for strengthening families among substantial segments of these populations, as Cherlin (see Chapter 3) has argued?

While we do not dismiss the importance of extrafamilial support that reduce parents' work–family conflict or the possibility that socioeconomic inequality might delay the growth in men's involvement in the family, we make a cultural argument that rests on the basic structural change in women's roles – the growth in labor force participation. We argue that changes underway reveal a broader shift in attitudes toward family roles and responsibilities that go beyond the effects of state policies and include, although often in surprising ways, members of both higher and lower classes, even in highly unequal societies. Fundamentally, there appears to be an expansion of men's roles to increasingly incorporate involvement with their homes and children in a broader array of roles than was found as recently as the mid-twentieth century. We consider studies examining whether, like other large social changes, behavioral changes linked with the gender revolution are first evident among the more educated, which can further exacerbate class differences, that then attenuate as attitude change diffuses to the wider population. We draw on examples from recent studies of gendered family behavior in order to assess the roles of family policy and inequality in delaying or accelerating the effects of the gender revolution on the family.

WHAT AFFECTS THE GENDER REVOLUTION?

Why might societies with weak or no family policies, or those with high levels of socioeconomic inequality be less likely to move toward completion of the two parts of the gender revolution? To address this question, we need to think about what factors underlie the progress of both halves of the gender revolution. We briefly summarize research on both its first part (the growth of female labor force participation) and then its second part (the growth in men's involvement in their homes and families), and see whether connections to generous family policies and low socioeconomic inequality emerge.

The Growth of Female Labor Force Participation

There is a substantial literature on factors favoring the growth of female labor force participation. In addition to the overwhelming effect of industrialization (see the review in Pampel and Tanaka (1986), in which they show that the relationship is actually curvilinear, as early increases in energy use actually forced women out of the labor force), the major classic studies have emphasized the importance of the growth in the demand for "female labor" beginning in the post-World War II years and accelerating in the later decades of the twentieth century (Goldin 1990; Mincer 1962; Oppenheimer 1970). Continued industrialization resulted in the emergence of occupations quite different from agricultural and early industrial jobs, which required both substantial physical strength and long hours. More recent research, however, has also emphasized the importance of the long-term rise in female education (Walters 1984), which began in the late nineteenth century, and led eventually to women surpassing men in the attainment of college degrees in the last few decades of the twentieth century (DiPrete and Buchman 2013). At least initially, in the late nineteenth and the first half of the twentieth century, this did not reflect reverse causality, in that the pursuit of educational attainment was justified as necessary for becoming a successful wife, mother, and homemaker (Walters 1984). Not until the growth in female labor force participation in the second half of the twentieth century did female education increase in response to the growth of economic opportunity.

The demographic transition from high to low fertility and mortality was also important, as it made it no longer feasible to define all of women's adult years as needed for childbearing and rearing (Stanfors and Goldscheider 2017; Watkins, Menken, and Bongaarts 1989). Increased earnings no doubt mattered as well, although analyses of the negative effects on earnings of women's concentration in "pink-collar" occupations (Cotter et al. 1997) suggest that women were eager to earn *anything* that could contribute more to their families than they were able to do with just their domestic skills and time. The crumbling of the "marriage bar" (Goldin 1990; Stanfors and Goldscheider 2017), which for so long prevented married women from taking many jobs, such as teaching, contributed as well.

The growth of female labor force participation emerged in response to these interrelated economic, social, and demographic changes primarily over the second half of the twentieth century. While women's employment has not reached parity with the labor force participation of men, it has reached the point where most women expect to spend much of their adult lives in employment (and most men expect their partners to do so as well). This creates an additional incentive for women to work, and to obtain more education in order to prepare for better jobs (e.g., those with more pay and better working conditions). It has also altered men's expectations of desirable attributes in a spouse; if their wives will be working, one who can earn more is preferred to one who is unlikely to earn much (Goldscheider and Kaufman 2006; Schwartz and Han 2014).

Clearly, these major changes in the structure of industrializing societies have been critical for increasing female labor force participation, and hence, are also likely to affect men's increasing involvement in the family, about which much less is known. However, if, as Cherlin and others argue, supportive family policies and socioeconomic inequality are also critical for encouraging or delaying the second half of the gender revolution, and perhaps also the first half, it is important to assess these impacts. How might social policies and greater socioeconomic inequality affect women's labor force participation, the first half of the gender revolution? We address these issues in the following sections, and then address the same issues for the second half of the gender revolution.

Family Policy and the First Half of the Gender Revolution

Until recently, few governments outside the (former) Soviet sphere of influence enacted policies explicitly to support women's employment.[1] Nevertheless, some policies developed for other purposes often affected women's likelihood of being employed, both positively and negatively. The most common direct policy involves the development of quality, subsidized child care, allowing women to outsource some of their family

---

[1] In the central and Eastern European countries under state socialism, policies supporting women's labor force participation were extensive: Child care, generous maternity leave, female education on par with male, pronatalist housing policies, birth and child allowances, and supposedly equal pay for women. Moreover, the inefficient economies created a high demand for labor, which was met by female labor (Frejka 2008). By 1990, all these countries had relatively high levels of female labor force participation, but with the abandonment of these policies, female labor force participation (and fertility) collapsed (Sobotka 2011), perhaps because none of the policies had encouraged men's participation in the tasks at home.

responsibilities (without having to involve their male partners). The United States developed an extensive network of child-care facilities during World War II, as women were needed to replace the men who had been conscripted (Skocpol 1995), although it was dismantled after the war ended.

Some other European countries encouraged female employment more permanently. The Scandinavian countries' initial response to the increased demand for labor in the post-World War II period was to encourage employment for mothers, going beyond the provision of subsidized, high-quality child care to provide up to a year of paid family leave, which allowed new mothers to maintain their connection with their employers while being able to care for their tiny infants. These countries preferred to meet the need for a growing labor force by supporting female employment rather than encouraging the immigration of male workers (while making it more likely that women would stay home), which was the policy choice taken by Germany in this period (Kamerman and Kahn 1991).

Policies with indirect effects on female labor force participation have primarily been those designed to increase fertility, although there are others, such as retirement plans and family-level vs. individual-level taxation, that have strong effects as well. As early as the 1930s, some countries experiencing dramatic fertility decline linked with the Great Depression, such as France, introduced baby bonuses, hoping to encourage more couples to take on the costs of childbearing. Others instituted family allowances and paid maternity leave, so that rather than the money being tied to childbearing, it was tied to (women's) child-rearing, often for an extended period, as in Germany.

In each case, the pro-fertility policies were designed to support a traditional division of labor in families, in which women stayed home, and could afford to stay home, to care for their families. Interestingly, there was little evidence that either of these policies was successful (Friedlander and Goldscheider 1979).[2,3] Research examining the relationship between length of parental leave and women's subsequent career progression has generally found that more

---

[2] In the 1960s, Romania took a more direct, heavy-handed approach to increasing fertility, banning abortion and contraception. While it had a dramatic short-term impact, as couples were forced to carry unwanted children to term, fertility shortly thereafter reestablished its downward trend (David 1970), as couples found alternative sources of birth control, essentially bootlegging contraception.

[3] Recent government exhortations designed to increase fertility have resulted in amused and indignant condemnation; even government officials retrospectively deride attempts to raise birth rates by appealing to nationalist sentiment. A September 2016 advertising campaign in Italy, designed to promote "Fertility Day," was withdrawn after an outraged backlash against the images. Even Prime Minister Matteo Renzi criticized the campaign: www.france24.com /en/20160903-italy-recalls-fertility-campaign-after-social-media-backlash

generous leave hampers longer-term earnings (e.g., Aisenbrey, Evertsson, and Grunow 2009).

Policies designed to reinforce mothers' ability to combine work and family might have a stronger effect on female employment, particularly by introducing subsidized, high-quality child care and job-protected, paid maternity leave. Although these policies tend to reinforce women's family roles by making the "second shift" less onerous, they also encourage the attainment of well-paid jobs, as the payments received during leave are normally tied to prebirth earnings. The need to attain a well-paid job before taking family leave also greatly reduces teen childbearing; job protection means a parent need not search for work after taking leave, which hastens the return to work even for the United States' unpaid Family and Medical Leave Act (Klerman and Leibowitz 1999).

Evidence that the provision of high-quality, subsidized child care supports female labor force participation also comes from a recent study comparing German-speaking residents in Belgium with those in an adjacent area in Germany (Klüsener, Neels, and Kreyenfeld 2013). These two regions' family patterns closely resembled each other prior to Belgium's introduction of family-friendly policies; thereafter, these two regions diverged in terms of both fertility (German fertility continued to fall while that of German-speaking Belgians did not because the German-speaking region of Belgium had much lower childlessness and higher completed family size than in Germany) and especially female labor force participation. By 2001, the proportion of mothers with children aged 0–2 in full- or part-time employment was only 30.1% in western Germany, compared with 60.5% of similar mothers in the German-speaking region of Belgium (Klüsener, Neels, and Kreyenfeld 2013). This is a clear case in which family-friendly policies not only support higher fertility but also, even more clearly, increase female labor force participation.

However, as we will discuss below in our consideration of the effects of policy on the second half of the gender revolution, policies that encourage men to share more of the family leave appear to have been even more successful in incorporating men into the care of their homes and families. Whether or not such policies are necessary for increasing men's involvement in the care of their homes and families, as we will see, they clearly help.

Inequality and the First Half of the Gender Revolution

Although the relationship between family policy and female labor force participation is fairly clear, that between socioeconomic inequality and female labor force participation is much less so. The primary studies have focused either on macro-level analyses of countries' levels of female labor force participation, mostly from the 1980s, or on more microstudies of how changes in inequality focused on how husbands affect married women's response. More problematic (and interesting) is the fact that given a rapid change in behavior, there is also a substantial change in the relationship between women's behaviors in the family and economic context.

The first major macrostudy (Semyonov 1980) undertook a comparative analysis of the social context of women's labor force participation. The study used data from sixty-one countries for the 1960s and 1970s and found that women were less likely to be economically active in societies where inequality was high. This was followed with an analysis of a much narrower set of countries (sixteen) but which included longitudinal data for five time points between 1955 and 1975 (Ward and Pampel 1985). In contrast to the broader analysis, however, this study found that increases in inequality increased female labor force participation. There were a number of other differences between the two studies, including the controls applied, however. It is not clear whether further studies of this question have been undertaken.

There are more, and more recent, analyses, primarily by economists, which examine how the labor force participation of married women responds to their husbands' earnings, motivated by the rapid increase in inequality in men's earnings and the initially high level of women's responsiveness to their family's economic well-being. Early studies of female labor force participation showed that family characteristics had a larger impact on married women's employment than the women's own characteristics. Small children were a major deterrent to married women's employment, as was husband's income; women were much more likely to work if they had no small children and their husbands' incomes were low (Blau and Kahn 2007). Hence, increases in inequality of male incomes have contributed to the increase in female labor force participation, as the growth-in-inequality losers (the number of men with low incomes) is always far greater than the growth-in-inequality winners (the number of men at the top of the earnings pyramid). The relationship between inequality in men's earnings and female labor force participation, however, is not strong, because while declines in male employment and earnings have been greatest for low-wage men, employment and earnings gains have been largest for wives of middle- and high-wage men (Juhn and Murphy 1997). This is because over the last few decades of the twentieth century, American women's labor force participation became much more responsive to their own characteristics (education, work experience) than they had been in the past (Leibowitz and Klerman 1995), so that in this way they became more like men. Further, educational homogamy has strengthened, so that inequality at the family level increased, as highly educated men and women married and both earned, while couples with few resources struggled (Karoly and Burtless 1995).

The Growth of Male Family Involvement

Any attempt to understand the growth of male involvement in the tasks of their families and homes must first recognize that not that long ago, men were highly involved in such tasks: Training their children and providing wood, water, and far more to their homes in the household-based agricultural economy. With industrialization came the construct of "separate spheres" as men left agriculture and took on the industrial and commercial jobs that were emerging in the new economy, leaving women behind in the home. It took more than a century until the social, economic, and demographic changes underway reached the point where women could join men in the public sphere as well. By then, the home had taken on its gendered nature, as a place for women and children (Stanfors and Goldscheider 2017), making it more challenging for men to include domestic tasks as part of their responsibilities.

Men resist not only the gendered tasks in the home, which causes a problem in their relationships, but also the gender-linked tasks in the labor market, which is a problem for their role as provider, given that, with the decline in agriculture, the decline in manufacturing has meant that the jobs "real men" used to take have been vanishing (see Chapter 3). We know much less about the factors that increase men's involvement in the home, and hence the progress of the second half of the gender revolution, than we do about the growth of women's labor force participation, but it is important to examine what we do know, particularly how it might be linked with family policy and socioeconomic inequality, as Cherlin worries (see Chapter 3).

Family Policy and the Second Half of the Gender Revolution

Many of the Scandinavian countries (and Quebec) have developed policies to address the second half of the gender revolution directly, by encouraging men to take a portion of what is now called "family" (rather than "maternity") leave (Duvander and Johansson 2015). Such policies require that, to gain, and not lose, the full benefit, each parent has to take some of the paid leave. If only one parent takes family leave, the duration is less than if each parent takes some, with lost leave ranging from one to three months. As a result, nearly all couples take at least the minimum required for the second parent (often called "daddy days," given that women continue to take most family leave). In Norway, 89% of fathers take most or all of the daddy days, with similar levels in Iceland (88%) and Sweden (86%) (Haas and Rostgaard 2011). Evidently, even managers in private industry do not want their workers to actually lose a paid benefit.

A major problem with assessing the impact of policies on citizens' behavior is whether the causal arrow is being correctly interpreted. Perhaps only more egalitarian countries enact egalitarian policies. Alternatively, men who take advantage of such policies may be selective, in that they are just more family-oriented than other men. In Sweden, for example, the fact that men who take more family leave with a first child are more likely to go on to have additional children than those who take less (Oláh 2003) might just reflect their greater family orientation. However, a recent study addressed this latter issue. Duvander (2014) has shown that although Swedish men with more familistic attitudes do indeed take more family leave, this is also the case for men with more egalitarian attitudes (controlling for their attitudes toward families).

The question of path dependency – that more egalitarian countries are more likely to enact egalitarian policies – is challenged by a recent analysis of trends in men's home involvement in the United States compared with the Scandinavian countries. Despite (or perhaps because of) the lack of policies reducing work–family conflict, the United States' levels and trends in men's share of housework and child-care time closely approximate those in Scandinavia (Stanfors and Goldscheider 2017). This is despite the fact that the ratio of female to male labor force participation is considerably lower in the United States than in the Scandinavian countries – about 85% in 2014 compared with ratios closer to 95% in Norway, Sweden, and Finland – reflecting the lack of public policies, such as child care, that support female labor force participation (Frejka, Goldscheider, and Lappegård 2018). This suggests that more US families are forced to depend on male involvement (perhaps coupled with shift work) to care for children while both parents are employed than in countries with policies reducing work–family conflict.

Another series of studies that attempt to hold cultural values (and hence path dependency) constant but vary potential family policies are "experiments" done in the United States (e.g., Pedulla and Thébaud 2015; Thébaud and Pedulla 2016). Respondents were young, unmarried, and childless, and were asked about their future work–family arrangements (essentially, who should be the primary earner and who the primary homemaker). In one study (Pedulla and Thébaud 2015), some respondents were randomly provided a scenario that asked them to imagine that there were policies in place that included paid family leave, subsidized child care, and the option to work flexible hours, and then asked about their preferred work–family balance. The results were dramatic, at least for women. More highly educated women (those with some college education or higher) who were told these policies would be virtually universal chose a work–family balance of equal sharing (94.5%) compared with similar women who did not receive this information (more than 30 percentage points less). Among less-educated women, the differences were also sharp, but smaller (82.2%, given the presence of these family-friendly policies; over 20 percentage points more than similar women who could not assume the presence of such policies).

Interestingly, men were much less responsive to the presence or absence of family-friendly policies (and differences were not significant). This finding suggests that men who had not confronted the possibility of work–family conflict had not really thought about it. Nevertheless, a substantial majority of men – both those with some college or more and those with high school or lower – gave egalitarian responses (about 70%).

A second study (Thébaud and Pedulla 2016) explored this gender difference, and established that men's preferred work–family arrangement was conditioned by their understanding of their peers' attitudes, not policy. The results showed that in scenarios where supportive work–family policies were available, men who were asked to assume that most of their peers preferred gender-egalitarian relationships were significantly more likely to prefer such arrangements for themselves. The researchers did not test to see whether similar results would have obtained if men had partners who did or did not prefer egalitarian relationships, or whether the families they had grown up in featured father involvement in the domestic sphere, which also has a strong impact on men's domestic participation (Lahne and Wenne 2012).

Inequality and the Second Half of the Gender Revolution

There is no question that in many parts of the industrialized world there are sharp differences in domestic sharing by socioeconomic status (Evertsson et al. 2009), as there are in other family patterns. In the United States, socioeconomic differences in family patterns seem to reflect nearly different universes (Lundberg and Pollak 2015), as Cherlin has dissected in his most recent book (Cherlin 2016), and as do Sassler and Miller (2017). The college-educated are currently far more likely to get and remain married, have children within marriage, and yet experience relatively egalitarian work–family relationships than those with educational levels of high school or lower, shaping what Sara McLanahan (2004) has termed the "diverging destinies" of young Americans from more and less advantaged backgrounds. Cherlin (2014) therefore argues that the second half of the gender revolution may only be emerging among the more educated (and perhaps most rapidly in a context of strong state support for families).

The issues revealed in recent research suggest that the patterns are extremely complex, which makes tracking class differences particularly challenging. Most fundamentally, the "private sphere" of family tasks is heterogeneous (like the public sphere), with the biggest divides between child care and housework, and within those two categories, between routine and less routine activities (Craig and Mullan 2013) and between taking responsibility and implementation (Raley, Bianchi, and Wang 2012). As we will show, men's entry into this complexity has varied over time and by class.

For example, men's time in child care and housework has been increasing more rapidly on weekends rather than weekdays (Neilsson and Stanfors 2014), a pattern that favors men with regular hours. Co-resident men are more involved than those who do not live with their children, which also favors the more educated, who are less likely to separate from their children, in part because their behaviors often undermine relationship stability as well as consistent child involvement (Barber et al. 2017; Cherlin, Chapter 3; Edin and Nelson 2013). Nevertheless, many non-co-residential fathers remain involved (Tach, Mincy, and Edin 2010).

Further, context appears to matter as well. Far more research is needed to disentangle these issues, but here we will focus on the effects of class (normally indicated by her education, but sometimes by his) on housework and child care, the second half of the gender revolution. We focus primarily on class differences and changes in child care. Child care is more consequential than housework, as perhaps the most fundamental domestic investment activity. Housework is both less problematic to ignore (beyond the most basic level) and easier to outsource. There is also considerable variation in how housework is measured over time, and too few studies have empirically explored class differences in the ways that dual career couples juggle family responsibilities.

The general finding is that fathers with more education are more involved with child care than fathers with less education. In the United States, more educated fathers have particularly increased their involvement in basic caregiving and teaching time, and have increased their belief in the importance of fathers in children's lives (Amato, Meyers, and Emery 2009; Hofferth et al. 2014; Raley, Bianchi, and Wang 2012; Sayer, Bianchi, and Robinson 2004). These findings are similar to those from a cross-national study of four countries (Australia, Denmark, France, and Italy) (Craig and Mullen 2013), that found, as well, that it was fathers' education rather than mothers' that mattered.

Nevertheless, a growing body of both quantitative and qualitative research is documenting that less-educated men are also viewing child care involvement as a central role (Carlson, Hanson, and Fitzroy 2016), but may perform their engagement differently than do fathers who are professionals (Edin and Nelson 2013; Shows and Gerstel 2009). Some research suggests that although men in the working/service classes express strongly gender-differentiated views, they often find themselves actually *living* quite egalitarian lives (Usdansky 2011). This finding reinforces a concern that such men might understate their household contributions.

THE CHANGING GENDER REVOLUTION

Might these effects of family policy and class on men's involvement in the tasks of their homes and families, the second half of the gender revolution, also be changing, much as changes have occurred in the determinants and consequences of women's labor force participation, the first half of the gender revolution? If so, do these changes suggest that we should be more or less worried about the necessity for supportive family policies and the problems of socioeconomic inequality for the possibility of gender equality in the home (Cherlin 2014; Cherlin, Chapter 3), and the demographic benefits of higher fertility and more stable unions gender equality seems to be linked with? This trend is a relatively new one, even newer than the growth of female labor force participation, and many changes take time.

That change takes time is evident in a study that focused on the effects of family policies, which appear to be strengthening, at least in Scandinavia. It addressed the question of under what circumstances couples adjust their balance of work and care in a more traditional direction after the birth of a child, and under what circumstances they do not. All research, starting with studies of United States couples of the 1970s (e.g., Morgan and Waite 1987), had found such a "traditionalization" until Dribe and Stanfors (2009) showed that while Sweden in the 1980s and 1990s had followed this pattern, this was no longer the case starting about 2000. Neilsson and Stanfors (2013) found the same pattern for the other Nordic countries. These are countries that had had such policies for nearly a generation, yet their impact was clearly increasing.

Neilson and Stanfors (2013) also explored changes for other countries, such as Germany, Italy, and Canada, where policies are less supportive of families, to see if similar changes were observed. They found that in all the non-Scandinavian countries they studied, gender differences had attenuated, at least to some extent, though the traditionalizing effect of parenthood had not totally vanished. In addition, in both Canada and Germany there was a considerable move toward equality on weekends, which is also the case in the United States (Yeung et al. 2001).

Further, there has been considerable growth in the prevalence of family supportive policies. New, stronger policies have been introduced in Canada (in Quebec), Germany, and the United Kingdom. Even in the United States, individual states have introduced policies that reduce work–family conflict by providing some paid family leave (California, New Jersey, New York as of 2018, Rhode Island, and perhaps the District of Columbia). Hence, to the extent that the growth in family-friendly policies supports the second half of the gender revolution, it seems unlikely that a major slowdown is in prospect.

The effects of socioeconomic inequality on sharing in the home also seem to be changing. A widely found pattern is that the more educated lead many types of social change, so that differences by education widen early in the change process and then attenuate as the new behavior diffuses more generally. More educated women led the decline in breastfeeding early in the twentieth century, and led, as well, its resurgence in the last third of that century, followed by the less-educated (Goldscheider and Waite 1991). Sullivan's (2010) research on men's involvement in the private sphere of the family supports this model. She examined changes in British and United States' men's contribution to domestic work and child care and found differences by education that were attenuating for housework, as the less-educated "caught up" with the more educated, yet differences were widening for child care, as the more educated led the later increase. In a further study, Sullivan, Billari, and Altintas (2014) found a fertility "catch-up" in countries with lowest-low fertility that also experienced recent increases in the contribution of younger, more highly educated fathers to child care and core domestic work. They interpret this result as suggestive evidence for a process of cross-national diffusion of more egalitarian domestic gender relations.

Other evidence comes from studies of gender-role attitudes. Most prominent among these are two analyses by Pampel (2011a,b). The first analyzes the relationships between education and gender-egalitarian attitudes in historical depth for the United States and finds for the range of cohorts born between 1900 and 1985 that structural change leads to adoption of new ideas and values supportive of gender equality by the more educated, but that the new ideas later diffuse to other groups through cultural processes. He obtains similar results in a cross-national study of roughly the same cohorts born in nineteen countries, showing that the effects of education first strengthen early in the growth of gender egalitarianism and then weaken as other groups come to accept the same views.

These results reinforce our view that studies indicating the power of educational differences in gender-related behavior are really showing a transient barrier to the progress of the gender revolution. Clearly, there is considerable resistance to men's sharing more at home, reflecting the continued strength of what is sometimes called "gender essentialism": the view that men and women are fundamentally different, making it appropriate that men should be providers and women carers. To the extent that men and women hold these views, men are less likely to want to share family responsibilities (and women are less likely to want them to do so).

However, while class appears to be linked with ideas about gender essentialism, with those in lower positions clinging more strongly to gender-typed behavior, it seems that these differences are changing and that there is class convergence. Unfortunately, ideas about gender essentialism are common not just among young adults making decisions about their planned work–family balance, but also among family scholars who promote ideational approaches to the analysis of gender roles. The most prominent in this group are Catherine Hakim (2001), Arland Thornton (2001), and Ron Lesthaeghe (2010).

Of these, Hakim is perhaps the most strident, claiming in her analysis of "preference theory" that most women would prefer to be employed no more than part-time, with little consideration that such a preference might reflect the lack of family-friendly policies (and sharing partners) that reduce women's work–family conflict. A recent test of Hakim's preference theory (Vitali et al. 2009), for example, examined links between individual-level preferences and both fertility outcomes and fertility intentions in a variety of settings. Counter to expectations based on the theory, they found that while there was the expected relationship between actual fertility and work–family lifestyle preferences, there was no relationship with fertility intentions.

Others have found no association between fertility intentions and employment outcomes among highly educated women, suggesting that constraints (discrimination), more than preferences (ideation), operate to shape women's employment choices (Cech 2016; Sassler et al. 2017). In fact, Hakim's argument that women's work decisions are predominantly based on their personal preferences has been met with fierce criticism (e.g., Crompton and Lyonette, 2005; Halrynjo and Lyng 2009; Hechter, Kim, and Baer 2005; McRae 2003; Stahli et al. 2009). Those who have used various data sets to test her theory generally find that country-level policies and social context play more important roles than preferences in women's employment retention or return after childbearing.

Thornton and Lesthaeghe are more oblique, in that Thornton sees gender equality as part of a set of ideas he calls the "developmental paradigm" (Thornton 2001) that falsely promotes the expectation for universal change, in this case, toward gender equality, while Lesthaeghe (2010) considers gender issues too minor to notice more than briefly. There is no question that attitudes toward gender essentialism have potency, at least in the short term. A recent paper (Brinton and Lee 2016) shows that an important factor in maintaining lowest-low fertility in southern Europe and East Asia is the high level of gender essentialism and hence the lack of supportive social policies in these regions that support male involvement in family roles.

Nevertheless, other research increasingly finds that young men coming of age in the early twenty-first century express desires for greater family involvement, even if they expect to assume the traditional provider role (Gerson 2010), and that more involvement is associated with positive outcomes, such as greater sexual frequency and satisfaction with sexual relationships (Carlson, Hanson, and Fitzroy 2016). There is also much evidence, including by Thornton and Young-DeMarco (2001), updating an earlier paper by Thornton and Freedman (1979), that gender essentialism eroded rapidly in the 1970s and 1980s in the United States. There remains, however, a substantial level of essentialism among young adults, particularly young men with less education (England 2011; Sassler and Miller 2011).

Although Cherlin (2014) argues that contemporary women will continue to reject young men who are unlikely to be strong providers as marital partners, there is a solid body of quantitative and qualitative evidence that such views do not preclude cohabiting unions (Kaufman 2000; Sassler and Goldscheider 2003; Sassler and Miller 2011; Smock, Manning, and Porter 2005) and childbearing (Edin and Kefalas 2005; Tach, Mincy, and Edin 2010). The increasing proportion of unions in which the female is the primary provider suggests the strength of these views is eroding (Raley, Mattingly, and Bianchi 2006; Vitali and Bruno 2016). Additionally, long-established views that men will be more educated than their partners have eroded as women surpass men in educational attainment; in fact, couples where the female partner has more education than the male partner are now no more likely to disrupt than when couples are educationally homogamous (Schwartz and Han 2014). Although the least economically attractive men may be less desirable as partners and parents, this may be more a result of their behaviors – substance abuse, violence, infidelity, and incarceration – than their role as providers (Barber et al. 2017).

Further, men who enter into marriage may increasingly be drawn from those who express and exhibit more gender-egalitarian views. Qualitative research on cohabiting couples in the early twenty-first century has found that men who anticipated more equal sharing of household chores, as well as men who actually participated more in household labor, were considerably more likely to become engaged over time, and their partners were more satisfied with their relationships, than were those who performed little household labor (Miller and Sassler 2010; Sassler and Miller 2017). This is a shift from what was found among those cohabiting in the 1970s and 1980s, when egalitarian men were more likely to cohabit than marry directly, relative to young adults expressing more gender-conventional views (Clarkberg, Stolzenberg, and Waite 1995). Further, 1980s cohabiting couples who exhibited more conventional divisions of labor had a greater likelihood of transitioning into marriage than their couple counterparts who engaged in more egalitarian divisions of labor (Sanchez, Manning, and Smock 1998). This is now much less the case (Miller, Sassler, and Kusi-Appouh 2011). Less-educated men, in contrast, often express a disinclination to assume responsibility for household labor (Sassler and Miller 2017). In fact, some have suggested that the weaker partnering options for the most economically disadvantaged men can, in part, be due to their rejection of available jobs that are often in gendered occupations like caregiving or nursing, where steady employment could translate into their becoming more marriageable (Reeves and Sawhill 2015). There is evidence that this, too, is changing, particularly among minority and immigrant men (Roos and Stevens 2018).

CONCLUSION

This review of studies examining the determinants of the two halves of the gender revolution, and in particular, the effects of family-friendly public policies and socioeconomic equality, does not strongly support Cherlin's concerns that the absence of these two features present a serious barrier to the ongoing gender revolution. Certainly, female labor force participation is facilitated by the availability of subsidized, high-quality child care, together with a program of family leave that keeps infants home for much of their first year of life. Yet the evidence from the United States of high male participation in family life suggests that these policies also substitute for male involvement in the home, delaying the second half of the gender revolution. Children gain when public policy promotes parental leave, because the combination of six to twelve months of family leave and high-quality child care gives children the developmentally ideal form of care – from parents in infancy and thereafter from skilled professionals in the company of other children as toddlers. An analysis of Nordic family policies concluded that the major gainers from these policies were children, who experience great continuity of care and high levels of parental investment, followed by men, who gained closer relationships with their children. Even in these countries, however, women still find themselves juggling the tasks of work and family, their long leave-taking delays their career development (Bjornberg 2013) and if they have more than one child (sequentially) reduces their earnings (Stanfors and Nystedt 2017).

Socioeconomic inequality might be more of a problem for the spread of gender egalitarianism, but the evidence suggests that it too can be addressed (see, for example, higher levels of paid leave provided for less economically advantaged parents in California). Nevertheless, even in the short term, the major problem with high levels of socioeconomic inequality, particularly in the absence of family-friendly policies, is that children suffer. What are needed are policies that ease not only women's work–family conflict but also men's good provider conflict. As Cherlin emphasizes, it is not just that men in the lower half of the income distribution are too "essentialist" to attract a modern partner, but that they are too poor to do so. They have increasing difficulty attracting a long-term partner, and hence the opportunity for any co-resident parental relationship. Further, the decrease in male, otherwise known as "good" jobs, that in the United States context come with health benefits, sick and family leave, and savings for eventual retirement, is increasingly a problem for men who want to form and maintain a family. As automation reduces the numbers of such jobs, policies that would make men's family lives better would have to include some sort of permanent income floor.

Thus it seems that inequality and the lack of family-friendly public policies will certainly not prevent the completion of the second half of the gender revolution, although they might impede its progress. With the ending of the separate spheres, many women will no longer be barred from more productive work to the economic benefit of their families and national economies. Further, many men will be able to develop richer and deeper relationships with their children as they can spend more time with them and with their partners, whose lives they can more fully share, benefiting them all. This does not mean that a totally equal life will be normatively required for all couples, which would likely be a straitjacket as confining as the separate spheres. As the gender-orientation revolution has allowed men and women to choose partners of whatever sex their fundamental biology has programed them for, and yet still be able to parent, so heterosexual men and women can chose lives and partners that let them express whatever balance of masculine and feminine characteristics they feel most comfortable with (Udry 1994).

10

Where's the Glue? Policies to Close the Family Gap

Richard V. Reeves

INTRODUCTION

When a childless couple divorces, how much should we care? If they are friends, we might feel sad for the individuals involved. The end of a romantic relationship almost always means some pain and some loss imposed on others. Equally, we might be relieved or happy that they are able to move on, perhaps to a happier relationship. Adult decisions affecting adults are one thing; it is quite another when children are affected. Hence the concern with *family* breakdown, rather than simply divorce or separation, especially among policymakers.

When addressing these issues, it is important to be as clear and specific as possible about the nature of the problem – or problems – being addressed. The "family divide" may refer to differences in rates of births outside marriage, rates of marriage, duration of marriage, rates of single parenthood, family stability, family structure, rates of divorce, parental engagement after divorce, parenting styles and investments, just to mention just a few. The gap can also be examined through the lenses of income, education, race, age, geography, and so on. Which gap, or gaps, are the ones that really count?

Answering that question requires us to answer another one first. What are we worried about? Poverty? For children, or adults too? Child development? Moral goodness? Well-being? Health? Rates of intergenerational mobility? Public expenditure? Given the strong interconnections between many of these, it may seem like splitting hairs, but unless we have a clear grasp of what problem we are trying to solve, and what success will look like, policy is likely to follow a scattergun approach and be less effective as a result.

I argue that we should care about family gaps because we care about poverty and inequality, and because we care about intergenerational mobility. Policy interventions may influence both of these, but more often aim at one more than the other.

I argue for policies of two kinds with regard to family stability, applicable to the United States and most European countries: Prevention and mitigation.

- *Preventing* family instability means helping families stay together in the first place, through policies that reduce unintended pregnancy rates, raise skills (especially through quality vocational training), and promote "family-friendly" work opportunities.
- *Mitigating* the family instability means attempting to limit the impact of family breakdown on the life chances of children. Mitigation can be achieved by reducing material poverty, supporting better parenting, and enhancing learning opportunities. Here, the need is for a "One Generation" approach, largely focused on children's outcomes.

I conclude with a note of humility. The reach of public policy is necessarily limited here. Sex, love, marriage, child-rearing; these are intimate, emotional, personal, and complex issues. By comparison to family policy, foreign policy is a breeze. The forces influencing changes in family life are tectonic, a combination of evolving social norms and public morality, and the shape and structure of the labor market. Still, there are policies that can and should be pursued. Strong families are not a quaint relic of the past. They are a necessary ingredient of a better future.

The "Family Gap"

Other contributors have detailed key trends in family life, especially the rise in nonmarital births, single parenthood, and increased relationship turnover. In the United States, four in ten children are born to unmarried parents; among women under 30, the number is closer to half. In most cases the mother is cohabiting; but only a minority of cohabitees are still with their partner by the time the child reaches five (McLanahan and Sawhill 2015). Two thirds have split up before their child reaches age 12, compared with a quarter of married parents (Kennedy and Bumpass 2008).

The "stability gap" between cohabiting and married couples can be seen in all countries and at every level of education (DeRose et al. 2017). In Norway, for example, children born to highly educated cohabiting mothers are twice as likely to see their parents' relationship end before the age of 12 as those born to highly educated married mothers (17 percent vs. 8 percent).

While there is a stability gap between married and cohabiting couples, there is also stability gap by social background. Rates of lone parenthood vary widely by education, race, and income. College graduates are unlikely to become single parents, compared to those with less education (Reeves 2017). Six in ten black children are in a single-parent family, almost double the rate for white and Hispanic children (Reeves and Rodrigue 2015a). The "retreat from marriage" has been much more rapid among less-educated, poorer Americans (Reeves 2014b).

Indeed, on every measure of family stability, including rates of unintended pregnancies and births, marriage, single parenthood, and divorce, there are wide, and in many cases, widening, gaps by education, income, and background. Trends in poverty, income inequality, or intergenerational mobility cannot be properly examined in isolation from trends in family life.

REASON TO CARE 1: POVERTY AND INEQUALITY

The economic circumstances of families are influenced by a wide range of factors, including rates of employment, levels of wages, welfare eligibility, job security, capacity to save, housing costs, and so on. One very simple factor – how many adults are in the household – has a significant impact. Two (or more) adults means two potential earners and two potential carers. Two adults living together reap big savings, since one home is cheaper than two. The way the federal government defines poverty gives some idea of that difference. Dispensing with the idea that either the mother or father has to be labeled the "head" of the household, it is clear that, other things equal, two heads are better than one.

The federal poverty levels, flawed in many ways though they are, put some numbers to these assumptions. The federal poverty level (FPL) for a single parent with two children in 2015 was $20,090, while for a family of two adults and two children, the FPL was $24,250 (US Department of Health and Human Services 2015). In other words, the additional adult only has to bring an additional income of just over $4,000 a year to enable the family to get above the official poverty line. It is no surprise then that almost 60 percent of children in poverty are being raised by a single mother, or that the household income of married parents is higher than for single parents (Entmacher et al. 2014; Thomas and Sawhill 2015).

From an economic point of view, the "two heads better than one" point is pretty obvious. A more interesting question is why the household income of married parents is so much higher than of cohabiting parents. Three main possibilities present themselves: (1) they are older, so have higher earnings; (2) their earnings are higher for reasons other than age (e.g., education, hours, or motivation); (3) their rates of employment are higher, with a higher chance of either of them working, of both working, and of one or both working full-time.

It looks like all of these factors play a role; but rates of employment are a big part of the story. Married women with children have increased their labor force participation rate faster than any other group, including single mothers (Engemann and Owyang, 2006). In 1970, about half of married couples with at least one child younger than 18 in the household had two paychecks coming into the home. By 2015, this had increased to two thirds (Parker and Livingston 2017). The model of twenty-first century marriage is of two breadwinners.

Sawhill and Karpilow (2013) highlight the strong link between household poverty and household structure. They model the impact on incomes for families in bottom third of the income distribution from various "what if" scenarios: More employment, higher wages, greater educational attainment, and more two-adult households. They estimate that the average single parent would see a 32 percent increase in her income if she were joined by another adult – far and away the biggest impact they report. None of this is to suggest, of course, that family structure is the principal cause of poverty, let alone that policies to promote family stability are the necessary response; indeed, the causes of poverty – for example lower education, poorer health, higher risks of incarceration – are also likely, other things being equal, to reduce marriage-ability and stability. However, it is fair to say that examining trends in poverty without taking into account changes in family structure results in an incomplete picture.

REASON TO CARE 2: LACK OF UPWARD INTERGENERATIONAL MOBILITY

At any particular time, the structure of family life will, then, influence rates of income poverty, and by extension income inequality. However, there are longer-term concerns, in particular, family stability has a strong influence on life chances and therefore on rates of intergenerational mobility. It may take a village to raise a child, but it takes a family, too.

Children of divorce have lower rates of both absolute and relative income mobility compared to kids whose mothers are continuously married between birth and nineteenth birthday. Children born to unmarried mothers have lower rates of relative mobility than kids of continuously married parents, though there are not significant differences in absolute mobility (Deleire and Lopoo 2010). Simple descriptive differences in relative mobility patterns for children raised in different family types are striking, as a number of studies (including my own) have shown (Reeves and Venator 2014), as seen in Figure 10.1.

(a)   **Growing up with a continuously married mother:**

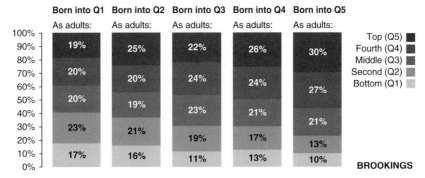

(b)   **Growing up with a non-continuously married mother:**

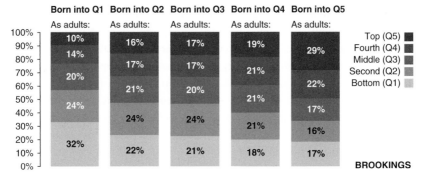

(c)   **Growing up with a never married mother:**

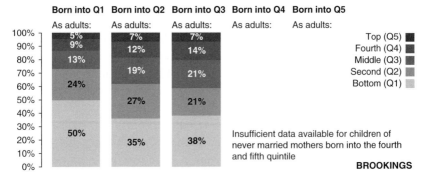

FIGURE 10.1 Intergenerational mobility by wealth quintile at birth
and family inequality

There are also quite big differences in the numbers of children falling into these three categories: 11 percent are raised by mothers who remain unmarried throughout their childhood (as far as our data constraints allow us to say), 39 percent by a mother married for at least part of their childhood, and 50 percent by continuously married mothers (Reeves and Venator 2014). The dismal mobility prospects of the first group – half of those born into the bottom quintile staying there – reflect a series of disadvantages that reach well beyond material poverty.

Children living with a single mother score lower on academic achievement tests, get lower grades, have a higher incidence of behavioral problems, and experience a greater tendency toward drug use and criminal activity (Autor and Wasserman 2013; McLanahan 2004). The impact of family breakdown appears to be greater when fathers lose contact. Daughters are more likely to have sex at a younger age and to become pregnant as a teenager (Ellis et al. 2003). Boys seem to be influenced most strongly by the absence of a father. Boys from single-mother-headed households are 25 percentage points more likely to be suspended in the eighth grade than girls from these households, compared to a 10 percentage point gap between boys and girls from households with two biological parents. Boys are also more likely to engage in delinquent behavior during adolescence and early adulthood if raised in single-parent household with no father in lives (Autor and Wasserman 2013). In his groundbreaking research drawing on administrative tax data, Professor Raj Chetty and his team show that rates of upward mobility are lowest in the areas with the highest proportion of single parents (Chetty et al. 2014a).

There is an important distinction here between family structure and family stability. What seems to harm children the most is a lack of stability, that is, a changing composition of the family unit, as different adults move in and out during childhood. As Manning (2015) concludes after a review of child health, "the family experience that has a consistent and negative implication for child health in both cohabiting and married parent families is family instability." However, certain family structures, namely marriage, are associated with greater stability. Married couples are very much more likely to stay together, and it is this family stickiness that provides a positive and stable environment for children, as seen in Figure 10.2.

It certainly looks as though marriage both expresses and enables the commitment of parents to raise their children together. The decision to marry in the twenty-first century is closely connected to a decision to become parents. As I have written elsewhere, for many married couples, especially the most-educated, marriage provides an important commitment device for shared child-rearing (Reeves 2014b). It should not be surprising then that most

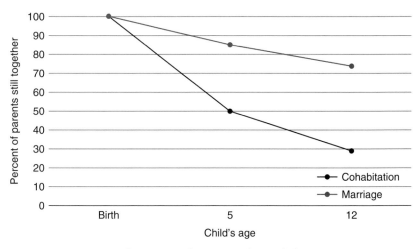

FIGURE 10.2 Staying together: married vs. cohabiting parents

pregnancies within marriages are planned, and that most pregnancies outside marriage are not.

Stability is more likely to come through marriage; but marriage and stable families are not the same thing. Take J.D. Vance as an example. In his best-selling book *Hillbilly Elegy*, he describes the chaos of his early childhood, with a drug-addicted mother perpetually moving between homes and partners (Vance 2016). In the end, he finds some family stability: With his grandmother (who he calls Mamaw):

> Now consider the sum of my life after I moved in with Mamaw permanently. At the end of tenth grade, I live with Mamaw, in her house, with no one else. At the end of eleventh grade, I live with Mamaw, in her house, with no one else. At the end of twelfth grade, I live with Mamaw, in her house, with no one else . . . What I remember most is that I was happy – I no longer feared the school bell at the end of the day, I knew where I'd be living the next month, and no one's romantic decisions affected my life. And out of that came the opportunities I've had for the past twelve years.

Mamaw becomes, in effect, Vance's single parent, having separated from her own husband. The point here is not that marriage does not matter, but that it matters most as a means to the end of family stability. "No one's romantic decisions affected my life." In a stable marriage, the romantic decision-making predates the arrival of the children.

Not all marriages are stable; not all stable homes feature a married couple. From an inequality perspective, it is striking that marriage is now strongest among the upper middle class, with college graduates much less likely to have a child outside marriage, more likely to be married, and more likely to make their marriages last (Blau and Winkler 2017). Although the most liberal on general social issues, including same-sex marriage, college graduates are now the most conservative on divorce (Reeves 2014b).

Upper middle-class families tend to be quite stable, but for low-income and, increasingly, middle-income Americans, family formation has become a more complex business. More parents now have multiple relationships while raising their children, a trend the sociologist Andrew Cherlin (2010) describes as a "Marriage-go-Round." As Sawhill (2014) puts it in her book, *Generation Unbound: Drifting into Sex and Parenthood without Marriage*, "family formation is a new fault line in the American class structure."

The rising disparity in earnings for both men and women is therefore amplified by class gaps in the chances of being in a relationship where resources and risks can be shared, but highly educated Americans are not just more likely to be married, they are more likely to be married *to each other*. This process, with the stunningly unromantic label of "assortative mating," means that college grads marry college grads. To the extent that cognitive ability is reflected in educational attainment and passed on genetically, assortative mating is likely to further concentrate advantage. As the British sociologist Michael Young (1958) put it in his book *The Rise of the Meritocracy*, "Love is biochemistry's chief assistant."

The class divide in family formation, structure and stability reflects and reinforces the opportunity gap vividly outlined by writers such as Robert Putnam (2015) in *Our Kids* and Charles Murray (2012) in *Coming Apart*.

WHAT TO DO 1: NARROWING THE GAP

So, what to do? The editors of this volume have asked me to "present policy solutions and cultural changes that will narrow the growing family divide in the West or minimize its effects on children." Nothing too difficult, then, but their framing is helpful, since it makes clear the difference between "policy solutions" and "cultural changes," as well as between those that "narrow the family divide" and those that "minimize its effects on children."

First, I will address some possible approaches toward narrowing the family gap, both in terms of policy and culture. My focus here is on the US policy context, though many of the lessons and dilemmas are more broadly applicable. In the next section, I will turn to some options for minimizing its effects on children.

One of the reasons policymakers often shy away from discussions of family structure and stability is that both issues feel beyond the reach of policy. The changes affecting family life are not only economic, but also cultural, as social norms regarding sex, gender relations and child-rearing have altered. Equally, economic shifts, for example in the earning power of women, have altered cultural norms around the timing of marriage, premarital sex, and divorce.

However, there are a number of ways in which policy could help to encourage and support family stability, especially in terms of reducing unintended pregnancy and childbearing; improving the quality of education and training for young adults not headed to four-year colleges; reducing the unpredictability of work schedules; and helping parents to balance paid work and family life through paid leave arrangements.

Supporting Family Planning

The vast majority of Americans become sexually active before marriage: To be precise, 95 percent compared to 80 percent in the 1970s. One in three has had at least six sexual partners before marrying (Daugherty and Copen 2016). Social norms on this issue have evolved even more quickly than behavior. Most Americans aged between 15 and 35 (58 percent of women and 68 percent of men) agree with the following statement: "It is all right for unmarried 18 year olds to have sexual intercourse if they have strong affection for each other" (Daugherty and Copen 2016).

Sex (between a man and woman) usually holds the promise – or threat – of resulting in pregnancy. Of course, effective contraception can prevent this, but not enough couples are being "planful," to use Paula England's phrase, about their fertility (England et al. 2016). There are now highly effective, convenient forms of contraception available, known in wonky circles as LARCs (long-acting reversible contraceptives), but only a minority use them. Over a five-year period, among those relying solely on condoms for contraception, 63 percent will get pregnant. For women using the best IUDs, the rate is just 1 percent (Reeves 2016), but progress toward greater promotion of LARCs among policymakers and health professionals has been slow. As a result, among sexually active women aged 15 to 24, just 10 percent use a LARC method of contraception. By comparison, around 20 percent of women in their early 20s report using an illegal drug in the previous month (US Department of Health and Human Services 2014). When there are twice as many young women using an illicit drug as using an effective contraceptive, we can be sure there is room for improvement.

We care because unintended childbearing is significantly associated with poorer child outcomes (Haskins, Sawhill, and McLanahan 2015; Sawhill 2015). It is hard to read Robert Putnam's book *Our Kids* and not notice the recurring pattern of chaotic starts to parenthood (Putnam 2015). Darleen got pregnant two months into a relationship with Joe, her boss at Pizza Hut. "It didn't mean to happen," she reports. "It just did. It was planned and kind of not planned." David, an 18-year-old in Port Clinton, Ohio (Putnam's home town), becomes a father. "It wasn't planned," David says. "It just kind of happened."

Given the rapid liberalization of social norms regarding sex but slow take-up of effective contraception, it should be no surprise to learn that 50 percent of pregnancies are unintended (Coleman and Garratt 2016), or that 60 percent of births to single women under age 30 are unplanned (Sawhill 2014). The high rate of unintended pregnancies and births, especially among women in their 20s, has serious implications for poverty, inequality, public spending, housing, and health care provision. There is a strong class dimension to this story too; women from affluent families are more likely to use contraception, much more likely to use the most effective kinds, and very much less likely to have an unintended pregnancy or birth (Reeves and Venator 2015). One reason for this is that young women from affluent families are more likely to be in regular contact with health providers, who often prescribe contraception for other health issues such as menstrual cramps. Although hard to pinpoint empirically, there is no doubt that unintended pregnancy and childbearing – what Sawhill and Venator (2015) call "drifting" into parenthood – is a very big factor influencing family stability. When a couple become parents by mistake, which is true of most cohabiting couples, it is little surprise that their relationship is less likely to endure than those who plan, as seen in Figure 10.3.

Ensuring access to affordable, effective contraception is the most powerful pro-family policy available. For a start, this means ensuring equal access to family planning services. Even if the Affordable Care Act (ACA) is repealed in the United States (which seems highly uncertain at the time of going to press) we must hope legislators see the value of this element of the plan. If not, geographic inequalities within the United States may deepen as many states are likely to bolster their own efforts in this area.

It is worth noting here that if all states had implemented Medicaid expansion under the ACA – at a cost to the federal government of around $952 billion over ten years – millions more low-income women would have been able to access family planning services more easily (Holahan et al. 2012; Ranji, Bair, and Salganicoff 2016). (Vice President Mike Pence, as Governor of Indiana, was one of ten Republicans accepting Medicaid expansion under the ACA.)

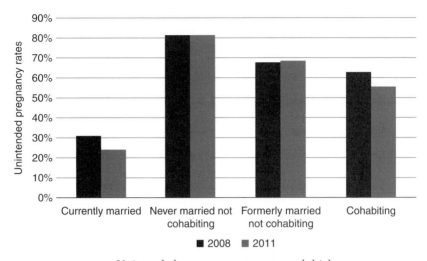

FIGURE 10.3 Unintended pregnancy rates are much higher among unmarried couples

There is also a need for greater awareness-raising and training among health professionals. Indeed, staff training alone seems to have a significant impact on the take-up of LARCs, according to a randomized control trial. The work of organizations like *UpStream* training providers in states including Ohio, New York, Texas, and Delaware is extremely promising.[1] Other steps can be taken to broaden access, including ensuring sufficient supplies in health clinics, simplifying billing procedures, and providing same-day service.

What is most needed here is a cultural shift, specifically with regard to responsibility around childbearing. Premarital sex among adults is now the norm, both in terms of attitudes and behavior. Nine in ten US adults under 44 now have sex before they marry (NSFG 2016). What is needed is a cultural shift toward more planfulness in childbearing, as Sawhill (2014) argues:

> The old norm was "don't have a child outside of marriage." The new norm should be "don't have a child before you want one and are ready to be a parent." If children were wanted and planned for, they would be better off.

I think this is exactly right. The key is to ensure that the liberalization of attitudes toward sex does not lead to a liberalization of attitudes toward the

---

[1] For a description of UpStream's approach, see www.upstream.org/impact/ (accessed March 22, 2017).

moral responsibility to plan when, how, and with whom we bring children into the world. Casual sex may be fine; casual childbearing is not.

Here the popular media is likely to be much more important than policy-makers or pundits. As work by Kearney and Levine (2015) shows, MTV's *16 and Pregnant* had a measurable impact on teen pregnancy rates.

There are, nonetheless, ways policymakers can nudge cultural change along toward more responsible parenting, and use of effective contraception. Sawhill and Venator (2014) propose social marketing campaigns to increase awareness of pregnancy risks and to inform individuals about the most effec-tive forms of contraception, modeled on Iowa's "Avoid the Stork," Colorado's "Prevention First," and other similar initiatives. Specifically, they propose that $100 million a year of Title X money be invested through the Office of Population Affairs to state-led campaigns. On fairly conservative assumptions, they predict $5 of savings from each $1 spent on well-crafted campaigns.

Skills and Education: Not Just BAs

Family poverty and instability are strongly associated with employment status, security, and wages, which in turn are greatly, and increasingly, tied to levels of education and skill. The United States is particularly weak in the area of vocational training, compared for example to most European countries. Germany provides a particularly strong model. One important step forward would be to elevate the status of vocational postsecondary learning. The obsessive focus on four-year degrees is now starting to do some real harm, as inexperienced, unprepared students are taking on debt in order to attend low-quality, often profit-seeking institutions. Many drop out, meaning that they end up with the downsides of debt without the upsides of higher earnings potential (Akers and Chingos 2016).

Community colleges, which have so much potential as an engine of upward mobility, remain "America's forgotten institutions," in Darrell West's (2010) phrase. "Two-year colleges are asked to educate those students with the great-est needs, using the least funds, and in increasingly separate and unequal institutions," was the conclusion of an expert task force assembled by The Century Foundation (2013). Fewer than half of those enrolling in com-munity colleges make it through their first year. Six in ten community college students need some extra developmental or remedial education when they arrive (Complete College America 2012).

Given the growing economic, racial, and social divide between two-year and four-year institutions in the United States, there is a strong case for some Title I-style federal investments in community colleges, increasing funds for those working with the most challenging students. Other important steps include simplifying and streamlining the pathway through community college, as Thomas Bailey, Shanna Jeggars, and Davis Jenkins (2015) argue in their book, *Redesigning America's Community Colleges* (Reeves and Rodrigue 2015b); improving transfer options from two-year to four-year colleges (Reeves and Rodrigue 2016); and providing more academic support (most community colleges are able to fund one academic adviser per 800 to 1,200 students). (Bailey, Jeggars, and Jenkins 2015).

Apprenticeships offer another promising alternative pathway to traditional college-based education, especially for young men. Improving earnings potential may increase the chances of family stability. Providing more vocationally oriented options at high school is a fruitful avenue too; it is striking that the only educational intervention shown to increase marriage rates among men is Career Academies (Kemple and Willner 2008). These typically work with around 200 students from grades nine to twelve, and combine academic and technical learning around a specific career theme. They also establish partnerships with local employers to provide work-based learning opportunities.

Family-Friendly Jobs

Many households now need two incomes; and huge changes in women's education opportunities, aspirations, and labor market participation have rendered the old breadwinner-male plus homemaker-wife model almost obsolete. Most families need to juggle paid work and raising children, but the workplace is still often constructed around previous norms. As a result both men and women can become stretched. Very often policy is focused on extending the school day, or providing child care at unusual hours, essentially attempting to create job-friendly families, rather than family-friendly jobs.

Two potential areas for policy illustrate the potential for promoting more family-friendly jobs. Paid leave for both mothers and fathers would ease the pressure on families, especially when children are young. There is some bipartisan interest in this issue, and right now, the United States is the only advanced country without a national paid leave policy. President Trump's proposals in this area are restricted to women. Senator Marco Rubio has proposed a 25 percent tax credit for companies that provide at least four weeks of paid leave to employees. A joint AEI-Brookings working group on this issue has recommended a new federally mandated right to paid leave. (AEI-Brookings 2017).

Another area of potential reform is in relation to the unpredictability of hours for paid work, especially in lower paid jobs. Four in ten hourly workers aged 26 to 32 learn their schedules less than a week in advance, according to a study by Lambert, Fugiel, and Henly (2014) at the University of Chicago, drawing on the National Longitudinal Survey of Youth (NLSY). Half of them have children. Among the 74 percent of workers who report weekly fluctuations in hours, average hours varied by 49 percent of their "usual" weekly hours. A 10-hour week can follow a 30-hour week. Half have no say over their hours.

Policymakers have some ideas about stabilizing hourly employees' schedules, some of which have been put into practice. San Francisco passed a bill requiring employers to set schedules at least two weeks in advance (Ludden 2014). Similar legislation has previously been introduced into the US Congress (Kasperkevic 2014). Some business-owners oppose these efforts, and successful legislation will have to balance the interests of employees and firms. Policymakers who are serious about family stability, though, have to be serious about job stability too.

It is worth mentioning here one area of policy that I have not argued for: Direct marriage promotion. This is partly because of a liberal sensibility about governments lecturing adults on how to conduct their lives, but also partly because such efforts rarely work. In the case of marriage promotion, extensive evaluations of various projects funded under the "Building Strong Families" (BSF) initiative have shown little if any impact. The summary of the evaluation reads as follows: "After three years BSF had no effect on the quality of couples' relationships and did not make couples more likely to stay together." As Haskins (2014) concludes:

> Given the resources invested in the Bush marriage initiative and the programs' quite limited success, there is little reason to be optimistic that programs providing marriage education and social services on a large scale will significantly affect marriage rates.

Of course, in just the same way that public individuals and institutions can use their voices to promote contraceptive use and responsible childbearing, they could also send out a much stronger pro-marriage message, to "preach what they practice," in Charles Murray's (2012) phrase. This was in fact one of the recommendations of a AEI-Brookings working group on poverty and opportunity (AEI-Brookings Working Group 2015).

My own view is that the way to promote marriage is to promote the things that predict and bolster marriage, rather than as a head-on goal of policy. Delayed, responsible childbearing; greater economic security and resources through better education; and more family-friendly workplaces. These will likely lead to more marriage, and to more stable families, which is what we are really after.

WHAT TO DO 2: MITIGATING THE EFFECTS OF THE FAMILY GAP ON CHILDREN

The second part of my brief is to examine policies and cultural changes that could "minimize the effects of the family divide on children." There have always been big differences in family background by social class, but these have become bigger, and likely more consequential, too. Given that so many children are being raised in families of different shapes and sizes, and with different levels of stability and resources, a key goal for policy is to reduce the impact of family instability, or lack of familial resources on the life chances of children. Otherwise family instability simply repeats itself, generation after generation.

Strategies to mitigate the effects of the family gap fall into three broad categories: Increase material resources to unmarried parents; improve parenting skills especially among the less educated; and enhance learning opportunities for children outside the home.

Enhance Material Resources

One reason children in single-parent, or cohabiting, or unstable households do less well is simply that they are more likely to be poor. A straightforward solution then is to give these families more money, through transfer payments, tax credits, higher minimum wages, or some combination of all of these. Great care however needs to be taken to structure support in a way that does not reduce incentives for paid work or for family formation.

The big question is how far extra money will go in producing better outcomes for the children, especially given that any increases are likely to be fairly modest. The evidence here is that cash does make a difference. Studies of the Earned Income Tax Credit (EITC), for example, show that in families receiving higher payments, test scores go up (Duncan, Morris, and Rodrigues 2011). Even college enrolment numbers seem to be positively affected (Manoli and Turner 2015). Russ Whitehurst summarizes a series of studies that link increased EITC payments to the performance in school of children in the home, and estimates that, for each $1,000 spent on a higher credit, bigger increases in test scores can be observed that in most studies of pre-K education or smaller class sizes (Whitehurst 2016), as seen in Figure 10.4.

These effects are not trivial, but they are not large either. Given the huge differences in outcomes between children from different backgrounds, the best we can hope for is a modest lessening of the disadvantages faced by children in poorer homes. It also seems likely that there will be considerable

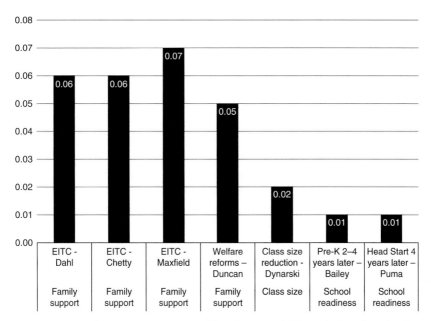

FIGURE 10.4 Impact on test scores of low-income children during the school years: reports in effect size of $1,000 of public expenditure on family support, class size reduction, or school readiness

heterogeneity in the relationship between additional income and child outcomes. EITC recipients, by definition, are active in the labor market, and while far from comfortable, financially speaking, they do not make up the poorest household, which typically lack wage income. There is however, some evidence that access to food stamps is associated with better health and, at least for women, better long-term economic outcomes (Hoynes, Schanzenbach, and Almond 2016).

Improve Parenting

To say that children are deeply influenced by their parents, for good and for ill, is to state the obvious. In earlier work with Kimberly Howard on the parenting gap, I showed stark inequalities in parent quality across class and family structure. Children from under-resourced, less stable families are more likely to have parents who are struggling to parent well, which hinders their opportunities (Reeves and Howard 2013). Waldfogel and Washbrook (2011) estimate that parenting behavior (including maternal sensitivity, reading to a child, out-of-home activities, parenting style, and expectations) explains about 40 percent of the income-related gaps in cognitive outcomes for children at age 4. There are large gaps on measures of parenting by income, education, race, and family structure (and of course these strongly overlap with each other). Focusing specifically on the last of these in Waldfogel and Washbrook's data, family structure, shows that the odds of being raised by a strong or weak parent (in fact, in these data, mother) varies significantly across household types. Single or cohabiting mothers are significantly more likely to fall into the weakest parents category. However, controlling for other variables, including income and education, the specific effect of being unmarried drops sharply. This suggests that it is the circumstances and traits that are associated with being an unmarried mother that are important, not just the fact of being unmarried itself. Nonetheless, improving the skills of parents, if this is possible, would go a long way to mitigating some of effects of the family gap on child outcomes.

Is it possible, though? Perhaps. Some home visiting programs, aimed at strengthening parenting, have shown positive results (Reeves and Rodrigue 2015c). Initiatives targeting reading, such as the Home Instruction for Parents of Preschool Youngsters (HIPPY) program, seem to improve literacy among children. For example, the DC Briya/Mary's Center program may be effective in giving parents skills and building clusters of opportunity in the mold of the Harlem Children's Zone (Butler, Grabinsky, and Masi 2015). This is a policy area where not only constant, high-quality evaluation is required but there also looks to be some real potential. Early indications are that the Trump administration is turning away from funding for home visiting. This would be premature and almost certainly counterproductive in terms of promoting family life.

Here too the cultural side is likely to have much stronger effects than policy. There are some signs that in some dimensions at least, such as reading to children, the parenting gap is beginning to close, as less-advantaged parents "catch up," resulting in some narrowing of school-readiness gaps, too (Reardon and Portilla 2016). That parenting styles diverge by class is hardly news. In recent decades, however, time investments in parenting toward the top of the distribution have increased, widening the gap. At the same time, the importance of parenting is now being appreciated more broadly, altering behavior more generally, and potentially narrowing the gap again (Ryan et al. 2015).

Enhance Learning Opportunities for Children Outside the Home

If children are negatively affected by their home and family circumstances, the natural inclination for policymakers is to try and improve those circumstances, for instance, through greater redistribution of money or by upskilling parents, as described above. However, it may be that mitigation for family circumstances will lie outside the family, in the shape of better formal education, access to mentors, stronger and safer communities, and so on.

Here I restrict my attention to two potential areas for nonfamily interventions to help mitigate the family gap: More intensive schooling and better communities. Schools can extend the length of their day, and the length of their year. Many charter schools do so. In many cases here the goal is, either explicitly or implicitly, to keep the children *away* from their families and neighborhoods. Going further still, some schools catering to students from very disadvantaged backgrounds have become boarding schools: The SEED schools in Baltimore, Washington, DC, and Miami provide one example, though there are many others. These schools are expensive, for obvious reasons; and research suggests a higher rate of return from extended-day charters (Curto and Fryer 2014). The effects are not trivial, though: "We show that attending a SEED school increases achievement by 0.211 standard deviations in reading and.229 standard deviations in math, per year of attendance." Boarding schools are likely to be most valuable to students from the most-disadvantaged, unstable backgrounds, but so far, little evaluation of impact for students of different types has been undertaken.

Another way to improve the nonfamily environment is through housing policy, and specifically through programs that allow and encourage low-income families to move to more affluent neighborhoods. Recent studies suggest that Moving to Opportunity (MTO), which provides vouchers that enable families to move, have positive long-term effects for children. Specifically, moving to a less poor neighborhood in childhood (i.e., before the age of 13) increased future annual income by the mid-twenties by roughly $3,500 (31 percent), enhanced marriage rates (by 2 percentage points), and raised both college attendance rates (by 2.5 percentage points) and quality of college attended. The age of the child moved was a critical factor: Moving to a less poor neighborhood in the teenage years had no significant impact on later earnings or other adult outcomes (Rothwell 2015).

The causal factors of these improved outcomes are inevitably hard to tease out. However, the wealth of sociological research on the importance of place suggests that a mixture of school quality, peer effects, social capital, physical security, and safety all likely played a part. Children of single parents benefit from moving to an area where they are the exception, rather than the rule. One important point about the MTO is that the short-term impact on the adults looked to be virtually nonexistent; it was the next generation who really benefited from the move.

CONCLUSION: THE NEED FOR JUDICIOUS POLICY

Wide gaps in the formation, structure, and stability of families contribute to the broader problems of inequality and poverty, and lack of upward intergenerational mobility. Weak families make for less equal societies, but these gaps are the result of deep, broad cultural shifts, many of which bring good news as well as bad news along with them. More liberal attitudes toward gender roles, sexuality, and sex have brought advantages, but for many they have also challenged family stability. Old norms about sex, gender, marriage, and work have weakened. New norms that promote both gender equality and family stability are developing, especially among more educated couples, but too slowly (Reeves and Sawhill 2015).

Public policy has a role to play, in both narrowing the family gap, and in mitigating its effects. Various strategies, from better contraception to more housing vouchers, have been discussed here, but we should be realistic. Public policy can only reach so far. Social norms are where most of the action is. There are reasons for optimism. Some traditional norms – for example, with regard to premarital sex, or specific gender roles – have evolved, but the fears of a descent into hedonistic, expressive individualism have not, by and large, been realized. Especially among the most-educated, affluent and powerful, marriage, adapted to gender egalitarianism, is if anything stronger than ever. The potential to improve family planning, with the emergence of LARCs, is very great – if the norms standing in the way of their adoption evolve quickly enough.

Restoring outdated family models is not the way to reduce the family gap. It is an old joke that conservatives want to bring back the family of the 1950s and liberals want to bring back the labor market of the 1950s. If this were true, both sides would be set for disappointment. That world is not coming back. (Though it is noteworthy that most of those who supported President Trump believe the United States has become a worse society since the 1950s.) Instead, we need to craft policies and support the development of a culture that is pro-family, without being anti-modern. Responsible childbearing, committed parenting, stable families – these are not antiquated ideas. Rather, they are necessary ingredients for giving children a strong start in life, which is more important than ever.

PART V

COMMENTARY AND CONCLUDING REFLECTIONS

The Pathology of Patriarchy and Family Inequalities

Lynn Prince Cooke[1]

Everyone in the world belongs to at least two families: The one in to which we were born and the ones we create in adulthood. Underlying this shared global experience is a wealth of individual diversity in how family shapes us emotionally, physically, and economically throughout our lives and, in turn, the lives of our children. The first goal of this chapter is to present a holistic conceptual frame for comparing the group inequalities in inputs, family processes, and outcomes discussed in the other chapters of this volume. Crucially, the frame highlights that relative group differences over time and across countries are configured at the intersections of family, market, and state institutions.

Much research in this area, including some of the chapters in this volume, implicitly or explicitly view recent family changes as examples of the "pathology of matriarchy" first raised in Moynihan's 1965 report on *The Negro Family: The Case for National Action*. The basis of this perspective is the strong and persistent correlation between female-headed families and negative outcomes for children (McLanahan, Tach, and Schneider 2013). The point to stress, though, is that these ill effects are particularly acute in the United States with its unique ideological acceptance of large class, gender, racial, and other group inequalities. As revealed in this and other chapters in the volume, the

[1] *Acknowledgements:* This chapter was prepared for an experts meeting in Rome, Italy, February 16–18, 2017, sponsored by the Social Trends Institute (STI) with assistance from the Institute for Family Studies (IFS). Thanks as well to Joe Devine, Anette Fasang, Rossella Icardi, Jane Millar, Rense Nieuwenhuis, and Mel Semple for comments on earlier drafts. The ideas developed in the chapter are part of a project that has received funding from the European Research Council (ERC) under the European Union's Horizon 2020 research and innovation program (grant agreement No. 680958). Opinions expressed here reflect only the author's view; the STI, IFS, and ERC are not responsible for any use that may be made of the information it contains.

magnitude of the family changes and especially their negative outcomes varies across cultural, economic, and political contexts.

The second goal of this chapter is to argue that the pattern of this cross-context variation does not point to an inherent pathology of matriarchy. Indeed, the differences in life chances across family types are minimized where institutional arrangements, unlike in the United States, support greater gender along with class equality (Nieuwenhuis and Maldonado 2018). Furthermore, gendered responses to the interrelated institutional changes over the past half-century suggest instead it is the pathology of *patriarchy* disproportionately hurting the life chances of boys and men. I draw broadly on Connell (1987; Connell and Messerschmidt 2005) to define patriarchy as men's historically institutionalized dominance over women in the family, labor market, and state.[2] As the institutional support for patriarchy gives way, a sizeable minority of men struggle to adapt in healthy ways, undermining family formation and stability.

Next I outline the conceptual frame for situating family processes and outcomes in their institutional contexts. Then I use the existing literature and other chapters in this volume to highlight how structural changes over the past half-century make patriarchal assumptions untenable for a growing proportion of men. In conclusion, I argue that only fully institutionalizing gender equality will minimize negative outcomes associated with family change. In part, fully-institutionalized gender equality ensures children have access to more economic and emotional resources regardless of family form. More importantly, fully institutionalized gender equality encourages development of new normative masculinities that support greater family stability in evolving institutional contexts.

DYNAMIC INSTITUTIONAL INTERSECTIONS

Figure 11.1 diagrams the "nested intersections" of institutions, family processes, and child and adult outcomes. The first box in the diagram indicates the socioeconomic structures that affect family formation and dissolution noted in the second box, which create the group differences in inequalities in individual outcomes outlined in the lower box. The structural effects occur at the

---

[2] Connell's concept of hegemonic masculinities from which I derive this definition of patriarchy not only incorporates the institutionalized patriarchal power relations between men and women but also the sexual, class, and racial–ethnic hierarchies among men vis-à-vis a hegemonic ideal (Connell and Messerschmidt 2005). Fully explicating this theoretically, vis-à-vis further group differences in family inequalities, is beyond the scope of this chapter.

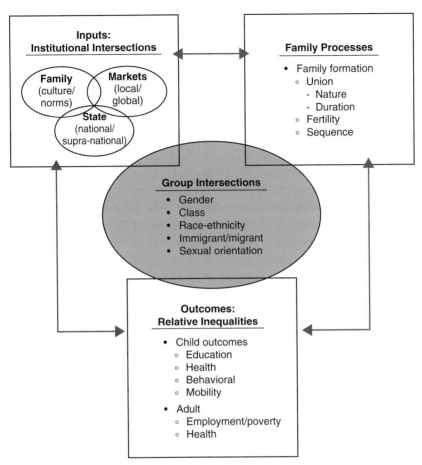

FIGURE 11.1 Nested intersections of institutions, family processes, and outcomes

intersections of family, market, and state institutions in a dynamic interplay that varies across and within national contexts over time.

Intersectionality is not commonly used to refer to institutional effects. Conventionally, intersectionality is a feminist paradigm emphasizing that no single master social category such as gender or class depicts the different experiences and social locations of all group members (McCall 2005). Consequently, intersectionality demands that we consider identities and experiences at the intersection of an individual's group memberships (Collins 2002; McCall 2005). Hence, Figure 11.1 includes a shaded circle spanning institutions, family processes, and outcomes to indicate that effects vary at the intersection of an individual's gender, class, race–ethnicity, immigrant status, sexual orientation, and the like. Due to space constraints, discussion in this chapter is primarily limited to gender and class differences, with education used as the main proxy for class.

Similarly, no master institution accounts for institutional effects on people's lives. Instead, individual and group differences are nested in the intersections of family, market, and state institutions, and supra-national institutions such as the European Union and World Bank. This may seem like common sense, but bears emphasizing when comparing possible causes and consequences of family inequalities across Europe and the Americas as done in this volume. For example, the institution of family includes norms about what or who constitutes a family, along with the expected behavior of family members. During early industrialization, the patriarchal heterosexual, nuclear, male breadwinner/female carer model of family became hegemonic in many, but not all Western economies.

Men's economic dominance under this model was theoretically enshrined in US economist Gary Becker's (1981) specialization theory of family. Becker argued that families in industrial societies optimize household production and reproduction when one partner specializes in paid work and the other in unpaid family work such as housework and child care. The math behind the theory is gender-neutral in that either partner could specialize in paid or unpaid work depending on their individual aptitudes and preferences. However, reflecting the patriarchal world in which he was raised, Becker (1981) ultimately concluded women's childbearing gives them a comparative advantage in family work, whereas the gender wage gap indicates men's comparative advantage in employment. Governments in most, but not all, countries reinforced the patriarchal order in the post-World War II expansion of employment-based welfare provisions payable to the primary breadwinner (Cooke 2011).

Perpetuation of the male breadwinner model of family, though, requires a labor market that enables all members of a family to survive on a single income. This became possible for the newly-created European and North American middle classes beginning in the nineteenth century (Cooke 2011). The possibility extended to the working classes as well in the brief postwar period when workers enjoyed the fruits of their growing productivity (Cherlin 2014; Gottschalk and Smeeding 1997). Since then, the evolution from industrial to postindustrial labor markets made the patriarchal male breadwinner model of family increasingly unsustainable.

Deindustrialization and deunionization made less-skilled men the first to lose their ability to support a family. High-wage manufacturing jobs disappeared, replaced by growing employment in low-wage service sector jobs

(Carlson, Chapter 1; Cherlin 2014). Neoliberal policies exacerbated less-skilled workers' labor market losses. For instance, in a bid to enhance employer flexibility in competitive global markets, some governments eased employment protections and allowed the real value of minimum wages to fall (Immervoll 2007). Wage inequalities widened further as returns to a university degree sharply increased beginning in the 1980s in the United States and Great Britain, and in the 1990s in other Western countries (Gottschalk and Smeeding 1997; Machin 2010).

Nonetheless, the middle classes are not safe either. Since the late 1980s, technological expansion has led to falling employment shares among middle-waged occupations in North America (Autor 2010) and Europe (Goos, Manning, and Salomons 2009), but the specific pattern of polarization varies across Western labor markets, as indicated in Table 11.1. The loss of middle-waged occupations in Austria, France, and Italy was offset by strong growth in the highest-waged occupations. In contrast, the middle-wage job loss in Finland and Norway was offset by growth in only low-wage occupations. In the United Kingdom as in the United States (Autor 2010), shrinking middle-wage employment was offset by approximately equal growth in both low- and high-wage jobs.

Consequently, to varying degrees, postindustrial labor markets no longer support the patriarchal male breadwinner model as did the postwar labor markets. In almost every OECD country, the employment rate of prime-age (25 to 54) men decreased since the 1970s (OECD 2016b; see also Eberstadt, Chapter 5). The trajectories of younger adults making critical decisions about education, employment, and family are more precarious than at any other time during the past half-century (Eurofound 2016). The evolving labor markets, coupled with cultural and policy shifts, eroded men's comparative advantage in employment. Simultaneously, gendered divisions of paid work narrowed.

EVOLVING FAMILY DIVISIONS OF LABOR

Any gender and other group hierarchies embedded in the institution of family are constantly contested (Connell and Messerschmidt 2005; Ferree 2010). In 1963, Friedan's book on *The Feminine Mystique* struck a chord with Western housewives who felt trapped, alienated, and vulnerable inside their homes and economically dependent on husbands. Friedan (1963) called for a revolution, for women to seize education and return to paid work. Friedan's timing was perfect, coinciding with the introduction of the birth control pill, coupled with the easing of anti-contraception laws in many Western nations (Cooke 2011).

TABLE 11.1 *Labor market polarization across Europe*

1993–2006 Percentage Point Change	Share of Hours Worked		
	Four Lowest-Paying Occupations	Nine Middle-Wage Occupations	Eight Highest-Paying Occupations
Continental Northern Europe			
Austria	−0.59	−14.58	15.17
Belgium	1.48	−9.50	8.03
France	−0.74	−12.07	12.81
Germany	3.05	−8.71	5.67
Netherlands	2.27	−4.68	2.41
Continental Southern Europe			
Greece	1.75	−6.08	4.34
Italy	−8.20	−9.08	17.28
Portugal	2.39	−1.13	−1.26
Spain	0.96	−7.04	6.07
Nordic			
Denmark	−0.96	−7.16	8.13
Finland	6.66	−6.54	−0.12
Norway	4.96	−6.52	1.57
Sweden	1.90	−6.93	5.03
English-Speaking (Liberal)			
Ireland	6.19	−5.47	−0.72
UK	5.77	−10.32	4.55
EU Average	1.58	−7.77	6.19

Source: Adapted from Goos, Manning, and Salomons 2009, Table 2; used with permission.

Women particularly embraced higher education. By the 1990s, women's educational attainment in most Western countries had caught up with men's. By 2011, college attainment among women aged 25–34 exceeded that of men in twenty-eight of thirty-four OECD countries (OECD 2013a). A consistent pattern across countries is that educated women are more likely to be employed than less-educated women (Cooke 2011; Harkness 2013; Pettit and Hook 2009). Nevertheless, growth of the service sector expanded job opportunities for less-skilled women, who take these jobs more often than similarly-skilled men (OECD 2016b). Consequently, and in contrast to men, women's labor force participation rates steadily increased from the 1970s, as shown in Table 11.2.

The intersection of the state with family and market institutions is evident in the regional variation in these trends. As noted earlier, most postwar welfare

TABLE 11.2 *Female labor force participation rates over time (age 25 to 54)*

	1975	1980	1990	2000	2010	2015	Part-time as % Women's Total 2015 Employment	2014 Gender Wage Gap (%)
Mexico	–	–	–	45.4	54.1	55.2	27.5	18
Costa Rica	–	–	38.7	47.7	61.0	64.2	29.8	–
Canada		60.0	75.5	78.5	82.3	82.0	26.4	19
UK	–	–	73.0	76.2	78.6	80.0	37.7	17
US	55.1	64.0	74.0	76.7	75.2	73.7	17.4	17
Belgium	–	–	60.8	72.7	80.4	80.2	30.2	6
France	–	–	72.2	78.6	83.4	83.0	22.3	14
Germany	52.8	56.6	63.4	76.9	81.3	82.5	37.4	17
Netherlands	28.5	36.7	58.5	72.7	82.3	82.1	60.7	19
Italy	31.3	39.9	53.9	57.9	64.5	65.9	32.8	6
Greece	–	–	51.5	62.0	72.4	77.7	16.3	9
Portugal	46.2	54.4	68.0	77.3	84.9	86.0	12.6	19
Spain	27.9	30.4	46.9	62.8	78.8	82.0	23.1	9
Czech Republic	–	–	–	81.8	79.8	81.4	7.4	16
Estonia	–	–	88.3	84.1	84.8	82.8	12.2	27
Denmark	–	–	87.8	84.0	85.3	83.4	25.8	7
Finland	78.5	82.7	86.4	85.0	84.4	83.5	16.4	20
Norway	55.3	68.9	79.2	83.5	84.4	83.9	27.6	6
Sweden	74.3	82.9	90.7	85.6	86.6	88.3	18.0	13

Source: From OECD statistics: http://stats.oecd.org/, accessed March 26, 2017. The gender wage gap is from OECD (2016b, p. 239) and is unadjusted – calculated as the difference between the unadjusted median earnings of men and the median earnings of women, relative to the median earnings of men. Part-time employment from OECD (2016b, p. 227).

state policies reinforced a male breadwinner model. The exception to this was the Nordic model offering extensive policy supports for maternal employment such as public provision of child care and paid parental leave (Cooke and Baxter 2010). Consequently, Finnish and Swedish women's labor force participation rates already exceeded 70% in 1975. The link between women's education and employment is also weaker in these more egalitarian countries (Harkness 2013; Pettit and Hook 2009). At the other end of the policy spectrum, the very low 1975 labor force participation rates of Dutch, Italian, and Spanish women reflected the national policy reinforcement of the male breadwinner model at that time.

The power of policy to change behavior across diverse cultural and historical contexts is evident in the wake of the European Union's 2000 Lisbon

Treaty. The Lisbon Treaty contained an explicit goal of 60% female labor force participation in all member states by 2010, supported by expansion of public child care and other family policies found in the Nordic model.[3] The over-time trends presented in Table 11.2 indicate the Lisbon strategy had some success. By 2015, the labor force participation rate of women in almost all European countries exceeded that in the United States. Yet one downside of the employment growth in the service economy is the increase in part-time rather than full-time jobs. In all countries, women are more likely than men to work part-time. Still, the percentage of women's total employment that is part-time varies from a low of 7.4% in the Czech Republic to a high of more than 60% among Dutch women (Table 11.2).

Persistent gender differences in hours employed contributes to the persistent gender wage gap in median earnings, indicated in the final column of Table 11.2. Even in the Nordic countries, the gender wage gap varies from a low of 6% in Norway, to a high of 20% in Finland. Finland's gender wage gap is in fact larger than the gender wage gap in the less-regulated British and US economies. Nevertheless, women's gains in employment and relative earnings over the past half-century are extraordinary, although gender employment equality remains elusive under even the most supportive policy framework to date.

One likely reason women made greater employment gains over the past few decades as compared with men is because of their greater predilection for education. Women might also navigate changing labor markets more successfully than men because of the growing employer demand for social in conjunction with cognitive skills (Deming 2015). The gender response to US job polarization provides an example of women's better adaptation. The decrease in middle-wage employment between 1979 and 2007 was more than twice as large for US women as men, 15.8% vs. 7%, respectively (Autor 2010, p. 10). Nevertheless, female employment overwhelmingly moved up the occupational wage distribution as middle-wage employment fell. The decrease in US men's middle-wage employment led to a more even split in employment growth in men's low- and high-wage occupations (Autor 2010). This highlights that the most-skilled men continue to make gains in the new economy, sustaining their advantage over high-skilled women. However, Autor (2010) found evidence of losses even among university-educated men, more of whom became employed in middle- and low-wage occupations. Future comparative work is needed to confirm

---

[3]   www.europarl.europa.eu/document/activities/cont/201107/20110718ATT24270/20110718AT
      T24270EN.pdf (Accessed January 4, 2017.)

whether these gender differences occurred in countries with varying patterns of polarization.

In any event, changing gender divisions of paid labor require some adaptation in how unpaid family work gets done. In this area as well, women have made greater behavioral changes than men. Unfortunately, men's failure to become full partners in unpaid family work encourages greater class inequality among women within and across labor markets.

Gender–Class Redistribution of Unpaid Work

Goldscheider and Sassler (see Chapter 9) laud the continuing gender revolution indicated by slow but somewhat steady increases in Western men's unpaid child care, most recently among less-educated men who historically professed the most conservative gender attitudes. Yet the decrease in women's total domestic time during the revolution has been greater than the increase in men's (Kan, Sullivan, and Gershuny 2011). Multinational time diary data from the early 1970s through the early 2000s are available for the Netherlands, Norway, the United Kingdom, and United States. These data show that women in these countries on average reduced their 337 minutes per day of housework and child care by 60 minutes between the two time periods. Men in these countries increased their 117 minutes per day domestic contribution by 40 minutes across the period (Kan, Sullivan, and Gershuny 2011, p. 236).

Not even the Nordic model has yet to eliminate gender inequality in unpaid work. Norwegian women in the early 2000s spent a similar amount of time as US women doing daily domestic tasks. Divisions were slightly more equal in Sweden, but because Swedish women spent appreciably less time doing these tasks than Norwegian or US women. The net result of these over-time shifts is that partnered women in all countries still perform 60% or more of household unpaid work. If future progress continues at the same rate as past progress – and this is a big "if" that Goldscheider and Sassler (see Chapter 9) fully embrace – gender equality in unpaid work would not be achieved for another half-century (Kan, Sullivan, and Gershuny 2011).

The void created by men's failure to contribute fully to family unpaid work is filled by the service sector, encouraging a growing class divide in women's domestic equality gains. Gupta and his colleagues (2010) found that high-wage German, Swedish, and US women spend significantly less time doing routine housework than their lower waged peers. The institutional context matters, as differences among women are greater where aggregate income inequality is greater as in the United States (Gupta et al. 2010). The demand for market substitutes for domestic work is undoubtedly one driver of the low-wage job growth in Great Britain and the United States.

Class and also racial–ethnic divisions among women increasingly span continents, as the use of migrant domestic workers in affluent economies surged since the 1990s (Williams 2012; Zimmerman, Litt, and Bose 2006). This includes an increase in the Nordic countries after governments introduced cash transfers to reduce the high cost of providing public care services (Williams 2012). As a result, the number of migrant care workers increased in Denmark, Norway, and Sweden as well as other European and North American countries (Williams 2012; Zimmerman, Litt, and Bose 2006).

The growth in migrant care work highlights that family inequalities in paid and unpaid work span First and Third World countries. If women in affluent economies struggle to balance employment and family, imagine the challenges for women doing so across national borders. Regardless of the care drain migrant work imposes on families in the sending countries, many governments actively encourage the migration of women over men (Williams 2012; Zimmerman, Litt, and Bose 2006). This is because migrant women on average send more of their earnings back to their families, which improves the national balance of payments required under international financial aid packages. Migrant male workers, in contrast, are more likely to spend more of their earnings in the host country (Zimmerman, Litt, and Bose 2006).[4]

Despite the downsides, all of the trends indicate that a growing number of women worldwide increasingly take advantage of postindustrial global labor markets. Of course, the highest-skilled men still benefit the most, but global markets increasingly tip the employment balance in favor of moderate- and less-skilled women over similar men. Global markets also allow high-wage women to fill the care deficit created by men's limited unpaid work by purchasing support from less-advantaged women. At the same time, the proportion of younger less-skilled women continues to shrink at a faster rate than men's (OECD 2013a). Policies also nudge women more than men. These evolving institutional effects shaping gender equality at its intersection with class (and race–ethnicity) are brought to bear on family formation patterns.

---

[4] This gender difference in family expenditures is not unique to the Third World. Lundberg, Pollack, and Wales' (1997) analysis of British family cash transfers found that expenditures on children's clothing increased when women received the transfers rather than men.

Becker (1981, 1985) believed that the mutual dependence created by gender specialization in paid or unpaid work enhances marital stability and fertility. Certainly, the three-institutional reinforcement of Becker's patriarchal model in the postwar decades reinforced a family formation sequence of marriage, childbearing, and children being raised by the two biological parents. This anomalous period in modern industrial history comprised the "golden age of marriage" in Western societies (Festy 1980). Couples married earlier, leading to a spike in fertility in many countries (Van Bavel and Reher 2013). Whether the sequence reflected choice or constraint is debatable. Few women had the independent economic resources to remain single or to leave an unhappy or abusive marriage. Conception outside marriage was deeply stigmatizing for both the mother and the child, and most often resulted in either a "shot-gun" wedding or putting the child up for adoption.

Yet institutional intersections are dynamic. They vary across countries at any given point in time, as well as over time within countries. Esteve and Florez-Paredes (see Chapter 2) note that marriage was not historically preeminent in Central and Latin America. Instead, cohabitation and union instability were structural dimensions of family life when marriage reached its zenith in the West (Esteve and Florez-Paredes, Chapter 2). During that time in the West, pronatalist policies combined with supports for maternal employment in Nordic and socialist countries correlated with higher nonmarital fertility rates (Cooke 2011; Perelli-Harris, Chapter 4). Relatedly, cohabitation in social democratic Denmark and Sweden began to increase in the 1960s, a decade ahead of other countries in Europe (Hall and White 2005, p. 30).

Over the past fifty years, more women throughout Europe and the Americas cohabit rather than marry and raise children outside marriage whether because of divorce or nonmarital childbearing (Carlson, Chapter 1; Esteve and Florez-Paredes, Chapter 2; Perelli-Harris, Chapter 4). What intrigues or worries many social scientists and policymakers are the educational and/or racial–ethnic disparities in these family patterns that reflect and/or magnify inequalities among families. For most Whites in the United States and non-Nordic European countries, avant-garde family arrangements in the 1960s such as cohabitation or divorce were the purview of a small elite. As alternative family forms became more culturally acceptable and legally possible, Goode (1970) anticipated they would become more prevalent among the less- rather than highly educated. His prediction has largely been borne out, although educational gradients in marriage, cohabitation, nonmarital childbearing, and divorce vary in their institutional context (Carlson, Chapter 1).

Within a patriarchal structure, men's economic capacity predicted by education still plays an important role in women's family choices as Cherlin argues here and elsewhere (Cherlin 2014). For example, Cherlin (see Chapter 3) attributes changes in the educational gradient in US single motherhood to the disparate gender earnings effects of job polarization. His prima facie case seems convincing. Recall that moderately educated women improved their earnings position in response to polarization while that of moderately educated men deteriorated (Autor 2010). The percentage of US children living with moderately educated single mothers increased in each decade since the 1980s, whereas that for both the least- and most-educated women remained fairly stable since the 1990s (Cherlin, Chapter 3).

However, education predicts much more than economic outcomes – even in the United States – that also have a bearing on family commitment and stability. These associations should not be given short shrift in discussions of educational gradients in family formation because they offer much deeper insights as to the causes as well as consequences of observed family patterns. To date, Kalmijn (2013) is the only demographer to explore the interplays between the institutional context and the possible meanings of education behind the gradients.

Beyond the Economics of Education

Kalmijn (2013) noted that education predicts not only economic prospects, but more egalitarian attitudes as well. He subsequently hypothesized that the degree of gender inequality in a society determines which aspect of education accounts for educational gradients in family formation. In the twenty-six European countries analyzed, Kalmijn found that highly educated women in male breadwinner contexts were less likely to have ever married and, if they married, more likely to have divorced. In contrast, less-educated women in these contexts have fewer nonmarital economic alternatives and hence were more likely to have married and less likely to have divorced. Education had little impact on men's marriage or divorce risks (Kalmijn 2013). This pattern is consistent with the educational scenarios in the United States at the height of the 1950s' male breadwinner model.

In more egalitarian contexts, however, highly educated women *and* men were more likely to have married and less likely to have divorced (Kalmijn 2013).[5] Kalmijn (2013) also found that highly educated individuals were more

---

[5] These results are consistent with Cooke et al.'s (2013) comparative study of harmonized national panel data, which reported that the reduction in divorce risk predicted by a wife's university degree was about as great in Finland, Norway, and Sweden as in the United States.

likely to be married to one another as gender equality increased. He concluded the stronger effect of men's education on marriage in egalitarian countries relates to its cultural rather than economic implications. Educated women married educated men because the latter are more involved in child care and hold more egalitarian attitudes about their wives' employment (Kalmijn 2013).

Missing from Kalmijn's study due to data limitations are the many other characteristics associated with education that also affect marriage probabilities. Lower education predicts a range of problems, from disability and poor health (Eurofound 2016), to greater illicit drug use and binge drinking, particularly among young men (Duncan, Wilkerson, and England 2006). Men with less education are more likely to commit domestic violence as well (Aizer 2010; Costa et al. 2016).

These associations do not mean that forcing men to gain additional education will reduce the negative behaviors, as the causal arrow goes in the other direction. Behavioral and socio-emotional factors account for both education and employment outcomes, and behavioral problems are more prevalent among boys than girls (see Bertrand and Pan 2013). Once young adults are engaged in illicit behaviors, they are the most difficult to reach with any education, training, or employment program (Eurofound 2016). At the same time, Cherlin (2014) summarized US qualitative research indicating that the persistent pressure on less-skilled men to fulfill the elusive patriarchal economic norm pushes them into illicit activities. This suggests outdated patriarchal norms do not support positive employment behavior among men.

Some academics and policymakers believe marriage "improves" men by encouraging them to give up bad habits and encourage their efforts to earn more money under the male breadwinner norm (Wilcox and Price, Chapter 8). For example, many studies find that married men earn more than either their single or divorced counterparts (Ahituv and Lerman 2007), although the magnitude of this marriage premium varies across countries (Schoeni 1995) and among men within countries (Cooke 2014). However, a growing body of research finds that it is more a case of "better" men selecting into marriage rather than a causal effect of marriage. Duncan, Wilkerson, and England (2006) found that US men's legal and illegal substance abuse significantly decreased before entering cohabitation or marriage, not after. In Norway, men who ultimately married had chosen higher wage occupations years before they partnered. Consequently, partnered men did not earn higher wages as compared with single men in the same occupations (Petersen, Penner, and Høgnes 2014). Similarly, US men tend to marry during periods of high wage growth, which plateaus (Dougherty 2006; Killewald and

Lundberg 2017) or even declines after the year of marriage (Loughran and Zissimopoulos 2009).

All in all, more desirable men are selected into stable marriages, either because men who are particularly keen to have a family actively prepare for it earlier in the life course, or because savvy women actively pursue such men for marriage. Women who remain in education have the greatest opportunity to meet a large number of potentially desirable partners over several years before deciding on one. As societal gender equality increases and cultural norms about family evolve, less-educated women feel less compelled to legally commit to someone from their pool of likely partners. Less-educated women do marry, of course, but women most frequently cite drug or alcohol abuse, domestic violence, as well as poor employment prospects as reasons for divorce (Härkönen 2014). The greater likelihood of these family-deleterious behaviors among less-educated men therefore contributes to educational gradients in marriage as well as divorce.

Patriarchy vs. Gender Equality

The body of evidence outlined above suggests the patriarchal norm of fathers as economic heads of households is incongruous with the educational and employment trends that highlight growing female advantage among low- to moderately educated adults. Men's paid work is still important for family formation and stability, but it is increasingly important for women as well. For example, studies cited in Cooke and Baxter (2010) found that the unemployment of either husbands *or* wives increased the risk of divorce in Finland and Norway. What is at odds with labor market trends is the assumption of men's wage advantage over women in general and their opposite-sex partner specifically.

A further problem with the patriarchal norm is that it precludes equally-valued roles for men's expressive as well as economic contribution to family. Indeed, a new norm of family men as emotionally engaged and domestically involved has become pervasive since the 1970s, but it still sits subordinate to the patriarchal norm of breadwinning (Gerson 1993; Segal 2007). As long as the patriarchal norm dominates, couples will find it culturally difficult to enact different divisions of household labor that might better suit their individual capabilities within postindustrial markets. Goldscheider and Sassler (see Chapter 9) discuss the compelling evidence that men in particular would enact more egalitarian domestic divisions if they believe that other men support these. This highlights that even the most-entrenched norms of masculinity can shift with public support from other men.

The economic and social trends together suggest that full institutional support for gender equality will ultimately support greater family stability in the postindustrial global economy. There is already some evidence that this is the case among younger cohorts. For example, US marriages where the woman has more education than the man are no longer more likely to divorce as they were a generation or two ago (Schwartz and Han 2014). At the same time, a US wife's employment still increases the risk of divorce (Cooke et al. 2013; Killewald 2016). This contrasts, however, with the effect of wives' employment in countries with greater policy support for equality. In Finland, Norway, and Sweden, wives' employment in fact lowers the risk of divorce (Cooke et al. 2013). Even within the United States, Cooke (2006) found that first marriages were most stable when couples had more equal divisions of paid and unpaid work. The optimal mix during the 1990s was when the wife contributed 40% to family earnings and the man 40% to unpaid domestic tasks (Cooke 2006).

However, it would be naïve to expect a smooth or rapid normative transition from patriarchal dominance to egalitarianism, particularly when some view the changes as entailing loss of public and private power. As noted by Carlson (see Chapter 1), cohabitation in lieu of marriage is widespread across the more egalitarian Nordic countries and cohabiting unions everywhere are less stable than married ones. In addition, Carlson's (see Figure 1.3) data showed that the 2014 divorce rate per 1,000 people was higher in Denmark than in the notoriously divorce-prone United States. Even when limiting comparisons to the smaller proportion of Nordic couples who marry, Finnish and Swedish divorce rates are among the top of the list, although not as high as in the United States and Russia (Fahey 2014, Figure 2).

In addition, other signs point to greater benefits of institutionalizing gender equality over patriarchy. Aizer (2010) found that US domestic violence decreased when the gender wage gap decreased, whereas a traditional grab for patriarchal power would have predicted an increase. Esping-Andersen and Billari (2015) highlight the recovery in fertility rates in the Nordic countries as compared with persistent low fertility in more gender-traditional European contexts.

Further aggregate evidence of a positive link between gender equality and partnered households is contained in Table 11.3. The first column displays the United Nations' Gender Inequality Index rating for numerous countries in Europe and the Americas. The index rates countries on women's reproductive health, empowerment, and economic status,[6] and ranges from zero,

---

[6]　Reproductive health is measured by the maternal mortality ratio and adolescent birth rates; empowerment includes the proportion of parliamentary seats occupied by women along with

TABLE 11.3 *Gender inequality, social expenditures, and percentage of children under 17 living in poverty in two- vs. single-parent families, circa 2010*

	Gender Inequality Index	% children in Single-Mother Families	% GDP Family Transfers	Poverty Rates (%)	
				Two-Parent Households	Single-Mother Households
Denmark	0.06	16.9	3.8	3.1	10.8
Finland	0.08	10.4	3.1	2.5	11.7
Norway	0.08	13.1	3.1	3.1	16.7
Sweden	0.05	18.0	3.4	3.3	10.4
Belgium	0.11	10.3	2.8	4.9	28.1
France	0.11	13.8	2.9	8.2	29.4
Germany	0.09	15.6	2.2	4.1	36.2
Greece	0.16	3.7	1.4	16.6	39.4
Italy	0.12	8.5	1.3	17.6	33.0
Netherlands	0.05	11.5	1.5	2.9	32.5
Spain	0.12	7.7	1.5	19.5	32.7
Czech Republic	0.14	12.2	2.4	7.4	32.2
Estonia	0.19	15.7	2.6	9.4	30.2
Hungary	0.24	14.6	3.4	11.5	18.6
UK	0.21	21.0	4.0	7.6	14.3
Canada	0.14	13.4	1.3	10.6	37.4
US	0.30	21.0	0.7	13.7	45.9
Brazil	0.45	19.2	*	27.8	40.5
Colombia	0.48	25.1	*	21.8	32.5
Dominican Republic	0.48	26.4	*	21.8	31.8
Guatemala	0.54	18.3	*	29.4	26.2
Mexico	0.45	16.0	1.1	25.3	22.3
Panama	0.49	22.6	*	29.7	38.9
Paraguay	0.48	17.6	*	27.6	33.8
Peru	0.42	16.2	*	30.7	52.0

Source: Gender Inequality Index (0 no inequality to 1 total inequality) from the 2010–15 average from UN Human Development Report 2011: http://hdr.undp.org/sites/default/files/reports/271/hd r_2011_en_complete.pdf; Social expenditure data for 2010 from OECD (2017): www.oecd.org/els /social/expenditure, retrieved March 24, 2017; Child poverty rates are the percentage of children under 17 living in households with less than 50% median household income, from LIS Key Figures for 2010 (2011) or the next earlier wave: www.lisdatacenter.org/lis-ikf-webapp/app/search-ikf-figures, accessed March 24, 2017. *Note:* Asterisk (*) indicates information not available.

the proportion of adult men and women aged 25 and older with at least some secondary education; and economic status encompasses the labor force participation rate of female and male populations aged 15 years and older. See http://hdr.undp.org/en/content/gender-inequality-index-gii (accessed March 3, 2017) for more detail.

indicating perfect gender equality, to one, indicating extreme gender inequality. The ratings confirm the high degree of gender equality in the Nordic countries, along with the Netherlands and Germany. Most of the rest of Europe along with Canada have moderately high gender equality, whereas it is noticeably lower in Hungary, the United Kingdom, and United States. It is lowest in familistic Latin America.

The second column displays the percentage of children under the age of 17 who are living in a single-mother household. The percentage is smallest in Greece at less than 4% and greatest in Colombia and the Dominican Republic where more than one quarter of children reside with a lone mother. The United Kingdom and United States are more similar to Latin America, with more than one fifth of young children residing in single-mother households. Overall, the percentage of children residing in single-mother households increases as gender *in*equality increases (correlation 0.64, p <0.000).

Whether institutionalized gender equality or patriarchy supports greater family stability in postindustrial societies is much more than an academic debate. The core issue behind the debate is the relationship between family forms and the individual outcomes noted in the bottom box of Figure 11.1 (see also Chapter 10). A sizeable literature documents that father absence predicts greater risks of behavioral, educational, and employment problems in the next generation. My final argument, building on an insight from Moynihan, is that any pathology associated with residing in single-mother households is an artifact of patriarchy that limits these households' access to resources. Proof of this conjecture is that the negative outcomes are minimized where cultural, market, and state institutions instead support greater gender equality.

INSTITUTIONAL INTERSECTIONS AND GROUP DIFFERENCES IN FAMILY OUTCOMES

Senator Moynihan's 1965 report for the US Department of Labor brought discussion of child outcomes associated with single-mother households into the public debate. In that report, he noted the very high divorce and nonmarital birth rates among African–American families as compared with Whites, and the strong correlations between father absence and children's low intelligence scores, school truancy, crime, drug addiction, etc. (Moynihan 1965). There were very strong educational gradients in effects that he attributed to the deep-seated US racism undermining African–American men's access to education and employment and, in turn, their relative employment advantage over African–American women. Moynihan (1965, p. 29) concluded the poor intergenerational outcomes were indicative of the "pathology of matriarchy" within a society that presumed and rewarded male leadership in public and private life. Moynihan did not consider patriarchy superior or inevitable, just normative at the time. One of his key insights was that it was the mismatch between individual and current normative circumstances that accounted for the ill effects, not a pathology inherent to matriarchy.

In this chapter, I have detailed the similar dismantling of economic rewards since Moynihan wrote his report for a growing proportion of men based on education, along with the sizeable increase in women's public participation and private power. Yet the assumed pathology of matriarchy persists in much of the US literature even as accumulating evidence indicates norms are giving way to more gender-egalitarian family arrangements. McLanahan (2004) gave it a less provocative name of "diverging destinies," with the likelihood of father absence predicated on mothers' education rather than race–ethnicity.[7]

To be sure, studies from a range of Western countries confirm that parental separation and subsequent family transitions predict some risk of negative effects on children's psychological well-being, behavior, grades, test scores, educational attainment, own early onset of sexual activity, early childbearing, and risk of divorce in adulthood (Garriga and Berta, Chapter 6; Härkönen, Bernardi, and Boertien 2017; McLanahan, Tach, and Schneider 2013; Perelli-Harris, Chapter 4). McLanahan (2004) contends the negative outcomes derive from the lower resources of single-parent households, in terms of both money and parental attention. As less-educated women are more likely to be single parents, their children face a larger resource deficit.

Confirming the causal direction of effects, however, is tricky (Autor et al. 2016; Perelli-Harris, Chapter 4). Lower socioeconomic status already predicts worse outcomes for children whether in two- or single-parent households. Another possibility is that some other characteristic might account for both family instability and children's outcomes (Autor et al. 2016; Perelli-Harris, Chapter 4). Analyses controlling for children's stable unobserved character-istics, prior behavior, or school performance indeed find smaller effects than when comparing across children (Härkönen, Bernardi, and Boertien 2017; McLanahan, Tach, and Schneider 2013). In other words, these children would have done worse regardless of family structure.

Furthermore, like patriarchy, the negative effects associated with spending time in a single-mother household are not inevitable. Most studies report "average"

---

[7]   Others point out that the educational gradients mainly mask the institutionalized racial–ethnic disadvantage originally noted by Moynihan (1965) (Autor et al. 2016; Esteve and Florez-Paredes, Chapter 2; Garriga and Berta, Chapter 6).

effects. In all countries, a sizeable minority if not majority of children experiencing family instability do just fine or perhaps better than had their fathers been present (Härkönen, Bernardi, and Boertien 2017). Furthermore, more redistributive welfare states and greater policy support for maternal employment minimize the negative intergenerational effects because they increase available resources (Härkönen, Bernardi, and Boertien 2017; Nieuwenhuis and Maldonado 2018). In Europe, this realization resulted in the adoption of a policy discourse around social investment rather than social protection. Whereas traditional welfare policies aimed to reduce current family poverty, social investment policies aim to break the intergenerational cycle of poverty (Jenson 2009). The goal is to ensure current and future employment growth within a (skilled) knowledge economy (Bonoli 2005). Patterned on the Nordic model, social investment policies stress greater education and skills for the next generation, simultaneous with current high levels of female labor force participation facilitated by more policy supports for employed parents and carers (Bonoli 2005; Jenson 2009).

The impact of public investment on families' economic resources is evident in the final three columns of Table 11.3. The third column indicates the percentage of GDP spent on family transfers in each of the countries (information not available for Latin America). Note the particularly low level of US public investment (0.7% of GDP in 2010) as compared with Europe and Canada. With this low level of public investment comes a high level of poverty even among US two-parent households – commensurate with the far less affluent Mediterranean countries struggling under austerity measures. The poverty rate for US single-mother households was a staggering 45.9% in 2010, exceeding that of any country in the table except Peru. In contrast, poverty rates of single-mother households in the redistributive Nordic countries were on average similar to the US poverty rate for two-parent households.

These aggregate differences manifest at the individual level. McLanahan, Tach, and Schneider's (2013) review consistently found significant negative effects of father absence on US children's educational and mental health outcomes, but effects were often weaker or entirely absent in other countries. For example, the educational penalty for father absence is twice as large in the United States as in Germany or the United Kingdom (Bernardi and Boertien 2017a). What research is just beginning to untangle is how child outcomes differ systematically at the intersection of gender and class (and race–ethnicity).

Gender–Class Gaps in Effects

Ascertaining possible gender or class differences in the impact of family structure on child outcomes is difficult because both characteristics

predict behavioral and educational differences irrespective of family structure. As already mentioned, children benefit from economic and parental
resources, the level of which increases as parents' education increases.
Consequently children of less-educated parents on average have more
behavioral problems and complete less education than children of highly
educated parents. Whether father absence magnifies this class disadvantage is unclear.

Two recent literature reviews found that approximately half of the reviewed
studies concluded that children of less-educated single parents fare worse,
whereas the other half concluded that the absence of a highly educated father
is more detrimental (Härkönen, Bernardi, and Boertien 2017; McLanahan,
Tach, and Schneider 2013). Bernardi and Boertien (2017a) contend the varying
conclusions stem from the different methods used in the analyses. Once
controlling for this, they found that father absence had the least impact on
the educational attainment of children of less-educated mothers in Germany,
Italy, the United Kingdom, and United States (Bernardi and Boertien 2017a).
Whether future research with similar attention to methodological issues will
reinforce this conclusion is an empirical question.

Gender differences in the impact of residing with a single mother are
apparent, however, at least in the United States. These develop from biological differences wherein boys do worse than girls on a range of noncognitive
measures affecting school success (Bertrand and Pan 2013). US boys are more
likely than girls to be diagnosed with attention deficit disorder and have lower
levels of inhibitory control and perceptual sensitivity, which equates to greater
aggression (see Bertrand and Pan 2013). US girls also have a slight but reliable
advantage in delaying gratification (Silverman 2003, cited in Bertrand and Pan
2013). Bertrand and Pan (2013) contend that some of the growing gender
differences in educational attainment discussed earlier can be traced to
these noncognitive gender differences in children.

The source of the gender behavioral differences may be biological, but as
with all essentialist differences, behaviors are responsive to environmental
factors. US evidence indicates that boys' outcomes deteriorate further with
the reduction in parenting resources of single-mother households (Bertrand
and Pan 2013; Cooper et al. 2011). Not only is there just one parent, but single
US mothers engage less with boys than girls from a very young age, although
parental time investment increases with mothers' education (Bertrand and
Pan 2013). Consequently, US girls generally fare better than boys in single-
parent households. Girls' greater resilience in the face of family change
contributes to their educational success and adaptability to changing labor
markets that demand high skills (Bertrand and Pan 2013).

Looking at effects at the intersection of gender and class using detailed Florida student records, Autor and colleagues (2016) found that the gender gaps in academic and behavioral outcomes in both single- and two-parent families shrink as parental socioeconomic status increases. Overall, boys' outcomes are more strongly contingent on family structure as well as economic resources, although high-quality schools can somewhat narrow the gender gap (Autor et al. 2016). The smaller impact of schools as well as neighborhoods on US boys' behavioral and academic outcomes indicates that Reeves' (see Chapter 10) suggestion of sending disadvantaged children to boarding schools would not rectify the inequalities. Doing so may particularly harm boys because it would remove both parents from their daily lives.

These gender differences in child outcomes may be another case of US exceptionalism, driven by the high levels of class and gender inequality in that country. Comparative research is needed to ascertain whether the more egalitarian policy contexts specifically minimize the negative impact of single motherhood on boys. It does seem likely that the perpetuation of the patriarchal norm in unequal contexts such as the United States contributes to the intergenerational gender differences. The expectation that men should be the primary family breadwinner in markets with a high degree of income inequality sharply reduces women's perceived benefit of committing to less-educated men. Men's failure to achieve the patriarchal ideal coupled with their biological predisposition to act out increases the risk they will engage in further negative behaviors that limit their time with residential or nonresidential children. The next generation of boys suffers the most from father absence in contexts of high inequality, perpetuating the cycle of maladaptation as institutional support for patriarchal entitlement in the family, market, and state continues to ebb. However, the solution is not to return to the patriarchal system built on gender inequality. Instead, what is needed is to fully institutionalize gender equality in which new, more adaptive masculinities can develop.

FAMILY FUTURES: MAKING GENDER EQUALITY A "COMPLETE"
INSTITUTION

In this chapter, I have highlighted how group inequalities configured at the intersections of family, market, and state institutions vary across place and evolve over time. My argument is that the institutional arrangements supporting patriarchy in the postwar decades have been crumbling for quite some time. A high-skill, technologically-driven global economy requires brains rather than brawn, and adaptable, socially engaged service providers. In Western societies, many of the requisite traits are traditionally feminine. Indeed, in the past half-century we have seen a remarkable ascendancy of women in the economic, social, and political order.

As the new institutional order unfolds, the value of education continues to increase (Autor 2010; Gottschalk and Smeeding 1997; Machin 2010). Education not only imparts skills, but encourages more egalitarian attitudes and predicts more positive social behaviors as well. Yet men's educational attainment has not kept pace with women's over the past few decades. Consequently a sizable proportion of men struggle to adapt to the new socio-economic demands in and outside the home.

The gender revolution is far from complete, but many women perceive themselves as sufficiently independent to go it alone at some stage of raising their children when their partners fall short of economic or behavioral expectations. Although much more comparative research is needed, available evidence finds that boys' essentialist behavioral problems magnify when fathers are absent from the household. These behavioral problems eclipse boys' educational development, which blunts the possibility that a larger proportion of the next generation can enjoy the greater family stability associated with greater educational attainment.

This vicious circle of intergenerational inequality down the male line does not indicate a pathology of matriarchy as initially suggested by Moynihan in the mid-1960s. It instead point to the growing pathology of patriarchy in postindustrial economies, because better institutional supports for gender along with class equality yield the best intergenerational outcomes. The reason we have not yet eradicated the risks is because gender equality remains an "incomplete institution" even in the most progressive contexts. I borrow this term from Cherlin's (1978) seminal article on remarriage after divorce. In that article, Cherlin argued that remarriages were less stable than first marriages because they lacked the institutional support in language, law, and custom that benefited first marriages. Similarly, I hold that the detrimental behaviors among boys and men will be staunched only once gender equality has become fully institutionalized in the family, market, and state. Institutionalizing gender equality eases the pressure on men to dominate paid work, allowing more adaptive masculinities to develop in which men's equal contributions to both paid and unpaid work support family stability. I conclude with some brief thoughts on the major market and policy challenges to achieving this.

The first challenge is to enhance children's and particularly boys' educational engagement from preschool that will carry them through to complete

higher levels of education. This perspective is core to the EU's social investment strategy, but as someone who worked on educational reform in her pre-
academic career, I can attest that the challenge is not the what, but the how.
Most compulsory educational systems developed with the assumption of an at-
home mother (Cooke 2011), and that children would adapt to the school
structures and processes. Both of these assumptions undermine academic
achievement.

Instead, educational processes need to adapt to children's and families'
needs. This includes additional public funding for more aides of both genders
in the classroom, innovative approaches to curriculum delivery, high-quality
care and learning opportunities before and after standard school days, further
supports for children with any type of special need (including behavioral), and
coordinated extracurricular activities that do not require parents to shuttle
children to and from venues. These supports should extend through adolescence, during which young persons are at greatest risk of becoming NEET –
not in education, employment, or training (Eurofound 2016).

The second challenge is that both parents need more workplace flexibility
to ensure they can be actively involved in their children's daily lives.
At present, organizations still reinforce patriarchal expectations of an ideal
worker without competing family demands (Acker 2006). These expectations
manifest in disparate gendered penalties when employees seek workplace
flexibility. For example, one US study found that male employees who
experienced a family conflict received lower performance ratings and lower
reward recommendations, whereas ratings of women were unaffected by
family conflicts (Butler and Skattebo 2004).

There is also a strong class dimension to organizational gendered expectations. Glass (2004) found that mothers in professional or managerial occupations incurred slightly larger wage penalties when they worked reduced hours
or worked from home, as compared with mothers in other occupations who
took up similar workplace options. Similarly, Brescoll, Glass, and Sedlovskaya
(2013) found that employers were more likely to grant low- than high-status
men's requests for flexible work schedules for family reasons. High-status men
were more likely to be granted leave for career development (Brescoll, Glass,
and Sedlovskaya 2013).

This nascent literature supports Goldscheider and Sassler's optimism (see
Chapter 9) that the second half of the gender revolution is now unfolding
among less-educated couples, which should ultimately reduce educational
gradients in marriage and divorce. At the same time, workplaces are stymying
further gender equality progress among the more highly educated, beyond
providing market alternatives for domestic production that widen class gaps

among women (Gupta et al. 2010). Persistent patriarchal advantage at the top of the class hierarchy blocks the thorough institutionalization of gender equality. One way to quell this is with more aggressive redistributive tax policies, the proceeds of which could be fed into the educational system.

Also needed are more aggressive positive discrimination policies, but targeted at the top of the occupational structure. Affirmative action entered US equality legislation with Johnson's 1965 Executive Order 11246, although it has subsequently come under fire as discriminating against unprotected groups. Positive discrimination is also allowed under the European Commission's 2006/54/EC directive on the implementation of the principle of equal opportunities and equal treatment of men and women in matters of employment and occupation. Again, however, many countries have argued against positive discrimination because in principle it violates men's rights to equality (Cooke 2011).

Gender equality at the executive level remains most elusive. The European Union is ahead of the Americas in tackling this with specific targets of increasing the percentage of women in key decision-making positions (European Commission 2016). In 2003, Norway mandated that 40% of non-executive board positions be filled by women. Although that controversial law is now considered a success, its implementation has not trickled down to increase the percentage of women in executive positions (Bertrand et al. 2015). Women's ability to succeed when appointed to executive positions is contingent on eliminating the patriarchal organizational norms for executives as noted above.

The resistance to positive discrimination highlights the cultural resistance to fully disavowing patriarchy, a cultural resistance that has proven slow to change. Goldscheider and Sassler (see Chapter 9) discuss the gender essentialism behind such resistance, so I will not repeat the arguments here. However, as they also argue and as indicated throughout this chapter, both markets and policies can drive us further along the path to gender equality and, in turn, better family outcomes. Only when gender equality is fully institutionalized in markets and policies can the family, however configured, and all of its members, thrive.

12

Concluding Reflections
What Does Less Marriage Have to Do with More Family Inequality?

W. Bradford Wilcox

This volume has explored the nature, causes, and consequences of family inequality in the Americas and Europe. Family inequality, measured both in economic terms and in family structure, can be found in many countries across these three regions, but it is most pronounced in the United States and Latin America (Boertien, Bernardi, and Härkönen, Chapter 7; Carlson, Chapter 1; Esteve and Florez-Paredes, Chapter 2). That is, although gaps in family income between more and less affluent families exist in all countries, they are especially large in the United States and Latin America (Carbone and Cahn, Chapter 13; Esteve and Florez-Paredes, Chapter 2). Likewise, single parenthood and family instability are now more common among those without a college education throughout most of the Americas and Europe, but inequalities in these particular dimensions of family structure seem to be especially prevalent in the United States and Latin America (Carlson, Chapter 1; Esteve and Florez-Paredes, Chapter 2; Perelli-Harris, Chapter 4). Overall, then, less-educated men, women, and their children in these three regions are more likely to be "doubly disadvantaged" – having fewer socioeconomic resources and less family stability, compared to their better-educated fellow citizens (McLanahan 2004; Perelli-Harris 2018) – and this pattern of double disadvantage is most common in the United States and Latin America.

Although this volume chronicles an array of economic, policy, and cultural factors that help to account for this dual pattern of economic and family inequality, it does not focus much on the role, if any, that the retreat from marriage unfolding across much of the globe since the 1960s (Goode 1993; Wilcox and DeRose 2017) has itself played in fueling both family economic inequality and family structure inequality between more- and less-educated Americans and Europeans. The major exception is Eberstadt's chapter (See

Chapter 5), which touches on the ways the decline of marriage among less-educated Americans may help explain the growing divergence in labor force participation among men with and without college degrees in the United States (Lerman and Wilcox 2014). Otherwise, not much attention is paid to the role that the decline of marriage may have played in fueling or locking in patterns of economic and family structure inequality.

Nevertheless, the retreat from marriage that has been unfolding in the Americas and Europe over much of the last half-century may well be an important contributor to growing inequality in family structure between more- and less-educated North Americans and Europeans – and high levels of family inequality between Latin Americans. That is because when marriage is less likely to anchor the adult life course, and less likely to ground and guide the bearing and rearing of children, family instability and single parenthood seem to follow in its retreating wake (Heuveline, Timberlake, and Furstenberg 2003). DeRose and colleagues (2017), for instance, find that in the United States and Europe, children born to cohabiting couples are, on average, about 90 percent more likely to see their parents split by age 12 compared to children born to married couples. Moreover, as cohabitation becomes more common and marriage becomes less common in countries across the globe, family instability generally increases (DeRose et al. 2017). In other words, less marriage seems to equal more family instability and single parenthood for children.

Why is this? Marriage is characterized by a distinctive set of norms, customs, and often legal rights and responsibilities that appear to make it more stable than cohabitation (Nock 1998). For instance, unlike cohabitation and dating, entry into marriage is marked by a collective ritual that signals to self, partner, friends, and family that a new state in life has been entered into. Above all, marriage is generally seen to signify greater commitment than the relational alternatives: It functions as a commitment device (Lundberg, Pollak, and Stearns 2016). Indeed, Perelli-Harris (see Chapter 4) notes that her focus groups with men and women across nine European countries indicate that "participants in all countries generally saw cohabitation as a less committed union than marriage." This, then, is probably why in countries as different as France, Italy, Norway, the United Kingdom, and the United States, children born to married parents enjoy markedly more stability than children born to cohabiting parents (DeRose et al. 2017).

In turn, the rise of cohabitation and the retreat from marriage seems to have affected the less-educated more than the college-educated in many American and European nations, at least as it relates to family instability and single parenthood. The number of families headed by single parents has increased and is markedly higher among those without college degrees in countries as different as Mexico, Sweden, and the United States (Carlson, Chapter 1; Esteve and Florez-Paredes, Chapter 2; Kennedy and Thomson 2010; Wilcox 2010). Although the negative relationship between education and family instability/single parenthood is not universal throughout Europe and the Americas, it does seem to be increasingly the norm (Carlson, Chapter 1; Perelli-Harris, Chapter 4).

Why is family structure increasingly patterned along educational lines? This development is true partly for economic reasons – for instance, less-educated men face higher levels of job instability, which affects both their marriageability and the stability of their families (Carbone and Cahn, Chapter 13; Perelli-Harris, Chapter 4; Wilcox, 2010). However, cultural reasons also seem to matter: The ethos of freedom and choice related to questions of sex, parenthood, and relationships valorized amidst the "second demographic transition," and the deinstitutionalization of marriage this ethos has fueled, can be more difficult for the less educated to navigate when it comes to childbearing, marriage, and the establishment of stable families (Cherlin 2004; Lesthaeghe and Neidert 2006; Sassler and Miller 2017). Future research will have to explore how much, and to what extent, the declining cultural, legal, and economic power of marriage has contributed to growing family structure inequality in much of the Americas and Europe.

Likewise, more needs to be learned about how the retreat from marriage, along with the increasingly stratified character of family structure, has affected economic inequality between families in Europe and Latin America. In the United States, growing family structure inequality appears to have played an important role in increases in family income inequality from the 1970s to the 2000s. The scholarship suggests that between about one fifth (Western, Bloome, and Percheski 2008) and four tenths (S. P. Martin 2006) of the growth in family income inequality over this period can be connected to the growing proportion of single-parent families among less-educated Americans. Because less-educated Americans have experienced much higher levels of family instability and single parenthood than their college-educated peers since the 1970s, their median family incomes are markedly lower than they would otherwise be, especially compared to their college-educated peers who are now much more likely to benefit from two incomes (Lerman and Wilcox 2014). By contrast, if they enjoyed levels of family stability as high as their college-educated fellow citizens, family income inequality in the United States would be smaller.

It is less clear, however, if and how increases in family structure inequality have influenced economic inequality in Europe and Latin America.

In Europe, it is possible that increasing family structure inequality may *not* have led to greater family economic inequality, at least when it comes to family income, because welfare state spending has increased commensurate with the growth in single-parent families (Huber and Stephens 2014). In Latin America, family income inequality has declined in recent years, largely because less-educated workers, including women, are working more and earning more, and welfare state spending has grown (Azevedo, Inchauste, and Sanfelice 2013; Lustig, Lopez-Calva, and Ortiz-Juarez 2013). However, given increases in women's labor force participation among less-educated women, it is possible family income inequality in Latin America would have been reduced even more than it was were it not for the fact that more and more Latin American mothers are single, especially the less-educated (Esteve and Florez-Paredes, Chapter 2). More research is needed to determine if growing family instability in Europe and Latin America has led to greater inequality in family economic well-being between the more and less-educated. Such research needs also to extend beyond income to include considerations of how changes in family structure may influence patterns of inequality in family assets between the highly educated and the less educated.

This volume shows that families across the Americas and Europe are more fragile. This is in part because marriage is less likely to anchor the adult life course, and to ground and guide the bearing and rearing of children in countries across these three continents. What is more, in many countries in the Americas and Europe, family life is particularly fragile among the less educated. This has led to family structure inequality in many countries – from Sweden to the United States – such that highly educated men and women continue to enjoy strong and stable families whereas their less-educated fellow citizens do not. However, it is not clear that growing inequality in family structure uniformly leads to growing family economic inequality in income and assets in these three continents. More research is needed to determine if public policies can and do minimize the economic fallout of growing family structure inequality on economic inequality in Europe and the Americas. In other words, it is not clear if less marriage always need equal more family economic inequality in nations across these three continents.

13

Commentary, Afterword, and Concluding Thoughts on Family Change and Economic Inequality

June Carbone and Naomi R. Cahn

Throughout the developed world, inequality is increasing and the family is changing. Yet, there is no agreement on the links between the two. Some claim that family change – particularly class-based increases in relationship instability, nonmarital cohabitation, and single-parent births – contributes to societal inequality. Accordingly, a renewed emphasis on marriage should be an important part of any solution. Others see economic change as the source of both greater inequality and family transformation, and favor solutions that provide greater support to those left behind – both for poverty alleviation and to enhance relationship stability. Both groups agree that a new information-based society has witnessed a series of overlapping changes: A greater demand for women's market labor, an elite shift to later marriage and relatively more egalitarian relationships, declining wages for unskilled men, greater tolerance for nonmarital sexuality, and lower overall fertility. Yet, they differ in the way they address the relationship between economic change and family values. Some scholars see the values change as a product of the economic changes; elite couples have delayed marriage and childbearing and embraced more cooperative and flexible parental roles in order to be able take advantage of dual career opportunities. We call this "blue" family values (Cahn and Carbone 2010). In accordance with this view, the instability in working-class families involves problems of transition; many societies do not provide sufficient support to systematize the advantages of the new family system, which depend on women's reproductive autonomy, the creation of meaningful social roles for blue-collar men, and greater parental security irrespective of family form. Others view the change in terms of values as independent of the economic changes, and favor stronger support for more responsible decisions about partnering and child-rearing. While the approaches overlap, they differ in their identification of causation, preferred family strategies, and proposed government interventions. Accordingly, while both see increasing working-class instability in employment, residences, and family composition as bad for children, they differ as to whether greater economic insecurity or cultural shifts in family composition play the larger role in increasing that instability.

Testing the relative merits of these viewpoints in a comparative context is challenging. Academic study of the increase in inequality is relatively new, and the study of the connections between inequalities of the family is even more contemporary. Moreover, while economies and families are changing almost everywhere, they are not necessarily changing everywhere in the same ways or at the same rates (Perelli-Harris, Chapter 4). Even within the same countries, for example, urban areas tend to be earlier adopters of the new family model than rural areas; and this may be true whether the urban areas are struggling or thriving (Cahn and Carbone 2010; Kurek 2011). Indeed, family scholars do not even agree on what to call the "new family behaviors" (Perelli-Harrris, Chapter 4), sometimes terming them the "deinstitutionaliza-tion of marriage" (Cherlin 2005), "the second demographic transition" (Lesthaeghe 2010), or something else entirely.

To make sense of the inquiry, an interdisciplinary and international group of scholars came to together in Rome, Italy. In this volume, they provide a comparative analysis of the relationship between growing economic inequal-ity in a large portion of the Western world and the process of family change. Unsurprisingly, they provide no comprehensive resolution of the debate over the implications of family change or the solution to economic inequality. Yet, they create a much more informed foundation for these discussions. Based on the contributions to this volume and our past scholarship in the area within this Commentary, we highlight where grounds emerge for at least tentative agreement, the issues likely to remain subjects of intense disagreement, and the areas which have yet to be fully explored. In doing so, we draw our examples primarily from the United States, although we recognize that it is often an outlier in both economic and family terms. Our goal is to shift the focus from the areas of disagreement toward positive policies with proven impact.

This Commentary breaks the debate down into three areas. We term the first "The View From 10,000 Feet." This section provides an overview of where some agreement is likely. A major part of the debate to date has been between those who see family change as a product of cultural shifts and those who view it as a reaction to a new, postindustrial economic model. Our response, which frames this Commentary and which we explore in this Section, is an emphatic "yes." Economic and cultural changes interact; viewing them as independent of each other is neither necessary nor sustainable. We conclude, therefore, that some agreement should be possible at the 10,000 foot level, and such agreement could involve recognition that the changes we see in the family are part of a transition to a new economy. There also seems to be agreement that this new economy causes reorganization of families' division of market and domestic work, with profound implications for investments in children.

In the second section, "The Nitty-Gritty," we consider the need to develop a dynamic analysis that examines the interaction of cultural, social, economic, and legal factors, rather than the isolation of individual causal agents. We note that determining causation in family change is always challenging. Nonetheless, most scholars agree that a significant factor underlying family composition is the status of women. However, accounting for the impact of change in women's roles is complicated because it involves not only relationships between men and women but also how those relationships affect both men's relative status among men, and women's ability to command societal support for their child-rearing efforts. We conclude that international, regional, and class comparisons are incomplete unless they take into account the societal and legal context for intimate relationships, as some chapters in this volume do.

In the third section, "Why Can't We All Get Along?" we observe the forces blocking comprehensive approaches to the family. If we see what is happening to the family as part of a process of economic and cultural change, the question should be whether it is desirable or possible to speed the transition to the new system of gender egalitarianism and public support for the transition to an information economy for those who might be left behind. In fact, some countries seem to have cushioned the transition to the new system; either because the values underlying the new system are more broadly shared, or because the society provides a greater degree of family support. In other countries however, the process of economic and family change has triggered greater divisions, blocking public support for a more comprehensive approach. We conclude by reviewing the proposals in this volume and their prospects for implementation.

THE VIEW FROM 10,000 FEET

Efforts to describe the family in comparative terms are a fraught enterprise, as they must account for cultural, economic, and legal changes in differing countries with diverse heritages. It is understandable therefore that the papers do not agree on an overall framework as to what exactly has caused changing family structures. Indeed, to the extent they agree on anything, it is most likely to be certain basic facts, and identification of the theories whose predictions *cannot* be validated. We therefore start with the factual assertions on which there is at least some agreement, then move on to the claims that do not stand up to examination, and close with the identification of the missing parts of a full analysis.

To the extent that there is a shared set of assumptions for this volume, they are basic. First, the family has changed. Between 1980 and 2000, fertility declined substantially across most of the developed world, though with greater variation after 2000. Nonmarital cohabitation and childbearing increased during the same period in every developed country. The patterns, however, are not uniform. Sweden and Iceland, which had much higher rates of nonmarital childbearing compared to other European countries in 1980, did not experience a sharp increase. The growth in nonmarital births is leveling off in both Sweden and Iceland (Perelli-Harris, Chapter 4, Figure 4.1).

Second, all developed countries experienced similar economic changes with a reduction in middle-wage jobs. The countries varied, however, in the degree to which they experienced a corresponding increase in higher or lower wage occupations (Cooke, Chapter 11, Table 11.1). France and Denmark, for example, experienced large increases in high-paying occupations, the Republic of Ireland and Finland saw their low-paying jobs expand most; while both high-paying and low paying jobs grew in the United Kingdom and the Netherlands.

Third, women's roles have changed, with women increasing their workforce participation throughout Europe and North America since 1960, although those rates have plateaued in many countries (Cooke, Chapter 11, Table 11.2). The impact of these changes on family, however, varies across countries and regions. In countries with patriarchal gender attitudes, for example, the highest-earning women are less likely to marry than women with less education while in countries with more egalitarian gender attitudes, the highest-earning women have become more likely to marry than other women (Cooke, Chapter 11). In addition, access to employment and contraception has given women greater independence, but the form that independence takes varies considerably. Comparatively, more patriarchal countries such as Italy and Greece may have relatively low levels of nonmarital childbearing, for example, but also have substantially lower fertility rates.

Fourth, the increase in family instability has not affected the well off to the same extent as the middle-class and low-income families, particularly in the countries that have experienced the sharpest increases in nonmarital births and cohabitation. While the class-based divergences are not universal (Garriga and Berta, Chapter 6), such differences are widespread and there is a shared concern that family change may exacerbate economic inequality (Wilcox and Price, Chapter 8).

Despite agreement on the basic facts, there is little agreement on cause or effect. Indeed, the greater theoretical agreement may be on the failure of existing theories to account for what has occurred. Initial studies of the changing family have treated it as a process of cultural change, with elite women among the first to question patriarchal marriage and to embrace a redefinition of intimate relationships. In economics, Gary Becker predicted that low-income couples would experience the greatest increases in relationship instability as they forewent the benefits of "specialization" in the respective spheres of home and market.[1] (Becker 1981) Demographers described the changes in terms of a shift in values toward greater individualization and search for self-fulfillment, with higher educated people leading the way (Lesthaeghe 2010; Van de Kaa 1987). The problem with these theories, however, is that they do not fit the evidence. In the United States in particular, elite families have seen little increase in nonmarital child-rearing and their families have experienced comparative stability (Lundberg, Pollack, and Stearns 2016) at the same time working-class groups with more traditional gender attitudes have experienced the most dramatic increases in relationship instability (Cherlin, Chapter 3). Thus, the authors in this volume share skepticism about the existing theories, but none offers a single, comprehensive, consensus-based alternative account.

Developing such a theory is particularly challenging because, as we have argued elsewhere, it involves integrating the economic and normative changes. The interaction between the two is a dynamic process in which causality likely flows in multiple directions. For example, industrialization made education the new pathway into the middle class (economic); and the family and women's roles within it changed to facilitate greater investment in children (normative) (Carbone and Cahn 2014; Lesthaeghe 2010). The hallmark of the middle class thus became women's ability to stay out of the paid labor market; a luxury beyond the reach of most of the working class until well into the twentieth century, except perhaps during the short-lived postwar economy of the 1950s.

Yet, the embrace of women's distinctive role in overseeing the moral training and development of the young occurred readily in only some places. In the United States for example, farmwives embraced the new gender model before the urban working class; viewing it as an elevation in women's status as they became the moral arbiters of family life (Carbone and Cahn 2014).

---

[1] This is despite the fact that the homemaker role of cook, cleaner, and career tends to be treated as a low-skill occupation that could be the epitome of generalization, while women's increased market labor in fact involves greater specialization among women (Carbone 2000).

European scholars associate similar increases in parental investment in children with greater parental affection (Lesthaeghe 2010), and view rural families as lagging behind urban ones in embracing the new values (Scott and Tilly 1975). On both continents, the shifts in "sentiment" associated with expressive individualism, the move away from arranged marriages, greater female status, and greater investment in children unfolded over centuries (Stone 1977, p. 198). In Europe, for example, women's ability to devote themselves to the home came earlier in Britain, with only 9% of married women in the labor market at the turn of the twentieth century, in contrast to France, where 38% of married women remained in the labor market during the same time period (Scott and Tilly 1975). Cherlin observes in this volume that the American working class acquired the ability to keep wives and children out of the workplace and to invest more heavily in children's education only after World War II (Cherlin, Chapter 3).

Today's information economy has created a similar long-term transformation in the relationship between home and family. The new, postindustrial economy has generated greater demand for women's market labor, making two-income families more important to middle-class status, and rewarding even greater investment in girls and boys. This has also required a reorganization of the family. To realize two incomes, college graduates embrace contraception and delay marriage and childbearing. When they do form families, they engage in a greater degree of assortative mating, with spouses choosing mates with similar interests and socioeconomic status. In managing children, the spouses trade off work force participation and child care, which requires a greater degree of trust and flexibility in managing relationships. We have previously termed this new system of family patterns as "blue" (Cahn and Carbone 2010).

Each of these new systems – one developing during the rise of industrialization and the other coinciding with the information economy – combine adaptation to new economies with new moral understandings. Yet, the process of universalizing these new systems can be slower if the new values are contested, or if the society is unwilling to support economic policies that allow transmission of the new model to those left behind. Unemployed men do not necessarily contribute to the creation of more egalitarian parenting relationships, even if they adore their children. Moreover, community health mediates the impact of growing economic inequality on family stability, with the result that close-knit communities built around shared religious or cultural values and communities with more robust safety nets may not see as much of an increase in family dysfunction. The result – at least in the short term – is greater income and educational inequality.

We have written about these shifts over the last twenty years in the United States (Cahn and Carbone 2010; Carbone 2000; Carbone and Cahn 2014), and we have tried to capture a 10,000-foot view of the nature of the changes. Our story involves the intersection of economic change with family organization and increased class divisions. We have argued that the changes that took place with the rise of industrialization involved the same issues that occur today – greater economic inequality as opportunities increase for some while remaining beyond the reach of others, changing women's roles that reallocate power in intimate relationships, and changing norms that become a source of tension in the recreation of culture. Cooke, with more of a European focus, describes the changes in similar terms (Cooke, Chapter 11). Underlying these changes has been the recreation of class advantage as the middle classes reorganize the family in order to realize the new opportunities – men's entry into the management positions and professions of the industrial economy, and women's similar expansion into the paid labor market today – while securing the investment in children necessary to realize these advantages (Lesthaeghe 2010). In the eighteenth and nineteenth centuries, this involved women's increased status within the home and greater emphasis on child-rearing. In the twenty-first century, it involves shared parenting and greater reliance on paid child care (Cooke, Chapter 11; Goldscheider and Sassler, Chapter 9). Seeing the changes as part of a long-term, unevenly disseminating process provides the basis for more in-depth explorations of the integration of economics and normative change.

Today's shifts – which involve investing in women as well as men's income opportunities, embracing the birth control pill and postponing childbearing, high investment in children based on intensive male and female parenting – also face a difficult challenge to greater acceptance. The reasons, however, lie not with the overall ideal – more egalitarian family practices appear to have won the day in principle throughout the developed world – but rather with the difficulties of implementation. These challenges involve what we label the "nitty-gritty," and they do help explain why analyses of the family remain so divisive.

THE "NITTY–GRITTY"

What we refer to here as "the nitty-gritty" involves the factors that explain how new normative systems spread, such as acceptance of new gendered roles. These factors are context-dependent – potentially varying substantially from rural Calabria to urban Stockholm for example. As explained below, the factors interact with each other in an iterative fashion. In short, they require a dynamic systems analysis, not just the isolation of individual causal agents. In this section, we identify a number of issues that complicate the analyses in this book and serve as important factors that explain differences in perspectives and outcomes. The factors involve men's status, women's sources of support for child-rearing, the legal treatment of intimate and child-rearing relationships, and the interaction between employment and migration in determining the composition of various communities.

Men's Status

All authors concur that declining prospects for working-class men contribute to family change (Cherlin, Chapter 3; Cooke, Chapter 11; Wilcox and Price, Chapter 8). Yet, there is no agreement on the mechanisms that translate a loss in income or employment into a decline in marriage, much less demonstration of a comparative effect across cultures. Indeed, Wilcox and Price (see Chapter 8) report that one of their more surprising findings is that societies with a higher rate of two-parent families do not necessarily have higher levels of male workforce participation.

Two missing pieces may contribute to the analyses: Men's reactions to more competitive status hierarchies and women's choice among possible partners (Carbone and Cahn 2014). In European societies, periods of higher unemployment correlate with lower marriage rates, but these studies do not necessarily track the impact of persistent unemployment or distinguish among subgroups who are more or less connected to stable employment (Kalmijn 2007). Ethnographic studies of low-income communities in the United States, where marriage rates have plummeted, generally indicate that women do not refuse to stay with low-income fathers because of their lack of income in itself. Instead, the women emphasize men's behavior. In one study, over half of the mothers listed domestic violence as a major reason why they were no longer with the fathers of their children (Edin and Kefalas 2005). A more recent study finds that domestic violence may also be a significant factor in younger women's likelihood of pregnancy in the context of unstable relationships (Barber et al. 2017); the violent men were more likely to father children than the women's other male partners. These studies further indicate that infidelity, criminality, and contact with the criminal justice system exacerbate relationship instability.

These correlations may well be a product of more unequal societies. In essence, societies with greater income inequality tend to also have higher levels of violence, imprisonment, and substance abuse (Wilkinson and Pickett 2009). Layoffs further aggravate domestic violence and substance abuse levels

(Carbone and Cahn 2014). In the United States, racial differences exacerbate the effect as communities of color tend to be disproportionate targets for criminal justice enforcement (Butler 2017), and have seen the most rapidly declining marriage rates. Moreover, as unequal societies tend to provide less comprehensive social safety nets, men may experience greater pressure to engage in illegal activities to raise money to support their families (Edin and Nelson 2013). A study of people's reasons for divorce in the Netherlands, a society with a stronger social safety net than the United States, also found that less-educated women were more likely to cite violence, substance abuse, and conflict over expenses as reasons for divorce than the better educated. Indeed, the Dutch women were four times more likely than men to list physical violence (26% women and 6% men) and alcohol and drug abuse (36% and 9%), problems that tend to increase with added stress (De Graaf and Kalmijn 2006). Yet, even the less-educated Dutch women do not cite these factors as often as unmarried American women as the reasons for their break-ups. The study further found that the Dutch women often stated that their husbands worked too much, and that sharing of household responsibilities had been a source of conflict, suggesting that tensions over the transition to more egalitarian family norms remain a factor.

The cumulative impact of these factors may be a series of reinforcing effects. Greater societal marginalization that results in higher levels of death, incapacitation, or incarceration reduces the number of available men (Carlson, Chapter 1). As women see the prospects for good relationships decline, they invest more in their own income opportunities. A paper examining the effect of incarceration on African–Americans, for example, finds that higher levels of incarceration tend to correlate with greater emphasis on women's education and work force participation (Mechoulan 2011). A cross-country comparison similarly found that where the available women outnumbered the men, the women became warier about commitment altogether (Stone, Shackelford, and Buss 2007, p. 297). This process does not just affect the individual woman who might have been partnered with a man who is arrested or otherwise unavailable.

The marginalization of a large number of men, effectively removed them from consideration as appropriate mates, may have similar effects. As Cooke notes, "more desirable men are selected into stable marriages, either because men who are particularly keen to have a family actively prepare for it earlier in the life course, or because savvy women actively pursue such men for marriage" (Cooke, Chapter 11). Where women enjoy the opportunity to select such men, they reinforce the desired characteristics, whether those characteristics are stable employment (Cherlin, Chapter 3), egalitarian attitudes

(Goldscheider and Sassler, Chapter 9), or a college degree, increasing the association of these characteristics with marriage. Where, however, women enjoy worse relationship prospects, they may become more reluctant to commit to any relationships (Carbone and Cahn 2014; Cooke, Chapter 11). Instead, they invest in themselves and their own income prospects and do not necessarily wait for the "right" partner, to whom they are willing to make a commitment before having children. Men within such communities may find that investment in themselves also has little effect on their relationship opportunities, and they may respond to the women's attitudes with greater distrust of their own (Edin and Nelson 2013; Wilson 1996, p. 99).

This combination of the effect of inequality on men's behavior and the corresponding reaction of the available women is harder to measure than the impact of declining employment prospects for men or even the prevalence of egalitarian gender attitudes. This dynamic may also contribute to the creation of distinct subgroups, such as African–Americans in racially and economically segregated communities in the United States, where the number of marriage-able men has declined precipitously with high rates of incarceration. In other communities with high poverty or unemployment rates, however, low-income men may not experience the same degree of societal marginalization. In these cases, relationship stability may not decline to the same extent. Accordingly, the question becomes identifying the filter that translates changing men's employment prospects into behavior that disrupts relationships, and produces women's strategies that move family formation efforts away from marriage or long-term cohabitation. While Goldscheider and Sassler (Chapter 9) are optimistic that middle-class norms will permeate lower income relationships, this seems unlikely in the absence of economic stability and decreasing incarceration rates – at least in the United States.

Sources of Support for Child-Rearing

The second factor that may connect economic change to relationship stability is the perceived source of support for child-rearing. Historically, marriage involved an exchange of men's financial support for recognition as the head of the household. In many countries, fathers could secure recognition of their paternity and right to a relationship to their children only through marriage. Likewise, mothers could claim paternal, societal, and often familial support for their children only if they married. Otherwise, they faced being ostracized (Carbone and Cahn 2014; Perelli-Harris, Chapter 4). Today however, sources of financial and emotional support for child-rearing vary widely. In this con-text, women who rely on their own earnings to provide for children may find marriage to an unreliable, abusive, or needy partner to be a more of a threat rather than an advantage in raising children.

The new ideal, as Cooke (see Chapter 11) and Goldscheider and Sasssler (see Chapter 9) suggest, may be an egalitarian one: Fathers and mothers trade off providing financial and carer contributions to the family. This changes marriage from a hierarchical relationship in which wives are expected to obey their husbands to partnerships that depend on greater degrees of trust, flexibility, and collaboration. This in turn changes the nature of relationship bargains making them far more individualized and more dependent on the relative positions of intimate partners, the legal and cultural context in which the bargain is struck, and the expected sources of support for child-rearing. Both men and women, for example, fear the consequences of divorce – which may be expensive and emotionally wrenching. Yet, different groups may fear divorce for different reasons.

High-income partners have long been wary of an intimate spouse's rights to leave a relationship and command continued spousal support. Mid- and low-income women may be more concerned about their ability to leave an abusive or unfaithful spouse without having to share decision-making power over their children. An American study that surveyed cohabiting couples in their twenties about their plans to marry indicated that wariness about marriage reflected class and gender differences. Among those with at least some college attendance, two thirds of the women while only about one third of the men reported that they planned to marry their current partners. Among individuals who did not attend college, the percentages were reversed: Two thirds of the men, but far fewer of the women planned to marry their current parents (Hymowitz et al. 2013).

The reasons may have to do with the legal consequences of marriage. In all countries, marriage is associated with a commitment to the other spouse (Perelli-Harris, Chapter 4). Couples who see cohabitation as a testing ground may be wary of whether the other partner is worthy of that commitment. The consequences can be stark. Two incomes are increasingly necessary to enjoy a comfortable family life, particularly in expensive cities such as London and New York. Marrying a partner who does not contribute a fair share to the household may threaten middle-class status. In addition, if the relationship does not last, the higher earning spouse may be subject to a substantial obligation for support, or an equal division of family property, making marriage an expensive proposition.

Yet, the impact of these considerations on relationship-form can be complex. In more traditional European countries, for example, the influence of religion is greater, divorce is rarer, and better-educated women may be less likely to marry than other women (Kamlijn 2007, 2013). These patterns suggest that marriage still reflects more traditional gender roles, which deter divorce – and in some countries, may simultaneously deter marriage and childbearing. In more egalitarian societies on the other hand, gender-based support obligations have disappeared, and more equal contributions to the relationship have become a more important source of stability (Carbone and Cahn 2014).

For those who are not wealthy, marriage has risks as well as benefits. In the United States, the median working-age household has approximately $5,000 in retirement savings (Elkins 2017); and more than half of Americans have less than $1,000 in the bank (Maxfield 2016). Commitment to a partner with an unstable income, who runs up the credit card bills, incurs large health care expenses in the absence of insurance, or needs to be bailed out of jail, can diminish family savings. Marriage entails a commitment – legally, financially and emotionally – to equally share the couple's joint resources (Miller, Sassler, and Kusi-Appouh 2011). For couples with unstable finances, particularly where one partner's contributions are more variable than the others, this commitment may be a source of peril – and this may be true even if the couple would be financially better off combining their resources. For the more reliable partner, it may only take one fender-bender, missed mortgage payment, or wrongful arrest to trigger a financial crisis. In the Republic of Ireland, the expense and inconvenience of divorce appears to have contributed to the self-selection of the stable into marriage as well as to greater legal and social acceptance of nonmarital unions (Fahey 2012).

Custody laws tend to further complicate the analysis. In all countries, marriage makes paternity recognition easier, even if unmarried couples can also receive acknowledgment, and for both mothers and fathers, fear of losing access to children may discourage divorce. In the United States, where courts increasingly award custody to both parents, mothers who fear loss of control over their children become less likely to file for divorce (Carbone and Cahn 2014). In Europe, this may discourage men from filing divorce, "possibly reflecting an anticipation of weaker postdivorce contact with their children" (Härkönen 2014, p. 15). Similar custody concerns may also affect a willingness to marry. In the United States for example, women frequently cite the difficulties and expense of divorce as a reason not to marry; and custody is a major part of their concern, particularly where shared parenting orders have become the norm at divorce while they are more difficult for unmarried men to obtain. . (Carbone and Cahn 2013).

Labor Market Effects and the Difficulties of Measurement

An additional factor complicating the relationship between inequality and the family is the impact of labor market policies in different societies. These policies may not only affect various groups within the same country differently, but the policies may also encourage migration to different regions which skews the results of statistical measures.

Underlying these different effects is employment stability. The ability to secure stable employment tends to increase marriage rates. Yet, we know less about the consequences of readily available, but insecure sources of employment. For example, a major difference between the United States and Europe is that European labor market regulations tend to produce more stable jobs, while increasing unemployment. These policies simultaneously create greater security for those with permanent jobs, incentives to postpone marriage and childbearing for people who hope to receive such jobs in the future, and greater emigration to other countries with better employment possibilities (Alderman 2017). In the United States, where there is less labor regulation, employment and income instability has increased on a more permanent basis for blue-collar workers. This has had at least some impact on people's abilities to create and maintain families (Pew Charitable Trusts 2017; Pugh 2017, p. 4). We have yet to see a comprehensive comparative study of the impact of this type of instability, but we would expect income instability to increase the reluctance to marry and undermine the level of commitment in lower income families.

A second issue is migration. In the United States, the states that enjoyed the greatest drops in teenage births were those that had the greatest in-migration of college graduates (Cahn and Carbone 2010). This changed the composition of both the origin states and the destination states. More recently, the end of net migration to the United States from Mexico appears to have made a significant contribution to the drop in overall fertility within the United States – with approximately half of the overall decline and an even greater percentage of the drop within teenage births coming from the changing fertility patterns of the Latino population (Cahn, Carbone, and Levine 2016). On the other hand, Germany has both the largest number of its citizens living abroad, and also the largest volume of immigration in Europe. Similarly, Italy has also experienced a loss of many of its most ambitious citizens aboard (Anelli and Peri 2016), and the Republic of Ireland has long claimed that its most prominent export is the Irish people (The *Irish Examiner* 2010). Indeed, even within countries, the differences between urban and rural areas may be influenced by migration of the young, the ambitious, and the adventurous to cities while those left behind tend to be older, more traditional, and more religious. Migration thus increases the cultural differences between rural and urban areas.

These migration patterns may affect not just the overall composition of particular countries, but gender ratios within regions. For example, a major factor depressing the marriage rates of well-educated minority women in American cities is the differential migration rates of men and women to those cities. In New York, 53% of women in their twenties working are college graduates in comparison to only 38% of the men, a gap greater for Blacks and Latinos than Whites (Carbone and Cahn 2014). Large diverse cities such as New York offer more employment opportunities than other places for both highly educated minority women and less-educated immigrant men (Carbone and Cahn 2014). Thus, overall statistics with respect to these cities may seem misleading.

A third issue concerns regional, cultural, and racial differences, factors that are considered in some of the contributors to the volume (e.g., Perelli-Harris, Chapter 4). Within the United States, the counties that have the highest proportion of single-parent families tend to be those which are racially and economically isolated (Chetty 2014a,b). Conversely in Europe, cultural differences may involve long-established cultural patterns, such as those between northwestern and southern Poland (Kurek 2011), or Northwestern and Southern Europe (Kalmijn 2011). Cultural differences that took root a century or more ago may continue to influence family patterns in ways that are difficult to tease out in cross-country comparisons.

All of these complexities present challenges to constructing an overall model of the feedback mechanisms between economic inequality and family change. The immediate challenge, however, is to develop policies that respond to the consequences of increasingly inequality.

"WHY CAN'T WE ALL GET ALONG?"

The predominant view of the contributions to this volume is that we are in the midst of a profound family change. The family instability we are witnessing could simply be an issue of transition. For example, comparative studies show that the higher the amount of cohabitation in a society, the more cohabitants resemble married couples (Soons and Kalmijn 2009). A more universal embrace of the new system could therefore improve stability, as couples once again internalize similar expectations about their relationships (Cooke, Chapter 11; Goldscheider and Sassler, Chapter 9). Alternatively, a move toward more egalitarian gender relationships may also provide single parents greater freedom to raise children on their own and more incentive for the state to support them. Greater variety may therefore become a more permanent feature of family life, but variety does not have to be associated with instability. In the meantime, we should do everything to mitigate the negative consequences of the transition; and to cushion the negative impact of greater economic inequality on children's life chances – an effort that other countries are undertaking (Boertien, Bernardi, and Härkönen, Chapter 7).

Three substantial obstacles complicate this process. First, there are cultural differences rooted in religion (Perelli-Harris, Chapter 4). The new egalitarian system rests on providing women substantial control of reproduction, partly through the availability of contraception and abortion. This postponement of family formation, and state support for the universalization of the means to do so, offends many religious teachings (Cahn and Carbone 2010). Where religious opposition becomes entrenched, as which occurred in the United States to systematic sex education and provision of contraception, or in the Republic of Ireland to divorce and abortion, the result tends to be the exacerbation of class and regional differences. In the case of abortion for example, the Irish elite evade the religiously based restrictions through travel abroad while the poor are subject to them (Aiken, Gomperts, and Trussell 2016). In the United States, the class-based differences in unintended pregnancies grew substantially between the early 1990s and 2009 at the same time that abortion rates fell for all groups (Carbone and Cahn 2014). The changes in unintended pregnancy rates correlated with the increasing class divergence in family formation practices, particularly among Whites and Latinos. Thus, while Reeves' proposals in this volume (see Chapter 10) for more universal access to contraception make eminent sense and have already produced impressive results in Colorado and many European countries in preventing early births, we believe universal adoption of such policies will be gradual. Indeed, the 2017 Trump Administration proposals would further undermine access to contraception, not just abortion, in the name of religious liberty.

The second obstacle increasing inequality pertains to the same practices lacking the same meanings throughout society. College graduate women, for example, have embraced an ethic that they should not have children with a partner they do not trust. In the United States, higher income women have relatively low levels of unintended pregnancies, and abort a higher percentage of unintended pregnancies than any other group (Guttmacher 2016). Their willingness to marry may in turn reflect acceptance of the egalitarian custody norms marriage now imposes, which include shared parenting and equal custody rights. In contrast, working-class women are more likely to have a child as a result of an unintended pregnancy or in circumstances where they view few available men as worthy of trust (Barber et al. 2017; Burton et al. 2009). In these circumstances, the egalitarian custody norms applicable at divorce may be inappropriate (Carbone and Cahn 2013). For example, an American study of divorcing couples found that the award of increased rates of shared parenting time correlated with increased domestic violence complaints, holding the other factors as constant (Brinig 2017). The author speculates "should the same logic hold true for unmarried parents, who as noted experience more domestic violence in their relationships, the concerns about insisting upon parenting orders for them at the time support is established would be justified" (Brinig 2017).

The third factor involves the lack of shared ways of discussing the cultural changes. Most studies find that greater family stability of all kinds, including more stable employment and income, fewer residential moves, and more stable household composition, benefits children. Further, while groups differ on the degree to which economic vs. cultural factors influence such stability, they agree that individual decisions play a role in family outcomes. Yet, different cultural groups fundamentally differ not just on the content, but the sources of individual responsibility and moral values. Modernist societies (which we have labeled "blue") differ from traditionalist ones (red) in the way they allocate discussions of morality to the public and private spheres. In modernist societies, the public virtues are equality and tolerance; notions of family form, consensual sexual behavior, and appropriate child-rearing practices are matters of private choice. More traditionalist societies insist on the importance of upholding shared values (such as childbearing within marriage) in the public square in order to reinforce the right values at home (Carbone 2017). Blue societies thus distrust a public emphasis on marriage per se, either because they associate with it with an older form of hierarchical gender roles or because they see it as a substitute for a process of individual selection of the right partner and the right values. Instead, they see family stability as coming from relationships premised on flexibility and trust. This in turn place much more emphasis on parental guidance in raising children who develop the individual moral codes, which they internalize as central to their personal integrity and which in turn make them trustworthy. These individual codes can vary, but responsible adulthood and personal self-respect depend on having one that orders a person's adult commitments and life choices, and that informs selection of an appropriate partner. Central to this process is avoiding childbearing until one is fully capable of assuming the responsibilities that comes with it in part because the system's success depends on a substantial degree of parental investment in children. Within this system, fully mature adults with well-developed personal codes do not need marriage; they would largely behave the same way without it. Also, without development of the underlying individual codes, marriage in an era in which it rests on flexibility and trust is unlikely to succeed. Indeed, within the United States, red states tend to have higher teen birth and divorce rates (Cahn and Carbone 2010; Glass and Levchak 2014).

Traditionalist societies often criticize the modernist approach as license. They associate tolerance in the public square with irresponsibility within the family. They prefer systems that seek to instill universal values that come from religious traditions or shared cultural norms. Historically, this system sought to insure family stability through marriage soon after completion of one's education, and socialization into adulthood through the assumption of gendered family roles (Cherlin 2005). Yet, this system also produced stability in part because of women's dependence. Today, such an approach works best with two parents who share the same traditionalist commitments, especially when the couple resides in a community that reinforces these values.

These two systems talk past each other, about both the source of moral values and the way to promote them. Traditionalists see moral failings as a product of insufficient public affirmation and private acceptance of responsibility; modernists see them as a product of the failure to create the conditions that promote individual flourishing. With greater inequality undermining both public support for family well-being and individual ability to live up to traditional precepts, the cultural clash between these views intensifies.

As a result, there are no easy policy prescriptions for increasing family stability because the interaction between economic changes and cultural norms is multi-causal, dynamic, and interactive (Cooke, Chapter 11), and there is no shared set of assumption for discussing the issues – other than an agreement that family stability is good for children. The evidence indicates that a narrow focus on family form, while it may produce benefits for relatively homogenous groups, does not work as a more universal public policy prescription. For example, in the United States, studies show that where both spouses are religious and attend the same church, divorce rates are low even if the spouses marry young. Other studies indicate, however, that in more religious communities in the United States, those who attend church less often have higher divorce rates than comparable couples in less religious communities. This is true in part because the religious practice of younger marriage in these communities tends to lower the average age of marriage for everyone, and marriage at younger ages carries with it a higher risk of divorce (Glass and Levchak 2014). While the selection effects make the picture more complicated, encouraging a return to marriage as the sole locale for child-rearing, for example, does not solve the problem of economic instability, which tends to weaken the resilience of most communities. In the United States, race tempers the financial benefits of marriage; as the St. Louis Federal Reserve reported, "when we focus on family-structure differences *within* racial or ethnic groups, rather than *between* groups, there is essentially no relationship at all" between family structure and wealth (Emmons & Rickett 2017). A cross-cultural study similarly found that differences in family structure have virtually no impact on children's educational attainment, after controlling for other factors (Bernardi and Boertien 2015). As Boertien, Bernardi, and Härkönen ask, in Chapter 7: "Does the result that family structure can explain little of socioeconomic background differences in educational attainment imply that family structure does not matter for socioeconomic inequality of opportunity in general?" They conclude that we simply do not know. The existing evidence on the relationship between family structure and educational attainment is simply too limited, with a small set of countries and time periods (Boertien, Bernardi, and Härkönen, Chapter 7).

Even if marriage were at least a partial solution, marriage promotion programs do not "affect marriage or poverty rates" for low-income couples (Randles 2017, p. 14), particularly in the absence of societal efforts to address the economic instability that correlates with unstable relationships (Cherlin, Chapter 3). Moreover, growing up in a single-parent family home has different effects on children's outcomes, depending on the country (Garriga and Berta, Chapter 6), or even the number of single-parent families in the community (Soons and Kalmijn 2009). Interventions strengthening children's well-being may be more effective than marriage promotion per se (Reeves, Chapter 10), and policies that support reproductive rights, greater access to health care, and improved workers' rights (such as a higher minimum wage) are also associated with family stability (Robbins and Fremstad 2016).

By presenting the complexity of variations between and within countries, this volume shows that generalizations about the impact of family structure do not work. Nonetheless, the weight of the evidence in this volume suggests that economic change is producing both family change and greater inequality, at different rates, in different forms across different societies. Cultural factors in these societies may, in turn aggravate or ameliorate the effects on family well-being; so too may societal interventions that cushion or worsen the consequences of greater economic inequality. All of these societies are moving toward at least slightly more egalitarian gender relationships as women's workforce participation has increased. Moreover, all societies are finding that it is difficult to maintain traditional understandings as a universal basis for family relationships. We conclude that, while there is much we still do not know about the interactions between changing families and changing economies, future family stability and the marshaling of resources necessary for children's well-being will require acceptance of at least a degree of family change and also a deeper integration of egalitarian relationships into our understanding of family function.

References

Aarskaug Wiik, Kenneth, Renske Keizer, and Trude Lappegård. 2012. "Relationship Quality in Marital and Cohabiting Unions across Europe." *Journal of Marriage and Family* 74(3): 389–398.

Acker, Joan. 2006. "Inequality Regimes: Gender, Class, and Race in Organizations." *Gender & Society* 20(4): 441–464.

Addo, Fenaba, Brienna Perelli-Harris, Stefanie Hoherz, Trude Lappegård, and Sharon Sassler. 2017. "Partnership Status and the Wage Premium in the United States, United Kingdom, Germany, and Norway: What Explains Differentials Between Married and Cohabiting Adults?" Population Association of America, Chicago, IL, USA, April 27–29, 2017.

AEI-Brookings Working Group on Paid Family Leave. 2017. *Paid Family and Medical Leave: An Issue Whose Times Has Come*. Washington, DC: AEI-Brookings.

AEI-Brookings Working Group on Poverty and Opportunity. 2015. *Opportunity, Responsibility, and Security: A Consensus Plan for Reducing Poverty and Restoring the American Dream*. Washington: DC: AEI-Brookings.

Aghion, Philippe, Leah Boustan, Caroline Hoxby, and Jerome Vandenbussche. 2009. "The Causal Impact of Education on Economic Growth: Evidence from US." [Unpublished.]

Ahituv, Avner and Robert I. Lerman. 2007. "How Do Marital Status, Work Effort, and Wages Interact?" *Demography* 44(3): 623–647.

Aiken, A. R. A., R. Gomperts, and J. Trussell. 2016. "Experiences and Characteristics of Women Seeking and Completing At-Home Medical Termination of Pregnancy through Online Telemedicine in Ireland and Northern Ireland: A Population-Based Analysis." *BJOG* 124(8): 1208–1215.

Aisenbrey, Silke, Marie Evertsson, and Daniella Grunow 2009. "Is There a Career Penalty for Mothers' Time Out? A Comparison of Germany, Sweden and the United States." *Social Forces* 88(2): 573–603.

Aizer, Anna. 2010. "The Gender Wage Gap and Domestic Violence." *The American Economic Review* 100(4): 1847–1859.

Akerlof, George A. 1998. "Men without Children." *The Economic Journal,* 108(447): 287–309.

Akers, Beth and Matthew M. Chingos. 2016. *Game of Loans: The Rhetoric and Reality of Student Debt*. Princeton, NJ: Princeton University Press.

Alamillo, Julia. 2016. *Family Structure and the Reproduction of Inequality: A Decomposition Approach*. Mathematica Policy Research Working Paper No. 49. Chicago, IL: Mathematica Policy Research.

Albertini, Marco and Jaap Dronkers. 2009. "Effects of Divorce on Children's Educational Attainment in a Mediterranean and Catholic Society." *European Societies* 11(1): 137–159.

Alderman, Liz. "Feeling 'Pressure All the Time' on Europe's Treadmill of Temporary Work." *The New York Times* February 9, 2017. www.nytimes.com/2017/02/09/busi ness/europe-jobs-economy-youth-unemployment-millenials.html?_r=0 (Retrieved March 1, 2018.)

Amato, Paul R. 1993. "Children's Adjustment to Divorce: Theories, Hypotheses, and Empirical Support." *Journal of Marriage and the Family* 55(1): 23–38.

Amato, Paul R. 2000. "The Consequences of Divorce for Adults and Children." *Journal of Marriage and Family* 62(4): 1269–1287.

Amato, Paul R. 2010. "Research on Divorce: Continuing Trends and New Developments." *Journal of Marriage and Family* 72(3): 650–666.

Amato, Paul R. and Christopher J. Anthony. 2014. "Estimating the Effects of Parental Divorce and Death with Fixed Effects Models." *Journal of Marriage and Family* 76 (2): 370–386.

Amato, Paul R., Alan Booth, Susan McHale, and Jennifer Van Hook, eds. 2015. *Families in an Era of Increasing Inequality*. National Symposium on Family Issues Volume 5. Switzerland: Springer International Publishing.

Amato, Paul R. and Joan G. Gilbreth. 1999. "Nonresident Fathers and Children's Well-Being: A Meta-Analysis." *Journal of Marriage and the Family* 61(3): 557–573.

Amato, Paul R., and Spencer James. 2010. "Divorce in Europe and the United States: Commonalities and Differences across Nations." *Family Science* 1(1): 2–13.

Amato, Paul R. and Bruce Keith. 1991. "Parental Divorce and Adult Well-Being: A Meta-Analysis." *Journal of Marriage and the Family* 61(3): 43–58.

Amato, Paul R., Catherine Meyers, and Robert Emery. 2009. "Changes in Nonresident Father-Child Contact from 1976 to 2002." *Family Relations* 58(1): 41–53.

Andersson, Gunnar. 2004. "Children's Experience of Family Disruption and Family Formation: Evidence from 16 FFS Countries." *Vienna Yearbook of Population Research* 2: 313–332.

Andersson, Gunnar, Elizabeth Thomson, and Aija Duntava. 2017. "Life-Table Representations of Family Dynamics in the 21st Century." *Demographic Research* 37(35): 1081–1230.

Anelli, Massimo and Giovanni Peri. June 2016. *Does Emigration Delay Political Change? Evidence from Italy during the Great Recession*. NBER Working Paper No. 22350. Cambridge, MA: National Bureau of Economic Research.

Antecol, Heather and Kelly Bedard. 2007. "Does Single Parenthood Increase the Probability of Teenage Promiscuity, Substance Use, and Crime?" *Journal of Population Economics* 20(1): 55–71.

Arias, Elizabeth and Alberto Palloni. 1999. "Prevalence and Patterns of Female Headed Households in Latin America: 1970–1990." *Journal of Comparative Family Studies* 30(2): 257–279.

Armingeon, Klaus. 2001. "Institutionalizing the Swiss Welfare State." *West European Politics* 24(2): 145–168.

Arriagada, Irma. 2004. "Transformaciones Sociales y Demograficas de las Familias Latinoamericanas." *Papeles de Población* 10(40): 71–95.

Arriagada Acuña, Irma. 2009. "La Diversidad y las Desigualdad de las Familias Latinoamericanas." *Revista Latinomaericana de Estudios de Familia* 1: 9–21.

Astone, Nan Marie and Sara S. McLanahan. 1991. "Family Structure, Parental Practices and High School Completion." *American Sociological Review* 56(3): 309–320.

Atkinson, Anthony B, Thomas Piketty, and Emmanuel Saez. 2011. "Top Incomes in the Long Run of History." *Journal of Economic Literature* 49(1): 3–71.

Aughinbaugh, Alison, Omar Robles, and Hugette Sun. 2013. "Marriage and Divorce: Patterns by Gender, Race, and Educational Attainment." *Monthly Labor Review* October: 1–18.

Augustine, Jennifer March. 2014. "Maternal Education and the Unequal Significance of Family Structure for Children's Early Achievement." *Social Forces* 93(2): 687–718.

Augustine, Jennifer March, and Robert Crosnoe. 2010. "Mothers' Depression and Educational Attainment and Their Children's Academic Trajectories." *Journal of Health and Social Behavior* 51(3): 274–290.

Autor, David. 2010. *The Polarization of Job Opportunities in the U.S. Labor Market: Implications for Employment and Earnings.* Washington, DC: Center for American Progress and the Hamilton Project of the Brookings Institution. https://economics .mit.edu/files/5554 (Retrieved March 15, 2017.)

Autor, David H. 2014. "Skills, Education, and the Rise of Earnings Inequality among the 'Other 99 Percent.'" *Science* 344(6186): 843–851.

Autor, David, David Dorn, and Gordon Hanson. 2018. *When Work Disappears: Manufacturing Decline in the Falling Marriage-Market Value of Young Men.* NBER Working Paper No. 23173. Cambridge, MA: National Bureau of Economic Research.

Autor, David, David Figlio, Krzysztof Karbownik, Jeffrey Roth, and Melanie Wasserman. 2016. *Family Disadvantage and the Gender Gap in Behavioral and Educational Outcomes.* NBER Working Paper No. 22267. Cambridge, MA: National Bureau of Economic Research.

Autor, David H., Lawrence F. Katz, and Melissa S. Kearney. 2008. "Trends in U.S. Wage Inequality: Revising the Revisionists." *Review of Economics and Statistics* 90 (2): 300–323.

Autor, David and Melanie Wasserman. 2013. *Wayward Sons: The Emerging Gender Gap in Education and Labor Markets.* Washington, DC: Third Way.

Azevedo, Joao Pedro, Gabriela Inchauste, and Viviane Sanfelice. 2013. *Decomposing the Recent Inequality Decline in Latin America.* Policy Research Working Paper No. 6715. Washington, DC: World Bank Group.

Bailey, Thomas R., Shanna Smith Jeggars, and Davis Jenkins. 2015. *Redesigning America's Community Colleges.* Boston: Harvard University Press.

Banco Interamericano de Desarrollo (BID). 1998. América Latina Frente a la Desigualdad: Progreso Económico y Social en América Latina, Informe 1998/1999. *Washington, DC: IDB.*

Barber, Jennifer, Yasamin Kusunoki, Heather Gatny, and Robert Melendez. 2017. "The Relationship Context of Young Pregnancies." *Law & Inequality: A Journal of Theory and Practice* 35(2): 175–198.

Baude, Amandine, Jessica Pearson, and Sylvie Drapeau. 2016. "Child Adjustment in Joint Physical Custody Versus Sole Custody: A Meta-Analytic Review." *Journal of Divorce & Remarriage* 57(5): 338–360.

Becker, Gary S. 1973. "A Theory of Marriage: Part I." *Journal of Political Economy* 81(4): 813–846.

Becker, Gary S. 1981. A Treatise on the Family. Cambridge, MA: Harvard University Press.

Becker, Gary S. 1985. "Human Capital, Effort, and the Sexual Division of Labor." *Journal of Labor Economics* 3(2): S33–S58.

Becker, Gary S. 1991. *A Treatise on the Family*, enlarged edn. Cambridge, MA: Harvard University Press.

Becker, Gary S. 1993. "Nobel Lecture: The Economic Way of Looking at Behavior." *Journal of Political Economy* 101(3): 385–409.

Berghammer, Caroline, Katrin Fliegenschnee, and Eva-Maria Schmidt. 2014. "Cohabitation and Marriage in Austria: Assessing the Individualization Thesis Across the Life Course." *Demographic Research* 31(37): 1137–1166.

Bernardi, Fabrizio and Diederik Boertien. 2016. "Understanding Heterogeneity in the Effects of Parental Separation on Educational Attainment in Britain: Do Children from Lower Educational Backgrounds Have Less to Lose?" *European Sociological Review* 32(6): 807–819.

Bernardi, Fabrizio and Diederik Boertien. 2017a. "Non-Intact Families and Diverging Educational Destinies: A Decomposition Analysis for Germany, Italy, the United Kingdom and the United States." *Social Science Research* 63: 181–191.

Bernardi, Fabrizio and Diederik Boertien. 2017b. "Explaining Conflicting Results in Research on the Heterogeneous Effects of Parental Separation on Children's Educational Attainment According to Social Background." *European Journal of Population* 33(2): 243–266.

Bernardi, Fabrizio, Diederik Boertien and Daria Popova. 2014. *Differential Effects of Parental Separation on Child Outcomes: Are Children from Higher Social Backgrounds Affected More?* EUI MWP Working Paper No. 6. Florence: Max Weber Programme, European University Institute.

Bernardi, Fabrizio, Juho Härkönen, Diederik Boertien, Linus Andersson Rydell, Kim Bastaits, and Dimitri Mortelmans. 2013. *State-of-the-art report. Effects of Family Forms and Dynamics on Children's Well-being and Life Chances: Literature Review.* Families and Societies. Working Paper Series No. 4.

Bernardi, Fabrizio and Jonas Radl. 2014. "The Long-Term Consequences of Parental Divorce for Children's Educational Attainment." *Demographic Research* 30(61): 1653–1680.

Berrington, Ann and Ian Diamond. 2000. "Marriage or Cohabitation: A Competing Risks Analysis of First–Partnership Formation among the 1958 British Birth Cohort." *Journal of the Royal Statistical Society: Series A (Statistics in Society)* 163(2): 127–151.

Berrington, Ann, Brienna Perelli-Harris, and Paulina Trevena. 2015. "Commitment and the Changing Sequence of Cohabitation, Childbearing, and Marriage: Insights from Qualitative Research in the UK." *Demographic Research* 33(12): 327–362.

Bertrand, Marianne, Sandra E. Black, Sissel Jensen, and Adriana Lleras-Muney. 2015. *Breaking the Glass Ceiling.* CEPR Discussion Paper No. DP10467. London: Centre for Economic Policy Research. https://ssrn.com/abstract=2575771 (Retrieved March 17, 2017.)

Bertrand, Marianne and Jessica Pan. 2013. "The Trouble with Boys: Social Influences and the Gender Gap in Disruptive Behavior." *AEJ: Applied Economics* 5(1): 32–64.

Biblarz, Timothy J. and Adrian E. Raftery. 1993. "The Effects of Family Disruption on Social Mobility." *American Sociological Review* 58(1): 97–109.

Billari, Francesco C. and Aart C. Liefbroer. 2010. "Towards a New Pattern of Transition to Adulthood?" *Advances in Life Course Research* 15(2–3): 59–75.

Billingsley, Sunnee and Tommy Ferrarini. 2014. "Family Policy and Fertility Intentions in 21 European Countries." *Journal of Marriage and Family* 76(2): 428–445.

Binstock, Georgina. 2010. "Tendencias Sobre la Convivencia, Matrimonio y Paternidad en Áreas Urbanas de Argentina." *Revista Latinoamericana de Población* 6: 129–146.

Bjarnason, Thoroddur and Arsaell M. Arnarsson. 2011. "Joint Physical Custody and Communication with Parents: A Cross-National Study of Children in 36 Western Countries." *Journal of Comparative Family Studies* 42(6): 871–890.

Björnberg, Ulla and M. H. Otteson. 2013. "Gender Equality and Nordic Family Policy." In *Challenges for Future Family Policy in the Nordic Countries.* Copenhagen: The Danish National Centre for Social Research, pp. 207–225.

Bjørnskov, Christian. 2012. "How Does Social Trust Affect Economic Growth?" *Southern Economic Journal* 78(4): 1346–1368.

Blank, Rebecca M. 1997. *It Takes a Nation: A New Agenda for Fighting Poverty.* Princeton, NJ: Princeton University Press.

Blank, Rebecca M. 2009. "Economic Change and the Structure of Opportunity for Less-Skilled Workers." In M. Cancian and S. Danziger, eds., *Changing Poverty, Changing Policies.* New York: Russell Sage Foundation, pp. 63–91.

Blau, Francine and Lawrence Kahn. 2007. "Changes in the Labor Supply Behavior of Married Women: 1980–2000." *Journal of Labor Economics* 25(3): 393–438.

Blau, Francine and Anne E. Winkler. 2017. *Women, Work, and Family.* NBER Working Paper No. 23644. Cambridge, MA: National Bureau of Economic Research.

Blossfeld, Hans-Peter and Andreas Timm. 2003. *Who Marries Whom?: Educational Systems as Marriage Markets in Modern Societies.* Vol. 12. Berlin: Springer Science & Business Media.

Boertien, Diederik. 2012. "Jackpot? Gender Differences in the Effects of Lottery Wins on Separation." *Journal of Marriage and Family* 74(5): 1038–1053.

Boertien, Diederik and Juho Härkönen. 2018. "Why Does Women's Education Stabilize Marriages? The Role of Marital Attractions and Barriers to Divorce." *Demographic Research.*

Bonoli, Giuliano. 2005. "The Politics of the New Social Policies: Providing Coverage against New Social Risks in Mature Welfare States." *Policy and Politics* 33(3): 431–449.

Brandolini, Andrea and Timothy Smeeding. 2006. "Patterns of Economic Inequality in Western Democracies: Some Facts on Levels and Trends." *PS: Political Science & Politics* 39(1): 21–26.

Brescoll, Victoria L., Jennifer Glass and Alexandra Sedlovskaya. 2013. "Ask and Ye Shall Receive? The Dynamics of Employer-Provided Flexible Work Options and the Need for Public Policy." *Journal of Social Issues* 69(2): 367–388.

Brinton, Mary and Dong-Ju Lee. 2016. "Gender-Role Ideology, Labor Market Institutions, and Postindustrial Fertility." *Population and Development Review* 42: 405–433.

Brady, David and Rebekah Burroway. 2012. "Targeting, Universalism, and Single-Mother Poverty: A Multilevel Analysis across 18 Affluent Democracies." *Demography* 49(2): 719–746.

Breen, Richard and Signe Hald Andersen. 2012. "Educational Assortative Mating and Income Inequality in Denmark." *Demography* 49(3): 867–887.

Brewster, Karen and Ron Rindfuss. 2000. "Fertility and Women's Employment in Industrialized Nations." *Annual Review of Sociology* 26(1): 271–296.

Brinig, Margaret F. 2017. "Chickens and Eggs: Does Custody Move Support, or Vice-Versa?" *Journal of American Academy of Matrimonial Law* 29: 269–294.

Brown, Susan L. 2000. "The Effect of Union Type on Psychological Well-Being: Depression among Cohabitors Versus Marrieds." *Journal of Health and Social Behavior* 41(3): 241–255.

Budig, Michelle J. and Paula England. 2001. "The Wage Penalty for Motherhood." *American Sociological Review* 66(2): 204–225.

Budig, Michelle.J., Joya Misra, and Irene Boeckmann. 2012. "The Motherhood Penalty in Cross-National Perspective: The Importance of Work–Family Policies and Cultural Attitudes." *Social Politics* 19(2): 163–193.

Burton, Linda M., Andrew Cherlin, D. M. Winn, A. Estacion, and C. Holder Taylor. 2009. "The Role of Trust in Low–Income Mothers' Intimate Unions." *Journal of Marriage and Family* 71(5): 1107–1124.

Butler, Adam B. and Amie Skattebo. 2004. "What is Acceptable for Women May Not Be for Men: The Effect of Family Conflicts with Work on Job-performance Ratings." *Journal of Occupational and Organizational Psychology* 77(4): 553–564.

Butler, Paul. 2017. *Chokehold: Policing Black Men*. New York: The New Press.

Butler, Stuart M., Jonathan Grabinsky, and Domitilla Masi. 2015. *Using Schools and Clinics as Hubs to Create Healthy Communities: The Example of Briya/Mary's Center*. Washington, DC: Brookings Institution.

Buvinić, Mayra and Geeta Rao Gupta. 1997. "Female-Headed Households and Female-Maintained Families: Are They Worth Targeting to Reduce Poverty in Developing Countries?" *Economic Development and Cultural Change* 45(2): 259–280.

Bzostek, Sharon H. and Lawrence M. Berger. 2017. "Family Structure Experiences and Child Socioemotional Development during the First Nine Years of Life: Examining Heterogeneity by Family Structure at Birth." *Demography* 54(2): 513–540.

Cabella, Wanda and Ignacio Pardo. 2014. "Hacia un Régimen de Baja Fecundidad en América Latina y el Caribe, 1990–2015." In S. Cavenaghi and W. Cabella, eds., *Comportamiento Reproductivo y Fecundidad en América Latina: Una Agenda Inconclusa*. Río de Janeiro: ALAP, pp. 13–31.

Cahn, Naomi and June Carbone. 2010. *Red Families v. Blue Families: Legal Polarization and the Creation of Culture*. Oxford: Oxford University Press.

Cahn, Naomi, June Carbone, and Howard Lavine. 2016. "A New Look at Demographics, Family Stability, and Politics." In *Two Perspectives on Demographic Change and the Future of the* Family. The States of Change: Demographics and Demography Project. Washington, DC: American Enterprise Institute, Brookings Institution, and Center for American Progress, pp. 1–25.

Cancian, Maria, Daniel R. Meyer and Steven T. Cook. 2011. "The Evolution of Family Complexity from the Perspective of Nonmarital Children." *Demography* 48(3): 957–982.

Carbone, June. 2000. *From Partners to Parents: The Second Revolution in Family Law.* New York: Columbia University Press.

Carbone, June and Naomi Cahn. 2013. "The Triple System of Family Law." *Michigan State Law Review* 4: 1185–1230.

Carbone, June, and Naomi Cahn. 2014. *Marriage Markets: How Inequality Is Remaking the American Family*. New York: Oxford University Press.

Carlson, Daniel, Sarah Hanson and Andrea Fitzroy. 2016. "The Division of Child Care, Sexual Intimacy, and Relationship Quality in Couples." *Gender & Society* 30 (3): 442–466.

Carlson, Marcia J. 2006. "Family Structure, Father Involvement, and Adolescent Behavioral Outcomes." *Journal of Marriage and Family* 68(1): 137–154.

Carlson, Marcia J. and Frank F. Furstenberg, Jr. 2006. "The Prevalence and Correlates of Multipartnered Fertility among Urban U.S. Parents." *Journal of Marriage and Family* 68(3): 718–732.

Carlson, Marcia J., James M. Raymo, Alicia G. VanOrman and Sojung Lim. 2014. "Cross-National Differences in Early Family Stability by Socioeconomic Status." Population Association of America, Boston, MA, USA, May 1–3, 2014.

Case, Anne C., I.-Fen Lin, and Sara S. McLanahan. 2003. "Explaining Trends in Child Support: Economic, Demographic, and Policy Effects." *Demography* 40(1): 171–189.

Castles, Francis G. 2003. "The World Turned Upside Down: Below Replacement Fertility, Changing Preferences and Family-Friendly Public Policy in 21 OECD Countries." *Journal of European Social Policy* 13(3): 209–227.

Cech, Erin A. 2016. "Mechanism or Myth? Family Plans and the Reproduction of Occupational Gender Segregation." *Gender & Society* 30(2): 265–288.

CELADE. 2013. *Observatorio Demográfico 2012. Proyecciones de Población*. Santiago de Chile: Comisión Económica para América Latina y el Caribe.

Centers for Disease Control and Prevention (CDC). 2016. *Key Statistics from theNational Survey of Family Growth: Premarital Sex. (Using data from 2011–2015.)* Atlanta, GA: National Center for Health Statistics/CDC. www.cdc.gov/nchs/nsfg /key_statistics/p.htm#premarital. (Accessed April 17, 2018.)

Century Foundation. 2013. *Bridging the Higher Education Divide: Strengthening Community Colleges and Restoring the American Dream*. Report of the Century Foundation Task Force on Preventing Community Colleges from Becoming Separate and Unequal. New York, NY: The Century Foundation.

Chandra, Amitabh. 2000. "Labor-Market Dropouts and the Racial Wage Gap: 1940–1990." *The American Economic Review* 90(2): 333–338.

Chant, Sylvia. 2003. *Female Household Headship and the Feminization of Poverty: Facts, Fictions and Forward Strategies.* New Working Paper Series Issue 9. London, UK: Gender Institute, London School of Economics and Political Science.

Chant, Sylvia. 2007. *Gender, Generation and Poverty: Exploring the Feminisation of Poverty in Africa, Asia and Latin America.* Gloucester, UK: Edward Elgar Publishing.

Cheadle, Jacob E., Paul R. Amato, and Valarie King. 2010. "Patterns of Nonresident Father Contact." *Demography* 47(1): 205–225.

Cherlin, Andrew J. 1978. "Remarriage as an Incomplete Institution." *American Journal of Sociology* 84(3): 634–650.

Cherlin, Andrew J. 1992. *Marriage, Divorce, Remarriage: Revised and Enlarged Edition.* Cambridge, MA: Harvard University Press.

Cherlin, Andrew J. 1999. "Going to Extremes: Family Structure, Children's Well-Being, and Social Science." *Demography* 36(4): 421–428.

Cherlin, Andrew J. 2004. "The Deinstitutionalization of American Marriage." *Journal of Marriage and Family* 66(4): 848–861.

Cherlin, Andrew J. 2005. "American Marriage in the Early Twenty-First Century." *The Future of Children* 15(2): 33–55.

Cherlin, Andrew J. 2009. *The Marriage-Go-Round: The State of Marriage and the Family in America Today.* New York: Random House.

Cherlin, Andrew J. 2010. "Demographic Trends in the United States: A Review of Research in the 2000s." *Journal of Marriage and Family* 72(3): 402–419.

Cherlin, Andrew J. 2014. *Labor's Love Lost: The Rise and Fall of the Working-Class Family in America.* New York: Russell Sage Foundation.

Cherlin, Andrew. 2016. "A Happy Ending to a Half-Century of Family Change?" *Population and Development Review* 42(1): 121–129.

Cherlin, Andrew J. and Frank F. Furstenberg, Jr. 1994. "Stepfamilies in the United States: A Reconsideration." *Annual Review of Sociology* 20(1): 359–381.

Cherlin, Andrew J., David C. Ribar, and Suzumi Yasutake. 2016. "Nonmarital First Births, Marriage, and Income Inequality." *American Sociological Review* 81(4): 749–770.

Chetty, Raj, Nathaniel Hendren, Patrick Kline, and Emmanuel Saez. 2014a. "Where Is the Land of Opportunity? The Geography of Intergenerational Mobility in the United States." *The Quarterly Journal of Economics* 129(4): 1553–1623.

Chetty, Raj, Nathaniel Hendren, Patrick Kline, Emmanuel Saez, and Nicholas Turner. 2014b. "Is the United States Still a Land of Opportunity? Recent Trends in Intergenerational Mobility." *The American Economic Review* 104(5): 141–147.

Clarkberg, Marin, Rafe Stolzenberg, and Linda Waite. 1995. "Attitudes, Values, and Entrance into Cohabitational Versus Marital Unions." *Social Forces* 74(2): 609–632.

Cohen, Philip N. 2015. "Divergent Responses to Family Inequality." In Amato, Paul R., Alan Booth, Susan M. McHale, and Jennifer Van Hook, eds., *Families in an Era of Increasing Inequality.* National Symposium on Family Issues Volume 5. New York: Springer, pp. 25–33.

Coleman, James S. 1988. "Social Capital in the Creation of Human Capital." *American Journal of Sociology* 94: 95–120.

Coleman, Priscilla K., and Debbie Garratt. 2016. "From Birth Mothers to First Mothers: Toward a Compassionate Understanding of the Life-Long Act of Adoption Placement." *Issues in Law & Medicine* 31: 139–166.

Collins, Patricia Hill. 2002. *Black Feminist Thought*, 2nd edn. New York: Routledge.

Complete College America. 2012. *Remediation: Higher Education's Bridge to Nowhere*. Washington, DC: Complete College America.

Conger, Rand D., Katherine J. Conger, and Monica J. Martin. 2010. "Socioeconomic Status, Family Processes, and Individual Development." *Journal of Marriage and Family* 72(3): 685–704.

Connell, R. W. 1987. *Gender and Power: Society, the Person and Sexual Politics*. Sydney: Allen and Unwin.

Connell, R.W. 1995. *Masculinities*. Cambridge, UK: Polity Press.

Connell, R. W. and James Messerschmidt. 2005. "Hegemonic Masculinity: Rethinking the Concept." *Gender & Society* 19(6): 829–859.

Cooke, Lynn Prince. 2006. "'Doing' Gender in Context: Household Bargaining and the Risk of Divorce in Germany and the United States." *American Journal of Sociology* 112(2): 442–472.

Cooke, Lynn Prince. 2011. *Gender-Class Equality in Political Economies*. Perspectives on Gender Series. New York: Routledge.

Cooke, Lynn Prince. 2014. "Gendered Parenthood Penalties and Premiums across the Earnings Distribution in Australia, the United Kingdom, and the United States." *European Sociological Review* 30(3): 360–72.

Cooke, Lynn Prince and Janeen Baxter. 2010. "Families in International Context: Comparing Institutional Effects across Western Societies." *Journal of Marriage and Family* 72(3): 516–536.

Cooke, Lynn Prince, Jani Erola, Marie Evertsson et al. 2013. "Labor and Love: Wives' Employment and Divorce Risk in Its Socio-Political Context." *Social Politics: International Studies in Gender, State & Society* 20(4): 482–509.

Coontz, Stephanie. 2005. *Marriage, A History: From Obedience to Intimacy, or How Love Conquered Marriage*. New York: Viking.

Cooper, Carey E., Cynthia A. Osborne, Audrey N. Beck and Sarah S. McLanahan. 2011. "Partnership Instability, School Readiness, and Gender Disparities." *Sociology of Education* 84(3): 246–259.

Costa, D., E. Hatzidimitriadou, E. Ioannidi-Kapolou et al. 2016. "Male and Female Physical Intimate Partner Violence and Socioeconomic Position: A Cross-sectional International Multicenter Study in Europe." *Public Health* 139: 44–52.

Cotter, David, JoAnn DeFiore, Joan M. Hermsen, Brenda Marsteller Kowalewski and Reeve Vanneman. 1997. "All Women Benefit: The Macro-Level Effect of Occupational Integration on Gender Earnings Equality." *American Sociological Review* 62(5): 714–734.

Council of Economic Advisers. 2016. *The Long-Term Decline in Prime-Age Male Labor Force Participation*. Washington, DC: Executive Office of the President.

Covre-Sussai, Maira, Bart Meuleman, Sarah Botterman, and Koen Matthijs. 2015. "Traditional and Modern Cohabitation in Latin America: A Comparative Typology." *Demographic Research* 32(32): 873–914.

Craig, Lyn and Killian Mullan. 2013. "How Mothers and Fathers Share Childcare: A Cross-National Time-Use Comparison." *American Sociological Review* 76(6): 834–861.

Crompton, Rosemary and Clare Lyonette, 2005. "The New Gender Essentialism: Domestic and Family 'Choices' and their Relation to Attitudes." *British Journal of Sociology* 56(4): 601–620.

Curtain, Sally C., Stephanie J. Ventura, and Gladys M. Martinez. 2014. *Recent Declines in Nonmarital Childbearing in the United States.* NCHS Data Brief No. 162. Hyattsville, MD: National Center for Health Statistics.

Curto, Vilsa E. and Roland G. Fryer Jr. 2014. "The Potential of Urban Boarding Schools for the Poor: Evidence from SEED." *Journal of Labor Economics* 32(1): 65–93.

Daugherty, J. and C. Copen. 2016. "Trends in Attitudes about Marriage, Childbearing, and Sexual Behavior: United States, 2002, 2006–2010, and 2011–2013." *National Health Statistics Reports* 92: 1–10.

David, Henry. 1970. *Family Planning and Abortion in the Socialist Countries of Central and Eastern Europe.* New York: The Population Council.

Davis, Evan F., Sarah J. Schoppe-Sullivan, Sarah C. Mangelsdorf, and Geoffrey L. Brown. 2009. "The Role of Infant Temperament in Stability and Change in Coparenting across the First Year of Life." *Parenting* 9(1–2): 143–159.

De Graaf, Paul M. and Matthijs Kalmijn. 2003. "Alternative Routes in the Remarriage Market: Competing-Risk Analyses of Union Formation after Divorce." *Social Forces* 81(4): 1459–1498.

De Graaf, Paul M. and Matthijs Kalmijn. 2006. "Divorce Motives in a Period of Rising Divorce: Evidence from a Dutch Life-History Survey." *Journal of Family Issues* 27(4): 483–505.

Deleire, Thomas and Leonard M. Lopoo. 2010. *Family Structure and the Economic Mobility of Children.* Economic Mobility Project. Philadelphia, PA: The Pew Charitable Trusts.

Deming, David J. 2015. *The Growing Importance of Social Skills in the Labor Market.* NBER Working Paper Series No. 21473. Cambridge, MA: National Bureau for Economic Research.

Demo, David H. and Mark A. Fine. 2010. *Beyond the Average Divorce.* Thousand Oaks, CA: Sage Publications.

DeNavas-Walt, Carmen, Bernadette D. Proctor, and Jessica C. Smith. 2010. *Income Poverty, and Health Insurance Coverage in the United States: 2009.* Washington, DC: US Bureau of the Census.

DeRose, Laurie, Mark Lyons-Amos, W. Bradford Wilcox and Gloria Huarcaya. 2017. *The Cohabitation-Go-Round: Cohabitation and Family Instability across the Globe.* World Family Map 2017: *Mapping Family Change and Child Well-being Outcomes.* New York: Social Trends Institute/Institute for Family Studies.

Detotto, Claudio and Edoardo Otranto. 2010. "Does Crime Affect Economic Growth?" *Kyklos* 63(3): 330–345.

De Vos, Susan. 1987. "Latin American Households in Comparative Perspective." *Population Studies* 41(3): 501–517.

Di Giulio, Paola, and Alessandro Rosina. 2007. "Intergenerational Family Ties and the Diffusion of Cohabitation in Italy." *Demographic Research* 16(14): 441–468.

DiPrete, Thomas A. and Claudia Buchman. 2013. *The Rise of Women: The Growing Gender Gap in Education and What It Means for American Schools.* New York: Russell Sage Foundation.

Dougherty, Christopher. 2006. "The Marriage Earnings Premium as a Distributed Fixed Effect." *The Journal of Human Resources* 41(2): 433–443.

Dribe, Martin and Maria Stanfors. 2009. "Does Parenthood Strengthen a Traditional Household Division of Labor? Evidence from Sweden." *Journal of Marriage and Family* 71(1): 33–45.

Drobnič, Sonja, Hans-Peter Blossfeld, and Götz Rohwer. 1999. "Dynamics of Women's Employment Patterns over the Family Life Course: A Comparison of the United States and Germany." *Journal of Marriage and the Family* 61(1): 133–146.

Dronkers, Jaap. 1999. "The Effects of Parental Conflicts and Divorce on the Well-being of Pupils in Dutch Secondary Education." *European Sociological Review* 15(2): 195–212.

Dronkers, Jaap, Gert-Jan M. Veerman, and Suet-Ling Pong. 2017. "Mechanisms Behind the Negative Influence of Single Parenthood on School Performance: Lower Teaching and Learning Conditions?" *Journal of Divorce & Remarriage* 58 (7): 471–486.

Duncan, Beverly, and Otis Dudley Duncan. 1969. "Family Stability and Occupational Success." *Social Problems* 16(3): 273–285.

Duncan, Greg J. and Jeanne Brooks-Gunn, eds. 1997. *The Consequences of Growing up Poor.* New York: Russell Sage Foundation.

Duncan, Greg J., Katherine Magnuson, Ariel Kalil, and Kathleen Ziol-Guest. 2012. "The Importance of Early Childhood Poverty." *Social Indicators Research* 108(1): 87–98.

Duncan, Greg J., P. A. Morris, and C. Rodrigues. 2011. "Does Money Really Matter? Estimating Impacts of Family Income on Young Children's Achievement with Data from Random-Assignment Experiments." *Developmental Psychology* 47(5): 1263–1279.

Duncan, S. and M. Phillips. 2008. "New Families? Tradition and Change in Modern Relationships." In A. Park et al., eds., *British Social Attitudes: The 24th Report.* London: Sage, pp. 1–28.

Duncan, Greg J., Bessie Wilkerson, and Paula England. 2006. "Cleaning Up Their Act: The Effects of Marriage and Cohabitation on Licit and Illicit Drug Use." *Demography* 43(4): 691–710.

Duncan, Greg J., Kathleen M. Ziol-Guest, and Ariel Kalil. 2010. "Early-Childhood Poverty and Adult Attainment, Behavior, and Health." *Child Development* 81(1): 306–325.

Duvander, Ann-Zofie. 2014. "How Long Should the Parental Leave Be? Attitudes to Gender Equality, Family, and Work as Determinants of Women's and Men's Parental Leave in Sweden." *Journal of Family Issues* 35(7): 909–926.

Duvander, Ann-Zofie and Mats Johansson. 2015. "What Are the Effects of Reforms Promoting Fathers' Parental Leave Use?" *Journal of European Social Policy* 22(3): 319–330.

Duvander, Ann-Zofie, Trude Lappegård, and Gunnar Andersson. 2010. "Family Policy and Fertility: Fathers' and Mothers' Use of Parental Leave and Continued Childbearing in Norway and Sweden." *Journal of European Social Policy* 20(1): 45–57.

Eberstadt, Nicholas. 2016. *Men without Work: America's Invisible Crisis.* Conshohocken PA: Templeton Press.

Edin, Kathryn and Maria Kefalas. 2005. *Promises I Can Keep: Why Poor Women Put Motherhood Before Marriage.* Berkeley, CA: University of California Press.

Edin, Kathryn and Timothy J. Nelson. 2013. *Doing the Best I Can: Fatherhood in the Inner City.* Berkeley: University of California Press.

Elkins, Kathleen. "Here's How Much the Average Family Has Saved for Retirement at Every Age." *CNBC* April 7, 2017. www.cnbc.com/2017/04/07/how-much-the-average -family-has-saved-for-retirement-at-every-age.html (Retrieved March 1, 2018.)

Ellis, Bruce J., John E. Bates, Kenneth A. Dodge et al. 2003. "Does Father Absence Place Daughters at Special Risk for Early Sexual Activity and Teenage Pregnancy?" *Child Development* 74(3): 801–821.

Ellwood, David T. and Christopher Jencks. 2004. "The Uneven Spread of Single-Parent Families: What Do We Know?" In K. M. Neckerman, ed., *Social Inequality.* New York: Russell Sage Foundation, pp. 3–78.

Elzinga, Cees and Aart Liefbroer. 2007. "De-standardization of Family-Life Trajectories of Young Adults: A Cross-National Comparison Using Sequence Analysis." *European Journal of Population* 23(3): 225–250.

Emens, Amie and Jane Lawler Dye. 2007. "Where's My Daddy? Living Arrangements of American Fathers." Presentation at the American Sociological Association Annual Meeting, New York, NY, August 11–14, 2007.

Emmons, William and Lowell Ricketts. "The Link between Family Structure and Wealth Is Weaker Than You Might Think." *St. Louis Fed On the Economy* blog May 9, 2017. www.stlouisfed.org/on-the-economy/2017/may/link-family -structure-wealth-weaker (Retrieved March 1, 2018.)

Engemann, Kristie M., and Michael T. Owyang. 2006. "Social Changes Lead Married Women into Labor Force." *The Regional Economist* April 2006: 10–11.

England, Paula. 2005. "Emerging Theories of Care Work." *Annual Review of Sociology* 31: 381–399.

England, Paula. 2011. "Reassessing the Uneven Gender Revolution and Its Slowdown." *Gender & Society* 25(1): 113–123.

England, Paula, Mónica L. Caudillo, Krystale Littlejohn, Brooke Conroy Bass, and Joanna Reed. 2016. "Why do Young, Unmarried Women Who do not Want to get Pregnant Contracept Inconsistently? Mixed-Method Evidence for the Role of Efficacy." *Socius* 2: 1–15.

Entmacher, Joan, Katherine Gallagher Robbins, Julie Vogtman, and Anne Morrison. 2014. *Insecure and Unequal: Poverty and Income among Women and Families 2000–2013.* Washington, DC: National Women's Law Center. www.nwlc.org/wp-content/uploads /2015/08/final_2014_nwlc_poverty_report.pdf. (Retrieved April 17, 2018.)

Erman, Jeylan and Juho Härkönen. 2017. "Parental Separation and School Performance among Children of Immigrant Mothers in Sweden." *European Journal of Population* 33(2): 267–292.

Esping-Andersen, Gøsta. 1990. *The Three Worlds of Welfare Capitalism.* Princeton, NJ: Princeton University Press.

Esping-Andersen, Gøsta. 2007. "Sociological Explanations of Changing Income Distributions." *American Behavioral Scientist* 50(5): 639–658.

Esping-Andersen, Gøsta. 2009. *The Incomplete Revolution: Adapting to Women's New Roles*. London: Polity Press.

Esping-Andersen, Gøsta. 2016. *Families in the 21st Century*. Stockholm: SNS Förlag.

Esping–Andersen, Gøsta and Francesco C Billari. 2015. "Re–theorizing Family Demographics." *Population and Development Review* 41(1): 1–31.

Esping-Andersen, G., D. Boertien, J. Bonke, and P. Gracia. 2013. "Couple Specialization in Multiple Equilibria." *European Sociological Review* 29(6): 1280–1294.

Esteve, Albert and Elizabeth Florez-Paredes. 2014. "Edad a la Primera Unión y al Primer Hijo en América Latina: Estabilidad en Cohortes más Educadas." *Notas de Población* 41(99): 39–65.

Esteve, Albert, Joan García-Román, and Ron Lesthaeghe. 2012. "The Family Context of Cohabitation and Single Motherhood in Latin America." *Population and Development Review* 38(4): 707–727.

Esteve, Albert and Ron J. Lesthaeghe, eds. 2016. *Cohabitation and Marriage in the Americas: Geo-Historical Legacies and New Trends*. New York, NY: Springer.

Esteve, Albert, Ron Lesthaeghe, and Antonio López-Gay. 2012. "The Latin American Cohabitation Boom, 1970–2007." *Population Development Review* 38(1): 55–81.

Esteve, Albert, Antonio López-Gay, Julián López-Colás et al. 2016. "A Geography of Cohabitation in the Americas, 1970–2010." In Albert Esteve and Ron J. Lesthaeghe, eds., *Cohabitation and Marriage in the Americas: Geo-historical Legacies and New Trends*. New York, NY: Springer, pp. 1–23.

Esteve, Albert, Ron J. Lesthaeghe, Julieta Quilodrán, Antonio López-Gay, Julián López-Colás. 2016. "The Expansion of Cohabitation in Mexico, 1930–2010: The Revenge of History?" In Albert Esteve and Ron J. Lesthaeghe, eds., *Cohabitation and Marriage in the Americas: Geo-historical Legacies and New Trends*. New York, NY: Springer, pp. 133–156.

Eurofound. 2016. *Exploring the Diversity of NEETs*. Luxembourg: Publications Office of the European Union.

European Commission. 2013. *Demography and Inequality: How Europe's Changing Population Will Impact Its Income Inequality*. Luxembourg: Publications Office of the European Union. http://europa.eu/epic/studies-reports/docs/eaf_policy_brief_-_demography_and_inequality_post_copy_edit_15.10.13.pdf (Retrieved August 15, 2017.)

European Commission. 2016. *Strategic Engagement for Gender Equality 2016–2019*. Luxembourg: Publications Office of the European Union. https://ec.europa.eu/anti-trafficking/sites/antitrafficking/files/strategic_engagement_for_gender_equality_en.pdf (Retrieved March 3, 2018.)

Evertsson, Marie, Paula England, Irma Mooi-Reci et al. 2009. "Is Gender Inequality Greater at Lower or Higher Educational Levels? Common Patterns in the Netherlands, Sweden, and the United States." *Social Politics* 16(2): 210–241.

Fahey, Tony. 2012. "Small Bang? The Impact of Divorce Legislation on Marital Breakdown in Ireland." *International Journal of Law Policy and the Family* 26(2): 242–258.

Fahey, Tony. 2014. "Divorce Trends and Patterns: An Overview." In J. Eekelaar and R. George, eds., *Routledge Handbook of Family Law and Policy*. Abingdon: Routledge, Chapter 2.2.

Fauve-Chamoux, Antoinette. 1984. "Les Structures Familiales au Royaume des Familles-Souches: Esparros." *Annales. Histoire, Sciences Sociales* 39(3): 513–528.

Fauve-Chamoux, Antoinette and Emiko Ochiai, eds. 2009. *The Stem Family in Eurasian Perspective: Revisiting House Societies.* Bern: Peter Lang.

Ferree, Myra Marx. 2010. "Filling the Glass: Gender Perspectives on Family." *Journal of Marriage and Family* 72(3): 420–439.

Ferrera, Maurizio. 1996. "The 'Southern Model' of Welfare in Social Europe." *Journal of European Social Policy* 6(1): 17–37.

Festy, Patrick. 1980. "On The New Context of Marriage in Western Europe." *Population and Development Review* 6(2): 311–315.

Firebaugh, Glenn. 2015. "Global Income Inequality." In Scott, Robert A. and Stephen M. Kosslyn, eds., *Emerging Trends in the Social and Behavioral Sciences: An Interdisciplinary, Searchable, and Linkable Resource*: John Wiley & Sons, Inc., pp. 1–14. (Accessed March 5, 2018.) DOI: 10.1002/9781118900772. etrds0149

Fischer, Tamar. 2007. "Parental Divorce and Children's Socio-Economic Success: Conditional Effects of Parental Resources Prior to Divorce, and Gender of the Child." *Sociology* 41(3): 475–495.

Flisher, Alan J., R. A. Kramer, R. C. Grosser et al. 1997. "Correlates of Unmet Need for Mental Health Services by Children and Adolescents." *Psychological Medicine* 27(5): 1145–1154.

Flood, Sarah, Miriam King, Steven Ruggles, and J. Robert Warren. 2015. "Integrated Public Use Microdata Series. Current Population Survey: Version 4.0." Minneapolis, MN: University of Minnesota.

Fokkema, Tineke and Aart C. Liefbroer. 2008. "Trends in Living Arrangements in Europe: Convergence or Divergence?" *Demographic Research* 19(36): 1351–1418.

Fomby, Paula and Andrew J. Cherlin. 2007. "Family Instability and Child Well-Being." *American Sociological Review* 72(2): 181–204.

Frank, Robert H., Adam Seth Levine, and Oege Dijk. 2014. "Expenditure Cascades." *Review of Behavioral Economics* 1(1–2): 55–73.

Frejka, Tomas. 2008. "Determinants of Family Formation and Childbearing during the Societal Transition in Central and Eastern Europe." *Demographic Research* 19 (7): 139–170.

Frejka, Tomas, Frances Goldscheider, and Trude Lappegård. 2018. *The Two-Part Gender Revolution, Women's Second Shift and Changing Cohort Fertility.* Stockholm Research Report in Demography SSRD 23. Stockholm: Demography Unit, Department of Sociology, University of Stockholm.

Friedan, Betty. 1963. *The Feminine Mystique.* New York: W.W. Norton.

Friedlander, Dov and Calvin Goldscheider. 1979. *The Population of Israel.* New York: Columbia University Press.

Furstenberg, Frank F. 2014. "Fifty Years of Family Change: From Consensus to Complexity." *Annals of the American Academy of Political and Social Science* 654: 12–30.

Furstenberg, Frank, F. and Rosalind Berkowitz King. 1999. "Multipartnered Fertility Sequences: Documenting an Alternative Family Form." Earlier version presented at the 1998 Annual Meetings of the Population Association of America, Chicago, IL.

Furstenberg, Frank F., Sheela Kennedy, Vonnie C. McLoyd, Ruben G. Rumbaut, and Richard A. Settersten, Jr. 2004. "Growing Up is Harder to Do." *Contexts* (Summer): 33–41.

Fussell, Elizabeth and Alberto Palloni. 2004. "Persistent Marriage Regimes in Changing Times." *Journal of Marriage and Family* 66(5): 1201–1213.

Gähler, Michael and Anna Garriga. 2013. "Has the Association between Parental Divorce and Young Adults' Psychological Problems Changed over Time? Evidence from Sweden, 1968–2000." *Journal of Family Issues* 34(6): 784–808.

Gähler, M. and E. L. Palmtag. 2015. "Parental Divorce, Psychological Well-Being and Educational Attainment: Changed Experience, Unchanged Effect among Swedes Born 1892–1991." *Social Indicators Research* 123(2): 601–623.

Galezewska, Paulina. 2016. Repartnering Dynamics and Fertility in New Partnerships in Europe and the United States. PhD Thesis, Southampton: Faculty of Social, Human and Mathematical Sciences, Division of Social Statistics and Demography, University of Southampton.

Garfinkel, Irwin, Lee Rainwater, and Timothy Smeeding. 2010. *Wealth and Welfare States: Is America a Laggard or Leader?* Oxford: Oxford University Press.

Garib, Geetha, T., Martin Garcia, and Jaap Dronkers. 2007. "Are the Effects of Different Family Forms on Children's Educational Performance Related to the Demographic Characteristics and Family Policies of Modern Societies?" *Changing Families and Their Lifestyles* 5: 27–50.

Garriga, Anna and Clara Cortina. 2017. "The Change in Single Mothers' Educational Gradient over Time in Spain." *Demographic Research* 36(61): 1859–1888.

Garriga, Anna, Sebastià Sarasa, and Paolo Berta. 2015. "Mother's Educational Level and Single Motherhood: Comparing Spain and Italy." *Demographic Research* 33(42): 1165–1210.

Garry, Eileen M. 1996. *Truancy: First Step to a Lifetime of Problems.* Juvenile Justice Bulletin. Washington, DC Office of Juvenile Justice and Delinquency Prevention, Office of Justice Programs, US Department of Justice.

Gash, Vanessa. 2009. "Sacrificing their Careers for their Families? An Analysis of the Penalty to Motherhood in Europe." *Social Indicators Research* 93(3): 569–586.

Gauthier, Anne H. 2007. "The Impact of Family Policies on Fertility in Industrialized Countries: A Review of the Literature." *Population Research Policy Review* 26: 323–346.

Geist, Claudia. 2006. *Payoff or penalty? A Comparison of the Marriage Wage Differential for Men and Women across 15 Nations* (No. 446). LIS Working Paper Series.

Gennetian, Lisa A. 2005. "One or Two Parents? Half or Step Siblings? The Effect of Family Structure on Young Children's Achievement." *Journal of Population Economics* 18(3): 415–436.

Gerson, Kathleen. 1993. *No Man's Land: Men's Changing Commitments to Family and Work.* New York: Basic Books.

Gerson, Kathleen. 2010. *The Unfinished Revolution: Coming of Age in a New Era of Gender, Work, and Family.* New York: Oxford University Press.

Gibson-Davis, Christina M., Kathryn Edin, and Sara S. McLanahan. 2005. "High Hopes and Even Higher Expectations: The Retreat from Marriage among Low-Income Couples." *Journal of Marriage and Family* 67(5): 1301–1312.

Glass, Jennifer. 2004. "Blessing or Curse? Work-Family Policies and Mothers' Wage Growth over Time." *Work and Occupations* 31(3): 367–394.

Glass, Jennifer and Philip Levchak. 2014. "Red States, Blue States, and Divorce: Understanding the Impact of Conservative Protestantism on Regional Variation in Divorce Rates." *American Journal of Sociology* 119(4): 1002–1046.

Gold, Rachel, Ichiro Kawachi, Bruce P Kennedy, John W Lynch, and Frederick A Connell. 2001. "Ecological Analysis of Teen Birth Rates: Association with Community Income and Income Inequality." *Maternal and Child Health Journal* 5(3): 161–167.

Goldani, Ana Maria and Aída CG Verdugo Lazo. 2004. "Brasil: Desafíos de las Políticas para las Familias." *En: Cambio de las Familias en el Marco de las Transformaciones Globales: Necesidad de Políticas Públicas Eficaces-LC/L*. 2230: 265–303.

Goldin, Claudia. 1990. *Understanding the Gender Gap: An Economic History of American Women*. New York: Oxford University Press.

Goldscheider, Frances K. 2000. "Men, Children and the Future of the Family in the Third Millennium." *Futures* 32(6): 525–538.

Goldscheider, Frances, Eva Bernhardt, and Trude Lappegård. 2015. "The Gender Revolution: A Framework for Understanding Changing Family and Demographic Behavior." *Population and Development Review* 41(2): 207–239.

Goldscheider, Frances and Gayle Kaufman. 2006. "Willingness to Stepparent: Attitudes toward Partners Who already Have Children." *Journal of Family Issues* 27(10): 1415–1436.

Goldscheider, Frances, Pierre Turcotte, and Alexander Kopp. 2001. "The Changing Determinants of Women's First Union Formation in Industrialized Countries: The United States, Canada, Italy and Sweden." *Genus* 57(3/4): 107–34.

Goldscheider, Frances and Linda Waite. 1991. *New Families, No Families: The Transformation of the American Home*. Los Angeles, CA: University of California Press.

Goldstein, Joshua R. and Catherine T. Kenney. 2001. "Marriage Delayed or Marriage Forgone? New Cohort Forecasts of First Marriage for U.S. Women." *American Sociological Review* 66(4): 506–519.

Goode, William J. 1962. "Marital Satisfaction and Instability. A Cross-Cultural Class Analysis of Divorce Rates." In Reinhard Bendix and Seymor Martin Lipset, eds., *Class, Status, and Power. Social Stratification in Comparative Perspective*. New York: The Free Press, pp. 377–387.

Goode, William J. 1970 [1963]. *World Revolution and Family Patterns*. New York: The Free Press.

Goode, William J. 1993. *World Changes in Divorce Patterns*. New Haven, CT: Yale University Press.

Goos, Maarten, Alan Manning, and Anna Salomons. 2009. "Job Polarization in Europe." *The American Economic Review* 99(2): 58–63.

Gornick, Janet C., Marcia K. Meyers, and Katherin E. Ross. 1997. "Supporting the Employment of Mothers: Policy Variation across Fourteen Welfare States." *Journal of European Social Policy* 7(1): 45–70.

Gornick, Janet C. and Branko Milanovic. 2015. *Income Inequality in the United States in Cross-National Perspective: Redistribution Revisited*. LIS Research Center Brief

(1/2015). New York: Luxembourg Income Study Center at the Graduate Center, City University of New York.

Gottschalk, Peter and Sheldon Danziger. 2005. "Inequality of Wage Rates, Earnings and Family Incomes in the United States: 1972–2002." *Review of Income and Wealth* 51(2): 231–254.

Gottschalk, Peter and Timothy M. Smeeding. 1997. "Cross-national Comparisons of Earnings and Income Inequality." *Journal of Economic Literature* 35: 633–687.

Granovetter, Mark. 1985. "Economic Action and Social Structure: The Problem of Embeddedness." *American Journal of Sociology* 91(3): 481–510.

Grätz, Michael. 2015. "When Growing Up without a Parent Does Not Hurt: Parental Separation and the Compensatory Effect of Social Origin." *European Sociological Review* 31(5): 546–557.

Gruber, Jonathan. 2004. "Is Making Divorce Easier Bad for Children? The Long-Run Implications of Unilateral Divorce." *Journal of Labor Economics* 22(4): 799–833.

Gupta, Sanjiv, Marie Evertsson, Daniela Grunow, Magnus Nermo, and Liana Sayer. 2010. "Does Class Matter? Economic Inequalities and Time Spent on Housework among Married Women in Germany, Sweden, and the U.S." In Judith Treas and Sonja Drobnič, eds., *Dividing the Domestic: Men, Women, And Household Work In Cross-National Perspective*. Stanford, CA: Stanford University Press, pp. 105–122.

Guttmacher Institute. 2016. *Unintended Pregnancy in the United States*. New York: Guttmacher Institute. www.guttmacher.org/fact-sheet/unintended-pregnancy -united-states (Accessed July 20, 2017.)

Guzmán, José Miguel, Jorge Rodríguez, Jorge Martínez, Juan Manuel Contreras, and Daniela González. 2006. "The Demography of Latin America and the Caribbean since 1950." *Population* 61(5): 519–620.

Guzzo, Karen Benjamin. 2014. "New Partners, More Kids: Multiple-Partner Fertility in the United States." *Annals of the American Academy of Political and Social Science* 654(1): 66–86.

Guzzo, Karen Benjamin and Cassandra Dorius. 2016. "Challenges in Measuring and Studying Multipartnered Fertility in American Survey Data." *Population Research and Policy Review* 35(4): 553–579.

Guzzo, Karen Benjamin and Frank F. Furstenberg, Jr. 2007a. "Multipartnered Fertility among American Men." *Demography* 44(3):583–601.

Guzzo, Karen Benjamin and Frank F. Furstenberg, Jr. 2007b. "Multipartnered Fertility among Young Women with a Nonmarital First Birth: Prevalence and Risk Factors." *Perspectives on Sexual and Reproductive Health* 39(1): 29–38.

Haas, Linda and Tine Rostgaard. 2011. "Fathers' Rights to Paid Parental Leave in the Nordic Countries: Consequences for the Gender Division of Leave." *Community, Work & Family* 14(2): 177–195.

Hair, N. L., J. L. Hanson, B. L. Wolfe and S. D. Pollak. 2015. "Association of Child Poverty, Brain Development, and Academic Achievement." *JAMA Pediatrics* 169(9): 822–829.

Hajnal, John. 1965. "European Marriage Patterns in Perspective." In D. V. Glass and D. E. C. Eversley, eds., *Population in History: Essay in Historical Demography*. Chicago: Aldine, pp. 101–143.

Hakim, Catherine. 2001. *Work-Lifestyle Choices in the 21st Century: Preference Theory*. Oxford: Oxford University Press.

Hall, Ray and Paul White, eds. 2005. *Europe's Population: Toward the Next Century.* London: University of College London Press.

Halryngo, Sigtona and Selma Therese Lyng. 2009. "Preferences, Constraints or Schemas of Devotion? Exploring Norwegian Mothers' Withdrawals from High Commitment Careers." *British Journal of Sociology* 60(2): 321–343.

Hamilton, Brady E., Joyce A. Martin and Michelle J.K. Osterman. 2016. *Births: Preliminary Data for 2015.* National Vital Statistics Reports, Vol. 65, No. 3. Hyattsville, MD: National Center for Health Statistics.

Hampden-Thompson, Gillian. 2013. "Family Policy, Family Structure, and Children's Educational Achievement." *Social Science Research* 42(3): 804–817.

Harkness, Susan. 2013. "Women's Employment and Household Income Inequality." In Janet Gornick and Markus Jantti, eds., *Income Inequality: Economic Disparities and the Middle Class in Affluent Countries.* Stanford, CA: Stanford University Press, Chapter 8.

Harkness, Susan and Jane Waldfogel. 2003. "The Family Gap in Pay: Evidence from Seven Industrialized Countries." In Solomon W. Polacheck, ed., *Worker Well-Being and Public Policy.* Research in Labor Economics Vol. 22. Bingley, UK: Emerald Publishing Limited, pp. 369–413.

Härkönen, Juho. 2014. "Divorce: Trends, Patterns, Causes, and Consequences." In Judith Treas, Jacqueline Scott, and Martin Richards, eds., *The Wiley Blackwell Companion to the Sociology of Families,* 1st edn. Chichester, UK: John Wiley & Sons, Chapter 15.

Härkönen, Juho. 2017. "Diverging Destinies in International Perspective: Education, Single Motherhood, and Child Poverty." *Stockholm Research Reports in Demography* No. 14. Stockholm: Stockholm University. https://www.su.se/polopoly_fs/1.340750.15 00967936!/menu/standard/file/WP_2017_04.pdf. (Retrieved April 17, 2018.)

Härkönen Juho. 2018. "Single-Mother Poverty: How Much Do Educational Differences in Single Motherhood Matter?" In R. Nieuwenhuis and L. Maldonado, eds., *The Triple Bind of Single-Parent Families.* Bristol: Policy Press, Chapter 1.

Härkönen, Juho, Fabrizio Bernardi, and Diederik Boertien. 2017. "Family Dynamics and Child Outcomes: An Overview of Research and Open Questions." *European Journal of Population* 33(2): 163–184. (Accessed April 17, 2018.) DOI: 10.1007/s10680-017-9424-6.

Härkönen, Juho and Jaap Dronkers. 2006. "Stability and Change in the Educational Gradient of Divorce. A Comparison of Seventeen Countries." *European Sociological Review* 22(5): 501–517.

Harper, Cynthia C. and Sara S. McLanahan. 2004. "Father Absence and Youth Incarceration." *Journal of Research on Adolescence* 14(3): 369–397.

Haskins, Ron. 2014. "Marriage, Parenthood, and Public Policy." *National Affairs* 19(1): 55–72.

Haskins, Ron, Isabel Sawhill, and Sara McLanahan. 2015. "The Promise of Birth Control." *The Future of Children* 25(2): 1–6.

Heaton, Tim B. and Renata Forste. 1998. "Education as Policy: The Impact of Education on Marriage, Contraception, and Fertility in Colombia, Peru, and Bolivia." *Social Biology* 45(3–4): 194–213.

Hechter, Michael, Hyojoung Kim, and Justin Baer. 2005. "Prediction Versus Explanation in the Measurement of Values." *European Sociological Review* 21(2): 91–108.

Heckman, James J. 2007. "The Economics, Technology, and Neuroscience of Human Capability Formation." *Proceedings of the National Academy of Sciences* 104(33): 13250–13255.

Hegewisch, Ariane and Janet C. Gornick. 2011. "The Impact of Work-Family Policies on Women's Employment: A Review of Research from OECD Countries." *Community, Work & Family* 14(2): 119–138.

Henz, Ursula and Elizabeth Thomson. 2005. "Union Stability and Stepfamily Fertility in Austria, Finland, France & West Germany." *European Journal of Population/ Revue Européenne de Démographie* 21(1): 3–29.

Heuveline, Patrick and Jeffrey M. Timberlake. 2004. "The Role of Cohabitation in Family Formation: The United States in Comparative Perspective." *Journal of Marriage and Family* 66(5): 1214–1230.

Heuveline, Patrick, Jeffrey M. Timberlake, and Frank F. Furstenberg. 2003. "Shifting Childrearing to Single Mothers: Results from 17 Western Countries." *Population and Development Review* 29(1): 47–71.

Hiekel, Nicole and Renske Keizer. 2015. "Risk-Avoidance or Utmost Commitment: Dutch Focus Group Research on Views on Cohabitation and Marriage." *Demographic Research* 32(10): 311–340.

Hiekel, Nicole, Aart C. Liefbroer, and Anne-Rigt Poortman. 2014. "Understanding Diversity in the Meaning of Cohabitation across Europe." *European Journal of Population* 30(4): 391–410.

Hofferth, Sandra, Joseph Pleck, Frances Goldscheider, Sally Curtin and Karen Hrapezynski. 2014. "Changing Family Structure and Men's Motivation for Parenthood and Parenting in the U.S." In Natasha J. Cabrera and Catherine S. Tamis-LeMonda, eds., *Handbook of Father Involvement: Multidisciplinary Perspectives*, 2nd edn. New York: Taylor and Francis, Inc, pp. 57–80.

Hoffman, Kelly and Miguel Angel Centeno. 2003. "The Lopsided Continent: Inequality in Latin America." *Annual Review of Sociology* 29(1): 363–390.

Hofstede, Geert and Michael Harris Bond. 1988. "The Confucius Connection: From Cultural Roots to Economic Growth." *Organizational Dynamics* 16(4): 5–21.

Hoherz, Stefanie, Brienna Perelli-Harris, Marta Styrc, Trude Lappegård, and Ann Evans. 2017. "Do Early Life Conditions Explain Differences in Subjective Well-Being Between Marriage and Cohabitation? A Comparison between Australia, the UK, Germany, and Norway." Population Association of America, Chicago, IL, USA, April 27–29, 2017.

Holahan, John, Matthew Buettgens, Caitlin Carroll, and Stan Dorn. 2012. *The Cost and Coverage Implications of the ACA Medicaid Expansion: National and State-by-State Analysis*. Washington, DC: The Henry J. Kaiser Family Foundation.

Holland, Jennifer A. and Elizabeth Thomson. 2011. "Stepfamily Childbearing in Sweden: Quantum and Tempo Effects, 1950–99." *Population Studies* 65(1): 115–128.

Hoynes, Hilary, Diane Whitmore Schanzenbach, and Douglas Almond. 2016. "Long-Run Impacts of Childhood Access to the Safety Net." *The American Economic Review* 106(4): 903–934.

Huber, Evelyne and John D. Stephens. 2014. "Income Inequality and Redistribution in Post-Industrial Democracies: Demographic, Economic and Political Determinants." *Socio-Economic Review* 12(2): 245–267.

Hughes, Mary Elizabeth and Linda J Waite. 2009. "Marital Biography and Health at Mid-Life." *Journal of Health and Social Behavior* 50(3): 344–358.

Human Development Report. 2011. *Sustainability and Equity: A Better Future for All.* New York: United Nations Development Programme.

Hymowitz, Kay, Jason S. Carroll, W. Bradford Wilcox, and Kelleen Kaye. 2013. "Knot Yet: The Benefits and Costs of Delayed Marriage in America." http://nationalmarria geproject.org/wp-content/uploads/2013/03/KnotYet-FinalForWeb.pdf (Accessed July 20, 2017.)

Immervoll, Herwig. 2007. *Minimum Wages, Minimum Labour Costs and the Tax Treatment of Low-wage Employment.* IZA Discussion Paper No. 2555. Bonn, Germany: Institute of Labor Economics (IZA).

Inglehart, Ronald. (1997). *Modernization and Postmodernization: Cultural, Economic, and Political Change in 43 Countries.* Princeton, NJ: Princeton University Press.

Irish Examiner, The. "Once More, Biggest Export Is Our People." December 3, 2010. www.irishexaminer.com/ireland/once-more-our-biggest-export-is-our-people-138338 .html (Retrieved March 1, 2018.)

Isen, Adam and Betsey Stevenson. 2010. *Women's Education and Family Behavior: Trends in Marriage, Divorce and Fertility.* NBER Working paper No. 15725. Cambridge, MA: National Bureau of Economic Research.

Isupova, Olga. 2015. "Trust, Responsibility, and Freedom: Focus-Group Research on Contemporary Patterns of Union Formation in Russia." *Demographic Research* 32 (11): 341–368.

Jacobs, Jerry A. and Kathleen Gerson. 2004. *The Time Divide: Work, Family, and Social Policy in the 21st Century.* Cambridge, MA: Harvard University Press.

Jejeebhoy, Shireen J. 1995. *Women's Education, Autonomy, and Reproductive Behaviour: Experience from Developing Countries.* Oxford: Clarendon Press.

Jenson, Jane. 2009. "Lost in Translation: The Social Investment Perspective and Gender Equality." *Social Politics* 16(4): 446–483.

Jones, Tonisha, Nicholas Lovrich, and Nichole R. Lovrich. 2011. *Updated Literature Review on Truancy: Key Concepts, Historical Overview, and Research Relating to Promising Practices—With Particular Utility to Washington State.* Seattle, WA: Center for Children & Youth Justice.

Jonsson, Jan O. and Michael Gähler. 1997. "Family Dissolution, Family Reconstitution, and Children's Educational Careers: Recent Evidence from Sweden." *Demography* 34(2): 277–293.

Juárez, Fatim, and Cecilia Gayet. "Transitions to Adulthood in Developing Countries." *Annual Review of Sociology* 40: 521–538.

Juby, Heather, Céline Le Bourdais, and Nicole Marcil-Gratton. 2005. "Sharing Roles, Sharing Custody? Couples' Characteristics and Children's Living Arrangements at Separation." *Journal of Marriage and Family* 67(1): 157–172.

Juhn, Chinhui and Keven Murphy. 1997. "Wage Inequality and Family Labor Supply." *Journal of Labor Economics* 15(1, Part 1): 72–97.

Kalil, Ariel. 2015. "Inequality Begins at Home: The Role of Parenting in the Diverging Destinies of Rich and Poor Children." In P. R. Amato, A. Booth, S. M. McHale, and J. Van Hook, eds., *Families in an Era of Increasing Inequality*, Vol. 5. National Symposium on Family Issues. Berlin: Springer International Publishing, pp. 63–82.

Kalil, Ariel, Rebecca Ryan and Michael Corey. 2012. "Diverging Destinies: Maternal Education and the Developmental Gradient in Time with Children." *Demography* 49(4): 1361–1383.

Kalmijn, Matthijs. 2007. "Explaining Cross-National Differences in Marriage, Cohabitation, and Divorce in Europe, 1990–2000." *Population Studies* 61(3): 243–263.

Kalmijn, Matthijs. 2011. "The Influence of Men's Income and Employment on Marriage and Cohabitation: Testing Oppenheimer's Theory in Europe." *European Journal of Population* 27(3): 269–293.

Kalmijn, Matthijs. 2013. "The Educational Gradient in Marriage: A Comparison of 25 European Countries." *Demography* 50(4): 1499–1520.

Kalmijn, Matthijs, Anneke Loeve, and Dorien Manting. 2007. "Income Dynamics in Couples and the Dissolution of Marriage and Cohabitation." *Demography*, 44(1): 159–179.

Kamerman, Sheila and Alfred Kahn. 1991. *Child Care, Parental Leave, and the Under 3s: Policy Innovation in Europe*. New York: Greenwood Publishing.

Kan, Man-Yee, Oriel Sullivan, and Jonathan Gershuny. 2011. "Gender Convergence in Domestic Work: Discerning the Effects of Interactional and Institutional Barriers from Large-Scale Data." *Sociology* 45(2): 234–251.

Karoly, Lynn and Gary Burtless. 1995. "Demographic Change, Rising Earnings Inequality, and the Distribution of Personal Well-Being, 1959–1989." *Demography* 32(3): 379–405.

Kasperkevic, J. "Elizabeth Warren to Help Propose Senate Bill to Tackle Part-Time Schedules." The *Guardian* July 23, 2014.

Katus, Kalev, Asta Põldma, Allan Puur, and Luule Sakkeus. 2008. "First Union Formation in Estonia, Latvia and Lithuania: Patterns across Countries and Gender." *Demographic Research* 17(17): 247–300.

Kaufman, Gayle. 2000. "Do Gender Role Attitudes Matter? Family Formation and Dissolution among Traditional and Egalitarian Men and Women," *Journal of Family Issues* 21(1): 128–144.

Kearney, Melissa S. and Phillip B. Levine. 2015. "Media Influences on Social Outcomes: The Impact of MTV's 16 and Pregnant on Teen Childbearing." *The American Economic Review* 105(12): 3597–3632.

Kearney, Melissa S. and Phillip B. Levine. 2017. *The Economics of Non-Marital Childbearing and the "Marriage Premium for Children"*. NBER Working Paper Series No. 23230. Cambridge, MA. National Bureau of Economic Research.

Kemple, James J. and Cynthia J. Willner. 2008. *Career Academies: Long-Term Impacts on Labor Market Outcomes, Educational Attainment, and Transitions to Adulthood*. New York, NY: MDRC.

Kennedy, Sheela and Larry Bumpass. 2008. "Cohabitation and Children's Living Arrangements: New Estimates from the United States." *Demographic Research* 19: 1663–1692.

Kennedy, Sheela and Elizabeth Thomson. 2010. "Children's Experiences of Family Disruption in Sweden: Differentials by Parent Education over Three Decades." *Demographic Research* 23(17): 479–508.

Kiernan, Kathleen. 1999. "Cohabitation in Western Europe." *Population Trends* (96): 25–32.

Kiernan, Kathleen. 2001. "The Rise of Cohabitation and Childbearing Outside Marriage in Western Europe." *International Journal of Law, Policy and the Family* 15(1): 1–21.

Kiernan, Kathleen, Sara McLanahan, John Holmes, and Melanie Wright. 2011. *Fragile Families in the U.S. and U.K.* Working Paper WP 11-04-FF. Princeton, NJ: Center for Research on Child Well-being, Princeton University.

Killewald, Alexandra. 2012. "A Reconsideration of the Fatherhood Premium: Marriage, Coresidence, Biology, and Fathers' Wages." *American Sociological Review* 78(1): 96–116.

Killewald, Alexandra. 2016. "Money, Work, and Marital Stability: Assessing Change in the Gendered Determinants of Divorce." *American Sociological Review* 8(4): 696–719.

Killewald, Alexandra and Ian Lundberg. 2017. "New Evidence against a Causal Marriage Premium." *Demography* 54(3): 1007–1028. (Accessed March 2017.) DOI: 10.1007/s13524-017-0566-2

King, Valarie, Kathleen Mullan Harris, and Holly E. Heard. 2004. "Racial and Ethnic Diversity in Nonresident Father Involvement." *Journal of Marriage and the Family* 66(1): 1–21.

Klärner, Andreas. 2015. "The Low Importance of Marriage in Eastern Germany-Social Norms and the Role of Peoples' Perceptions of the Past." *Demographic Research* 33 (9): 239–272.

Klerman, Jacob and Arleen Leibowitz. 1999. "Job Continuity among New Mothers." *Demography* 36(2): 145–155.

Klüsener, Sebastian. 2015. "Spatial Variation in Non-Marital Fertility across Europe in the Twentieth and Twenty-First Centuries: Recent Trends, Persistence of the Past, and Potential Future Pathways." *The History of the Family* 20(4): 593–628.

Klüsener, Sebastian and Joshua R. Goldstein. 2014. "A Long–Standing Demographic East–West Divide in Germany." *Population, Space and Place* 22(1): 5–22.

Klüsener, Sebastian, Karel Neels, and Michaela Kreyenfeld. 2013. "Family Policies and the Western European Fertility Divide: Insights from a Natural Experiment in Belgium." *Population and Development Review* 39(4): 587–610.

Klüsener, Sebastian, Brienna Perelli-Harris, and Nora Sánchez Gassen. 2013. "Spatial Aspects of the Rise of Nonmarital Fertility across Europe since 1960: The Role of States and Regions in Shaping Patterns of Change." *European Journal of Population* 29(2): 137–165.

Knijn, Trudie, Claude Martin, and Jane Millar. 2007. "Activation as a Common Framework for Social Policies towards Lone Parents." *Social Policy & Administration* 41(6): 638–652.

Kobrin, Frances E. 1976. "The Fall of Household Size and the Rise of the Primary Individual in the United States." *Demography* 13(1): 127–138.

Kollmeyer, Christopher. 2013. "Family Structure, Female Employment, and National Income Inequality: A Cross-National Study of 16 Western Countries." *European Sociological Review* 29(4): 816–827.

Konietzka, Dirk and Michaela Kreyenfeld. 2002. "Women's Employment and Non-Marital Childbearing: A Comparison between East and West Germany in the 1990s." *Population (English)* 57(2): 331–358.

Korpi, Walter and Joakim Palme. 1998. "The Paradox of Redistribution and Strategies of Equality: Welfare State Institutions, Inequality, and Poverty in the Western Countries." *American Sociological Review* 63(5): 661–687.

Kostova, Dora. 2007. "The Emergence of Cohabitation in a Transitional Socio-Economic Context: Evidence from Bulgaria and Russia." *Demografia* 50(5): 135–162.

Kurek, Slawomir. 2011. "Population Changes in Poland: A Second Demographic Transition View." *Procedia – Social and Behavioral Sciences* 19: 389–396.

Lahne, Oscar and Richard Wenne. 2012. *Hur Skapas Jämställda Attityder? Effekten av egen Utbildning, Föräldrars Utbildning och Föräldrars Fördelning av Hushållsarbete. [How Are Egalitarian Attitudes Created? The Effects of Own Education, Parental Education, and Parents' Distribution of Domestic Work.]* YAPS Working Paper 01/12. Stockholm: Demography Unit, Department of Sociology, University of Stockholm. www.suda.su.se/yaps (Retrieved March 2, 2018.)

Lamb, Kathleen A, Gary R Lee, and Alfred DeMaris. 2003. "Union Formation and Depression: Selection and Relationship Effects." *Journal of Marriage and Family* 65 (4): 953–962.

Lambert, Susan J., Peter J. Fugiel, and Julia R. Henly. 2014. "Schedule Unpredictability among Early Career Workers in the US Labor Market: A National Snapshot." Chicago, IL: Employment Instability, Family Well-being, and Social Policy Network, University of Chicago.

Lamont, Michèle. 2000. *The Dignity of Working Men: Morality and the Boundaries of Race, Class, and Immigration.* Cambridge, MA: Harvard University Press.

Laplante, Benoît, Teresa Castro-Martín, Clara Cortina, and Teresa Martín-García. 2015. "Childbearing within Marriage and Consensual Union in Latin America, 1980–2010." *Population and Development Review* 41(1): 85–108.

Lappegård, Trude, and Turid Noack. 2015. "The Link between Parenthood and Partnership in Contemporary Norway: Findings from Focus Group Research." *Demographic Research* 32(9): 287–310.

Lappegård, Trude and Marit Rønsen. 2013. "Socioeconomic Differences in Multipartner Fertility among Norwegian Men." *Demography* 50(3): 1135–1153.

Lareau, Annette. 2003. *Unequal Childhoods: Class, Race, and Family Life.* Berkeley: University of California Press.

Laslett, Peter. 1970. "The Comparative History of Household and Family." *Journal of Social History* 4(1): 75–87.

Law Commission. 2007. *Cohabitation: The Financial Consequences of Relationship Breakdown.* LAW COM No. 307. London, UK: The Law Commission. https://assets.publishing.service.gov.uk/government/uploads/system/uploads/attachment_data/file/228881/7182.pdf. (Retrieved April 17, 2018.)

Lee, Dohoon and Sara McLanahan. 2015. "Family Structure Transitions and Child Development: Instability, Selection, and Population Heterogeneity." *American Sociological Review* 80(4): 738–763.

Leibowitz, Arleen and Jacob Alex Klerman. 1995. "Explaining Changes in Married Mothers' Employment over Time." *Demography* 32: 365–378.

Leonard, Andrew "The Hourglass Economy." *Salon.* September 13, 2011 (Sep 13). www.salon.com/2011/09/13/the_hourglass_economy/ (Accessed February 24, 2017.)

Leopold, Liliya and Thomas Leopold. 2016. *Maternal Education, Divorce, and Changes in Economic Resources: Evidence from Germany.* SOEP Papers on Multidisciplinary Panel Data Research No. 836. Rochester, NY: Social Science Research Network.

Lerman, Robert. I. 2011. "Economic Perspectives on Marriage: Causes, Consequences, and Public Policy." In Lloyd R. Cohen and Joshua D. Wright, eds., *Research Handbook on the Economics of Family Law.* Cheltenham, UK: Elgar Publishing Limited, pp.72–95.

Lerman, Robert I. and W. Bradford Wilcox. 2014. *For Richer, for Poorer: How Family Structures Economic Success in America.* Washington, DC: American Enterprise Institute. www.aei.org/wp-content/uploads/2014/10/IFS-ForRicherForPoorer-Final _Web.pdf (Retrieved March 3, 2018.)

Lerman, Robert I., Joseph Price, Adam Shumway, and W. Bradford Wilcox. 2018. "Marriage and State-Level Economic Outcomes." *Journal of Family and Economic Issues* 39(1): 66–72. (Accessed March 3, 2018.) doi: 10.1007/s10834-017-9540-9

Lerman, Robert I., Joseph Price, and W. Bradford Wilcox. 2017. "Family Structure and Economic Success across the Life Course." *Marriage & Family Review* 53(8): 744–758.

Lesthaeghe, Ron J. 1995. "The Second Demographic Transition in Western Countries: An Interpretation." In K. O. Mason and A.-M. Jensen, eds., *Gender and Family Change in Industrialized Countries.* Oxford: Oxford University Press, pp. 17–62.

Lesthaeghe, Ron. 2010. "The Unfolding Story of the Second Demographic Transition." *Population and Development Review* 36(2): 211–251.

Lesthaeghe, Ron J. and Lisa Neidert. 2006. "The Second Demographic Transition in the United States: Exception or Textbook Example?" *Population and Development Review* 32(4): 669–698.

Lesthaeghe, Ron and Johan Surkyn. 1988. "Cultural Dynamics and Economic Theories of Fertility Change." *Population and Development Review* 14(1): 1–45.

Lesthaeghe, R. and Johan Surkyn. 2002. *New Forms of Household Formation in Central and Eastern Europe: Are They Related to Newly Emerging Value Orientations?* Brussels, Belgium: Interface Demography (SOCO) Vrije Universiteit Brussel.

Levy, Frank and Peter Temin. 2010. "Institutions and Wages in Post–World War II America." In Clair Brown, Barry J. Eichengreen, and Michael Reich, eds., *Labor in the Era of Globalization.* Cambridge: Cambridge University Press, pp. 15–30.

Lewis, Jane E. 1997. *Lone Mothers in European Welfare Regimes: Shifting Policy Logics:* London, UK: Jessica Kingsley Publishers.

Li, L. J-C. A. and L. L. Wu. 2008. "No Trend in the Intergenerational Transmission of Divorce." *Demography* 45(4): 875–883.

Lichter, Daniel T., Kathryn Michelmore, Richard N. Turner, and Sharon Sassler. 2016. "Pathways to a Stable Union? Pregnancy and Childbearing among Cohabiting and Married Couples." *Population Research and Policy Review* 35(3): 377–399.

Liefbroer, Aart C. and Edith Dourleijn. 2006. "Unmarried Cohabitation and Union Stability: Testing the Role of Diffusion Using Data from 16 European Countries." *Demography* 43(2): 203–221.

Liu, Chia, Albert Esteve, and Rocío Treviño. 2016. "Female-Headed Households and Living Conditions in Latin America." *World Development* 90: 311–328.

Liu, Hui, and Debra J. Umberson. 2008. "The Times They Are a Changin': Marital Status and Health Differentials from 1972 to 2003." *Journal of Health and Social Behavior* 49(3): 239–253. (Retrieved March 3, 2018.) DOI: 10.1177/0022146508049000301

Liu, Ruth X. and Zeng-yin Chen. 2006. "The Effects of Marital Conflict and Marital Disruption on Depressive Affect: A Comparison between Women in and out of Poverty." *Social Science Quarterly* 87(2): 250–271.

Lloyd, Cynthia B., ed. 2005. *Growing up Global: The Changing Transitions to Adulthood in Developing Countries.* Washington, DC: National Academies Press.

Loughran, David S. 2002. "The Effect of Male Wage Inequality on Female Age at First Marriage." *Review of Economics and Statistics* 84(2): 237–250.

Loughran, David S. and Julie M. Zissimopoulos. 2009. "Why Wait? The Effect of Marriage and Childbearing on the Wages of Men and Women." *The Journal of Human Resources* 44(2): 326–349.

Lucas Jr, Robert E. 1988. "On the Mechanics of Economic Development." *Journal of Monetary Economics* 22(1): 3–42.

Ludden, Jennifer. "San Francisco Proposes Predictable Scheduling to Help Hourly Workers." *National Public Radio (NPR)* November 21, 2014. www.npr.org/2014/11/21/365762020/san-francisco-proposes-predictable-scheduling-to-help-hourly-workers (Retrieved April 22, 2017.)

Lundberg, Shelly, and Robert A. Pollak. 2015. "The Evolving Role of Marriage: 1950–2010." *Future of Children* 25(2): 29–50.

Lundberg, Shelly, Robert A. Pollak, and Jenna Stearns. 2016. "Family Inequality: Diverging Patterns in Marriage, Cohabitation, and Childbearing." *The Journal of Economic Perspectives* 30(2): 79–101.

Lundberg, Shelly, Robert A. Pollak, and Terence J. Wales. 1997. "Do Husbands and Wives Pool Their Resources?" *Journal of Human Resources* 32(3): 463–480.

Lupton, Joseph P. and James P. Smith. 2003. "Marriage, Assets, and Savings." In Shoshana A. Grossbad, ed., *Marriage and the Economy: Theory and Evidence from Advanced Industrial Societies.* Cambridge, UK: Cambridge University Press, pp. 129–152.

Lustig, Nora, Luis F. Lopez-Calva, and Eduardo Ortiz-Juarez. 2013. "Declining Inequality in Latin America in the 2000s: The Cases of Argentina, Brazil, and Mexico." *World Development* 44: 129–141.

Luxembourg Income Study (LIS) Database. 2011. *Inequality and Poverty Key Figures.* Esch-Belval, Luxembourg: LIS: Cross-National Data Center in Luxembourg.

Lyngstad, Torkild Hovde, and Marika Jalovaara. 2010. "A Review of the Antecedents of Union Dissolution." *Demographic Research* 23: 257–291.

Lyngstad, Torkild Hovde, Turid Noack, and Per Arne Tufte. 2010. "Pooling of Economic Resources: A Comparison of Norwegian Married and Cohabiting Couples." *European Sociological Review* 27(5): 624–635.

Machin, Stephen. 2010. "Changing Wage Structures: Trends and Explanations." In Paul Gregg and Jonathan Wadsworth, eds., *The Labour Market in Winter – The State of Working Britain 2010.* Oxford: Oxford University Press, pp. 155–169.

Mandel, Hadas and Moshe Semyonov. 2005. "Family Policies, Wage Structures, and Gender Gaps: Sources of Earnings Inequality in 20 Countries." *American Sociological Review* 70(6): 949–967.

Mandemakers, Jornt J. and Matthijs Kalmijn. 2014. "Do Mother's and Father's Education Condition the Impact of Parental Divorce on Child Well-Being?" *Social Science Research* 44(March): 187–199.

Mandemakers, Jornt J. and Christiaan W. S. Monden. 2010. "Does Education Buffer the Impact of Disability on Psychological Distress?" *Social Science & Medicine* 71(2): 288–297.

Manning, Wendy D. 2013. *Trends in Cohabitation over Twenty Years of Changes, 1987–2010*. National Center for Family and Marriage Research Family Profiles FP-13-12, Bowling Green, OH: Bowling Green State University.

Manning, Wendy D. 2015. "Cohabitation and Child Well-Being." *Future of Children* 25(2): 51–66.

Manning, Wendy D., Susan L. Brown, and Krista K. Payne. 2014. "Two Decades of Stability and Change in Age at First Union Formation." *Journal of Marriage and Family* 76(2): 247–260.

Manoli, Day and Nick Turner. 2015. "Cash-on-Hand and College Enrollment: Evidence from Population Tax Data and the Earned Income Tax Credit." http://www.daymanoli.com/wp-content/uploads/2014/04/Manoli_Turner1.pdf (Retrieved April 17, 2017.)

Marginson, Simon. 2011. "Higher Education in East Asia and Singapore: Rise of the Confucian Model." *Higher Education* 61(5): 587–611.

Mariani, Elena, Berkay Özcan, and Alice Goisis. 2017. "Family Trajectories and Well-Being of Children Born to Lone Mothers in the UK." *European Journal of Population* 33(2): 185–215.

Martin, Molly A. 2006. "Family Structure and Income Inequality in Families with Children, 1976 to 2000." *Demography* 43(3): 421–445.

Martin, Molly A. 2012. "Family Structure and the Intergenerational Transmission of Educational Advantage." *Social Science Research* 41(1): 33–47.

Martin, Steven P. 2006. "Trends in Marital Dissolution by Women's Education in the United States." *Demographic Research* 15(20): 537–560.

Martín, Teresa Castro. 2002. "Consensual Unions in Latin America: Persistence of a Dual Nuptiality System." *Journal of Comparative Family Studies* 33(1): 35–55.

Martín, Teresa Castro and Fatima Juárez. 1995. "The Impact of Women's Education on Fertility in Latin America: Searching for Explanations." *International Family Planning Perspectives* 21(2): 52–80.

Matysiak, Anna, Marta Styrc, and Daniele Vignoli. 2014. "The Educational Gradient in Marital Disruption: A Meta-Analysis of European Research Findings." *Population Studies* 68(2): 197–215.

Maxfield, John. "How Much Does the Average American Have in Their Savings Account?" *The Motley Fool* September 25, 2016. www.fool.com/investing/2016/09/2 5/how-much-does-the-average-american-have-in-their-s.aspx (Retrieved March 1, 2018.)

McCall, Leslie. 2005. "The Complexity of Intersectionality." *Signs: Journal of Women in Culture in Society* 30(3): 1771–1800.

McLanahan, Sara. 1997. "Parent Absence or Poverty: Which Matters More." In G. J. Duncan and J. Gunn-Brooks, eds., *Consequences of Growing up Poor*. New York: Russell Sage Foundation, pp. 35–48.

McLanahan, Sara. 2004. "Diverging Destinies: How Children Are Faring under the Second Demographic Transition." *Demography* 41(4): 607–627.

McLanahan, Sara. 2011. "Family Instability and Complexity after a Nonmarital Birth: Outcomes for Children in Fragile Families." M. J. Carlson and P. ngland, eds., In *Social Class and Changing Families in an Unequal America*. Stanford: Stanford University Press, pp. 108–133.

McLanahan, Sara and Wade Jacobsen. 2015. "Diverging Destinies Revisited." In P. R. Amato, A. Booth, S. M. McHale, and J. Van Hook, eds., *Families in an Era of Increasing Inequality: Diverging Destinies*. New York: Springer, pp. 3–23.

McLanahan, Sara and Christine Percheski. 2008. "Family Structure and the Reproduction of Inequalities." *Annual Review of Sociology* 34: 257–276.

McLanahan, Sara S. and Gary Sandefur. 1994. *Growing up with a Single Parent: What Hurts, What Helps*. Cambridge, MA: Harvard University Press.

McLanahan, Sara and Isabel Sawhill. 2015. "Marriage and Child Wellbeing Revisited: Introducing the Issue." *The Future of Children* 25(2): 3–9.

McLanahan, Sara, Laura Tach, and Daniel Schneider. 2013. "The Causal Effects of Father Absence." *Annual Review of Sociology* 39(1): 399–427.

McNamee, Catherine and R. Kelly Raley. 2011. "A Note on Race, Ethnicity and Nativity Differentials in Remarriage in the United States." *Demographic Research* 24: 293–312.

McNeal, Ralph B. 1999. "Parental Involvement as Social Capital: Differential Effectiveness on Science Achievement, Truancy, and Dropping Out." *Social Forces* 78(1): 117–144.

McRae, Susan. 2003. "Constraints and Choices in Mothers' Employment Careers: A Consideration of Hakim's Preference Theory." *British Journal of Sociology* 54(3): 317–338.

Mechoulan, Stéphane. 2011. "The External Effects of Black Male Incarceration on Black Females." *Journal of Labor Economics* 29(1): 1–35.

Medeiros, Marcelo and Joana Costa. 2008. "Is There a Feminization of Poverty in Latin America?" *World Development* 36(1): 115–127.

Meyer, Daniel R., Maria Cancian, and Steven T. Cook. 2005. "Multiple-Partner Fertility: Incidence and Implications for Child Support Policy." *Social Service Review* 79(4): 577–601.

Michelmore, Katherine. 2016. "The Earned Income Tax Credit and Union Formation: The Impact of Expected Spouse Earnings." *Review of Economics of the Household* [Online First Article.] (Retrieved March 15, 2017.) DOI: 10.1007/s11150-016-9348-7

Mikolai, Julia, Brienna Perelli-Harris, and Ann Berrington. 2014. "The Role of Education in the Intersection of Partnership Transitions and Motherhood in Europe and the United States." Population Association of America, Boston, MA, May 1–3, 2014.

Miller, Claire Cain. "Why Men Don't Want the Jobs Done Mostly by Women." The *New York Times* January 4, 2017. www.nytimes.com/2017/01/04/upshot/why-men-dont-want-the-jobs-done-mostly-by-women.html (Accessed January 4, 2017.)

Miller, Amanda J. and Sharon Sassler. 2010. "Stability and Change in the Division of Labor among Cohabiting Couples." *Sociological Forum* 25(4): 677–701.

Miller, Amanda J., Sharon Sassler, and Dela Kusi-Appouh. 2011. "The Specter of Divorce: Views from Working- and Middle-Class Cohabitors." *Family Relations* 60(5): 602–616.

Mincer, Jacob. 1962. "Labor Force Participation of Married Women." In H. Gregg Lewis, ed., *Aspects of Labor Economics*. National Bureau of Economic Research Special Conference Series No. 14. Princeton, NJ: Princeton University Press, pp. 63–105.

Mincy, Ronald B. and Hillard Pouncy. 1999. "There Must Be Fifty Ways to Start a Family: Public Policy and the Fragile Families of Low Income Non-Custodial Fathers." In W. Horn, D. Blankenhorn, and M. B. Pearlstein, eds., *The Fatherhood Movement: A Call to Action*. New York: Lexington Books, pp. 83–104.

Minnesota Population Center. 2015. "Integrated Public Use Microdata Series, International: Version 6.4." Minneapolis, MN: University of Minnesota. (Retrieved March 4, 2018.) DOI: 10.18128/D020.V6.4.

Monte, Lindsay M. 2017. *Fertility Research Brief*. Household Economic Studies Current Population Reports P70BR-147 Washington, DC: US Census Bureau.

Mooyaart, Jarl E. and Aart C. Liefbroer. 2016. "The Influence of Parental Education on Timing and Type of Union Formation: Changes over the Life Course and Over Time in the Netherlands." *Demography* 53(4): 885–919.

Morgan, S. Philip and Linda Waite 1987. "Parenthood and the Attitudes of Young Adults." *American Sociological Review* 52(4): 541–547.

Moser, Caroline. 2010. "Moving beyond Gender and Poverty to Asset Accumulation: Evidence from Low-Income Households in Guayaquil, Ecuador." In Chant, Sylvia. ed., *The International Handbook of Gender and Poverty: Concepts, Research, Policy*. Gloucester, UK: Edward Elgar Publishing, pp. 391–398.

Moynihan, Daniel Patrick. 1965. *The Negro Family: The Case for National Action*. Washington, DC: US Department of Labor.

Murray, Charles. 2012. *Coming Apart: The State of White America, 1960–2010*. New York: Crown Forum.

Musick, Kelly and Larry Bumpass. 2012. "Reexamining the Case for Marriage: Union Formation and Changes in Well-Being." *Journal of Marriage and Family* 74(1): 1–18.

Musick, Kelly and Katherine Michelmore. 2015. "Change in the Stability of Marital and Cohabiting Unions Following the Birth of a Child." *Demography* 52(5): 1463–1485.

Musick, Kelly and Katherine Michelmore. 2016. "Cross-National Comparisons of Union Stability in Cohabiting and Married Families with Children." Presented at the Annual Meeting of the Population Association of America, Washington, DC, USA, March 31-April 2, 2016. www.cpc.cornell.edu/html/research/WP_musick_mi chelmore_demog_102116.pdf (Retrieved April 17, 2018.)

Mynarska, Monika, Anna Baranowska-Rataj and Anna Matysiak. 2014. "Free to Stay, Free to Leave: Insights from Poland into the Meaning of Cohabitation." *Demographic Research* 31(36): 1107–1136.

Neilsson, Jeffrey and Maria Stanfors. 2013. "Re-Traditionalisation of Gender Relations in the 1990s? The Impact of Parenthood on Gendered Time Use in Three Scandinavian Countries." *Journal of Contemporary European Studies* 21(2): 269–289.

Neilsson, Jeffrey and Maria Stanfors. 2014. "It's About Time! Gender, Parenthood, and Household Divisions of Labor under Different Welfare Regimes." *Journal of Family Issues* 35(8): 1066–1088.

Neyer, Gerda and Gunnar Andersson. 2008. "Consequences of Family Policies on Childbearing Behavior: Effects or Artifacts?" *Population and Development Review* 34 (4): 699–724.

Nieuwenhuis, Rense and Laurie C. Maldonado. 2018. *The Triple Bind of Single-Parent Families*. Bristol: Policy Press.

Nock, Steven L. 1998. *Marriage in Men's Lives*. New York: Oxford University Press.

OECD. 2011a. *Divided We Stand: Why Inequality Keeps Rising*. Paris: OECD Publishing.

OECD. 2011b. *The Future of Families to 2030. Projections, Policy Challenges and Policy Options: A Synthesis Report*. International Futures Programme. Paris: OECD. www .oecd.org/futures/49093502.pdf (Retrieved August 5, 2017.)

OECD. 2012. *Settling in: OECD Indicators of Immigrant Integration 2012*. Paris: OECD Publishing. (Accessed April 17, 2018.) doi: 10.1787/9789264171534-en.

OECD. 2013a. *Education at a Glance 2013*. Paris: OECD Publishing.

OECD. 2013b. *PISA 2012 Results: Excellence through Equity (Volume II): Giving Every Student the Chance to Succeed*. Paris: OECD Publishing.

OECD. 2015. *In It Together: Why Less Inequality Benefits All*. Paris: OECD Publishing.

OECD. 2016a. *OECD Family Database*. Paris: OECD Publishing. www.oecd.org/els /family/database.htm (Accessed October 16, 2016.)

OECD. 2016b. *Employment Outlook 2016*. Paris: OECD Publishing.

OECD. 2017. *OECD Social Expenditure Data. 4*. Paris: OECD Publishing. www.oecd .org/els/social/expenditure (Accessed April 17, 2018.)

OECD. 2017a. *Family Database*. Paris: OECD Publishing. http://www.oecd.org/els /family/database.htm (Accessed February 2, 2017.)

Oláh, Livia Sz. 2003. "Gendering Fertility: Second Births in Sweden and Hungary." *Population Research and Policy Review* 22(2): 171–200.

Oppenheimer, Valerie. 1970. *The Female Labor Force in the United States: Demographic and Economic Factors Governing its Growth and Changing Composition*. Population Monograph Series No. 5. Berkeley, CA: University of California.

Oppenheimer, Valerie Kincade. 1988. "A Theory of Marriage Timing." *American Journal of Sociology* 94(3): 563–591.

Osborne, Cynthia and Sara McLanahan. 2007. "Partnership Instability and Child Well-Being." *Journal of Marriage and Family* 69(4): 1065–1083.

Padovano, Fabio and Emma Galli. 2001. "Tax Rates and Economic Growth in the OECD Countries." *Economic Inquiry* 39(1): 44–57.

Pampel, Fred. 2011a. "Cohort Changes in the Socio-Demographic Determinants of Gender Egalitarianism." *Social Forces* 89(3): 961–982.

Pampel, Fred. 2011b. "Cohort change, diffusion, and support for gender egalitarianism in cross-national perspective." *Demographic Research* 25: 667–694.

Pampel, Fred and Kazuko Tanaka. 1986. "Economic Development and Female Labor Force Participation: A Reconsideration." *Social Forces* 64(3): 599–619.

Parker, Kim and Gretchen Livingston. 2017. "6 Facts about American Fathers." June 15, Pew Research Center. www.pewresearch.org/fact-tank/2017/06/15/fathers-day-facts/ (Retrieved February 18, 2018.)

Parsons, Talcott and Robert F. Bales. 1955. *Family, Socialization, and the Interaction Process*. New York: The Free Press.

Pedulla, David S. and Sarah Thébaud. 2015. "Can We Finish the Revolution? Gender, Work-Family Ideals, and Institutional Constraint." *American Sociological Review* 80(1): 116–139.

Perelli-Harris, Brienna. 2014. "How Similar Are Cohabiting and Married Parents? Second Conception Risks by Union Type in the United States and Across Europe." *European Journal of Population* 30(4): 437–464.

Perelli-Harris, Brienna and Laura Bernardi. 2015. "Exploring Social Norms around Cohabitation: The Life Course, Individualization, and Culture." *Demographic Research* 33(25): 701–732.

Perelli-Harris, Brienna, Ann Berrington, Nora Sánchez Gassen, Paulina Galezewska, and Jennifer A. Holland. 2017a. "The Rise in Divorce and Cohabitation: Is There a Link?" *Population and Development Review* 43(2): 303–329.

Perelli-Harris, Brienna, M. Kreyenfeld, and K. Kubisch. 2010. *Harmonized Histories Manual for the Preparation of Comparative Fertility and Union Histories*. MPIDR Working Papers No. 2010–011. Rostock, Germany: Max Planck Institute for Demographic Research (MPIDR).

Perelli-Harris, Brienna, Michaela Kreyenfeld, Wendy Sigle-Rushton et al. 2012. "Changes in Union Status during the Transition to Parenthood in Eleven European Countries, 1970s to Early 2000s." *Population Studies* 66(2): 167–182.

Perelli-Harris, Brienna and Mark Lyons-Amos. 2015. "Changes in Partnership Patterns across the Lifecourse: An Examination of 14 countries in Europe and the United States." *Demographic Research* 33(6): 145–178.

Perelli-Harris, Brienna and Mark Lyons-Amos. 2016. "Partnership Patterns in the United States and across Europe: The Role of Education and Country Context." *Social Forces* 95(1): 251–282.

Perelli-Harris, Brienna, Monika Mynarska, Caroline Berghammer et al. 2014. "Towards a Deeper Understanding of Cohabitation: Insights from Focus Group Research across Europe and Australia." *Demographic Research* 31(34): 1043–1078.

Perelli-Harris, Brienna and Nora Sánchez Gassen. 2012. "How Similar Are Cohabitation and Marriage? Legal Approaches to Cohabitation across Western Europe." *Population and Development Review* 38(3): 435–467.

Perelli–Harris, Brienna, Wendy Sigle–Rushton, Michaela Kreyenfeld et al. 2010. "The Educational Gradient of Childbearing within Cohabitation in Europe." *Population and Development Review* 36(4): 775–801.

Perelli-Harris, Brienna and Marta Styrc. 2018. "Mental Well-Being Differences in Cohabitation and Marriage: The Role of Childhood Selection." *Journal of Marriage and Family* 80(1): 239–255.

Perelli-Harris, Brienna, Marta Styrc, Fenaba Addo et al. 2017b. *Early Life Conditions and the Benefits of Cohabitation and Marriage for Health in Mid-Life: Is the Relationship Similar across Countries?* CPC Working Paper Series No. 84. Southampton, UK: Centre for Population Change (CPC).

Petersen, Trond, Andrew Penner, and Geir Høgnes. 2014. "From Motherhood Penalties to Husband Premiums: The New Challenge for Gender Equality and Family Policy, Lessons from Norway." *American Journal of Sociology* 119(5): 1434–1472.

Pettit, Becky and Jennifer Hook. 2005. "The Structure of Women's Employment in Comparative Perspective." *Social Forces* 84(2): 779–801.

Pettit, Becky and Jennifer L. Hook. 2009. *Gendered Tradeoffs: Family, Social Policy, and Economic Inequality*. New York: Russell Sage Foundation.

Pew Charitable Trusts, The. 2017. *How Income Volatility Interacts with American Families' Financial Security: An Examination of Gains, Losses, and Household Economic Experiences*. Issue Brief. www.pewtrusts.org/~/media/assets/2017/03/in comevolatility_and_financialsecurity.pdf (Accessed July 20, 2017.)

Piketty, Thomas and Emmanuel Saez. 2003. "Income Inequality in the United States, 1913–1998." *The Quarterly Journal of Economics* 118(1): 1–41.

Plümper, Thomas and Christian W. Martin. 2003. "Democracy, Government Spending, and Economic Growth: A Political-Economic Explanation of the Barro-Effect." *Public Choice* 117(1–2): 27–50.

Pong, Suet-ling, Jaap Dronkers, and Gillian Hampden-Thompson. 2003. "Family Policies and Children's School Achievement in Single- Versus Two-Parent Families." *Journal of Marriage and Family* 65(3): 681–699.

Poortman, Anne-Rigt. 2007. "The First Cut Is the Deepest? The Role of the Relationship Career for Union Formation." *European Sociological Review* 23(5): 585–598.

Pryor, Jan and Bryan Rodgers. 2001. *Children in Changing Families. Life after Parental Separation*. Hoboken, NJ: Blackwell Publishers.

Pugh, Alllison J., ed. 2016. "Introduction: The Broader Impacts of Precariousness." In *Beyond the Cubicle: Job Insecurity, Intimacy, and the Flexible Self*. Oxford: Oxford University Press, pp. 1–21.

Pugh, Allison J. 2017. "What Happens at Home When People Can't Depend on Stable Work." *Harvard Business Review* April 4. https://hbr.org/2017/04/whathappens-at -homewhen-people-cantdepend-on-stablework. (Accessed April 17, 2018.)

Putnam, Robert D. 2015. *Our Kids: The American Dream in Crisis*. New York: Simon and Schuster.

Quilodran, Julieta. 1999. "The Free Union in Latin America: Recent Aspects of a Secular Phenomenon." *Cahiers Quebecois de Demographie* 28(1–2): 53–80.

Quisumbing, Agnes. R., Lawrence Haddad, and Christine Peña. 2001. "Are Women Overrepresented among the Poor? An Analysis of Poverty in 10 Developing Countries". *Journal of Development Economics* 66(1): 225–269.

Rackin, Heather and Christina M. Gibson-Davis. 2012. "The Role of Pre- and Postconception Relationships for First-Time Parents." *Journal of Marriage and Family* 74(3): 526–539.

Raley, R. Kelly and Larry L. Bumpass. 2003. "The Topography of the Divorce Plateau: Levels and Trends in Union Stability in the United States after 1980." *Demographic Research* 8: 245–260.

Raley, Sara, Suzanne Bianchi, and Wendy Wang. 2012. "When Do Fathers Care? Mothers' Economic Contribution and Fathers' Involvement in Child Care." *American Journal of Sociology* 117(5): 1422–1459.

Raley, Sara, Marybeth Mattingly, and Suzanne Bianchi. 2006. "How Dual Are Dual-Income Couples? Documenting Change from 1970–2001." *Journal of Marriage and Family* 68(1): 11–28.

Randles, Jennifer M. 2017. *Proposing Prosperity? Marriage Education Policy and Inequality in America*. New York; Columbia University Press.

Range, Bret G., Debra Ann Davenport Yonke, and Suzanne Young. 2011. "Preservice Teacher Beliefs about Retention: How Do They Know What They Don't Know?" *Journal of Research in Education* 21(2): 77–99.

Ranji, Usha, Yali Bair, and Alina Salganicoff. 2016. *Medicaid and Family Planning: Background and Implications of the ACA.* Issue Brief. Menlo Park, CA: Henry J Kaiser Family Foundation.

Raymo, James M., Marcia J. Carlson, Alicia VanOrman, Sojung Lim, and Isabel Pike. 2016. "Cross-National Differences in Child Poverty: The Role of Family Structure Revisited." [Unpublished.]

Reardon, Sean F. and Ximena A. Portilla. 2016. "Recent Trends in Socioeconomic and Racial School Readiness Gaps at Kindergarten Entry." *AERA Open* 2(3): 1–18. (Retrieved February 17, 2018.) DOI: 10.1177/2332858416657343

Reeves, Richard. 2014a. *Saving Horatio Alger: Equality, Opportunity, and the American Dream.* Washington, DC: Brookings Institution.

Reeves, Richard. 2014b. "How to Save Marriage in America." The *Atlantic* February 13, 2014. www.theatlantic.com/business/archive/2014/02/how-to-save-marriage-in-america/283732/ (Retrieved February 18, 2018.)

Reeves, Richard. 2016 *Bipartisanship in Action: Evidence and Contraception.* Brookings Social Mobility Memos. Washington, DC: Brookings Institution.

Reeves, Richard. 2017. *Dream Hoarders: How the American Upper Middle Class Is Leaving Everyone Else in the Dust, Why That Is a Problem, and What to Do About It.* Washington, DC: Brookings Institution.

Reeves, Richard and Kimberly Howard. 2013. *The Parenting Gap.* Washington, DC: Center on Children & Families at the Brookings Institution.

Reeves, Richard and Edward Rodrigue. 2015a. Five Bleak Facts on Black Opportunity. *Brookings Social Mobility Memos.* Washington, DC: Brookings Institution.

Reeves, Richard and Edward Rodrigue. 2015b *Memo to Hillary Clinton: More Choice Can Thwart Community College Students.* Brookings Social Mobility Memos. Washington, DC: Brookings Institution.

Reeves, Richard and Edward Rodrigue. 2015c. *Home Visiting Programs: An Early Test for the 114th Congress.* Brookings Social Mobility Memos. Washington, DC: Brookings Institution.

Reeves, Richard and Edward Rodrigue. 2016. *Transfer Season: Lowering the Barrier Between Community College and Four-Year College.* Brookings Social Mobility Memos. Washington, DC: Brookings Institution.

Reeves, Richard and Isabel Sawhill. "Men's Lib!" Sunday Review/Opinion, The *New York Times* November 14, 2015.

Reeves, Richard and Joanna Venator. 2014. *Saving Horatio Alger: The Data behind the Words (and the Lego Bricks).* Brookings Social Mobility Memos. Washington, DC: Brookings Institution.

Reeves, Richard and Joanna Venator. 2015. *Sex, Contraception, or Abortion? Explaining Class Gaps in Unintended Childbearing.* Washington, DC: Brookings Institution.

Reher, David Sven. 1998. "Family Ties in Western Europe: Persistent Contrasts." *Population and Development Review* 24(2): 203–234.

Rindfuss, Ronald R., David K. Guilkey, S. Philip Morgan, and Øystein Kravdal. 2010. "Child-Care Availability and Fertility in Norway." *Population and Development Review* 36(4): 725–748.

Robbins, Katherine Gallagher and Fremstad, Shawn. 2016. *4 Progressive Policies that Make Families Stronger*. Washington, DC: Center for American Progress.

Rodríguez Vignoli, Jorge. 2005. "Reproducción en la Adolescencia: el Caso de Chile y sus Implicaciones de Política." *Revista de la CEPAL* 86: 123–146.

Roos, Patricia and Lindsay Stevens. 2018. "Integrating Occupations: Changing Occupational Sex Segregation in the U.S. from 2000 to 2014." *Demographic Research* 38(5): 127–154.

Rosero Bixby, Luis, Teresa Castro Martín, and Teresa Martín-García. 2009. "Is Latin America Starting to Retreat from Early and Universal Childbearing?" *Demographic Research* 20(9): 169–194.

Rothwell, Jonathan. 2015. *Sociology's Revenge: Move to Opportunity (MTO) Revisited.* Brookings Social Mobility Memos. Washington, DC: Brookings Institution.

Ruggles, Steven. 1988. "The Demography of the Unrelated Individual: 1900–1950." *Demography* 25(4): 521–536.

Rumberger, Russell W. and Katherine A. Larson. 1998. "Student Mobility and the Increased Risk of High School Dropout." *American Journal of Education* 107(1): 1–35.

Ryan, Mary P. 1981. *Cradle of the Middle Class: The Family in Oneida County, New York, 1790–1865*. Interdisciplinary Perspectives on Modern History. Cambridge, UK: Cambridge University Press.

Ryan, Rebecca M., Amy Claessens, and Anna J. Markowitz. 2015. "Associations between Family Structure Change and Child Behavior Problems: The Moderating Effect of Family Income." *Child Development* 86(1): 112–127.

Ryan, Rebecca, Ariel Kalil, Kathleen Ziol-Guestet al. 2015. "Preschool-Age Skills Gaps and the Changing Technology of Parenting." Panel paper presented at the 37th Annual Association for Public Policy and Management Fall Research Conference, Chicago, IL, November 12–14, 2015.

Rychtaříková, Jitka. 2008. "Twenty Years of Single Motherhood in the Czech Republic (1986–2005)." *Czech Demography* 2(2): 34–45.

Sampson, Robert J. 1987. "Urban Black Violence: The Effect of Male Joblessness and Family Disruption." *American Journal of Sociology* 93(2): 348–382.

Sampson, Robert J., John H. Laub, and Christopher C. Wimer, 2006. "Does Marriage Reduce Crime? A Counterfactual Approach to Within-Individual Causal Effects." *Criminology* 44(3): 465–508.

Samuelson, Paul A. and Franco Modigliani. 1966. "The Pasinetti Paradox in Neoclassical and More General Models." *The Review of Economic Studies* 33(4): 269–301.

Sanchez, Laura, Wendy Manning, and Pamela Smock. 1998. "Sex-Specialized or Collaborative Mate Selection? Union Transitions among Cohabitors." *Social Science Research* 27(3): 280–304.

Sánchez Gassen, Nora and Brienna Perelli-Harris. 2015. "The Increase in Cohabitation and the Role of Union Status in Family Policies: A Comparison of 12 European Countries." *Journal of European Social Policy* 25(4): 431–449.

Sandefur, Gary D., Sara McLanahan, and Roger A. Wojtkiewicz. 1992. "The Effects of Parental Marital Status during Adolescence on High School Graduation." *Social Forces* 71(1): 103–121.

Sassler, Sharon, Fenaba Addo, Trude Lappegård et al. 2016. "The Consequences of Partnered Childbearing for Mothers' Mid-Life Health." Population Association of America, Washington, DC, March 31–April 2, 2016.

Sassler, Sharon, Jennifer Glass, Yael Levitte, and Katherine Michelmore. 2017. "The Missing Women in STEM? Gender Differentials in the Transition to First Jobs in STEM." *Social Science Research* 63: 192–208.

Sassler, Sharon and Amanda J. Miller. 2011. "Waiting to be Asked: Gender, Power, and Relationship Progression among Cohabiting Couples." *Journal of Family Issues* 32 (4): 482–506.

Sassler, Sharon and Amanda J. Miller. 2017. *Cohabitation Nation? Gender, Class, and the Remaking of Relationships*. Oakland, CA: University of California Press.

Sawhill, Isabel V. 2014. *Generation Unbound: Drifting into Sex and Parenthood without Marriage*. Washington, DC: Brookings Institution.

Sawhill, Isabel. 2015. *The Best New Year's Resolution: Intentional Childbearing*. *Brookings Social Mobility Memos*. Washington, DC: Brookings Institution.

Sawhill, Isabel and Quentin Karpilow. 2013. *Strategies for Assisting Low-Income Families*. Washington, DC: Brookings Institution.

Sawhill, Isabel and Adam Thomas. 2005. "For Love and Money? The Impact of Family Structure on Family Income." *Future of Children* 15(2): 57–74.

Sawhill, Isabel and Joanna Venator. 2014. "Proposal 3: Reducing Unintended Pregnancies for Low-Income Women." In Melissa S. Kearney, Benjamin H. Harris, and Karen Anderson, eds., *Policies to Address Poverty in America*. Washington, DC: The Hamilton Project at the Brookings Institution, pp. 37–46.

Sawhill, Isabel and Joanna Venator. 2015. *Improving Children's Life Chances through Better Family Planning*. CCF Brief No. 55. Washington, DC: Center on Children and Families at The Brookings Institution.

Sayer, Liana and Suzanne M. Bianchi. 2000. "Women's Economic Independence and the Probability of Divorce: A Review and Reexamination." *Journal of Family Issues* 21(7): 906–943.

Sayer, Liana, Suzanne Bianchi, and John Robinson. 2004. "Are Parents Investing Less in Children? Trends in Mothers' and Fathers' Time with Children." *American Journal of Sociology* 110(1): 1–43.

Schoen, Robert, Nan Marie Astone, Young J. Kim, Kendra Rothert, and Nicola J. Standish. 2002. "Women's Employment, Marital Happiness, and Divorce." *Social Forces* 81(2): 643–662.

Schoeni, Robert F. 1995. "Marital Status and Earnings in Developed Countries." *Journal of Population Economics* 8(4): 351–359.

Schwartz, Christine R. 2010. "Earnings Inequality and the Changing Association between Spouses' Earnings." *American Journal of Sociology* 115(5): 1524–1557.

Schwartz, Christine R. and Pilar Gonalons-Pons. 2016. "Trends in Relative Earnings and Marital Dissolution: Are Wives Who Outearn Their Husbands Still More Likely to Divorce?" *RSF* 2(4): 218–236.

Schwartz, Christine R. and Robert D. Mare. 2005. "Trends in Educational Assortative Marriage from 1940 to 2003." *Demography* 42(4): 621–646.

Scott, Joan W. and Louise A. Tilly. 1975. "Women's Work and the Family in Nineteenth-Century Europe." *Comparative Studies in Society and History* 17(1): 36–64.

Scott, Mindy E., Laurie F. DeRose, Laura H. Lippman, and Elizabeth Cook. 2013. "Two, One, or No Parents?" World Family Map 2013: *Mapping Family Change and Child Well-Being Outcomes*. Bethesda, MD: Child Trends.

Shannon, Sarah, Christopher Uggen, Jason Schnittker, Melissa Thompson, Sara Wakefield, and Michael Massoglia. 2017. "The Growth, Scope, and Spatial Distribution of People with Felony Records in the United States, 1948 to 2010." *Demography* 54: 1795–1818. (Accessed April 17, 2018.) DOI: 10.1007/s13524-017-0611-1

Shows, Carla and Naomi Gerstel. 2009. "Fathering, Class, and Gender: A Comparison of Physicians and Emergency Medical Technicians." *Gender & Society* 23(2): 161–187.

Schwartz, Christine R. and Hongyun Han. 2014. "The Reversal of the Gender Gap in Education and Trends in Marital Dissolution." *American Sociological Review* 79(4): 605–629.

Segal, Lynne. 2007. *Slow Motion: Changing Masculinities, Changing Men*. Basingstoke, UK: Palgrave Macmillan.

Seltzer, Judith A. 1991. "Relationships between Fathers and Children Who Live Apart: The Father's Role after Separation." *Journal of Marriage and the Family* 53(1): 79–101.

Seltzer, Judith A. 2000. "Child Support and Child Access: Experiences of Divorced and Nonmarital Families." In J. T. ldham and M. S. Melli, eds., *Child Support: The Next Frontier*. Ann Arbor: University of Michigan Press, pp. 69–87.

Seltzer, Judith A. 2004. "Cohabitation in the United States and Britain: Demography, Kinship, and the Future." *Journal of Marriage and Family* 66(4): 921–928.

Semyonov, Moshe. 1980. "The Social Context of Women's Labor Force Participation: A Comparative Analysis." *American Journal of Sociology* 86(3): 534–550.

Shin, Jung Cheol. 2012. "Higher Education Development in Korea: Western University Ideas, Confucian Tradition, and Economic Development." *Higher Education* 64(1): 59–72.

Sigle-Rushton, Wendy, John Hobcraft, and Kathleen Kiernan. 2005. "Parental Divorce and Subsequent Disadvantage: A Cross-Cohort Comparison." *Demography* 42(3): 427–446.

Sigle-Rushton, Wendy and Sara McLanahan. 2004. *Father Absence and Child Wellbeing: A Critical Review*. New York: Russell Sage Foundation.

Skocpol, Theda. 1995. *Protecting Soldiers and Mothers*. Cambridge, MA: Harvard University Press.

Smock, Pamela, Wendy Manning, and Meredith Porter. 2005. "'Everything's There Except Money': How Money Shapes Decisions to Marry among Cohabitors." *Journal of Marriage and Family* 67(3): 680–696.

Sobotka, Thomáš. 2011. "Fertility in Central and Eastern Europe after 1989. Collapse and Gradual Recovery." *Historical Social Research* – Special issue *Fertility in the 20th Century: Trends, Policies, Theories, Discourses)* 36(2): 246–296.

Sobotka, Thomáš and Laurent Toulemon. 2008. "Overview Chapter 4: Changing Family and Partnership Behavior: Common Trends and Persistent Diversity across Europe." *Demographic Research* 19(6): 85–138.

Soons, Judith P. M. and Matthijs Kalmijn. 2009. "Is Marriage More Than Cohabitation? Well-Being Differences in 30 European Countries." *Journal of Marriage and Family* 71(5): 1141–1157.

Stähli, Michèle, Jean Marie Le Goff, René Levy, and Eric Widmer. 2009. "Wishes or Constraints? Mothers' Labour Force Participation and Its Motivation in Switzerland." *European Sociological Review* 25(3): 333–348.

Stanfors, Maria and Frances Goldscheider. 2017. "The Forest and the Trees: Industrialization, Demographic Change, and the Ongoing Gender Revolution in the US, 1870–2010." *Demographic Research* 36(6): 173–226.

Stanfors, Maria and Paul Nystedt. 2017. "Two for the Price of One? Economic Consequences of Motherhood in Contemporary Sweden." Paper presented at the Annual Meeting of the Population Association of America, Chicago, IL, April 27–29, 2017.

Stevenson, Betsey and Justin Wolfers. 2007. "Trends in Marital Stability." Wharton School, University of Pennsylvania. http://users.nber.org/~bstevens/papers/Marital_Stability.pdf. (Accessed March 2, 2018.)

Stone, Emily A., Todd K. Shackelford, and David M. Buss. 2007. "Sex Ratio and Mate Preferences: A Cross-Cultural Investigation." *European Journal of Social Psychology* 37(2): 288.

Stone, Lawrence. 1977. *The Family, Sex and Marriage in England 1500–1800*. New York: Harper and Row.

Stykes, Bart, and Seth Williams. 2013. Diverging Destinies: Children's Family Structure Variation by Maternal Education. Bowling Green, OH: National Center for Marriage and Family Research, Bowling Green State University. https://www.bgsu.edu/content/dam/BGSU/college-of-arts-and-sciences/NCFMR/documents/FP/FP-13-16.pdf. (Accessed April 17, 2018.)

Sullivan, Oriel. 2010. "Changing Differences by Educational Attainment in Fathers' Domestic Labour and Child Care." *Sociology* 44(4): 716–733.

Sullivan, Oriel, Francesco Billari, and Evrim Altintas. 2014. "Father's Changing Contributions to Child Care and Domestic Work in Very Low Fertility Countries: The Effect of Education." *Journal of Family Issues* 35(8): 1048–1065.

Sweeney, Megan M. 2002. "Two Decades of Family Change: The Shifting Economic Foundations of Marriage." *American Sociological Review* 67(1): 132–147.

Sweeney, Megan M. 2010. "Remarriage and Stepfamilies: Strategic Sites for Family Scholarship in the 21st Century." *Journal of Marriage and Family* 72(3): 667–684.

Tach, Laura, Ronald Mincy, and Kathryn Edin. 2010. "Parenting as a 'Package Deal': Relationships, Fertility and Nonresident Father Involvement among Unmarried Parents." *Demography* 47(1): 181–204.

Thébaud, Sarah and David Pedulla. 2016. "Masculinity and the Stalled Revolution: How Gender Ideologies and Norms Shape Young Men's Responses to Work-Family Policies." *Gender & Society* 30(4): 590–617.

Therborn, Göran. 2004. *Between Sex and Power: Family in the World, 1900–2000*. London, UK: Routledge.

Therborn, Göran. 2014. "Family Systems of the World: Are They Converging?" In Judith Treas, Jacqueline Scott, and Martin Richards, eds., *The Wiley-Blackwell Companion to the Sociology of the Family*. West Sussex: John Wiley & Sons, pp. 3–19.

Thévenon, Olivier. 2011. "Family Policies in OECD Countries: A Comparative Analysis." *Population and Development Review* 37(1): 57–87.

Thomson, Elizabeth. 2014. "Family Complexity in Europe." *The Annals of the American Academy of Political and Social Science* 654(1): 245–258.

Thomson, Elizabeth and Helen Eriksson. 2013. "Register-Based Estimates of Parents' Coresidence in Sweden, 1969–2007." *Demographic Research* 29: 1153–1186.

Thomson, Elizabeth, Thomas Hanson, and Sara S. McLanahan. 1994. "Family Structure and Child Well-Being: Economic Resources versus Parental Behaviors." *Social Forces* 73(1): 221–224.

Thomson, Elizabeth, Trude Lappegård, Marcia Carlson, Ann Evans, and Edith Gray. 2014. "Childbearing across Partnerships in Australia, the United States, Norway, and Sweden." *Demography* 51(2): 485–508.

Thomson, Elizabeth and Sara S. McLanahan. 2012. "Reflections on Family Structure and Child Well-Being: Economic Resources vs. Parental Socialization." *Social Forces* 91(1): 45–53.

Thomson, Elizabeth, Maria Winkler-Dworak, Martin Spielauer, and Alexia Prskawetz. 2012. "Union Instability as an Engine of Fertility? A Microsimulation Model for France." *Demography* 49(1): 175–195.

Thornton, Arland. 2001. "The Developmental Paradigm, Reading History Sideways, and Family Change." *Demography* 38(4): 449–465.

Thornton, Arland and Deborah Freedman. 1979. "Changes in the Sex Role Attitudes of Women, 1962–1977: Evidence from a Panel Study." *American Sociological Review* 44(5): 831–842.

Thornton, Arland and Linda Young-DeMarco. 2001. "Four Decades of Trends in Attitudes toward Family Issues in the United States: The 1960s through the 1990s." *Journal of Marriage and the Family* 63(4): 1009–1037.

Torche, Florencia. 2014. "Intergenerational Mobility and Inequality: The Latin American Case." *Annual Review of Sociology* 40: 619–642.

Trost, Jan 1978. "A Renewed Social Institution: Non-Marital Cohabitation." *Acta Sociologica* 21(4): 303–315.

Udry, J. Richard. 1994. "The Nature of Gender." *Demography* 31(4): 561–573.

US Census Bureau. 1940. "Census of Population: The Labor Force." (Sample Statistics.)

US Census Bureau. 2012. "1940 Census of Population."

US Census Bureau. 2015. "Educational Attainment in the United States: 2015."

US Census Bureau. 2016. "Estimated Median Age at First Marriage, by Sex: 1890 to the Present." www.census.gov/hhes/families/data/marital.html (Retrieved October 30, 2017.)

US Bureau of Labor Statistics. "BLS Data Finder 9.0." https://beta.bls.gov/dataQuery /search (Retrieved April 22, 2017.)

US Bureau of Labor Statistics. "Current Population Survey. Series: LNS12300025 and LNS12300061." http://data.bls.gov/pdq/querytool.jsp?survey=ln (Retrieved May 16, 2016.)

US Bureau of Labor Statistics. "Current Population Surve y. Series: LNS12000061 and LNU00000061." www.bls.gov/data (Retrieved April 22, 2017.)

US Bureau of Labor Statistics. "Current Population Survey. Series: LNS13000061 and LNU05000061." www.bls.gov/data. (Retrieved June 19, 2015.)

US. Bureau of Labor Statistics. "Current Population Survey. January 1994–September 2015." https://dataferrett.census.gov/ (Retrieved October 20, 2015.)

US Bureau of Labor Statistics. "Current Population Survey: Labor Force Statistics from the Current Population Survey Data Tool." http://data.bls.gov/pdq/querytool.jsp?survey=ln (Retrieved June 21, 2016.)

Usdansky, Margaret. 2011. "The Gender-Equality Paradox: Class and Incongruity Between Work-Family Attitudes and Behaviors." *Journal of Family Theory and Research* 3(3): 163–178.

US Department of Defense. 1956. *Selected Manpower Statistics*. Washington, DC: Progress Reports and Statistics Division, United States Department of Defense. www.dtic.mil/dtic/tr/fulltext/u2/a954007.pdf (Retrieved August 5, 2016.)

US Department of Health and Human Services. 2014. "2013 National Survey on Drug Use and Health (NSDUH)." Rockville, MD: The Substance Abuse and Mental Health Services Administration. www.samhsa.gov/data/sites/default/files/NSDUHresultsPDFWHTML2013/Web/NSDUHresultsAlts2013.htm#fig2.5 (Accessed .)

US Department of Health and Human Services. 2015. "2015 Poverty Guidelines." https://aspe.hhs.gov/2015-poverty-guidelines#threshholds (Accessed .)

Uunk, Wilfred. 2004. "The Economic Consequences of Divorce for Women in the European Union: The Impact of Welfare State Arrangements." *European Journal of Population* 20(3): 251–285.

Vanassche, Sofie, Martine Corijn, Koen Matthijs, and Gray Swicegood. 2015. "Repartnering and Childbearing after Divorce: Differences According to Parental Status and Custodial Arrangements." *Population Research and Policy Review* 34(5): 761–784.

Van Bavel, Jan and David S. Reher. 2013. "The Baby Boom and Its Causes: What We Know and What We Need to Know." *Population and Development Review* 39(2): 257–288.

Vance, J. D. 2016. *Hillbilly Elegy*. New York, NY: Harper Collins.

Van de Kaa, Dirk. 1987. "Europe's Second Demographic Transition." *Population Bulletin* 42(1): 1–59.

Vignoli, Daniele, and Silvana Salvini. 2014. "Religion and Union Formation in Italy: Catholic Precepts, Social Pressure, and Tradition." *Demographic Research* 31(35): 1079–1106.

Vikat, Andres, Elizabeth Thomson, and Jan M. Hoem. 1999. "Stepfamily Fertility in Contemporary Sweden: The Impact of Childbearing before the Current Union." *Population Studies* 53(2): 211–225.

Vitali, Agnese, Francesco Billari, Alexia Prskawetz, and Maria Testa 2009. "Preference Theory and Low Fertility: A Comparative Perspective." *European Journal of Population* 25(4): 413–438.

Vitali, Agnese and Arpino Bruno. 2016. "Who Brings Home the Bacon? The Influence of Context on Partners' Contributions to the Household Income." *Demographic Research* 35(41): 1213–1244.

Waite, Linda and Maggie Gallagher. 2000. *The Case for Marriage: Why Married People Are Happier, Healthier and Better Off Financially*. New York, NY: Doubleday.

Waldfogel, J., T.-A. Craigie, and J. Brooks-Gunn. 2010. "Fragile Families and Child Wellbeing." *Future of Children* 20(2): 87–112.

Waldfogel, Jane and Elizabeth Washbrook. 2011. *On Your Marks: Measuring the School Readiness of Children in Low-to-Middle Income Families*. London, UK: Resolution Foundation.

Walters, Pamela. 1984. "Occupational and Labor Market Effects on Secondary and Postsecondary Educational Expansion in the United States: 1922 to 1979." *American Sociological Review* 49(5): 659–671.

Ward, Kathryn and Fred Pampel. 1985. "Structural Determinants of Female Labor Force Participation in Developed Nations, 1955–75." *Social Science Quarterly* 66(3): 654–667.

Watkins, Susan, Jane Menken, and John Bongaarts. 1987. "Demographic Foundations of Family Change." *American Sociological Review* 52(3): 346–358.

Wax, Amy L. 2014. "Diverging Destinies Redux." *Michigan Law Review* 112(6): 925–955.

Weitoft, G. R., A. Hjern, B. Hagland, and M. Rosén. 2003. "Mortality, Severe Morbidity, and Injury in Children Living with Single Parents in Sweden: A Population-Based Study." *Lancet* 361(9354): 289–295.

West, Darrell M. 2010. *Community Colleges: America's Forgotten Institutions of Higher Education.* Washington, DC: Brookings Institution.

Western, Bruce, Deirde Bloome, and Christine Percheski. 2008. "Inequality among American Families with Children, 1975 to 2005." *American Sociological Review* 73(6): 903–920.

White, Lynn and Stacy J. Rogers. 2000. "Economic Circumstances and Family Outcomes: A Review of the 1990s." *Journal of Marriage and Family* 62(4): 1035–1051.

Whitehurst, Grover J. 2016 *Family Support or School Readiness? Contrasting Models of Public Spending on Children's Early Care and Learning.* Washington, DC: Brookings Institution.

Wiik, Kenneth Aarskaug. 2009. "'You'd Better Wait!'— Socio-economic Background and Timing of First Marriage versus First Cohabitation." *European Sociological Review* 25(2): 139–153.

Wilcox, W. Bradford, ed. 2010. "When Marriage Disappears: The Retreat from Marriage in Middle America." In *The State of our Unions: Marriage in America.* New York, NY: Institute for American Values and Charlottesville, VA: The National Marriage Project, University of Virginia, pp. 13–60.

Wilcox, W. Bradford and Laurie DeRose. "Ties that Bind: Childrearing in an Age of Cohabitation." *Foreign Affairs* February 14, 2017. www.foreignaffairs.com/articles/2017-02-14/ties-bind (Retrieved February 18, 2017.)

Wilkinson, Richard and Kate Pickett. 2009. *The Spirit Level: Why More Equal Societies Almost Always Do Better.* London: Allen Lane.

Williams, Fiona. 2012. "Converging Variations in Migrant Care Work in Europe." *Journal of European Social Policy* 22(4): 363–376.

Wilmoth, Janet and Gregor Koso. 2002. "Does Marital History Matter? Marital Status and Wealth Outcomes among Preretirement Adults." *Journal of Marriage and Family* 64(1): 254–268.

Wilson, William J. 1987. *The Truly Disadvantaged: The Inner City, the Underclass, and Public Policy.* Chicago: University of Chicago Press.

Wilson, William J. 1996. *When Work Disappears: The World of the New Urban Poor.* New York: Vintage Books.

Wong, Siu Kwong. 2011. "Reciprocal Effects of Family Disruption and Crime: A Panel Study of Canadian Municipalities." *Western Criminology Review* 12: 43–64.

World Bank. 2003. *Inequality in Latin America and the Caribbean: Breaking with History?* Washington: The International Bank for Reconstruction and Development/The World Bank.

Wu, Huijing. 2017. *Trends in Births to Single and Cohabiting Mothers, 1980–2014.* Bowling Green, OH: National Center for Marriage and Family Research, Bowling Green State University.

Xie, Yu, James M. Raymo, Kimberl Goyette, and Arland Thornton. 2003. "Economic Potential and Entry into Marriage and Cohabitation." *Demography* 40(2): 351–367.

Yeung, W. Jean, Miriam R. Linver, and Jeanne Brooks–Gunn. 2002. "How Money Matters for Young Children's Development: Parental Investment and Family Processes." *Child Development* 73(6): 1861–1879.

Yeung, W. Jean, John Sandberg, Pamela Davis-Kean, and Sandra Hofferth. 2001. "Children's Time with Fathers in Intact Families." *Journal of Marriage and Family* 63(1): 136–154.

Young, Michael D. 1958. *The Rise of Meritocracy.* London: Thames and Hudson.

Young, Alwyn. 1995. "The Tyranny of Numbers: Confronting the Statistical Realities of the East Asian Growth Experience." *The Quarterly Journal of Economics* 110(3): 641–680.

Zartler, Ulrike and Katrin Grillenberger. 2017. "Doubled Homes—Doubled Social Ties? Children's Relationships in Post-Divorce Shared Residence Arrangements." *Children & Society* 31(2): 144–156.

Zimmerman, Mary K., Jacquelyn S. Litt, and Christine E. Bose. 2006. *Global Dimensions of Gender and Carework.* Stanford, CA: Stanford University Press.

Index

affirmative action, 260
apprenticeships, 228
abortion, 48, 203, 279
achievement tests, 145, 221
AEI-Brookings working group, 228, 229
Affordable Care Act (ACA), 225
Akerlof, George, 183
assortative mating, xvi, 2, 24, 223, 270
Australia. *See* Chapters 1, 4, 5, 6, 7 & 9
Austria. *See* Chapters 1, 4 & 6
Autor, David, 193
Avoid the Stork, 227

Baltics, 87
Becker, Gary, 240
Belarus, 88
Belgium. *See* Chapters 6, 9 & 11
birth control. *See* contraception
boarding schools, 233, 257
Brazil. *See* Chapters 2 & 11
Building Strong Families, 229
Bulgaria, 29, 87, 306
Bureau of Labor Statistics, 106, 109, 110, 320, 321

Canada. *See* Chapters 1, 5, 6, 7, 8 & 11
Career Academies, 228, 304
Catholic Church, 58, 87, 93
children of divorce, 219
community colleges, 227
cohabitation
    focus group, 8, 86, 92, 93, 94, 95, 96
    heterogeneity of, 8, 97, 101, 145, 146
    legal recognition of, 89
    life satisfaction, 8, 98, 98
Colombia. *See* Chapters 2 & 11
compensatory hypothesis, 146

contraception
    anti-contraception laws, 241
    effective contraception, 14, 224, 225, 227
    IUDs, 224
    LARCs, 224, 226, 234
    religious opposition, 279
criminal activity
    married men, 180, 187, 188, 221
    two-parent families, 188, 189, 194
cultural diffusion, 11
Current Population Survey (CPS), 106, 109, 128, 297, 320, 321
Czech Republic, 23, 169, 171, 243, 244, 252, 316

DC Briya/Mary's Center, 232
Daddy Days, 207
deindustrialization, 23
deinstitutionalization of marriage, 69, 263, 266
Demographic and Health Surveys (DHS), 182, 190
Denmark. *See* Chapters 1, 4, 6, 7, 9 & 11
developmental paradigm, 213
diverging destinies, 2, 4, 5, 10, 13, 21, 33, 41, 103, 144, 161, 165, 166, 175, 208, 254
domestic violence, 249, 250, 251, 272, 280
domestic work, 7, 12, 76, 211, 246, 267
drug addiction, 253
dual nuptiality system, 5

Earned Income Tax Credit (EITC), 230
earnings gap, 71, 72
economic inequality and family structure, 1, 15, 261
educational homogamy, 206
effects of family structure, 156

according to socioeconomic background, 171–173

test scores, 33, 145, 146, 148, 150, 156, 162, 166, 172, 173, 177, 180, 181

egalitarianism, 13, 170, 211, 215, 234, 251, 267, 312

England, Paula, 224, 289, 294, 296

Europe. *See* Chapters 1, 4, 5 & passim
  family policy, 14, 18, 88, 200, 204, 206, 210, 217, 225
  landscape of nonmarital fertility, 86–89
  patterns of family change, 83–89

euthanasia, 48

extended households, 43, 47, 48, 53, 59, 61

Family and Medical Leave Act, 204

family gap, 216, 223, 230, 232, 233, 234

family policy
  baby bonuses, 203
  family allowances, 203
  Nordic model, 243, 244, 245, 255
  paid maternity leave, 203, 204
  subsidized child care, 202, 204, 208

family structure effects, 145, 146, 149, 164, 177, 178

family structure inequality, 261, 263, 264

father absence, 253, 254, 255, 256, 257

female-headed households, 45, 49, 174

feminization of poverty, 50

Finland. *See* Chapter 6 & 9

floor effect hypothesis, 146

focus group project, 92–96

France. *See* Chapters 1, 4, 5, 6, 7, & 9

gender essentialism, 212, 213, 260

gender revolution, 12, 13, 41, 199, 200, 202, 204, 206, 209, 210, 211, 212, 214, 215, 245, 258, 259

General Social Survey, 76, 77

Germany. *See* Chapters 1, 4, 6, 7, 9 & 11

globalization, 16, 23, 79, 136

grade repetition, xiii, xiv, 9, 145, 151, 154, 155, 156, 157, 159, 162, 163

Great Depression, 7, 71, 76, 80, 111, 117, 203

Greece. *See* Chapters 1, 4, 5, 6 & 11

Gruber, Jonathan, 189

Hakim, Catherine, 212

Harlem Children's Zone, 232

hegemonic masculinity, 79

Home Instruction for Parents of Preschool Youngsters (HIPPY), 232

home visiting programs, 232

homogamous marriages, 24

homosexuality, 48

household complexity, 3, 43, 47, 50, 59

housing policy, 233

Hungary, 35, 171, 252, 253, 312

Iceland, 29, 87, 171, 207, 268

intact married families, 149

Integrated Public Use Microdata Series-International (IPUMS-I), 190

intergenerational mobility, 13, 33, 216, 218, 219, 234

International Standard Classification of Education (ISCED), 152

intersectionality, 239

Ireland. *See* Chapters 1, 6, 7 & 11

Italy. *See* Chapters 1, 4, 5 & passim

Japan, 112, 179

Lamont, Michèle, 73

Latin America. *See* Chapters 2 & 11
  double disadvantage, 261
  family systems, xvii, 42
  family trends, 45–55
  Maps, ix, 44
  paradoxes of Latin American family change, 56–58
  union and childbearing calendars, 3, 43

Lesthaeghe, Ron, 212

Lithuania, 27, 29, 35, 87, 304

Lucas, Robert, Jr., 180

Luxembourg. *See* Chapters 1 & 6

Luxembourg Income Study (LIS) Database, 144, 308

male breadwinner model, 41, 91, 240, 241, 243, 248

marriage
  among highly educated women, 52, 212
  educational gradient in, 34, 35, 37
  retreat from, 6, 7, 15, 16, 34, 82, 111, 146, 184, 199, 218, 261, 262, 263

marriage and economic growth, 180–187

marriage bar, 201

marriage premium, 172, 184, 249

marriage promotion, 229, 282

marriageable men, 23, 274

Medicaid, 225, 302, 315

Mediterranean countries, 153, 255

men and work
  education effect, 136
  in the United States, 183
  marriage effect, 134, 136
  married prime-age men, 122, 125, 126, 130, 134, 136
  never-married prime-age men, 122
Mexico. *See* Chapter 2
motherhood penalty, 186
Moving to Opportunity (MTO), 233
MTV's *16 and Pregnant*, 227
multipartnered fertility, 3, 4, 30, 31, 36, 38
Murray, Charles, 223, 229

National Longitudinal Survey of Youth (NLSY), 229
Netherlands. *See* Chapters 1, 4, 6, 7 & 11
New Zealand. *See* Chapters 5 & 6
nonmarital childbearing
  births to lone mothers, 5
  class divide in nonmarital childbearing, 8
  in cohabiting unions, 5, 52, 70
North America, 2, 181, 185, 241, 268
Norway. *See* Chapters 1, 4, 6, 9 & 11

OECD countries, ix, 22, 25, 26, 27, 29, 150, 242
Organization for Economic Co-operation and Development (OECD), 112, 182

PACS, 90, 92
paternity, 91, 274, 276
pathology of matriarchy, 237, 238, 254, 258
pathology of *patriarchy*, 15, 238, 258
Pence, Mike, 225
Poland, 23, 29, 35, 88, 93, 94, 278, 306, 311
Portugal, 88, 151, 153, 155, 156, 158, 159, 160, 162, 242, 243
preference theory, 212
premarital sex, 224, 234
Prevention First, 227
Programme for International Student Assessment (PISA) of 2012, 145
Putnam, Robert, 223, 225

red states, 281
Redesigning America's Community Colleges, 228
relationship stability, 15, 209, 265, 274
Rubio, Marco Senator, 228
Russia, 37, 93, 95, 169, 251, 303, 306

Sawhill, Isabel, 13, 301, 310, 315
  Generation Unbound, 223
Scandinavia, 12, 207, 210
second demographic transition, 3, 17, 21, 25, 33, 36, 38, 41, 48, 80, 81, 83, 165, 199, 263, 266
SEED schools, 233, 293
Serbia, 88, 171
single motherhood
  and mother's education, xiii, xiv, 154, 155, 158, 159, 160, 161
  mother's tertiary education, 156, 162
  negative effects of, 144, 145, 147, 148, 150, 156, 163, 255
single-mother households, 253, 255, 256
  percentage of children residing in. *See* Table 11.3
Slovenia, 29
Social Trends Institute, xix, 2, 21, 181, 237, 293
Spain. *See* Chapters 1, 4, 6 & passim
stability gap, 217
stepparent, xvii, 151, 167, 168
Survey of Income and Program Participation (SIPP), 121
Sweden. *See* Chapters 1, 4, 6, 7, 9 & 11
Switzerland. *See* Chapters 1, 4 & 6

teen pregnancy rates, 227
The Century Foundation, 227, 290
The Negro Family: The Case for National Action, 237
Thornton, Arland, 212, 323
Title X, 227
truancy, xiii, xiv, 9, 17, 145, 151, 154, 155, 156, 157, 160, 161, 162, 163, 253

unintended pregnancy, 13, 217, 224, 225, 279
union instability, 4, 14, 17, 37, 38, 41, 59, 81, 182, 247
United Kingdom. *See* Chapters 1, 4, 6, 7, 9 & passim
United Nations Office on Drugs and Crime (UNODC), 188
United Nations Statistics Division as well as the World Values Survey (WVS), 190
United States. *See* Chapters 1, 3, 5, 7, 8, 9, & passim
  changes in family patterns, 5, 23, 25, 136, 139
  class divide in marriage, 8
  decline of work for American men, 106–112

work rates and family structure, 125–139
universal preschool, 12
upper middle class, 223
UpStream, 226

Vance, J.D., 222
vocational apprenticeships, 14

West, Darrell, 227
Western Ukraine, 88
work-based learning, 228
work–family conflict, 12, 199, 200, 207, 208, 211, 212, 215
working class, 269
World Bank, 40, 182, 185, 186, 191, 240, 286, 323